European Yearbook of Constitutional Law

Volume 4

D1826741

The *European Yearbook of Constitutional Law* (EYCL) is an annual publication devoted to the study of constitutional law. The yearbook provides a forum for in-depth analysis and discussion of new developments in constitutional law in Europe and beyond. Each issue is dedicated to a specific theme. Papers are subject to editorial and double-blind peer review. The yearbook is published by T.M.C. ASSER PRESS in cooperation with Springer Publishers.

Contact

To get in touch, please send an e-mail to eycl@tilburguniversity.edu

Jurgen de Poorter · Gerhard van der Schyff ·
Maarten Stremler · Maartje De Visser ·
Ingrid Leijten · Charlotte van Oirsouw
Editors

European Yearbook
of Constitutional Law 2022

A Constitutional Identity for the EU?

Editors

Jurgen de Poorter
Department of Public Law and Governance
Tilburg Law School
Tilburg, The Netherlands

Gerhard van der Schyff
Department of Public Law and Governance
Tilburg Law School
Tilburg, The Netherlands

Maarten Stremler
Department of Public Law
Faculty of Law
Maastricht University
Maastricht, The Netherlands

Maartje De Visser
SMU School of Law
Singapore, Singapore

Charlotte van Oirsouw
Department of Constitutional
and Administrative Law
Utrecht University
Utrecht, The Netherlands

Ingrid Leijten
Department of Public Law and Governance
Tilburg Law School
Tilburg, The Netherlands

ISSN 2405-6111   ISSN 2405-612X (electronic)
European Yearbook of Constitutional Law
ISBN 978-94-6265-597-3   ISBN 978-94-6265-595-9 (eBook)
https://doi.org/10.1007/978-94-6265-595-9

Published by T.M.C. ASSER PRESS, The Hague, The Netherlands www.asserpress.nl
Produced and distributed for T.M.C. ASSER PRESS by Springer-Verlag Berlin Heidelberg

This T.M.C. ASSER PRESS imprint is published by the registered company Springer-Verlag GmbH, DE, part of Springer Nature
The registered company address is: Heidelberger Platz 3, 14197 Berlin, Germany

Preface

We are privileged to announce that Prof. Ingrid Leijten has joined the editorial board of the *European Yearbook of Constitutional Law*. She holds the chair of Dutch and European Constitutional Law at Tilburg Law School. Professor Leijten's academic insights and expertise will without a doubt be most valuable to the *Yearbook* as it grows from strength to strength.

In addition, we are happy to share with our readers that Charlotte van Oirsouw LL.M. has become one of the *Yearbook's* managing editors. She is currently working towards her Ph.D. at Utrecht Law School, having previously worked at Tilburg Law School.

Tilburg/Maastricht/Utrecht/Singapore   The Editors
The Netherlands/Singapore
April 2023

Contents

Editors and Contributors

About the Editors

Jurgen de Poorter is Professor of Administrative Law in the Department of Public Law and Governance at Tilburg University, The Netherlands. His research focuses in particular on constitutional dialogues, public interest litigation and methods of judicial lawmaking.

Gerhard van der Schyff is Associate Professor in the Department of Public Law and Governance at Tilburg University, The Netherlands. His research interests include constitutional law and fundamental rights, especially from a comparative and European perspective.

Maarten Stremler is Assistant Professor of Constitutional Law at the Faculty of Law of Maastricht University, The Netherlands. His research interests are comparative constitutional law and constitutional theory.

Maartje De Visser is Associate Professor at the Yong Pung How School of Law, Singapore. Her current research focuses on constitutional engagement by courts and non-judicial actors, transnational judicial dialogues in Europe and Asia, and means to improve constitutional literacy.

Ingrid Leijten is Professor of Dutch and European Constitutional Law in the Department of Public Law and Governance at Tilburg University, The Netherlands. Her research primarily deals with the changing role and meaning of fundamental rights against the background of broader (comparative) constitutional law developments.

Charlotte van Oirsouw is doctoral researcher at the Institute of Jurisprudence, Constitutional and Administrative Law at Utrecht University. Her research concerns the regulation of algorithmic decision-making by Dutch constitutional and administrative law. Her research combines legal doctrinal and empirical research approaches.

Contributors

Erika Arban Melbourne Law School, Centre for Comparative Constitutional Studies, Melbourne, Australia

Robert Böttner University of Erfurt, Erfurt, Germany

Tímea Drinóczi Faculty of Law, Federal University of Minas Gerais, Belo Horizonte, Brazil

Pietro Faraguna Department of Constitutional Law, University of Trieste, Trieste, Italy

Jakob Gašperin Wischhoff DFG Graduate Program DynamInt, Humboldt-Universität zu Berlin, Berlin, Germany

Dieter Grimm Humboldt University Berlin, Berlin, Germany; Wissenschaftskolleg zu Berlin, Institute for Advanced Study, Berlin, Germany

Gohar Karapetian Faculty of Law, University of Groningen, Groningen, The Netherlands

Emil Martini College of Europe, Bruges, Belgium

Alberto Nicòtina Government and Law Research Group, Faculty of Law, University of Antwerp, Antwerp, Belgium

Giuliano Vosa Department of Law, University of Catania, Catania, Italy

Chapter 1
Introduction: Exploring the Concept of a Constitutional Identity for the European Union

Gerhard van der Schyff, Ingrid Leijten, Charlotte van Oirsouw, Jurgen de Poorter, Maarten Stremler and Maartje De Visser

Contents

The original version of this chapter was revised: The wrong abstract and keywords have been removed from the online version and replaced by the correct abstract. The correction to this chapter is available at
https://doi.org/10.1007/978-94-6265-595-9_11

G. van der Schyff (✉) · I. Leijten · J. de Poorter
Tilburg University, Tilburg, The Netherlands
e-mail: g.vdrschyff@tilburguniversity.edu

I. Leijten
e-mail: a.e.m.leijten@tilburguniversity.edu

J. de Poorter
e-mail: j.c.a.depoorter@tilburguniversity.edu

C. van Oirsouw
Utrecht University, Utrecht, The Netherlands
e-mail: c.c.k.vanoirsouw@uu.nl

M. Stremler
Maastricht University, Maastricht, The Netherlands
e-mail: m.stremler@maastrichtuniversity.nl

M. De Visser
Singapore Management University, Singapore, Singapore
e-mail: mdevisser@smu.edu.sg

© T.M.C. ASSER PRESS and the authors 2023, corrected publication 2023
J. de Poorter et al. (eds.), *European Yearbook of Constitutional Law 2022*,
European Yearbook of Constitutional Law 4,
https://doi.org/10.1007/978-94-6265-595-9_1

1.1   Constitutional Identity Beyond the Member States

Globalisation has not only impacted trade and markets, but also the constitutional conditions under which public power is exercised. The role played by states in modern-day constitutionalism, although still important, is increasingly being qualified by multilevel legal regimes.

In the search for a constitutional model to give effect to such regimes, the European Union (EU) deserves particular attention. The reality of this shared constitutional space is that of a multilevel order characterised by a heterarchical or pluralist relationship between the EU level and the level of the Member States.[1] An emerging element of the multilevel exchanges in this shared space is the concept of "constitutional identity".[2] The notion of identity often refers to the expression of a legal entity's individuality in deciding on and developing its fundamental constitutional features and values.[3]

A lacuna in the debate on identity seems to be the notion of an EU constitutional identity, hence the topic of this volume of the *European Yearbook of Constitutional Law*. To date scholarship and case law have mostly focussed on the constitutional identities of the Member States.[4] This can probably be explained by the fact that since the Maastricht Treaty of 1992, the Treaty of European Union (TEU) has required the EU to respect the "national identities" of its Member States.[5] This term, which is widely interpreted as covering the identities of states' constitutional orders, is today contained in Article 4(2) TEU.[6] This provision requires the EU to respect such identities as they inhere in states' "fundamental structures, political and constitutional, inclusive of regional and local self-government".[7] In addition, Member States' highest or constitutional courts have shown themselves increasingly willing to articulate and protect the respective constitutional identities under their jurisdiction, also or even especially in the context of European integration.[8]

The attention paid to Member State constitutional identity stands in contrast to the notion of an EU constitutional identity. Such an identity features very little in

---

[1] For an account of the EU as a multilevel constitutional order, see Pernice 2002.

[2] For studies of the concept in the EU legal space, see among other sources the special edition of European Public Law by Fromage and De Witte 2021; Drinóczi 2020; Schnettger 2020; Van der Schyff 2020; Belov 2017; Faraguna 2017; Polzin 2017; Claes and Reestman 2015; Blanke 2013; Von Bogdandy and Schill 2011.

[3] Calliess and Van der Schyff 2020a, b, p. 7.

[4] See the country studies in Calliess and Van der Schyff 2020a, b; Claes and Reestman 2015, pp. 919–931, 941–967.

[5] On the various treaty incarnations of the identity provision, see Claes and Reestman 2015, pp. 932–933; Von Bogdandy and Schill 2011, pp. 1421–1422; Besselink 2010, pp. 40–42.

[6] For a different view, namely that Article 4(2) TEU is intended to protect "national identity" in a first order sense and not "constitutional identity", see Cloots 2015, 2016.

[7] For various views on the scope and meaning of Article 4(2) TEU, see De Witte 2021; Blanke 2013; Van der Schyff 2012.

[8] See the country studies in Calliess and Van der Schyff 2020a, b; Claes and Reestman 2015, pp. 919–931, 941–967.

academic literature.[9] As to case law, until 16 February 2022 it had only been referred to by Advocates-General of the CJEU on a couple of occasions.[10] This situation changed on that date, when the CJEU handed down two judgements dealing with the annulment proceedings brought respectively by Hungary and Poland against the Regulation on a general regime of conditionality for the protection of the EU budget of 16 December 2020.[11] The aim of the Regulation is to protect the EU's budget against rule of law breaches by Member States by limiting their access to funding.[12] Poland and Hungary complained, among other grounds, that the reference to the "rule of law" in Article 2 TEU was not precise enough to sanction breaches of the concept by the Member States.[13] In the two judgements, the CJEU not only rejected Hungary and Poland's complaints that the rule of law as a concept was too vague, but also made it clear that the EU could take measures to defend its "identity as a common legal order".[14] These two judgements herald a new phase in the study of EU constitutional law through the lens of identity. Whereas the language of identity was until recently closely linked to Member States' constitutional orders, either through Article 4(2) TEU or case law, it has now been applied explicitly to the legal order of the EU too.

The migration of the language of identity in the EU from the national plane to the supranational plane raises several questions that need to be addressed. Various contributions to this volume factor in this migration, while they all deal with the wider questions of whether or if so, how the language of constitutional identity should be applied to the EU.

---

[9] For discussion of constitutional identity in the context of the EU, see Faraguna and Drinóczi 2022; Van der Schyff 2016, 2021, 2022; Martinico 2016; Van Damme 2015; Sarmiento 2013; Sadurski 2006.

[10] View of Advocate General Kokott of 13 June 2014 regarding Opinion procedure 2/13, ECLI:EU:C:2014:2475, para 168; Opinion of Advocate General Cruz Villalón of 14 January 2015 in CJEU, Case C-62/14, *Gauweiler*, ECLI:EU:C:2015:7, para 61; Opinion of Advocate General Szpunar of 14 January 2020 in CJEU, Case C-641/18, *LG v. Rina SpA, Ente Registro Italiano Navale*, ECLI:EU:C:2020:3, paras 141, 144.

[11] CJEU, Case C-156/21, *Hungary v. Parliament and Council*, judgement of 16 February 2022, ECLI:EU:C:2022:97; CJEU, Case C-157/21, *Poland v. Parliament and Council*, judgement of 16 February 2022, ECLI:EU:C:2022:98.

[12] See especially Articles 4(1) and 5(1) of Regulation (EU, Euratom) 2020/2092 of the European Parliament and of the Council of 16 December 2020 on a general regime of conditionality for the protection of the Union budget.

[13] *Hungary v. Parliament and Council*, para 205; *Poland v. Parliament and Council*, para 313.

[14] *Hungary v. Parliament and Council*, para 127; *Poland v. Parliament and Council*, para 145.

1.2   A Constitutional Identity for the EU?

What is to be made of the characterisation of the EU in terms of constitutional identity? While it is often accepted that the constitutional orders of Member States can be studied using the lens of constitutional identity, the question of whether the EU legal order lends itself to similar study is more open to debate and controversy.[15]

In this regard, Dieter Grimm in Chap. 2 distinguishes between constitutional identity as denoting difference between constitutions, as referring to the core elements of a constitution and as a symbolic value which captures people's identification with a constitution. For analytical purposes the last two types of identity are the most interesting. In further exploring the term, Grimm notes that an identity attaches to a *constitution*, raising the question whether the EU can lay claim to a constitution, and hence an own identity. We learn from his analysis that the EU is fundamentally a treaty organisation which is dependent on its constituent states. The EU is "hetero-determined" through its Member States, and not "self-determined" by a constituent people. The result is that the Treaties evidence a "quasi-constitutional character", which means that the EU only possesses what may be termed a "functional constitution". The identity of the Treaties therefore derives mainly from the fact that they do not form a constitution in the sense of state constitutions. Interestingly, Grimm remarks that it seems insufficient to reduce a European constitutional identity only to the common values in Article 2 TEU, as is sometimes proposed. The four economic freedoms are located as a part of the Treaties' core, as well as the Charter of Fundamental Rights. On the whole, we learn from Grimm's analysis that the term "constitutional identity" when applied to the EU does not carry the same meaning as when applied to states and their constitutions. The mere fact that the Treaties might be labelled as "constitutional", as the failed Constitutional Treaty of 2004 attempted, does not change this situation. What would be needed for a fully-fledged EU constitutional identity to take shape is for the EU to be transformed into a European state, a prospect which is deemed highly unlikely under current conditions. Grimm concludes that in the absence of such a transformation, the EU has to be appreciated and identified with what it is, namely an unprecedented political entity that lies in between traditional nation states on the one hand and modern supranational organisations on the other.

Apart from the chapter by Dieter Grimm, other chapters also investigate the very idea of conceptualising the EU in terms of constitutional identity. In this regard, in Chap. 3 Jakob Gašperin Wischhoff is also critical of imagining the EU in such terms, based on five considerations. First, in his view, it is impossible to determine objectively what the identity of the EU is, also given the existence of different narratives about this identity. Further, the notion of constitutional identity at the national level seems to serve mainly as a substitute for sovereignty, so that application of this notion at the EU level may upset Member States and may suggest misplaced neo-colonial ambitions. Third, identity does not denote a self-standing fact, but a relationship in

---

[15] On whether the term "constitutional identity" should be used as such, see Scholtes 2021; Fabbrini and Sajó 2019. Compare also Perju 2020.

which a person identifies with an idea, which implies that there would be a multitude of European constitutional identities. Moreover, constitutional identity suggests the existence of an immutable constitutional core, which goes against the ideal of democratic revisability and is problematic in light of the open future of the EU. Fifth and finally, Gašperin Wischhoff argues that if the purpose behind constructing a constitutional identity for the EU lies in defending the EU's values—such as democracy, the rule of law and human rights—it is better to simply call these values by their names.

Against the backdrop of the two more sceptical or critical contributions mentioned above, Tímea Drinóczi and Pietro Faraguna in Chap. 4 are more accepting of the EU possessing a constitutional identity of its own. These authors discuss the term constitutional identity as applied to the Member States of the EU, and to the EU itself. In this regard they distinguish the application of the term by the constitutional courts of Germany and Italy from the term's use by the constitutional courts of Hungary and Poland. The first two countries are noted for their dialogical approach in using the term in the context of the EU, while the latter two countries are criticised for abusing the term. Furthermore, we learn from their analysis that the EU also possesses a constitutional identity and not just its Member States. This identity, the authors explain, can be derived from the immutability of some of the EU's core values such as human rights, democracy and the rule of law. Support for this claim is also drawn from the fact that the CJEU, in its twin landmark judgements dealing with the rule of law conditionality regime mentioned earlier, affirmed that Article 2 TEU defined the "very identity of the European legal order" and that the Member States may not deviate from the EU rule of law standard.[16]

The contribution by Gerhard van der Schyff (Chap. 5) also supports the view that the EU possesses a constitutional identity of its own. Building on the concept of an EU citizenship, he argues that the EU has a type of sovereign non-statehood. As a result, its constitutional order is not simply a derivate of the Member States' constitutional orders, but is an order in its own right. The effect is that the EU project is composed of 28 constitutional identities in total. These are the 27 individual identities of the Member States' constitutional orders and the common identity of the EU's constitutional order. When it comes to settling disputes between the common EU identity and those of the Member States, he argues that the common identity has to prevail if the EU is to function in a meaningful way.

---

[16] *Hungary v. Parliament and Council*, paras 127, 232–233; *Poland v. Parliament and Council*, paras 145, 264–265.

1.3   The Content and Scope of a Constitutional Identity for the EU

Apart from addressing the very notion of an EU constitutional identity, several contributions to this volume also consider the content or scope of such an identity. In other words, if the EU were to be conceptualised as possessing a constitutional identity, what would that identity cover?

The contributions by Dieter Grimm, Tímea Drinóczi and Pietro Faraguna, as well as Gerhard van der Schyff all touch on the content of an EU constitutional identity, in addition to investigating the notion as such. As mentioned above, in distinguishing the identity of the EU from that of the Member States, Drinóczi and Faraguna limit their analysis to Article 2 TEU in investigating the EU's core, while Grimm notes that the core of the Treaties is wider than the values in Article 2 TEU. In this regard, he also refers to the four economic freedoms and the Charter of Fundamental Rights as belonging to the EU's core and hence as being part of the EU's identity. Van der Schyff, in his chapter, argues that the EU's constitutional identity consists of two inter-related pillars. The first of which guarantees the autonomy of EU law, through doctrines such as the direct effect and primacy of EU law, while the second pillar covers its fundamental values, as protected in Article 2 TEU.

A number of contributions focus on the content of the constitutional identity of the EU as such. In Chap. 6, Gohar Karapetian examines EU citizenship from the perspective of Christian theological literature, particularly St. Augustine's political thought. Karapetian argues that some of the main issues EU citizenship is dealing with in the current EU constitutional debate, specifically in its relation with the national citizenship of the Member States, were touched upon in the fifth century AD by St. Augustine concerning the relationship between Christian citizenship and secular citizenship. According to Karapetian, St. Augustine's thought on the structure of Christian citizenship may help us in answering the question why the CJEU qualifies EU citizenship as the fundamental status of the citizen, and why EU citizenship, thus, transcends national citizenship from the CJEU's point of view. From an Augustinian perspective, in attaching value to the EU's and its citizenship's final destination, the CJEU ruled that EU citizenship is destined to be the fundamental status of the citizen. Additionally, similar to the relationship of Christian citizenship with worldly citizenship as developed by St. Augustine, in facilitating the coexistence of EU citizenship with the citizenship of the Member States, the CJEU confirms the intimate relationship the citizen has with the legal and political order of his Member State. The city of God's eschatology and the EU's final destination are, in Karapetian's conclusion, from an Augustinian perspective crucial in comprehending the (secular) transcendence of both Christian citizenship and EU citizenship over other existing citizenships.

In Chap. 7, Erika Arban turns her attention to solidarity as an important principle in relation to the constitutional identity of the EU. She notes that the EU is facing various challenges, and that solidarity, which is explicitly taken up in Article 2 TEU, plays a role in this regard as well as in shaping the constitutional identity of the EU. Starting from the literature on constitutional identity, Arban develops a "thick" concept of constitutional identity that combines aspirations and commitments based on the past, and that is fluid and changeable in order to deal with contradictions and imbalances. She argues that taking solidarity seriously can form an impetus to invigorate EU integration and curb the tensions traversing the continent. Other than in Article 2 TEU, references to solidarity can also be found in other articles of the TEU as well as in the Charter of Fundamental Rights. On the basis of her theoretical approach, combined with doctrinal and comparative insights, Arban shows how solidarity is linked to the idea of a constitutional identity of the EU, and as such can forge a constitutional identity that can help tackle the EU's various crises.

In further exploring what an EU constitutional identity might entail, Robert Böttner in Chap. 8 alerts us to the importance of the twin values of "unity" and "diversity" in the context of European integration. Instead of focussing on a substantive value and its meaning in order to understand constitutional identity in connection with the EU, Böttner investigates the EU's identity as an interaction between the forces unifying EU law and those allowing for diversity in EU law. "Unity", we learn, is exemplified by "legal unity" which covers concepts such as the primacy of EU law. In addition to such legal homogeneity, the EU has evolved into a "Union of values" exemplified by its foundational values protected in Article 2 TEU. Completing the triptych of unifying forces, the establishment of the common market is treated as the start and core of European integration in a strict sense. Uniform integration, however, was not a goal in itself, and became more difficult to achieve as more states joined the EU. In this regard, Böttner investigates how the EU legal order came to be characterised by national diversity and differentiation in both primary and secondary law. Various provisions of EU law are discussed, such as Article 4(2) TEU which allows for legal and institutional pluralism in the EU. However, instead of seeing unity and diversity as incompatible forces, he suggests that they are in fact two sides to the same coin. Unity is the ideal of European integration, while diversity is the strength of the EU.

1.4 The Function and Operation of a Constitutional Identity for the EU

Conceptualising the constitutional identity of the EU also begs the question as to its function or operation. Or, to put it differently, what end does the device of constitutional identity of the EU serve? In this regard, a number of contributions consider the added value of the concept in studying European integration.

The most straightforward answer to the question of its use relates to the *descriptive* value of constitutional identity. Deploying the concept helps us to debate and classify the core values or elements of EU law. A survey of the contributions reveals that Article 2 TEU is generally considered to fit the category of constitutional identity, while additional elements can also be considered such as the four economic freedoms at the base of European integration. But as the discussion in the previous section illustrated, the device of identity can be put to a much broader use in describing and understanding the content of EU law, such as in focussing on the moulding forces of unity and diversity.

The device of identity can also entail more than describing or classifying a constitutional order. In addition to description, constitutional identity can for instance also serve a *benchmark function* in the EU's multilevel legal system.[17] This becomes apparent from the contribution of Tímea Drinóczi and Pietro Faraguna. These authors point to the possibility of "unconstitutional constitutional identities", by which they mean that the EU is required to respect national constitutional identities only insofar as such identities do not violate the constitutional identity of the EU. The EU's duty in Article 4(2) TEU to respect a Member State's constitutional identity so finds its limit in the identity of the EU, the enforcement of which serves not only to reject a particular state's illiberalism, but also as a way of affirming common EU constitutional values. Van der Schyff comes to a similar conclusion, he argues that while the EU is called upon to respect the "national identities" of the Member States according to Article 4(2) TEU, such respect is to be conditioned by the "identity of the European Union as a common legal order".

The contribution by Giuliano Vosa (Chap. 9) also delves into the function or application of constitutional identity in the EU. In this respect his contribution argues in favour of endowing such an identity with legal, normative force, grounded in the values laid down in Articles 2, 4(2) and 9 TEU. Vosa's interest lies with the implications thereof for the primacy of EU law, and here he advances the claim that there should be respect for and concordance with national democratic self-government, which contributes to the creation of a multi-layered public sphere where conflicts between the two levels can find a satisfactory solution. Rather than conceiving of such a normative identity as an instrument of fully-fledged federal supremacy, Vosa suggests that it can "unveil the delicate mechanisms that bind together people's sovereignty and protection of rights" in a supranational context, which may be useful in reviewing EU measures that are insufficiently supported by (the peoples of) the Member States, including through discussions on the *political* and not only the judicial plane.

Importantly, the related question of the implementation of an EU constitutional identity requires attention. In other words, how does or should identity operate in practice? In this regard, Chap. 10 by Alberto Nicòtina and Emil Martini provides some valuable insights regarding what is termed "peer to peer judicial dialogue". According to the authors, the notion of EU identity finds a definition and consolidates itself in the institutional capacity of national and supranational courts to engage in a fruitful dialogic relationship with each other. In this respect, they look beyond the preliminary reference mechanism and provide comparative inspiration for the discussion about possible institutional instruments to enhance the judicial dialogue among courts. More precisely, they look to the US practice of federal courts asking states' supreme courts for a "certification" of questions of state law. It is pointed out

---

[17] Van der Schyff 2021, pp. 5–6.

that EU law already leaves room for such "reverse preliminary references" and that this should be explored further.

1.5 Constitutional Identity in the EU and Beyond

Three general comments can be made in drawing the discussion of the contributions related to constitutional identity of the EU to a close for present purposes.

Firstly, although a relatively new topic, the study of constitutional identity is likely to gain traction. Until quite recently Gary Jacobsohn could still note that constitutional theorists have relatively little to say about the identity of the constitutions that they study.[18] While this observation might still hold true for some legal orders and their constitutions, its relevance for the study of European integration is rapidly diminishing. The traditional study of constitutional identity as a device in relation to the constitutional orders of the Member States of the EU is now increasingly augmented by the study of such identity in the context of the EU legal order. The inquiry into identity is no longer restricted to the interpretation of the EU's duty to respect the "national identities" of its Member States, as enshrined in Article 4(2) TEU, or to national supreme court or constitutional court rulings protecting their respective "constitutional identities". The extension to the supranational level does not mean though that applying the term "constitutional identity" to the EU is widely accepted or without controversy, as amply illustrated by various contributions to this volume. What it does show is that the question is no longer at the fringes of EU constitutional law. Accounts of EU constitutional law will in future have to take a stance on whether the concept is to be applied to the EU as such, and if so under what conditions.

Secondly, the study of constitutional identity in relation to the EU shows that the legal nature of European integration is still fundamentally contested. The use of the term is not simply a superficial exercise; rather, its use reveals distinct approaches to discussing and understanding what the EU is about and how legal conflict should be settled. In this regard, constitutional identity can serve as a functional device with which to compare the constitutional similarities between the nature and content of the legal orders of the EU and its Member States, but importantly, also their differences. The contribution by Grimm shows the potential differences very clearly in distinguishing between the "constitutions" of the Member States on the one hand, and the "functional constitution" of the EU on the other. On this reading, national constituent authority is fundamental to conceptualising the EU as a legal entity. This stands in contrast to conceptions which view the EU as possessing its own original legal order, which is not simply derived from the states and their constitutions.[19] As an analytical device, constitutional identity can be useful in navigating this debate and delineating the various positions and arguments on the constitutional relationship

---

[18] Jacobsohn 2011, p. 129.

[19] Van der Schyff 2021, p. 4; Pernice 2002, pp. 518–519.

between the EU and its Member States. For instance, the device of identity has proven very useful in refining the debate on the primacy of EU law. On the Member State level, it has been used to articulate national limits to such primacy in the event of a violation of constitutional fundamentals, while on the EU level it has been used to locate and affirm common values which are to be enforced against all Member States. The mere use of term "constitutional identity" does not entail settling the discussion on primacy in favour of Member States or the EU, but it does offer a common vocabulary with which to classify and evaluate the various positions.[20]

Thirdly, although this volume focussed its attention on constitutional identity in the context of the EU, there might be something to be said for the term's application to other multilevel legal regimes where appropriate. The example of the EU shows that a common grammar about the core values or elements underlying a common legal order and its constituent parts can help identify constitutional fault lines to be considered in the application and study of such arrangements. For example, the European Court of Human Rights recently allowed a Member State to rely on its constitutional identity as a legitimate aim in treating citizens and non-citizens differently in a case about pension rights.[21] Arguably, the concept of constitutional identity could be relevant not only from the perspective of the Member States of the Council of Europe, but also when conceptualising the core of the European Convention on Human Rights, or similar regional organisations in other parts of the world that are committed to close legal integration, be it in the field of human rights or beyond.[22]

References

Belov M (2017) The Functions of Constitutional Identity Performed in the Context of Constitutionalization of the EU Order and Europeanization of the Legal Orders of EU Member States. Perspectives on Federalism 9:72–97

Besselink L F M (2010) National and Constitutional Identity Before and After Lisbon. Utrecht Law Review 6:36–49

Blanke H F (2013) Article 4: The Relations Between the EU and the Member States. In: Blanke H F, Mangiameli S (eds) The Treaty on European Union (TEU). A Commentary. Springer, Heidelberg, pp 185–253

Calliess C, Van der Schyff G (eds) (2020a) Constitutional Identity in a Europe of Multilevel Constitutionalism. Cambridge University Press, Cambridge

---

[20] Compare Von Bogdandy and Schill 2011, p. 1435 on the benefits of a common vocabulary in fostering a dialogue between the EU and the Member States, and between the Member States themselves.

[21] ECtHR Case No. 49270/11, judgement of 9 June 2022 (*Savickis and Others v. Latvia*), para 198. Also, even though in their joint dissenting opinion judges O'Leary, Grozev and Lemmens were critical of relying on constitutional identity arguments in this instance and cautious about their use in general, they were careful not to reject the validity of such arguments categorically (para 27).

[22] Consider, for instance, the view of the ECtHR Case No. 2346/02, judgement of 27 July 2002 (*Pretty v. The United Kingdom*), para 65 that the "very essence of the Convention is respect for human dignity and human freedom".

Calliess C, Van der Schyff G (2020b) Constitutional Identity Introduced. In: Calliess C, Van der Schyff G (eds) Constitutional Identity in a Europe of Multilevel Constitutionalism. Cambridge University Press, Cambridge, pp 3–8

Claes M, Reestman J H (2015) The Protection of National Constitutional Identity and the Limits of European Integration at the Occasion of the Gauweiler Case. German Law Journal 16:917–970

Cloots E (2015) National Identity in EU Law. Oxford University Press, Oxford

Cloots E (2016) National Identity, Constitutional Identity, and Sovereignty in the EU. Netherlands Journal of Legal Philosophy 45:82–98

De Witte B (2021) Article 4(2) TEU as a Protection of the Institutional Diversity of the Member States. European Public Law 27:559–570

Drinóczi T (2020) Constitutional Identity in Europe: The Identity of the Constitution. A Regional Approach. German Law Journal 21:105–130

Fabbrini F, Sajó A (2019) The Dangers of Constitutional Identity. European Law Journal 25:457–473

Faraguna P (2017) Constitutional Identity in the EU—A Shield or a Sword? German Law Journal 18:1617–1640

Faraguna P, Drinóczi T (2022) Constitutional Identity in and on EU Terms. VerfassungsBlog, 21 February 2022, https://verfassungsblog.de/constitutional-identity-in-and-on-eu-terms/, DOI: https://doi.org/10.17176/20220222-001059-0

Fromage D, De Witte B (eds) (2021) Special Issue of European Public Law 27:411–628

Jacobsohn G J (2011) The Formation of Constitutional Identities. In: Ginsburg T, Dixon R (eds) Comparative Constitutional Law. Edward Elgar, Cheltenham/Northampton, pp 129–142

Martinico G (2016) Building Supranational Identity: Legal Reasoning and Outcome. In: Kadi I (ed) Opinion 2/13 of the Court of Justice. Italian Journal of Public Law 8:235–267

Perju V (2020) Identity Federalism in Europe and the United States. Vanderbilt Journal of Transnational Law 53:207–273

Pernice I (2002) Multilevel Constitutionalism in the European Union. European Law Review 27:511–529

Polzin M (2017) Constitutional Identity as a Constructed Reality and a Restless Soul. German Law Journal 18:1595–1615

Sadurski W (2006) European Constitutional Identity? Working Paper, EUI LAW, 2006/33

Sarmiento D (2013) The EU's Constitutional Core. In: Saiz Arnaiz A, Alcoberro Llivinia C (eds) National Constitutional Identity and European Integration. Intersentia, Cambridge/Antwerp/Portland, pp 177–204

Schnettger A (2020) Article 4(2) TEU as a Vehicle for National Constitutional Identity in the Shared European Legal System. In: Calliess C, Van der Schyff G (eds) Constitutional Identity in a Europe of Multilevel Constitutionalism. Cambridge University Press, Cambridge, pp 9–37

Scholtes J (2021) Abusing Constitutional Identity. German Law Journal 22:534–556

Van Damme T A J A (2015) Advies 2/13 en de constitutionele identiteit van de EU: Over de (niet-)toetreding tot het EVRM van een federale "non-staat". SEW, Tijdschrift voor Europees en economisch recht 63:616–627

Van der Schyff G (2012) The Constitutional Relationship Between the European Union and Its Member States: The Role of National Identity in Article 4(2) TEU. European Law Review 37:563–583

Van der Schyff G (2016) Exploring Member State and European Union Constitutional Identity. European Public Law 22:227–241

Van der Schyff G (2020) Member States of the European Union, Constitutions, and Identity a Comparative Perspective. In: Calliess C, Van der Schyff G (eds) Constitutional Identity in a Europe of Multilevel Constitutionalism. Cambridge University Press, Cambridge, pp 305–347

Van der Schyff G (2021) Constitutional Identity of the EU Legal Order: Delineating Its Roles and Contours. Ancilla Iuris 1–12

Van der Schyff G (2022) The Need for an Explicit EU Constitutional Identity: The Flipside of the Polish Constitutional Tribunal Judgment K 3/21. NederlandRechtsstaat, 14

January 2022, https://www.nederlandrechtsstaat.nl/the-need-for-an-explicit-eu-constitutional-identity-the-flipside-of-the-polish-constitutional-tribunal-judgment-k-3-21/
Von Bogdandy A, Schill S (2011) Overcoming Absolute Primacy: Respect for National Identity Under the Lisbon Treaty. Common Market Law Review 48:1417–1453

Chapter 2
Three Meanings of Constitutional Identity and Their Prospects in the European Union

Dieter Grimm

Contents

Abstract In a rather banal understanding, constitutional identity means that each constitution is singular in the sense that no constitution looks exactly like the other. In a more prescriptive sense, identity refers to the fundamental principles of a constitution and the basic structure of the order it designs; in short, those provisions without which the constitution would no longer be the same. In a symbolic sense, it means that the people who live under a certain constitution accept it as a more or less good order and can identify with it. The EU has no constitution in the strict sense, but the European Treaties fulfil a number of functions that, within states, are fulfilled by their constitution. The Treaties may, therefore, be called a functional constitution. As such, they have an identity in the two first meanings of the term. However, an important part of this identity is derived from the fact that the EU is not a state, but an unprecedented supranational organization. Different from the identity of Member States' constitutions, which fulfil a defensive function vis-à-vis the EU, this European constitutional identity up to now remains legally speaking latent. The functional European constitution lacks, however, symbolic identity. But not many state constitutions have been able to mobilize this form of identity either. It requires special conditions that are absent in the EU. The hope to increase the acceptance and legitimacy of the EU by transforming the functional constitution into a veritable constitution in the strict

D. Grimm (✉)
Humboldt University Berlin, Berlin, Germany
e-mail: grimm@wiko-berlin.de

Wissenschaftskolleg zu Berlin, Institute for Advanced Study, Berlin, Germany

© T.M.C. ASSER PRESS and the authors 2023
J. de Poorter et al. (eds.), *European Yearbook of Constitutional Law 2022*,
European Yearbook of Constitutional Law 4,
https://doi.org/10.1007/978-94-6265-595-9_2

13

sense would most likely be in vain. It would inescapably transform the EU into a state and thereby aggravate the legitimacy problems rather than solve them.

Keywords Constitutional identity · National identity · European identity · Constitution · European Union · Nation state · European Treaties · Symbolic effect · European Court of Justice · Federal Constitutional Court (Germany)

2.1   Forms and Functions of Constitutional Identity

"Constitutional identity" is not a term that one would find in the text of constitutions. Constitutions do not speak about their own identity. They have it, if only in the sense that no constitution is exactly like the other. The multiple identities are the basis of comparative constitutional research. For purposes of constitutional doctrine and adjudication, identity in this rather banal sense is of little interest. Constitutional provisions can be interpreted and applied without a reference to identity. Even if the predominant legal method favours a contextual instead of an isolated approach to constitutional interpretation and adjudication, it is not the identity of the constitution in this sense that plays a role.

In a narrower and legally momentous sense, the term "constitutional identity" refers to the core elements of the constitution, which determine its type, its basic structure and leading principles, in short, those provisions without which the constitution would no longer be the same, whereas there are numerous other rules whose change or even abolition would leave constitutional identity unaffected. Often, the core elements enjoy a special legal status. In Germany, for instance, they are exempted from amendment by Article 79(3) Basic Law, the so-called eternity clause. The German Constitutional Court locates the identity of the Basic Law exactly in this article and thus gives the notoriously fuzzy notion a relatively clear legal meaning.

Finally, one can speak of constitutional identity in the sense that the people who live under a certain constitution regard it as a lasting expression of the popular will as to how their political rule and social relations should be ordered. This popular perception does not depend on a detailed knowledge of the constitution, but on a general awareness of its basic elements and practical relevance as well as on the conviction that it constitutes altogether a good order under which it is worth living, so that the majority of citizens can identify themselves with it. This form of constitutional identity, although dependent on the effectiveness of the constitution, is but loosely coupled with its legal nature. It rather operates on the symbolic level.

Applied to the very core or the symbolic effect of a constitution, constitutional identity is by no means banal. It is high-toned and as such inapt for everyday use. It will rather remain latent most of the time. There is no need to resort to it as long as the identity of a constitution can be taken for granted. Conversely, if it comes to the fore, this will often indicate that the integrity of a constitution is questioned or threatened. It is thus not by chance that the German Constitutional Court mentioned the term "identity of the constitution" for the first time in connection with the threat that European law posed to the integrity of national constitutional law after the European Court of Justice had proclaimed the priority of European law over national law, including the constitutions of the member states.[1]

In the famous Solange I-decision of 1974, the Court gave the term legal relevance by ruling that Article 24 of the Basic Law, which authorizes Germany to transfer powers ("Hoheitsrechte") to international organizations, does not permit a change of "the constitution's basic structure ("Grundstruktur") on which its identity is founded".[2] Consequently, Germany may not ratify an international treaty that would negatively affect the identity of the Basic Law. Moreover, the Court declared that the primacy of European law ends where the identity of the constitution begins. As a consequence, each interpretation of a Treaty provision by the European authorities including the CJEU, which gives it a meaning not compatible with the identity of the Basic Law may not take effect in Germany.

In Solange I, the Constitutional Court counted the protection of fundamental rights among the basic structure and derived from this assumption its own power to review European laws or legal acts as to their compatibility with the Bill of Rights of the Basic Law, at least as long as ("solange") a similarly effective protection of fundamental rights was lacking on the European level. Twelve years later, in the Solange II-opinion, the Court suspended this power because it found that meanwhile a sufficient standard of European fundamental rights protection had been developed by the CJEU. Yet, the power was not abandoned, but can be activated whenever the conditions change.[3]

The Court emphasized this power again in its decision on the Lisbon-Treaty.[4] Here, the Court found support in Article 4(2) TEU, according to which the EU respects the national identity of the member states "inherent in their fundamental structures, political and constitutional". In addition, the Court derived from the identity as expressed in Article 79(3) BL in connection with national sovereignty a barrier against abandoning the right to self-determination and transforming the EU into a state. Even a constitutional amendment would not be able to overcome this barrier. According to the Court, a decision of such a magnitude can only be taken by the people themselves in a new constitution.[5]

As these decisions show, constitutional identity has mainly assumed a defensive function on the national level. While internally, Article 79(3) BL was sufficient to protect the core of the Basic Law against amendments after which the constitution would have no longer been the same, the eternity clause seemed insufficient vis-á-vis external threats. Here, a stronger notion was deemed necessary to establish a barrier against claims of foreign law that were regarded as threat to the integrity of the national constitution. Identity offered this added value, because it postulates the

---

[1] Court of Justice of the European Union, *Van Gend & Loos*, judgment of 5 February 1963, ECLI:EU:C:1963:1; CJEU, *Costa v. ENEL*, judgment of 15 July 1964, ECLI:EU:C:1964:66.

[2] BVerfGE 37, 271, *Solange I*, judgement of 29 May 1974.

[3] BVerfGE 73, 339, *Solange II*, judgement of 22 October 1986.

[4] BVerfGE 123, 267, *Lisbon*, judgement of 30 June 2009, para 353.

[5] BVerfGE 123, 267, *Lisbon*, judgement of 30 June 2009, para 347.

constitution not just as a body of high-ranking legal norms, but an expression of the national will and a formative element of the nation's identity.

2.2 The EU Treaties as a "Functional" Constitution

While the identity of national constitutions has been widely discussed after the German Court's Lisbon-judgment, a similar discussion about European constitutional identity is missing. The editors of the Yearbook are aware of this and want to initiate such a discourse. They ask, whether a supranational entity like the EU can have or may even need a constitutional identity, which function it fulfils or effect it has, and what it might consist of. However, all these questions make sense only if the first one can be answered in the affirmative. Should constitutions be limited to states, the following questions would be superfluous. Constitutional identity presupposes a constitution. Does the EU have a constitution?

The legal basis of the EU is a treaty concluded by sovereign states under international law. However, this treaty fulfils a number of functions which, within states, are fulfilled by the constitution. The Treaty of Rome established the then European Economic Community, defined its purpose, equipped it with powers necessary to pursue the purpose, provided the EEC with organs, defined their function, and determined the conditions under which they may exercise their power. Insofar, the Treaties follow the constitutional pattern. They also enjoy precedence over secondary European law and, according to the CJEU, also over national law and thereby share an essential characteristic of constitutions.

What then distinguishes the European Treaties from a state constitution? First, their appearance is not that of a constitution. They are much longer. The explanation is that the provisions which fulfil a constitutional function are a small minority in the Treaties, and the Charter of Fundamental Rights that was added to the Treaties in 2009 did not change this substantially. The vast majority of provisions concern matters that no state regulates in its constitution, but in ordinary law. So, the whole law of economic competition is part of the Treaties, not of secondary European law. This is not a misconception of the member states, but a consequence of the fact that they did not have a constitution in mind when they drafted the Treaties.

Secondly and even more important, state constitutions are today generally regarded as acts of self-determination of a nation, a people or a society as to the form of its political existence and the modalities of political rule. This essential element of modern constitutionalism is missing in the EU. The EU does not give itself a constitution, it owes its existence to the will of states and receives its legal basis from them by way of agreement. The people of the EU are not involved nor is the Treaty attributed to them as the source of all public authority. With regard to its existence, purpose, competencies, organization, procedures etc., the EU is not self-determined, but hetero-determined.

One might assert that there are constitutions which were enacted by a treaty of sovereign states, such as the constitution of the German Empire of 1871. But here, the treaty was only the mode by which a constitution for a newly created state was brought about. In the treaty, the founding states gave up the constituent power and transferred it to the new entity. The nature of a treaty was thus consummated with its conclusion. The new entity was from the very moment of treaty conclusion onwards self-determined. Even if the founding states retained a share of the amendment power for themselves, they exercised it as an organ of the new political entity, not as sovereign states.

Nothing like that has happened in the EU. Up to now, the member states are not prepared to hand the constituent power over to the EU. Amendments to the European Treaties require the conclusion of another international treaty that has to be ratified in all member states according to the provisions of their national constitutions. Discussed in terms of sovereignty, this means that the member states transfer certain sovereign rights to the EU, but not sovereignty itself. The EU exercises public authority, but cannot claim to be sovereign. It seems difficult to argue that a political entity that depends on others with regard to its existence, its purpose, its powers, etc., is sovereign.[6]

This would have been so even if the failed Constitutional Treaty of 2004 had entered into force. While it is true that the member states changed the procedure for amendments by admitting new actors in the stage of preparation, nothing was changed regarding the final decision. In particular, the EU citizenry was not involved. The amendment power remained in the hands of the member states. The failed document would not have endowed the EU with the right to self-determination about its legal foundation. Like the preceding treaties, the treaty of 2004 would have been an international treaty with the only difference that it was labelled a "constitution".

Still, what matters is not the label, but the legal nature, and this continues to be that of a treaty. Hence, if one looks for a basis of a European constitutional identity, it can only be found in the Treaties. One may call them "constitution" in a functional sense. But then it is necessary to keep the difference in mind. It is a thin notion of constitutionalism, with the democratic origin, that is an integral part of the achievement of constitutionalism, left out. Among the various meanings of the term "constitutional identity", certainly the symbolic meaning is directly linked to the democratic element of constitutionalism. Are the Treaties nevertheless capable of serving as a basis for a specific European constitutional identity? And why would the EU need such an identity in the first place?

2.3 Weakness of European Constitutional Identity

The Treaties mention "identity" only in connection with the member states, not the EU, and they do not speak of constitutional identity, but of national identity. The EU is obliged to respect it. This shows that the member states as the authors of the Treaties saw their identity endangered by the EU, not the other way round.

---

[6] Grimm 2017, p. 39.

Constitutional identity comes in insofar as national identity is declared to be "inherent in the fundamental structures of the member states, political and constitutional". The relationship appears more clearly in the German text where the national identity "finds expression" in the fundamental political and constitutional structures. The constitutions are seen in an auxiliary position regarding national identity, a difference that disappears in the jurisprudence of the CJEU.[7]

However, one cannot conclude from the silence of the Treaties with regard to a European constitutional identity that it does not have one. The national constitutions do not stipulate a constitutional identity either. Nevertheless, they have it, however it is defined and what it entails. There is no principal obstacle against a European constitutional identity to the extent that the Treaties may be called a constitution. If their quasi-constitutional character is accepted, albeit reduced in comparison to the achievement of constitutionalism,[8] their identity can hardly be doubted, in any case in the banal sense of the term. But also the form of identity that is constituted by the basic structure or the core elements can be ascertained in the Treaties.

However, the Treaties draw their identity mainly from the fact that they are not a constitution in the sense of state constitutions. Rather, their supranational elements are what accounts for the identity of the European quasi-constitution. Among these core elements is the fact that the European public authority is not entrusted to the EU organs by a European people, but by states that preserve their sovereignty and only transfer a number of sovereign powers to the EU. This is the reason for the contractual nature of the quasi-constitution, and following from that for the competence-competence of the member states and, as its safeguard, the principle of conferral. It also finds an expression in the organizational structure with the Council and not the Parliament in the centre.

Substantively, the four economic freedoms form part of the core. The Lisbon Treaty added the values of the Union, which all member states have to adhere to. Together with the Charter of Fundamental Rights, they are also part of the core of the European legal foundation.[9] While the supra-national elements distinguish the legal foundation of the EU from the member states' constitutions, they share the values and a bill of rights. Just as the EU has to respect the constitutional identity of the member states, the member states are obliged to acknowledge these values. Like in many state constitutions, legal consequences are attached to these provisions. Non-compliance with Article 2 TEU may trigger the sanctions provided for in Article 7 TEU.

However, these items are rarely discussed in terms of a European constitutional identity. If the experiences in the member states are valid also for the EU, the reason may be that until recently the integrity of the Treaties was not under a threat which

---

[7] Wischmeyer 2015, p. 442; Burgorgue-Larsen 2013, p. 282.

[8] Grimm 2016, p. 357.

[9] It seems insufficient to reduce the European constitutional identity to the common values in Article 2 TEU, like in Mlynarski 2021, p. 15, with further references, and prominently in CJEU, Hungary v. European Parliament, Council of the EU, and Poland v. European Parliament and Council of the EUR, judgements of 16 February 2022, Cases 156/21 and 157/21.

made it necessary to resort to identity. As far as the member states are concerned, every expansion of transferred competences by way of Treaty interpretation limits the scope and impact of national constitutions. The EU is less affected from the side of the member states because they do not have the last word in determining the meaning of European law. However, it is telling that the CJEU felt compelled to invoke European identity as defined in Article 2 TEU vis-à-vis Poland and Hungary when these member states questioned some of the values of the EU.[10]

Remains the symbolic identity. Like in Article 4(2) TEU that seeks to protect the national identity and only indirectly the constitutional identity of the member states, the point of reference is the identity of the EU as expressed in and supported by the Treaties as Europe's functional constitution. Constitutional identity in the symbolic sense refers not so much to the specific legal character of the constitution, but to its capability to generate an identification of the European citizens with the EU. The EU as the object of identification must be distinguished from the constitution as the means to bring forth or contribute to the acceptance by the people. Yet, in terms of acceptance, the EU lags far behind the member states.

What explains the difference? States are the political form of existence of a nation or society, to which one belongs regardless of the differences in interests and ideals, wealth and education, town and country, etc. In Germany, the word "Schicksalsgemeinschaft" is in use. The EU is not perceived as a "Schicksalsgemeinschaft" by its citizens. It is an artificial entity composed of states with limited tasks. Up to now, it has not been able to generate a sense of belonging among its citizens similar to that of states. States may be criticized, the performance of their rulers contested, even their political system questioned. But this leaves their right to existence unaffected. Rejection of a government, even attempts to change the political system can go along with a deep affection for the country.

The EU, to the contrary, is constantly confronted with doubts about its necessity or utility. A growing number of citizens regard it as a threat to the national identity. There is a revival of national identity within the member states of the European Union, not only in some new ones, but also in the founding states. It does not remain in the private sphere, but is organized politically and attracts votes in national and European elections. But even where the existence of the EU and its usefulness in general is not contested—and this seems still to be a significant majority of the EU citizens—no feeling of belonging and no solidarity across borders comparable to that within the states has developed. The "ever closer Union" lacks a solid popular basis.

---

[10] See the judgments mentioned in fn. 9.

2.4   Different Sources of Identity

Could an increase of symbolic constitutional identity help to solve Europe's legitimacy problem? And why is it now perceived as a problem, whereas it did not bother
the people and the European institutions very much in the earlier periods of European
integration? The turning point seems to be the moment in history when people began
to notice that the EU was no longer just a common market with a lot of advantages for
the majority of citizens, but had become a political project, that affected the conditions of people's life more and more, but was not based on an expressed will of the
citizenry. Rather, where the citizens were asked to endorse the progress of European
integration, such as with the Constitutional Treaty of 2004, it was rejected.

The immense progress that European integration had made over time, had come
by stealth, to a very large extent through the jurisprudence of the CJEU, that is to say,
incrementally in a non-political mode and without public debate.[11] Stealth had been
a condition of the progress of integration, but the more the integration advanced the
more did stealth become a problem. The legitimacy resources that were sufficient for
the common market are not sufficient for the political entity that the EU has become
over time. These are some reasons for the rise of the identity discussion in Europe,
whereas the current identity discussion in many member states is rather caused by the
increasing rift within national societies, on the one hand, and the threat to national
identity that emanates from the EU, on the other.

The question is whether there are sources for a European identity and in particular, whether there are chances that the European Treaties or perhaps a European
constitution in the full sense could fill the identity gap of the EU. In order to answer
this question, it may be helpful to change the perspective for a moment and ask what
serves as basis for the identity of states. Mostly still the nation, its uniqueness or
otherness, often hand in hand with an assumed superiority over other nations, the
grand periods in national history, the nation's achievements like military victories
or its persistence in spite of existential crises, its culture and religion, science and
technological inventions that were produced in the country, even sporting success.

The constitution does not figure in this list, and, as a matter of fact, national identity based on a country's constitution is rare. Constitutions are expected to function
legally. Their function is fulfilled if their provisions are complied with. That it serves,
in addition, as a basis for national identity is not the rule. Yet, under favourable conditions, juridically successful constitutions may exceed their regulatory function and
contribute to the integration of society. This happens if the people see their aspirations and conceptions of a just order reflected in the constitution and thus develop
not only a utilitarian, but also an emotional relationship towards the constitution, so
that it becomes a part of the national identity.[12]

Still, there are examples of states whose constitutions have played an important
role in the formation of national identity, the most conspicuous one being the United

---

[11] Grimm 2017, pp. 1 and 21.

[12] See, e.g., Vorländer 2002.

States. Why is that so? The US emerged from a triumphant revolution against a colonial power, for which the Declaration of Independence stands, and it was established as a state by adopting the Constitution in 1787. It had had no independent history, culture, faith on which it could have built its own identity. It rather comprised immigrants of very different national traditions and cultures. The Constitution was what they shared and were proud of, being the first political entity based on a constitution in the modern sense, and it promised them a better life than in their countries of origin, which they had to leave.

Another example is West Germany. The identity of the Federal Republic before unification was to a large extent based on the Basic Law. However, different from the US, it emerged from a national catastrophe that had destroyed the traditional sources of national identity. The nation was divided, the history was loaded with the Holocaust, the cultural heritage was needed as the last remaining bond around the two German states. The Constitution succeeded in filling this gap. It symbolized the rise of the country after a devastating defeat, its return into the circle of civilized nations and in addition the better alternative compared to the other German state under communist rule.[13]

However, this success would not have been possible without the Federal Constitutional Court whose jurisprudence bestowed on the Basic Law a degree of relevance for political behaviour and social relations that no previous German constitution had had, and it made this relevance constantly visible for the people. The Constitutional Court is the institution that the public trusts most. Even judgments that greatly irritated the people and drew heavy protest lowered the approval for moments, but left the general popularity of the institution unaffected. In the end, something as rare as a "constitutional patriotism" could emerge, a term that will hardly be found in other countries.[14]

However, the post-World War II-conditions of West Germany's constitutional patriotism are so unique that they cannot serve as a model for the EU. But couldn't the US be a model? The EU shares with the US its multinational and multicultural citizenry. But it differs from the US in that European people did not leave their home countries and were ready to start anew in a different environment. Rather, they stay in their traditional national environment and remain part of its tradition, culture and education, its political system, its national discourse. It is true that the EU guarantees every European citizen free movement in the EU, but the vast majority of citizens is not keen on living in a different country and under unfamiliar conditions.

---

[13] See Grimm 2001, p. 107.
[14] Müller 2007.

2.5   Auspices for a European Constitutional Identity

If one asks, based on this insight, what the auspices for a European constitutional identity are, it will be seen that almost all preconditions that contributed to the symbolic effect of state constitutions are missing. The beginnings are not marked by a "constitutional moment".[15] It is true that European integration had hardly been possible without the devastating consequences of World War II. But the War had ended twelve years before the European Economic Community was founded, and the peace that has existed ever since among the member states, although an important achievement, is no longer attributed to the Union. Even if one imagines Europe without the EU, the consequence is not war.[16] The economic integration, with which it began, does not furnish the emotional basis on which identity can be built.

Moreover, the European Treaties are not of a sort to acquire the symbolic function that state constitutions may fulfil under favourable conditions. Not conceived as a constitution, they did not appeal to the people's emotions. They were technical law that does not easily lend itself to veneration. They contained detailed rules for the common market, but lacked any emphatic exclamation like "Die Würde des Menschen ist unantastbar", that helps to root a constitution in the minds and hearts of people. The people could not perceive them as a constitution. When the EU found that the time had come for a Constitutional Treaty, it failed in two referenda, because it looked like more Europe, where a majority found that there was already too much Europe.

In addition, the sheer amount of provisions in the Treaties, which has increased, not decreased over time, makes it difficult to recognize them as a constitution, because most of them are not of a constitutional nature. The Treaties do not observe the difference between constitutional law and ordinary law that is crucial for constitutionalism. Constitutional law contains the fundamental principles and basic rules for the political process and for political decision-making. But it leaves the decisions themselves to the political process and to the preferences of those political groups which obtained a majority in the election, whereas in the EU, many of these decisions are already taken in the Treaties. This explains their excessive volume, compared to state constitutions.

One should not play this down as a matter of legal aesthetics. It is a cause of Europe's legitimacy problem. All those rules, although far from what one would expect in a constitution, participate in the constitutionalization of the Treaties in the wake of the two ground-breaking judgments of the CJEU in 1963 and 1964.[17] They are withdrawn from the political process. The winner is the CJEU. It can interpret and shape them according to its perception of the Common Market. The member states as well as the European Parliament are not only side-lined, they cannot change the result, even if they think that it has little to do with their intention or is detrimental.

---

[15] See Ackerman 1989, p. 546; further elaborated in Ackerman 1991, 1998, 2014.

[16] It remains to be seen whether the war in the Ukraine will bring the achievement of peace to the fore once again and to what extent it will be attributed to the EU or rather to NATO.

[17] See fn. 1.

As far as the constitutionalized Treaties reach, elections do not matter. This is one of the biggest, but least noticed sources of the European democratic problem.[18]

Would it then be helpful to revive the idea of a European constitution in the full sense of the term? This would require two fundamental changes. The first one would be to relieve the Treaties from the big number of provisions that are not of a constitutional nature and to downgrade them to ordinary law, so that that they are again open for democratic decision-making, while on the constitutional level only those provisions would remain, which resemble a constitution in the general understanding. Secondly, it would be necessary to root the legal basis of the EU in an act of self-determination of the European citizens. After a long history of European integration without participation of the citizenry, this would be a precondition of the symbolic effect of constitutions, not a guarantee.

However, before taking this step, one has to be aware that it would mean a transformation of the European Union into a European state. As soon as the member states hand the constituent power over to the EU itself they turn it into a state, regardless of whether this is intended or not. As a consequence, the EU would be transformed from a supranational organization established and supported by states into a self-supporting political entity. No longer would the states decide which competences they transfer to the EU, but the EU would decide which competences it takes from the states. The Council in which the member states are represented would become a second house of the Parliament and no longer be responsible for the degree and pace of the integration.

Under current conditions, it seems highly unlikely that this is what a majority of the people want. But irrespectively of popular sentiments and also of the prohibition by the Basic Law, one has to ask whether it is desirable. The major question is how the EU would generate the increased democratic legitimacy that it needs when turned into a state. Up to now, the legitimacy of the EU flows mainly from the democratic process in the member states, whereas the EU's own legitimacy that flows from the European elections is rather low. Where are the sources for a genuine European legitimacy in a state that lacks the societal preconditions of a lively democratic process, the European intermediaries between the electorate and the institutions and the Europe-wide political discourse?

One should rather realize that the identity, even the uniqueness, that distinguishes the EU from all other political entities lies in its unprecedented nature as an entity between traditional nation states on the one hand and modern supranational organizations on the other. It handles, on the one hand, the growing number of problems that can no longer be efficiently solved within the narrow framework of nation states, but it leaves, on the other, the responsibility for the purposes and powers of the EU as well as the bulk of political decision-making to the national level where the prospects for democratic legitimation and accountability are better than on the supranational

---

[18] Grimm 2017, p. 81.

level. This unique model is the more promising basis for a genuine European identity than a constitution.[19]

References

Ackerman B (1989) Constitutional Politics/Constitutional Law. Yale Law Journal 99:453–547
Ackerman B (1991) We the People, Vol. 1. Harvard University Press, Cambridge, MA
Ackerman B (1998) We the People, Vol. 2. Harvard University Press, Cambridge, MA
Ackerman B (2014) We the People, Vol. 3. Harvard University Press, Cambridge, MA
Burgorgue-Larsen L (2013) A Huron at the Kirchberg Plateau. In: Saiz Arnaiz A, Alcoberro Llivina C (eds) National Constitutional Identity and European Integration. Intersentia, Cambridge, pp. 275–287
Grimm D (2001) Die Verfassung und die Politik. C.H. Beck, Munich
Grimm D (2016) Constitutionalism. Past, Present and Future. Oxford University Press, Oxford
Grimm D (2017) The Constitution of European Democracy. Oxford University Press, Oxford
Haltern U (2002) Europäische Verfassung und Europäische Identität In: Elm R (ed) Europäische Identität: Paradigmen und Methodenfragen. Nomos, Baden-Baden, pp. 239–290
Mlynarski M (2021) Zur Integration staatlicher und europäischer Verfassungsidentität. Mohr Siebeck, Berlin
Müller J-W (2007) Constitutional Patriotism. Princeton University Press, Princeton
Vorländer H (ed) (2002) Integration durch Verfassung. VS Verlag für Sozialwissenschaften, Wiesbaden
Wischmeyer T (2015) Nationale Identität und Verfassungsidentität. Archiv des öffentlichen Rechts 140:415–460

---

[19] See Haltern 2002, p. 289, "Das Potential eines verfassten Europas besteht gerade darin, auf eine Verfassung zu verzichten."

Chapter 3
A Plaidoyer Against the Sisyphean Endeavour to Imagine the Constitutional Identity of the EU

Jakob Gašperin Wischhoff

Contents

Abstract Claims of national constitutional identity, within the European Union, are primarily reactions to constitutional conflicts among the Member States and the Union itself. One the one hand, respect for the national identities—that are inherent in the fundamental political and constitutional structures of the Member States— forms part of EU law. On the other hand, the Member States are ultimately bound to respect the principle of primacy. These constitutional tensions may thereby often

J. Gašperin Wischhoff (✉)
DFG Graduate Program DynamInt, Humboldt-Universität zu Berlin, Berlin, Germany
e-mail: j.gasperin.wischhoff@posteo.eu

© T.M.C. ASSER PRESS and the authors 2023
J. de Poorter et al. (eds.), *European Yearbook of Constitutional Law 2022*,
European Yearbook of Constitutional Law 4,
https://doi.org/10.1007/978-94-6265-595-9_3

be resolved through dialogue; in the sense of engagement and loyal cooperation. However, the imprudent and prematurely artificial construction of a constitutional identity of the European Union finds itself in a completely different context. Imagining in good faith a constitutional identity of the EU may imply striving for a more robust and enhanced commitment to essential liberal constitutional values, such as democracy, human rights, and the rule of law, but good will alone cannot replace the likely pitfalls of such an endeavour. This chapter considers the pitfalls and examines the potential risks of imagining a European constitutional identity, questions the underlying motivation for such a formation, and seeks to demonstrate the unsuitability of identity-related terminology in constitutional law. Moreover, it explores the conceptual history of the constitutional identity argument and delves into the inherent tensions between democracy and identity. Finally, it argues that, rather than denominating essential constitutional commitments as a constitutional identity, in order to elevate their argumentative strength, one can facilitate their enforcement by taking existing constitutional principles seriously while simply calling them by their proper names.

Keywords Changeability · Democratic (ir)reversibility · Essential constitutional values · European constitutional identity · Hierarchy of norms · Identity as relation · Multitude of identities · National constitutional identity · Sovereignty

3.1 Introduction

What is the purpose of artificially construing the possible meanings around the conceptual conundrum of the constitutional identity of the European Union (hereafter also: 'EU' or 'Union')? Why would the EU need to imagine its constitutional identity? And what are the potential and real pitfalls of such an undertaking? This chapter argues against the misguided Sisyphean attempt to artificially invent a constitutional identity of the European Union while developing the following five considerations.

First, *identity as knowing thyself*. As the Oracle of Delphi from ancient Greece suggests,[1] knowing thyself is not an easy task. But knowing the identity of the European Union may be even problematic, due to the various possible narratives and characteristics. Moreover, should one only understand identity in legal terms, as *the essential constitutional features of a legal entity*,[2] what is the purpose of identifying it for the EU? Is it to be able to compare and differentiate itself from the 'Other'? And if so, with what and for what purpose should the EU compare itself with? Or alternatively, should knowing the essence of itself only serve to symbolically strengthen the EU's constitutional commitments and, perhaps, even limit the Member States from potential departure from common and shared constitutional values (Sect. 3.2)?

---

[1] Hard 2019, pp. 146–165.

[2] Van der Schyff 2021, p. 3.

Second, *identity is a conceptual substitute for sovereignty—nihil novum sub sole.* Since the Treaties[3] completely omitted the word sovereignty and introduced an obligation to respect the national identities of the Member States, conceptually the latter have somewhat replaced it. Yet, bringing the conceptual substitute for sovereignty to the level of the Union may upset the Member States, as well as imply global ambitions for the Union, which are at odds with its current constitutional design (Sect. 3.3).

Third, *identity as a relation.* In the legal sphere, identity vocabulary is generally misunderstood in its full scope. Consequently, one of the essential meanings of the word *identity* is usually overlooked when implanting the concept into the constitutional arena. Identity is not just a characteristic or a feature of a subject (uniqueness or collective sameness) but mostly a relation between a specific subject[4] and what it is not, which is firstly *identified* and then internalized, practiced and potentially rejected. Moreover, the semantics of identity reveal that its construction requires an active agent, capable of creating a relationship. Hence, application of identity as a descriptive measure is manifestly unsuitable for constitutional law, generally producing mystification, incoherence and confusion (Sect. 3.4).

Fourth, *there is a deep tension between democracy and identity.* Designating a subject in terms of identity implies an essential nature which is so paramount that it is immune to any potential challenge or change. Democracy, on the other hand, is open to constitutional contestation and modification.[5] Tension between democracy and identity is, thus, inevitable, even though constitutional identity often paradoxically claims to safeguard the very principles of democracy.[6] Proclaiming and thus *conserving* the constitutional identity of the EU would potentially halt the very essence of the Union itself—its constant evolution.[7] The EU is perpetually changing, not only with respect to its institutional design and membership but also as a matter of its *raison d'être*—towards forming an ever-closer Union. There is hardly any persuasive reason to sustain the current status quo and to immunize some of its parts from further progressive development. In addition, a designation of some norms as the real constitutional identity of the EU can introduce a hierarchy of constitutional norms.[8] If so, that may radically modify constitutional adjudication practices beyond the established practice and the initial intention of the Member States and the Treaties (Sect. 3.5).

Finally, *let us call the essential constitutional principles by their name.* If one aims to declare the EU's constitutional essentials to be the EU's identity, in order

---

[3] The Treaty of Lisbon, amending the Treaty on European Union and the Treaty establishing the European Community, signed at Lisbon, 13 December 2007, OJ C 306, 17.12.2007, pp. 1–271.

[4] Troitskaya 2021.

[5] Hohnerlein 2020, pp. 11–73.

[6] German Federal Constitutional Court (Bundesverfassungsgericht, Zweiter Senat), *2 BvE 2/08* (*Lissabon-Urteil*), judgment of 30 June 2009, para 249.

[7] Article 1(2) TEU: '[T]he process of creating an ever closer union among the peoples of Europe [...]'.

[8] Pinelli 2016.

to just strengthen our commitments to them, there is perhaps a better approach to take. Let us simply call them by their names: human dignity, freedom, the rule of law, democracy, fundamental rights, pluralism, solidarity and equality. 'Elevating' them into an identity does not equate them with any further and more compelling normative standards. These values are, properly understood, already imperative and transcendent,[9] and need to be taken seriously on their own (Sect. 3.6).

3.2 The Oracle of Delphi

The following section challenges the notion that one can objectively determine the constitutional identity of the European Union (Sect. 3.2.1). Additionally, a European (constitutional) identity could be construed on the basis of contrastive methodological narratives (Sect. 3.2.2). Furthermore, constitutional identity is itself an evasive and disputed concept (Sect. 3.2.3). Finally, in the absence of clear methodological guidance, one would merely project one's own idea of constitutional identity and thus create a meaning according to one's own ideological aspirations (Sect. 3.2.4). In addition, identity serves as a comparison whereas the Member States and the Union are sharing their essential constitutional commitments (Sect. 3.2.5).

3.2.1 Know Thyself

Pythia, the major oracle in Delphi, was consulted about the most important decisions in ancient Greece. Carved into the stone above her temple, one could read the maxim: 'Know thyself'.[10] Pythia knew that knowing oneself is not an easy task, especially in light of the fact that everything and everyone is constantly changing. And nothing is isolated, coherent and indivisible on its own. Thus, can one ever truly know one's own identity as such? Furthermore, are we indeed capable of articulating the identity of Europe, a subject matter of abundant and highly complex relations, achievements, nations, peoples, histories and aspirations? And, as lawyers, are we capable of determining what the *constitutional* identity of the European Union is?

Think of the following three perspectives regarding the identity of the Union. According to the first perspective, the European Union was built on the principle of a common market and four fundamental freedoms. With capital and labour intrinsically connected via the states and nations of the Union, wars and conflicts would no longer be profitable, if at all possible. Economic cooperation has brought peace and material prosperity. Henceforth, the basic constitutional identity of the Union is a liberal market, as provided for and protected in the Treaties. Everything else is simply an

---

[9] Rawls 1993.

[10] There were apparently three maxims carved: Know thyself, nothing to excess, and certainty brings insanity. See also Hard 2019, pp. 146–165.

appendix, constitutional accessories. After all, the majority of the most important decisions are (still) taken by the heads of states behind closed doors, guided mainly by the demands of the common currency and common market, notwithstanding the limitations of the Treaties. The identity of the EU is, then, not primarily linked to democracy, human rights and the rule of law but, rather, economic cooperation of the Member States to facilitate the common market and, thereby, the enhancement of the economic advantages it provides.

Alternatively, the European Union would never be possible if one were to simply put together 27 states and prescribe them specific forms of cooperation. The very prerequisite for such successful and unique supranational union has been European history, as seen from a broader perspective; including hundreds of years of common ideas, exchanging cultures, shared literature, education, wars and peaceful trading. The perpetual movement of borders and peoples, the immense intellectual force of the Ancient Greek and Roman philosophies and ideas, the unifying political and religious authority of the Church(es) and Judeo-Christian traditions, the Enlightenment of the French revolution have all contributed. Consequently, the constitutional identity of the EU is comprised of such *European* traditions and values, based on Christianity, humanism and ideas of human dignity. As Pope John Paul II wrote: '*In order to build Europe on solid foundations it necessarily has to be based upon authentic values, rooted in the common moral law, as inscribed in the heart of every human. […] The Christian inspiration may turn a political, cultural and economic gathering into a community in which every European would feel at home and create a family of nations, that could be a fruitful impulse for other regions of the world.*'[11] Hence, European constitutional identity is based on (legal) values derived out of genuine European religious and humanistic traditions.

Finally, the European Union can be first and foremost seen as a *legal* community. Based on the Treaties, and developed further through the progressive jurisprudence of the Court of Justice of the European Union and the occasional resistance of the national apex courts. It is the community of law[12] which shares the common constitutional traditions of the Member States. Accordingly, it is also a Union of principles and values,[13] as currently articulated in Article 2 of the Treaty on European Union (hereinafter: 'TEU') but initially established already by the Copenhagen criteria of 1993.[14] From this perspective, European constitutional identity is solely a legal phenomenon which, arguably, does not have anything to do with any necessary connecting links of identification among the people(s) of the Union. After all, the membership of the Union is constantly changing, and there is no need for the kind of

---

[11] John Paul II 2003, Adh. Ap. Ecclesia in Europa, pp. 116, 121.

[12] W. Hallstein, Speech at the University of Padua, March 1962. 'The European Economic Community is a community of law ... because it serves to realize the idea of law. The founding treaty, which may not be terminated, forms a kind of a Constitution for the Community'.

[13] Von Bogdandy et al. 2017b, pp. 218–233.

[14] Copenhagen criteria. The Copenhagen European Council in 1993 and strengthened by the Madrid European Council in 1995. https://www.europarl.europa.eu/summits/copenhagen/co_en.pdf, p. 12. Accessed 1 December 2021.

communal feeling of belonging and solidarity which is often considered a prerequisite for successful democratic participation and contestation—the component which
enables and facilitates the collective self-governing of a nation state. Hidden and
distanced from the *political*, European constitutional identity enjoys the privileges
of *legal* phenomena being determined and interpreted by the courts for reasons of
adjudication of constitutional conflicts alone. Hence, the constitutional identity of
the EU is considered to be solely a legal matter, articulated as the essential liberal
constitutional principles, as reflected, *inter alia*, in Article 2 of the TEU.

Surely, most readers would probably subscribe to at least one of the above-
sketched examples of what a potential European constitutional identity should consist
of, not to mention many other possibilities which are not broached here. However,
it would be categorically wrong to simply project one's own ideological preferences
regarding the Union and its potential status according to one's personal (here, legal)
intuition under the pretext of seemingly scientific, objective legal deductive interpretation. A lack of predictably valid methods, as well as the enigmatic meaning
of (constitutional) identity should compel us to be cautious when setting off to the
uncharted journey of discovering and imagining the constitutional identity of the
European Union.[15]

3.2.2   European (Constitutional) Identity—Two Contrastive Methodological Narratives

The idea to articulate the European identity is not new.[16] As it is not unambiguous.
One can construe the European, and consequently the European *constitutional*
narrative, from at least two distinctive methodological perspectives. One is closely
connected with, and limited to the birth of the European Union as an 'institution'.
The second narrative is more holistic and goes beyond the mere institutionalized
project of European cooperation.

The European Union (as it is called today) initially connected the steel industries
of the two biggest continental European powers for the reason to prevent the next
devastating future war on the European continent and beyond. As a response to World
War II, the EU project commenced with the Treaty of Paris (1951), the creation of the
European Coal and Steel Community, and mostly with the Schuman declaration,[17]
declaring two European core principles: peace and solidarity. Or in the words of
Robert Schuman: 'Europe will not be made all at once, or according to a single
plan. It will be built through concrete achievements which first create a de facto

---

[15] Fabbrini and Sajó 2019, p. 469.

[16] Checkel and Katzenstein 2012, pp. 213–227; Kaina et al. 2016; Bergbauer 2018; Drace-Francis
2013; Jacobs and Maier 1998.

[17] The Schuman Declaration (Paris, 9 May 1950), https://www.cvce.eu/en/recherche/unit-content/
-/unit/b9fe3d6d-e79c-495e-856d-9729144d2cbd/e3a3d62f-ceb2-4202-9d66-6dd88b316931/Res
ources#9cc6ac38-32f5-4c0a-a337-9a8ae4d5740f_en&overlay. Accessed 1 December 2021.

solidarity.'[18] And also: '[T]he establishment of a common economic system; it may be the leaven from which may grow a wider and deeper community between countries long opposed to one another by sanguinary divisions.' That was the birth of Europe as a political entity, 'laying the true foundation of an organised Europe.'[19] Since the initial practical perspective, with regards to the economic terms among the six founding Member States, it has become a progressive and sophisticated political project of today with 27. Every new treaty or its revision has brought the Member States closer, and at the peak of the optimism the European Union had its own draft of the European Constitution and 28 Member States. Today, the EU has its own EU Charter of Fundamental Rights, a provision in the Treaties where the basic values are articulated, and a formal commitment[20] to be open for new memberships. In principle, it is open to anyone who is willing and ready to adhere to the common European constitutional values. Or at least to the 'enlargement countries' from the Western Balkans—although 'Realpolitik' demonstrates the immense reservations to any further expansions at this particular stage.[21]

The first identity narrative is constructed around the legal and economic story of the gradual and progressive evolvement of the European Union and its current state. The second narrative is broader. (European) history had not started in 1950, not with the rivalry of Germany and France, and the project of the European Union today is not disconnected with the intertwined European history in political, economic and historical aspects for several hundreds of years. The scope of the chapter is not meant to go deeper, but one ought to think of at least some of the most important milestones of the European intertwined narratives. The Ancient Greek philosophy and mythology from the sixth century BC has influenced our thinking until today. One could say that '[t]he European philosophical tradition consists of a series of footnotes to Plato.'[22] The Roman Empire had defined and spread the application of the civil law with the level of unprecedented sophistication. In fact, even today we are mostly applying the same rules and principles as developed by the Roman jurists.[23] In the sixth century AC, in the Eastern Roman Empire Justinian the Great had codified a collection of fundamental jurisprudence in the Corpus Iuris Civilis, considered to be the encyclopaedia of the writings of the Roman jurists, which is the foundation of the Western civil legal tradition. The oldest university in the world, the University of Bologna (founded in 1088), has first taught the Justinian's code and had remained the dominant centre for law studies through the High Middle Ages.

---

[18] Ibid.

[19] Joint Declaration of the Ministers signatory to the Treaty establishing the European Coal and Steel Pool (18 April 1951). https://www.cvce.eu/en/obj/joint_declaration_by_the_signatory_ministers_18_april_1951-en-a5bee6ca-6506-48bb-9bd5-c1aa8487bdfd.html. Accessed 1 December 2021.

[20] European Council in Copenhagen—21–22 June 1993—Conclusions of the presidency—https://ec.europa.eu/commission/presscorner/detail/en/DOC_93_3. Accessed 1 December 2021.

[21] See the political reservations concerning Albania, Bosnia and Herzegovina, North Macedonia, Montenegro, Kosovo and Serbia.

[22] Whitehead 1929, Part II, Chap. I, Sect. I.

[23] Zimmermann 2015, pp. 452–480.

Furthermore, the Napoleonic Code, mostly still in force, was the next biggest pan-European project attempting to modernize and defeudalize the countries. It had a vast influence throughout the Napoleonic Wars and it is considered as one of the few documents that have influenced the entire world.[24]

But there are many additional European narratives which have strongly influenced and connected Europe. The role of the Church and religion in particular. One should not undermine the European identity building through that narrative, as the writings of Erasmus of Rotterdam convey. He wrote in the Querela pacis (1521): 'How very wrong this is! A geographical name of no importance divides them... In earlier times the Rhine divided the French and the Germans, but it does not separate one Christian from another. The Pyrenees separate Spaniards and Frenchmen, but they do not undo the communality of the church. The sea flows between the English and the French but can in no way split the unity of faith.'[25]

Furthermore, some authors argue that the wrathful religious wars in response to the Reformation and the following Westphalian 'sovereignty' created the modern myth of the nation-state,[26] which continues to remain until today the predominant political entity.

Finally, it cannot be overemphasized how the era of Enlightenment with the French and American revolutions and the processes of nation building have fundamentally changed Europe. The principles of individual freedom, solidarity and equality, even if *de facto* at first only for some, have posited the values which have remained our inspiration and commitment to this very day. The will of the people, as expressed through and via the notion of a nation state has secured the highest legitimacy. And it remains the only and the highest authority even today.

In addition, the Bill of Rights (1689), the Declaration of the Rights of Man and of the Citizen (1789), and finally, after two shattering world wars, the Universal Declaration of Human Rights (1948). These ground-breaking documents, exhibiting the political achievements of their time, not without stark opposition, have all significantly influenced and co-shaped the self-image that we hold of ourselves today, politically and legally.

These aspects of European history, along with gradual and mutual integration, cannot be completely omitted when constructing the European (constitutional) identity. But at the same time, it is also not clear to what extent one should include or omit them when defining the *legal* aspect of constitutional identity.

To sum up, both narratives are not mutually exclusive. But is there a clear answer as to which one is the right one? Or what kind of combination of them? For they surely impact one another. But within the scope of constitutional law, what kind of role have these historical, political, philosophical and economic aspects for the anticipated endeavour to articulate the constitutional identity of the European Union? One is left without a clear methodological approach in how to define the constitutional identity of the Union.

---

[24] Holtman 1981.

[25] Erasmus 1917, p. 60.

[26] Cavanaugh 2009, pp. 142–180.

3.2.3 (Constitutional) Identity as an Evasive Concept

An alternative approach to define the constitutional identity of the EU is to scrutinize scholarly theoretical accounts and/or the national jurisprudence of the Member States that contain arguments about 'constitutional identity', and define the meaning of constitutional identity accordingly. Subsequently, one would simply apply the definition also for the Union.

Yet, the survey of claims of national constitutional identity among the Member States exhibits quite diverse case law. From identity claims which are in deep contrast even with basic liberal commitments,[27] to the extra-legal arguments of culture and history.[28] Constitutional identity can be a peculiar and idiosyncratic interpretation of fundamental rights,[29] or a general commitment to human rights and democracy.[30] It can be a different name for sovereignty,[31] or an argument how to legalize the political question of the scope and intensity of the European integration process.[32] Finally, national apex courts may adhere to identity arguments simply because it gives them flexibility to extend their competences against EU law due to its conceptual vagueness. As argued by Fabbrini and Sajó, once "identity is left to the constitutional courts, the scope, content and sphere of applicability becomes a matter of identity conjecture". "[I]ts application becomes unforeseeably and easily arbitrary in the hands of constitutional judges."[33]

Henceforth, there is little what we can learn from the Member States as to the potential all-encompassing definition and the contents of the concept of constitutional identity. Due to the case law, one is almost more confused as at the beginning of the journey. Is constitutional identity just the most essential 'DNA' of the political system? Essentials of political community, like the principle of democracy, the rule of law, human rights, solidarity, welfare state and prohibition of discrimination? One

---

[27] Scholtes 2021, p. 551. Constitutional Court of Hungary (Alkotmánybíróság), *Decision 22/2016 on joint exercise of competences with the EU. (XII. 5.)*, Decision of 5 December 2016, Decision 22/ 2016. (XII. 5.), para 66.

[28] Court of Justice of the European Union (Grand Chamber), *Joined Cases C-643/15 and C-647/15 Slovak Republic and Hungary v Council of the European Union*, judgement of 6 September 2017, ECLI:EU:C:2017:631, at 302.

[29] Court of Justice of the European Union (Grand Chamber), *Case C-42/17, M.A.S., M.B. (Tarico II)*, judgement of 5 December 2017, ECLI:EU:C:2017:936.

Court of Justice of the European Union (Second Chamber), *Case C-208/09 Ilonka Sayn-Wittgenstein*, judgement of 22 December 2010, ECLI:EU:C:2010:806.

[30] Czech Constitutional Court (Ústavní soud), PL. ÚS 36/01: BANKRUPTCY TRUSTEE, judgement of 25 June 2002, Pl. US 36/01. Available in English at: https://www.usoud.cz/fileadmin/user_ upload/ustavni_soud_www/Decisions/pdf/Pl%20US%2036-01.pdf. Accessed 1 December 2021.

[31] Polish Constitutional Tribunal (Trybunał Konstytucyjny), Polish Lisbon Decision, judgement of 24 November 2010, Ref. No. K 32/09, published on 6 December 2010 in the Journal of Laws—Dy. U. No. 229, item 1506, at 2.1, pp. 23, 38, 41. Available in English at: https://trybunal.gov.pl/filead min/content/omowienia/K_32_09_EN.pdf. Accessed 1 December 2021.

[32] German Federal Constitutional Court (Bundesverfassungsgericht, Zweiter Senat), *2 BvE 2/08 (Lissabon-Urteil)*, judgement of 30 June 2009, paras 249, 252.

[33] Fabbrini and Sajó 2019, p. 471.

could call these 'essentials' the constitutional identity.[34] Although, if every Member
State would be the same, there would be no need to claim an identity. Is constitutional identity then something unique, something which makes every Member State
a special and idiosyncratic case? A way to differentiate itself from others? Or again
the other way around, is the aim of identity to find everybody who shares the same
constitutional identity?

Some scholars have called these different faces identity as *sameness* and identity
as *differentiation*.[35] But then again, is constitutional identity just the peculiar and
special, context-specific, and locally sensitive *interpretation* of the shared values
of liberal constitutionalism? Is constitutional identity only a unique understanding
of *universal* human rights in a concrete case? Or is constitutional identity the bits
and pieces which are within the scope of common values, but completely new and
different, with no variation of it among other Member States? Or, after all, all of the
above?[36]

The Aristotelian understanding of identity which conflates national identity with
the identity of the polis no longer corresponds to the contemporary liberal understanding of a state and liberal constitutionalism.[37] Francis Fukuyama argues that
national identity covers both the legal and sociological aspects of a state. It is
embodied in formal laws and institutions, in language, but it also extends into the
realm of culture and values, the stories that people tell about themselves and their
shared historical memories.[38] J. H. H. Weiler wrote that "constitutions are said to
encapsulate fundamental values of the polity and this, in turn, is said to be a reflection
of our collective identity as a people, as a nation, as a state, as a community, or as
a union."[39] Or even more poetic, in his influential book on constitutional identity,
Gary Jacobsohn argued that "a constitution acquires an identity through experience,
that this identity exists neither as a discrete object of invention nor as a heavily
encrusted essence embedded in a society's culture, requiring only to be discovered.
Rather, identity emerges dialogically and represents a mix of political aspirations
and commitments that are expressive of a nation's past, as well as the determination of those within the society who seek in some ways to transcend that past. It is
changeable but resistant to its own destruction, and it may manifest itself differently
in different settings."[40]

Considering the above-described incoherent definitions, it seems to me that the
methodology of transferring the meaning of constitutional identity from the various
theoretical accounts as well as from the national acquis to the supranational EU

---

[34] Sarmiento 2013, pp. 177, 187.

[35] Rosenfeld 2012, pp. 762–766.

[36] See Kumm 2012b, p. 323. Also Habermas 1996, pp. 125–137.

[37] Aristotle 1962, p. 99.

[38] Fukuyama 2018, p. 8.

[39] Weiler 2005, p. 184.

[40] Jacobsohn 2010, p. 7.

level does not bring us the desired result. There is simply no unified, coherent and persuasive meaning of national constitutional identity.[41]

3.2.4 An Endeavour of Numerous Projections—Following the Intuition and Creating the Meaning

If neither scholars nor the national apex courts and the Court of Justice of the European Union (hereinafter: 'CJEU') have come up with the one clear and unambiguous definition of constitutional identity yet, how can one with all the necessary gravity and in good faith pursue the aim of articulating the European constitutional identity?

Surely, one can subjectively decide for one's own preferred definition. According to Faraguna, the main pillars of constitutional identity of the EU are the principles of primacy of EU law and direct effect.[42] For Calliess and van der Schyff, 'constitutional identity is […] defined as the core or fundamental elements or values of a particular state's constitutional order as the expression of its individuality.'[43] Or, constitutional identity as essentials, which are not, and cannot be subject to change.[44] Or alternatively, the constitutional identity of the Union is the common and shared constitutional traditions or values of all its Member States. Or the constitutional identity of the Union will rather be developed and articulated by the CJEU, as the recent application of identity terminology by the CJEU indicates. "The values contained in Article 2 TEU have been identified and are shared by the Member States. They define the very identity of the European Union as a common legal order. Thus, the European Union must be able to defend those values, within the limits of its powers as laid down by the Treaties."[45] Or again differently in the negative sense, the constitutional identity of the Union, as it differentiates itself from the other ideological and political regimes in the world, where individuals are not the supreme authority of legitimate power, where democracy (if at all) is not exercised together with the freedom of press and respect for minorities and human rights.

These are but a few projections which can be more or less legitimately subscribed to the identity conception. For the conception is lacking any coherent meaning within a theoretical and normative account which would at least generally be shared among legal scholars and supported by the case law practice.[46] But as indicated above, one can even go further, beyond the alleged limits of the strict legal confines. European constitutional identity could be construed around the fundamental freedoms and the

---

[41] Belov 2017, p. 79. See also Millet 2021, pp. 571–596.

[42] Faraguna 2017, p. 1624.

[43] Calliess and van der Schyff 2019, p. 7.

[44] About the account of unchangeability, see Polzin 2017, pp. 1595–1616.

[45] Court of Justice of the European Union, Case C-157/21 (*Republic of Poland v European Parliament and Council of the European Union*) Judgment of 16 February 2022, ECLI:EU:C:2022:98, para 145.

[46] Fabbrini and Sajó 2019, p. 471.

common market. One could plausibly make the case for it and evaluate the *constitutional* case law of the CJEU with the arguably economic and market preferences, vis-à-vis the human rights and other constitutional principles. The latter ideas are more or less to calm down the German Constitutional Court and its Solange jurisprudence,[47] as mere beauty corrections, or so the argument goes. Ergo, the cynical projection could articulate well the *constitutional* identity of the Treaties as the practical advancement of the market and the preservation of some of the geo-strategic powers, which only a select few of the Member States had in abundance in the past.

The presented dilemma is threefold. First, if one is to imagine the constitutional identity of the European Union, who would that be? Scholars, the CJEU, or rather the Member States as the 'Masters of the Treaties'? Furthermore, according to what kind of methodology? As we have seen, the meaning of constitutional identity cannot be unambiguously extracted from the judicial practices of national apex courts, nor from the CJEU.[48] Second, would that endeavour not necessarily privilege a specific normative projection of the observer on the Union, an action which is predominately political in nature?

Finally, is the articulation of the constitutional identity of the European Union a legal or a political task? Does the 'legalization' by the apex courts turn the disputed political issues into a legal matter?[49] Or the other way around—does the legal intervention of articulation of the constitutional identity of the Union rather politicizes the issue, which prior were not on the political agenda as a matter of political dispute?[50] In my opinion, one should avoid both avenues, regardless of the question which of both potential interpretations is analytically better suited.

3.2.5   Shared Constitutional Traditions—Comparison and Differentiation

Let us assume, even if just for the sake of the argument, that the constitutional identity of the European Union has the following meaning: the community of values (*Wertegemeinschaft*)[51] in light of the recent case law of the CJEU. According to the

---

[47] German Federal Constitutional Court (Bundesverfassungsgericht, Zweiter Senat), BvL 52/71, (*Solange I*), Judgment of 29 May 1974. Also Polzin 2018, pp. 199–209.

[48] See for example Calliess and van der Schyff 2019. Even the recent case law of the CJEU which applies the terminology of identity avoids connecting it with 'constitutional' or 'national'. See Court of Justice of the European Union, Case C-157/21 (*Republic of Poland v European Parliament and Council of the European Union*) judgement of 16 February 2022, ECLI:EU:C:2022:98, para 145.

[49] Polish Constitutional Tribunal (Trybunał Konstytucyjny), judgement of 7 October 2021, Ref. No. K 3/21. Available in English at: https://trybunal.gov.pl/en/hearings/judgments/art/11662-ocena-zgo dnosci-z-konstytucja-rp-wybranych-przepisow-traktatu-o-unii-europejskiej. Accessed 1 December 2021.

[50] German Federal Constitutional Court (Bundesverfassungsgericht, Zweiter Senat), *2 BvR 859/15* (*PSPP*), judgement of 5 May 2020, paras 1–237.

[51] See also Calliess 2004, pp. 1033–1045; Von Bogdandy 2021, pp. 73–97.

CJEU, "Article 2 TEU is not merely a statement of policy guidelines or intentions, but contains values which […] are an integral part of the very identity of the European Union as a common legal order, values which are given concrete expression in principles containing legally binding obligations for the Member States."[52] These values have an important feature—they are 'common to the Member States'.[53] Human dignity, freedom, democracy, equality, the rule of law, respect for human rights, protection of minorities, pluralism, non-discrimination, tolerance, justice, solidarity and equality between women and men. All the cited values are concurrently the values of the Member States and the Union.[54] Consequently, the constitutional identity of the European Union is the same as the constitutional identity of the Member States. That follows basic logic. Alas, that cannot be, something in this equation must be wrong.

The function of identity usually serves to create a distinction between *I/We* and *They*. If one knows oneself, then one is able to see the differences as well as the similarities in relation to the other. The same identity of the subjects connects them, and it also divides them in relation to everybody else who does not share the same identity. In other words, identity serves comparison and differentiation.[55]

In the European constitutional context, the (national constitutional) identity argument has the same role. Moreover, the very reason why identity was, and perhaps still is, celebrated so much is the conciliatory role that it might have in the light of the potential conflicts among the heterarchical constitutional orders, national and supranational, in the light of constitutional pluralism.[56] It was a promised tool which would have the capacity to articulate important constitutional issues and bring them to the fore in the frame of engagement. Why? Because a national constitutional identity is inherently a *national* matter, subject to determination solely by the respective Member State and its (judicial) institutions, but at the same time subject to evaluation and potential acceptance by the CJEU in the light of its duty to respect national identities. Naturally, weighted and balanced with all the other relevant principles and rights in the respected situation. Or to put it simply, the identity tool was the door between the supranational and national constitutional systems for rare and exceptional circumstances, when unforeseeable constitutional conflicts would arise.

From that functional perspective on the identity argument, one can critically reflect on the current endeavour to articulate the constitutional identity of the European Union from two viewpoints. From the perspective of sameness, and from the perspective of distinctiveness. Both perspectives are inherently problematic.

---

[52] Court of Justice of the European Union, Case C-156/21 (*Hungary v European Parliament and Council of the European Union*) judgement of 16 February, ECLI:EU:C:2022:97, para 232.

[53] Article 2 TEU.

[54] The meaning of values and principles should not be understood in Habermasian sense (Habermas 1997, pp. 255 ff.), where the values as opposed to principles lack the legal normativity, but rather as similar and interchangeable concepts in the sense of Alexy. See Alexy and Rivers 2009, pp. 86, 91, 378.

[55] See also Faraguna 2017, p. 1632.

[56] See Häcker et al. 2012; Kumm 2012a, pp. 39 ff.; Avbelj 2017, pp. 44–61.

The first perspective concerns sameness in an inward direction. In light of the above assumed fundamental values pursuant to Article 2 TEU, as the assumed constitutional identity of the EU, there is simply no differentiation among the Member States and the Union. The value of the European constitutional identity for the purpose of active engagement with potential differences among the heterarchical constitutional systems within the EU is therefore considerably limited. Except in one scenario, where a Member State would distance itself from the fundamental principles of liberal democracy. The scenario which indeed might slowly become a painful reality.[57] This might even be the underlying reason for the scholarly attempts to create a European constitutional identity. However, such a 'Reverse Solange'[58] against 'rouge States' requires, in my opinion, more than a scholarly account of constitutional identity. It needs a robust and fully transparent mechanism as foreseen in the Article 7 TEU[59] procedure. The political sensibility to 'punish' one of your own is just too gargantuan to put it on scholarly notions like identity, as will be further suggested in the last section.

The second perspective, concerning distinctiveness, is construed in an outwards direction. The constitutional identity of the EU, as liberal fundamental principles and values can be posited against regimes, states and political actors that are pursuing different ideological commitments. Religious, autocratic, communistic, monarchic, military, etc. It is in that sense that the EU may exhibit its distinctiveness. Hence the question: to what extent do the European values limit and guide the EU when it conducts, trades, communicates, and acts with others? This question opens a completely new avenue of exploration which exceeds the scope of this chapter. However, it is doubtful that in order to answer this question, one would have to define the constitutional identity of the Union first.

To summarize, even if we agree on the most apparent definition of the constitutional identity of the European Union, namely, the shared fundamental values as articulated in Article 2 TEU, that in itself still does not prove to benefit the engagement relationship between the Member States and the Union, as well as with others.

3.3 Identity as Conceptual Substitute for Sovereignty—Nihil Novum Sub Sole

The underlying issue behind the constitutional identity phenomenon is firstly explored through conceptual history (Sect. 3.3.1). Furthermore, sovereignty has not been fully replaced, but rather used together with identity, either as a substitute or an addition (Sect. 3.3.2). Finally, bringing the sovereignty concept to the level of the European Union might imply the neo-colonial delusions and create tensions with the Member States (Sect. 3.3.3).

---

[57] Pech et al. 2021, pp. 1–43.

[58] 'Reverse Solange', see von Bogdandy et al. 2017a, pp. 218–233.

[59] Besselink 2017, pp. 128–144.

3.3.1 Conceptual History

The underlying issue behind the (new) conception of constitutional identity is essentially an old and well-known phenomenon. The quest to justify and maintain the supreme importance of the political order in relation to the others, and at the same time the necessary coordination of and commitment to the inescapable cooperation, constitutional conflict solving, and solidarity. The story is as old as the political systems.[60]

The advent of the rhetoric of national constitutional identity in the last ten years[61] has only reframed and conceptualised the underlying problem differently.[62] Ergo, *nihil novum sub sole.*

The first attempt to conceptually develop the respective multileveled constitutional structures has been undertaken by the ECJ. As the simplified vision that all constitutional orders of the Member States will simply fall into the beautiful and geometrically perfect pyramid of the norms. A perfect Kelsenian monistic order, where EU law would have the undeniable primacy and supremacy. The push was strong enough because it was built on the practical implications of (dis)functionality, where the EU norms remain only as the buffet, an open invitation to freely choose from. Every Member State would take what it pleases and when it pleases, and there would be no common, effective and binding rules across the Union.[63] The idea has been in principle accepted by the Member States, but it soon became slightly absolute, considering the early and underdeveloped constitutional design of the Union.[64]

Henceforth, the apex courts of the Member States have asserted an alternative approach. Partially because they were afraid of the ever-increasing competence gain of the Union through the progressive adjudication, and partially due to the fear that the national highest courts would consequently no longer be the most important judicial actors. Or would at least have to share the highest judicial powers. The Union was therefore alternatively interpreted, and thus reduced, to be the subject of the Member States, *Herren der Verträge*, which in itself does not possess any legal autonomy and democratic legitimacy. It is the derivative structure, which is fully subordinated to the sovereign control of the Member States. With the emphasis on the principle of sovereignty.

But the Member States (and their apex courts) have forgotten about the nature of sovereignty, which is not a black-or-white concept with solely two categories, having it or not, but rather a linear conception. The concept, where the degree of its realisation always correlates to the normative and factual circumstances. The concept which cannot be blind to the fact that nobody is alone in this world, and that without the principle of *pacta sunt servanda* no fair cooperation is possible.

---

[60] See also Kumm 2012c, p. 219.

[61] Fabbrini and Sajó 2019, p. 471.

[62] Weiler 2005, pp. 173–184.

[63] ECJ, Case 26/62, (*van Gend & Loos*), Judgement of 5 February 1963, ECLI:EU:C:1963:1. ECJ, Case 6-64, (*Costa v E.N.E.L.*), judgement of 15 July 1964, ECLI:EU:C:1964:66.

[64] See Kumm 2011, pp. 605–628; Klabbers et al. 2009.

Accordingly, the Union could not accept this conceptual alternative either. Disrespecting the primacy would severely endanger the legal order of the EU, its *raison d'être*, which could become an existential problem for the Union. It is not a coincidence after all, that on the 145-pages of the Lisbon Treaty the word sovereignty is not mentioned one single time.

Public international law demands compliance with the freely undertaken international obligations, regardless of the inner constitutional requirements, which leaves the States with only two options. To withdraw or to change their national constitutional requirements in order to achieve compliance with international law. Not to mention that the nature of the Union goes far beyond those of an international organisation.[65] The autonomous legal system of the Union, the Union's foundations of shared constitutional traditions, and its democratic features, although with no doubt still with many shortcomings, are demanding more than just to comply with the Treaties. The Treaties have become *constitutionalised*[66] and they are directly applicable across every Member State, in parallel to national constitutions and within the scope of the conferred competences.

While accepting this, the only question remains is who has the last word; the concerns of the *ultra vires* dilemma, and the refusal to confer on the Union the power to determine its own competences, the so called *Kompetenz-Kompetenz*.[67] But, as the BVerfG correctly stated in the past case law of *Honeywell*,[68] the Member States can only refuse to comply with EU law, should the violation of conferred competences appear *manifest* (obvious and not a question of reasonable legal disagreement), structurally significant, and only after they engage into a dialogue with the CJEU concerning the respective subject matter, issuing a preliminary reference proceedings.

Finally, the alternative conceptual attempt to navigate the heterarchical constitutional relationships was the identity concept. Praised at the beginning,[69] as the engagement mechanism that would bring the two misleading perspectives together. Away from absolute primacy, but also away from complete control by the Member States. And in light of the heterarchical constitutional pluralism, which is only *shallow* and based on the basic common commitments, it would promise to bridge the constitutional systems in a unique and context-sensitive way.

3.3.2   Sovereignty and Identity Together

The engagement tool of (constitutional) identity has yet to adequately fulfil its potential promise. Perhaps because the concept never had any comprehensive meaning

---

[65] Walker 2008, pp. 247–267.

[66] Arcari and Ninatti 2017, pp. 11–41; Piris 2006, pp. 192–197.

[67] Gehring 2020, pp. 155–222.

[68] German Federal Constitutional Court (Bundesverfassungsgericht, Zweiter Senat), *2 BvR 2661/ 06*, (*Honeywell*), judgement of 6 July 2010.

[69] See for example constitutional identity as a norm of convergence, Millet 2013, pp. 239–256.

which would be subject to a clear definition. Or because it was too often applied in *mala fide*. Or rather due to the reserved and quite cautious adjudications of the CJEU, not daring to embrace the term and define its limits. Be that as it may, the Member States have slowly realised that identity vocabulary might be worth a shot, but that it has been also quite rarely picked up by the CJEU anyway. As a consequence, they have started to add to identity vocabulary also other concepts, notably the notion of sovereignty, all with the aim to be successful in the claims to be allowed to apply EU law. Or as Fabbrini and Sajó wrote, the use of constitutional identity 'signals that certain courts uttering "identity" are really reclaiming sovereignty.'[70]

The Polish Constitutional Court, in its Lisbon decision, has simply merged the significance of constitutional and systemic identity with the sovereignty of the Member States, while allegedly summarising the common characteristics of the other national apex courts adjudications.[71] The Lithuanian court connected protection of the state language with the preservation of the nation's identity which, *inter alia*, ensures the expression of national sovereignty.[72] The Hungarian Constitutional Court stated, that 'Hungary can only be deprived of its constitutional identity through the final termination of its sovereignty […] Accordingly, sovereignty and constitutional identity have several common points, thus their control should be performed with due regard to each other in specific cases.'[73] Additionally, apart from the specific identity review in France, the French Conseil examined the compatibility of the EU treaties with the French Constitution according to the criterion of 'the essential conditions for the exercise of national sovereignty'.[74] A condition which refers to matters which limit national sovereignty, such as monetary policy, immigration, foreign policy, defence. Moreover, a condition which also limits national sovereignty in procedural terms, such as for example qualified majority voting.[75] Similar is the Danish example, where the Danish constitution (subject to a potential change) limits the scope of transfer of sovereignty which is in practice then concretely articulated by the legislative branch, stating the specific exemptions from European integration. Namely, security, defence, criminal law, migration and asylum, citizenship, and fiscal policy, which can all be understood as matters of core national sovereignty, but in the

---

[70] Fabbrini and Sajó 2019, p. 471.

[71] Polish Constitutional Tribunal (Trybunał Konstytucyjny), *Polish Lisbon Decision*, judgement of 24 November 2010, Ref. No. K 32/09, published on 6 December 2010 in the Journal of Laws—Dy. U. No. 229, item 1506, at 2.1.

[72] Court of Justice of the European Union (Second Chamber), *Case C-391/09 (Runevič-Vardyn)*, judgement of 12 May 2011, ECLI:EU:C:2011:291, paras 84, 86.
  Constitutional Court of The Republic of Lithuania (Lietuvos Respublikos Konstitucinis Teismas), *Byla 2A-1579-577/2013*, judgement of 9 October 2013, https://eteismai.lt/byla/279788 36282048/2A-1579-577/2013. Accessed 1 December 2021.

[73] Constitutional Court of Hungary (Alkotmánybíróság), *decision 22/2016 on joint exercise of competences with the EU. (XII. 5.)*, decision of 5 December 2016, decision 22/2016. (XII. 5.), para 67.

[74] Millet 2019, p. 139.

[75] Millet 2019, p. 139.

words of Helle Krunke also as the expression of national constitutional identity.[76] Finally, the German BVerfG has similarly developed the notion of the European Union as 'an association of sovereign states (*Staatenverbund*)', where these states can only remain *sovereign* by retaining control over specific essential areas. The guarantee to remain sovereign, according to the BVerfG, is even reflected in the Treaties, pursuant to Article 4(2) TEU. Concretely, the German legislator has to claim control over substantial and procedural criminal law; monopoly on the use of force by the police and the military (war and peace); taxation, public revenue, expenditures and fiscal decisions; social policy considerations or welfare; and culture, education and religion.[77]

The examples above only demonstrate that the argument of identity often shares the room with sovereignty. Sometimes as an additional element, another time as a substitute.

Henceforth, one cannot think of (national constitutional) identity without an awareness that many apex courts have already made a substantial step to either connect the phenomenon with national sovereignty, or to even replace the sovereignty principle with the identity vocabulary while addressing the same underlying challenges.

3.3.3   European Sovereignty and Neo-Colonial Delusions

What would happen if we assume that the connection between sovereignty and identity, as depicted above, would continue to exist even when construing the European constitutional identity? Would not that in turn award to the Union the European sovereignty? And if so, how would that impact the relationship between the Union and the Member States?

The argument will be explored from two perspectives. What does it mean for the EU to assume its own sovereignty in a legal sense? And, how can this rhetoric bring about the imperial tensions from a political perspective?[78]

If constitutional identity is nothing else than a different pretext for sovereignty, then imagining European constitutional identity logically assumes the sovereignty of the latter. The European legal order is already legally established as autonomous,[79] and there is a close and complicated link between the autonomy and sovereignty.[80] But what would a creation of European sovereignty mean? Is it that the EU can no longer give away some of its attained competences and powers, if European integration would in the future take the road back to more disconnected and loose

---

[76] Krunke 2019, p. 132.

[77] German Federal Constitutional Court (Bundesverfassungsgericht, Zweiter Senat), *2 BvE 2/08* (*Lissabon-Urteil*), judgement of 30 June 2009, paras 249, 252.

[78] See also De Witte 2006, pp. 1–29.

[79] Weiler and Haltern 1996, p. 411.

[80] Eckes 2020, pp. 1–19.

cooperation? Or that it must have the power to determine its own powers, the *Kompetenz-Kompetenz*?

The European Union has the legal subjectivity to be the holder of the rights and obligations in the public international sphere. Would the notion of sovereignty increase the power and legitimacy of the Union? Would it facilitate the relationships with the other international subjects? Would it enhance the current integration process?

And in turn, how would the Member States, the *Herren der Verträge*, respond to this notion? The Union does not have its own territory, its Member States are constantly changing, and European citizenship has only an auxiliary nature. Yet, the Union assumes to have the constitutional characteristics resembling the sovereignty of a state.

As Mattias Kumm argued, thinking of the European Union in terms of 'Legal Monism',[81] state-developed conceptions would seriously undermine the purpose and the nature of the Union as it *is* and as it *ought to be*. However, can we avoid that trap if one is determined to bring the identity vocabulary to describe the Union? Can constitutional identity on the level of the Union completely be detached from the underlying sovereignty concept, which constitutional identity is only half-hearted trying to replace?

In addition, sovereignty assumes a certain degree of independence. It assumes its own power. And since it is clear that in the twenty-first century, the European countries are only small and almost insignificant reflection of its previous global influence, often obtained due to dubious moral and legal standards, and even the biggest members can no longer independently shape the global politics and economy; the European Union can at least partially correct that picture. It gives the size and the capacity to have a say in the world once again. That shall not be, in any possible way, the *raison d'être* or the side effect of the European integration. And every time when talks occur about the fact that Europe is losing influence, or has to (re)gain the primary seat among the big powers once more, the EU has been instrumentalized as a vehicle for neo-colonial delusions, expressed only in a different form. Equally, the argument of imagining the European constitutional identity and the underlying European sovereignty follows the same distorted narrative. Instead of simply engaging with fundamental rights, the rule of law, and democracy from within.

3.4 Identity as a Relation

According to Newman, 'We are all safer when language is specific; it improves our chances of knowing what is going on.'[82] In brief, language matters. If jurisprudence were to be more like a natural science, perhaps we could get away without words, dealing solely with numbers and symbols. Yet, legal science is intrinsically connected

---

[81] Kumm 2011, pp. 11–138, 2013, p. 220.

[82] Newman 1976.

with language and its interpretation. Hence, one must first determine the meaning of a legal term in order to use it justly.

But what is the meaning of a legal concept? As Danny Crane famously put it: 'The Constitution says whatever the Supreme Court says it says.'[83] That is certainly true. But words still have meanings on their own. Without words, the courts would not have any means to articulate what the given words are supposed to mean. And, in reality, we can discuss H.L.A. Hart's 'vehicles in the park'[84] problem as long as we please, but one fact remains. A common, regular car is definitely included under the definition of 'vehicles'. In other words, even in the world of legal language, where everything can be disputed and misinterpreted, some basic 'rules of gravity' cannot be denied.

This brings us to the discussion about the meaning of identity and its transposition in the era of identity politics, from the social and psychological spheres into constitutional law. Despite the courts and legal scholarship trying to imagine, and artificially construe the *legal* meaning of (constitutional) identity, the merciless rules of gravity have the last words, meaning that certain contents of the original meaning of identity cannot be ignored. For it is not the creation of new meanings that bewilders me but, rather, the purposeful ignorance of a discernible core of identity.

Hence, I put forth an argument that due to its intrinsic original meaning, the use of identity vocabulary regarding the constitutional identity of the European Union misguides and convolutes such efforts. First, because identity is a relational and not descriptive phenomenon (Sect. 3.4.1). Second, an idea such as the European Union, as an identifying subject of the many, cannot be objectively and accurately articulated according to just one narrative (Sect. 3.4.2). Lastly, identity phenomena are never single but actually comprised of a chord of multitudes (Sect. 3.4.3).

3.4.1 Identity as Relational, not Descriptive

Identity is a relational concept.[85] And that has two distinctive consequences. Firstly, it requires an active agent that is capable to create a *connection*. And secondly, identity is the connection itself, the belonging, rather than the identifying subject matter.

The subsequent two trivial examples can illustrate this point. If one would say: I have a German and Christian identity, the identity would not be the Federal Republic of Germany or Christianity itself. Rather, it would be the connection that one is able and willing to make to the mentioned subject matter. German identity is not Germany itself. It is the relation to Germany. Henceforth, identity phenomena are not simply a matter that one can describe and depict, but rather a relation to a specific matter of identification.

---

[83] From the TV Series Boston Legal, Dances With Wolves, Season 5, Episode 3. Broadcast: 6 October 2008, written by Susan Dickens and David E. Kelley.

[84] Hart 1958, p. 607.

[85] See also Williams 1979, pp. 81–100.

Furthermore, what is the identity of the respective car? It is a diesel, red, it has luxurious leather seats, and a rearing horse on the top of the bonnet.

You might confidently say a Ferrari, but the answer would be wrong. A car has no identity. It has a name, one can describe its main features, and one can even relate to it. But the car itself cannot. It is not an agent, it cannot identify itself with anything, it is not capable of creating an active connection.

Arguably, the identity concept cannot be used as a substitute for descriptive endeavours with the aim to characterise the subject. A constitution has no identity. Because it is not capable of creating a relation. Constitutional identity could only be, theoretically, a Habermasian constitutional patriotism (*Verfassungspatriotismus*),[86] which would describe the identity of the respective constitutional subjects of those who identify themselves with the constitution. But to the best of my knowledge, no one has tried to ascribe the meaning of constitutional identity in this manner. Alternatively, a constitution could articulate the national identity of the people. But then we should talk about *national* identity as potentially *described* in the constitution. But that meaning has even less sense when one is trying to describe the common identity of the peoples of 27 nations. The conventional assumption of constitutional identity rather refers to the constitution which has its own identity, like that of a Ferrari.

Accordingly, the use of the word identity when *describing* a constitution, a lifeless legal text, creates confusion and misleading expectations. It ignores the basic gravity rule that the core meaning of identity requires an *agent*, one capable of creating an active *relation*.

3.4.2 Identified Subject Matter as Idea or Narrative

When one identifies with the subject matter, the subject matter inherently influences the identifying agent in turn. Somewhat like a circle. The identity relation is not just *liking* the subject matter, but partially, and to a certain degree, the rediscovering of the identified subject matter in some form also in itself.

The situation however changes, when the identified subject matter is no longer in a materialized form, but represents an idea or a narrative. The identified idea is then adopted by the agent as its own version. In the society of many-many individuals that process is multiplied, and suddenly one has the feeling of belonging to the idea, and of others belonging to this idea, simply by sharing this same narrative. Yet, with the multitude of processes of adopting an idea, the idea itself is no longer singular. It lives in every single individual on its own, and it no longer has only one proper form and context. The identity in this form is then by definition lacking coherence. And even if one would try to identify the true definition of the idea and would empirically ask the multitude of individuals about it, the answers would be neither the initial idea itself, nor something which would overlap among the interlocutors. Rather, one

---

[86] Habermas 1995, p. 851.

would get thousand versions of identity. Like the children's game 'the telephone', where the initial message always becomes garbled along the way.

The nature of identity phenomena, as described above, illustrates the tension of the concept with legal science, where the expectations and the rules are radically different. The entire legal undertaking is dedicated to making the language and its meaning as clear and predictable as possible. The introduction of identity vocabulary, on the other hand, is by its definition the opposite. The meaning which cannot be encapsulated into one single narrative,[87] the toothpaste which cannot be squeezed back into the tube.

3.4.3 Singleness and Multitude of Identities

Finally, the conventional legal knowledge of (national) constitutional identity somehow assumes that one agent bears just one identity. In other words, the assumption that there *is* a constitutional identity. One German, one Italian, one European. Yet, due to the initial meaning of identity, nothing could be further from the truth.

Every agent has a multitude of identities, identities *are*. The European, national, regional, local, professional, etc. One agent can have it all. Or if it pleases, none. Yet, the legal constitutional discourse consistently assumes that a constitutional identity is just one phenomenon, only waiting to be discovered and articulated. As if it would be only due to the lack of good scholarship and case law that we are still missing the final, unified, and coherent theoretical account of it.[88]

The question of compatibility between the multitude of identities in the sociological and psychological meaning on the one hand, and the assumed singleness of constitutional identity on the other, is not a trivial one. If national constitutional identity, or the European constitutional identity, could have several identities, what would be the purpose of construing them? How would they relate to one another? For example, fundamental rights identity as incorporated in the Charter. Common market identity as developed due to the fundamental freedoms. Weak democratic identity according to the current design of institutions, etc. And then we could compare them, or make combinations of them. But is that really the intended purpose when trying to construe the European constitutional identity? And if there has to be just one main identity, how is that compatible with the initial meaning which has clearly never intended to monopolize just one relation?

Once again, the identity vocabulary brings to lawyers way more difficult questions than guiding answers. Does it really make sense to export all these dilemmas further to the EU level?

---

[87] Fabbrini and Sajó 2019, p. 467.

[88] See also Doroga 2020, pp. 91–116.

3.5 Tensions Between Identity and Democracy

The construction of identity is especially delicate regarding the question of permanence and change. Is identity a *perpetuum mobile*, a constant reinvention of itself, or a stable and unchangeable feature, a subject matter which simply cannot be alternated (Sect. 3.5.1)? Moreover, how does the conventional constitutional understanding of constitutional identity relate to this particular feature of identity change (Sect. 3.5.2)? And, accordingly, what kind of tensions then arise between the principle of democratic reversibility and the notion of unchangeable constitutional identity (Sect. 3.5.3)?

3.5.1 Identity as Perpetuum Mobile

Heraclitus stated, about 2500 years ago; '*You cannot step into the same river twice.*'[89] This beautiful metaphor is perfect to describe the whimsicalness of every moment, ever changing human nature, the inevitability of change in time and space, and thereby of one's identity.

Judith A. Howard put it more fittingly: '*The basic premise of symbolic interaction is that people attach symbolic meaning to objects, behaviours, themselves, and other people, and they develop and transmit these meanings through interaction. People behave toward objects on the basis not of their concrete properties, but of the meanings these objects have for them. Because meanings develop through interaction, language plays a central part. […] Identities locate a person in social space by virtue of the relationships that these identities imply, and are, themselves, symbols whose meanings vary across actors and situations.*'[90]

Identities in their initial meanings are thus all but stable and fixed phenomena. They are not motionless or finished products, but rather 'the problematic ongoing process of access to an image of totality.'[91] Finally, identities are never *a priori* absolute and isolated in an ivory tower, but rather continuously forced to adopt in accordance with the societal notions of narrative, intelligibility and accountability.[92]

The character Meursault in Camus' novel *L'Étranger* is a powerful example of this duality of identity.[93] On the one hand, what somebody *is* in relation to the outside evaluation. On the other, how society demands from an individual to adopt to the social standards and norms. Meursault, while on the trial because he was not crying at his mother's funeral, is a *stranger* to society, as much as society is *strange* to him. 'What Meursault displays is a passive threat to society, albeit what society does is a

---

[89] Plato 360 BCE, Cratylus, para 402a.

[90] Howard 2000, p. 371.

[91] Bhabha 1994, p. 73.

[92] Taylor 1992, p. 218.

[93] The reference to Camus' character in relation to identity (change) was made at the WZB Colloquium Global Constitutionalism by Mattias Kumm.

major threat to his individuality.'[94] Thus, understanding as well as navigating one's 'identity is highly depended on the social construction a person hails from.'[95]

3.5.2   (Dis)Ability of Change and the Hierarchy of Norms

Constitutional identity, on the other hand, assumes the opposite. Constitutional identity often imitates unchangeability. The very reason that the Member States are putting so much into the claims of constitutional identity, against the application of EU law, is the nature of the argument which assumes inability of change. The argument of constitutional identity is only strong, when the Member States can say: 'Sorry, but we are simply not able to change this feature of our constitutional law, because it is identity. It is not *possible* to change it.'

For example, when the German Basic Law conflicted with the application of the EU law Directive on equal treatment within employment,[96] because the German constitutional provision provided only for men to serve in the army, Germany had to change the respective constitutional norm.[97] This was not seen as a constitutional problem, because the constitutional norm was not declared to be a matter of constitutional identity. But when a constitutional norm which is also constitutional identity conflicts with EU law, a Member State cannot simply change it. Because it is identity, and identity cannot be simply changed by new legislation. And that is precisely the power of the constitutional identity argument, it gives the Member States the grounds to refuse compliance with EU law. Not because they do not want to, but because they supposedly cannot.

The unamendable core of the constitution, or such constitutional identity, has two important consequences. First, it is not subject to change. That is a highly problematic notion in light of the democracy principle, as it will be further elaborated below. The national apex courts are then able to navigate and block the constitutional changes in the society. And as far as this 'safety brake' may primarily aim to prevent a potential escalation into an autocratic or undemocratic catastrophe, it can also circumvent democratic decision making, enabling the judges to gain the power beyond the constitutional confines of judiciary. And second, and more important, it creates a constitutional hierarchy of norms.[98] Declaring something as constitutional

---

[94] Devi 2020, p. 355.

[95] Devi 2020, p. 351.

[96] Council Directive 76/207/EEC of 9 February 1976 on the implementation of the principle of equal treatment for men and women as regards access to employment, vocational training and promotion, and working conditions (OJ 1976 L 39, p. 40).

[97] Court of Justice of the European Union, *Case C-285/98 (Tanja Kreil v Bundesrepublik Deutschland)*, judgement of 11 January 2000, ECLI:EU:C:2000:2.

[98] Roznai 2019.

identity eventually creates a constitutional hierarchy which clearly privileges some constitutional norms over others.[99]

3.5.3 Law and Democratic Reversibility

The initiative of scholars to designate the values of Article 2 TEU as European constitutional identity will potentially create two significant problems.

The first one is the problem of reversibility. To use the vocabulary of identity, the identity of the European Union and European legal integration is most likely 'the change' itself. The famous metaphor of the EU and its reforms as the bicycle which has to be continuously pushed forward, not to fall on either side, is illustrative in that regard. Every crisis brings new challenges which demand new solutions. That is translated into the new treaties, which bring about new institutional designs. Or as cited at the beginning, the actual connection of economies and the creation of the common market will create real and tangible results and establish connections; these connections will create solidarity, and this solidarity will lead into a more integrated and successful society. But declaring some articles of the current Treaties as constitutional identity could freeze this process. It would wrongfully presume that the EU stands at its final stage and is no longer open to progressive change. That is, after all, the most important feature of democracy; the ability to stay agile and flexible in order to evolve with time. European constitutional identity could well stop that process. It could freeze the current modest level of protection of human rights as sufficient, it would signal that we may be satisfied with the current state of the art, where social rights are only articulated as soft law,[100] where the European Parliament for example has a position which is almost only a mere observer or a correcting mechanism, without any real power to initiate a legislative process on its own. It would signal that we can be satisfied with the current level of democratic participation.

On the other hand, if the European constitutional identity would be articulated as broadly and in general terms, as for example the commitment to democracy, human rights, and the rule of law, what could that general articulation of European constitutional identity offer in the legal sense? For what purpose of differentiation, since the same commitments are already shared among the Member States?[101]

The second problem concerns the hierarchy of norms. If declaring Article 2 TEU as the European constitutional identity, how would that elevation of the norm create impact on the adjudicative process of the European judiciary in relation to other constitutional principles and norms? Would that give the CJEU the possibility to give clear priority to the rule of law over other principles, such as the principle of

---

[99] Passchier and Stremler 2016.

[100] Interinstitutional Proclamation on the European Pillar of Social Rights, OJ C 428, 13.12.2017, pp. 10–15.

[101] Gašperin Wischhoff forthcoming, p. 101.

sincere cooperation, or respect for national identity, or the principle of conferral?[102] Would the principle of prohibition of discrimination as part of Article 2 TEU thereby automatically overweigh the fundamental freedoms because of its higher rank as identity? Or over the principle of 'freedom to conduct business'?

Constitutional law is cautious not to prioritize among constitutional norms. It requires judges to exercise the real work. To put all the elements into the equation and to balance them; to find the least intrusive way of limiting one's right as to enable the widest possible exercise of the other. Designating some norms with the constitutional identity label could demolish that fragile equilibrium of constitutional adjudication. And once again, it would arguably create more problems than it promised to solve.

3.6 Call the Essential Constitutional Commitments by Their Name

Confucius was once asked, what is the beginning of wisdom, and what would he do first should he become a governor? His reply was: 'Call things by the right names.'[103]

In Analects one reads: 'If names be not correct, language is not in accordance with the truth of things. If language be not in accordance with the truth of things, affairs cannot be carried on to success.'[104]

At the beginning we have asked the question what is the purpose of construing the European constitutional identity? One clear answer could be: to strengthen the essential constitutional commitments of the Union. To give them true legal meaning, to make them judicially applicable,[105] to be able to enforce them, and thereby to protect the Union as the Community of values.[106]

One way of identifying the basic constitutional values of the Union is to refer to Article 2 TEU. 'The Union is founded on the values of respect for human dignity, freedom, democracy, equality, the rule of law and respect for human rights, including the rights of persons belonging to minorities. These values are common to the Member States in a society in which pluralism, non-discrimination, tolerance, justice, solidarity and equality between women and men prevail.'[107]

Additionally, many other principles could also qualify as 'essential constitutional commitments of the Union'. Most notably, the four fundamental freedoms of the common market as the pivotal practical reason of the Union's existence. Furthermore, the special *sui generis* nature with no comparable constitutional structure in the world

---

[102] This proposition is advocated by Spieker 2021, pp. 237–268.

[103] Confucius 1998, Book XIII, Chapter 3, verses 4–7, para 13.3.

[104] Confucius 1998, Book XIII, Chapter 3, verses 4–7, para 13.3.

[105] Spieker 2021, pp. 237–268.

[106] For a somewhat more balanced approach against the Schmittian 'Tyranny of Values', see von Bogdandy 2021, pp. 74–97.

[107] Article 2 TEU.

could also qualify as an essential constitutional element, just like the principles of primacy, of subsidiarity, of conferral, and of sincere cooperation, to name but a few.

Yet, there is a missing link when one aims to answer the initial research question. Why would denomination of identified (potentially *these* particular) essential constitutional values of the Union as the *European constitutional identity* in any way contribute to the gravity and significance of their existence? Truly, would such denomination *elevate* them normatively? Qualify them as the highest normative standards and thus improve their protection and enforcement?

Here, I argue the opposite. Or at least raising cautious concerns relating to the potential pitfalls of such endeavour. As indicated above, there are many reasons why the identity vocabulary might bring about more confusion and additional challenges. Apart from the lack of any intelligible methodology as to identification and creation of such (constitutional) identity, henceforth subjectively projecting and *imagining*[108] it. In fact, the semantics of the identity terminology suggest the complete omission of the phenomena as unsuitable for the purposes of *describing* the essential elements of constitution.

But even more importantly, there are no reasons why such denomination would in fact enhance the respect for the essential constitutional values. Whereas facilitating the argument of constitutional identity from the Member States at least makes sense due to the fact that the Union itself is bound to respect national identity. And thus, gives the Member States some leverage in negotiating the potential constitutional tensions, as there is no such reference for the identity of the EU.

Alternatively, I suggest to follow the advice of Confucius. Let us call the things by their right names. Let us truly take the essential constitutional commitments of the EU seriously, simply by using their names as they have them already. In light of the ongoing backsliding by some of the Member States, respect for the rule of law has already been taken more seriously by the CJEU.[109] Initially, in the ASJP[110] decision of the Portuguese judges, in the *obiter dictum*, the CJEU has boldly introduced the protection of the rule of law, not just as programmatic or ideological guidelines which allegedly cannot be enforceable, but as indispensable legal structures that enables the functioning of the EU. It has recognized that '*the effective judicial review* […] *is of the essence of the rule of law.*'[111] Subsequently, it has only strengthened the initial position further. Just a few months later, it issued the *Celmer*[112] decision. Thus, confirming the chosen trajectory to give life to the rule of law as enforceable principle, and not just a programme-based phrase. In addition, the CJEU has not only

---

[108] Anderson 1991.

[109] See also Spieker 2019, pp. 1182–1213.

[110] Court of Justice of the European Union (Grand Chamber), Case C-64/16, (*Associação Sindical dos Juízes Portugueses v Tribunal de Contas, ASJP*), judgement of 27 February 2018, ECLI:EU:C:2018:117.

[111] Court of Justice of the European Union (Grand Chamber), Case C-64/16, (*Associação Sindical dos Juízes Portugueses v Tribunal de Contas, ASJP*), judgement of 27 February 2018, ECLI:EU:C:2018:117, para 36.

[112] Court of Justice of the European Union (Grand Chamber), Case C-216/18 PPU, (*LM*), judgement of 25 July 2018, ECLI:EU:C:2018:586, paras 48–51.

started to develop the contents of the rule of law, but also of other values pursuant to Article 2 TEU, as for example the principle of democracy within the latest case law concerning the Catalan politicians and their immunities.[113] Finally, the most recent case law of the CJEU concerning the infringement proceedings, as to the Polish judiciary *reform*, has only confirmed the true dedication of the CJEU to secure and protect the principles and values pursuant to Article 2 TEU.[114]

In my opinion, this is a much better way of the robust commitment to the essential constitutional principles and values of the EU. And if the CJEU will continue to take these legal values seriously, that in itself is the preferred way of *constitutionalisation*[115] of the Union without clinging to equivocal terminology of identity.[116] Because these principles and values are already properly understood, imperative and transcendent. We just have to take them seriously and simply call them by their names.

3.7 Conclusion

Imagining the constitutional identity of the European Union is much like Alice going down the rabbit hole. To enter into unknown territories and not knowing how deep the rabbit hole goes.

The chapter at hand is therefore a five-step plaidoyer, to highlight the potential traps of the arguably misguided Sisyphean endeavour to imagine the constitutional identity of the EU while asking the following question: What is the purpose, the additional value, and what are the pitfalls to artificially construe meaning around this conceptual conundrum?

The task is Sisyphean, because it is pointless and interminable. The denomination of essential constitutional values of the EU, to the qualifying standard of constitutional identity, elevates the respective principles. That in itself creates a subjective hierarchy of constitutional norms and therefore generates tensions with the democratic principle of reversibility. Moreover, it invites confusion as to the methods, consequences and the meaning of constitutional identity.

Furthermore, the semantics of identity phenomena strongly argue for the omission of any correlation with the term in the field of constitutional law. This is due to its

---

[113] Court of Justice of the European Union (Grand Chamber), *Case C-502/19*, judgement of 19 December 2019, CLI:EU:C:2019:1115, paras 63, 83.

[114] Pech et al. 2021, pp. 1–43. Court of Justice of the European Union, Case C-156/21 (*Hungary v European Parliament and Council of the European Union*) Judgment of 16 February, ECLI:EU:C:2022:97, para 232. Court of Justice of the European Union, Case C-157/21 (*Republic of Poland v European Parliament and Council of the European Union*) judgement of 16 February 2022, ECLI:EU:C:2022:98, para 145.

[115] Kumm 2013, pp. 605–628.

[116] For a more nuanced view on the limits of the CJEU's jurisprudence to solve the current democracy and rule of law crisis, see Schneider 2020, pp. 4–28.

specific nature, which presupposes an agent, capable of establishing a *relation* with the respective subject matter as an undertaking of identification.

Conclusively, rather than constitutional identity, one should embrace the principles and values of the Union by their names. Already imperative and transcendent, they might present a more fruitful way of the true *constitutionalisation* of the Union and the potential qualitative evolvement of European integration, as well as its democratic standards.

References

Alexy R, Rivers J (2009) A Theory of Constitutional Rights. Oxford University Press, New York/ Oxford

Anderson B (1991) Imagined Communities: Reflections on the Origin and Spread of Nationalism. Verso, London/New York

Arcari M, Ninatti S (2017) Narratives of Constitutionalization in the European Union Court of Justice and in the European Court of Human Rights' Case Law. ICL Journal 11(1):11–41

Aristotle (1962) The Politics of Aristotle (Barker E (ed) (transl)). Oxford University Press

Avbelj M (2017) Pluralism and Systemic Defiance in the EU. In: Jakab A, Kochenov D (eds) The Enforcement of EU Law and Values: Ensuring Member States' Compliance. Oxford University Press, pp 44–61

Belov M (2017) The Functions of Constitutional Identity Performed in the Context of Constitutionalization of the EU Order and Europeanization of the Legal Orders of EU Member States. Perspectives on Federalism 9(2):72–97

Bergbauer S (2018) Explaining European Identity Formation. Springer, Berlin

Besselink L (2017) The Bite, the Bark, and the Howl: Article 7 TEU and the Rule of Law Initiatives. In: Jakab A, Kochenov D (eds) The Enforcement of EU Law and Values: Ensuring Member States' Compliance. Oxford University Press, pp 128–144

Bhabha H K (1994) The Location of Culture, 2nd edn. Routledge, London/New York

Calliess C (2004) Europa Als Wertegemeinschaft — Integration Und Identität Durch Europäisches Verfassungsrecht? JuristenZeitung 59(21):1033–1045

Calliess C, van der Schyff G (eds) (2019) Constitutional Identity Introduced. In: Calliess C, van der Schyff G (eds) Constitutional Identity in a Europe of Multilevel Constitutionalism. Cambridge University Press, Cambridge, pp 3–8

Cavanaugh W (2009) The Myth of Religious Violence: Secular Ideology and the Roots of Modern Conflict. Oxford University Press, Cambridge

Checkel J T, Katzenstein P T (2012) Conclusion – European Identity in Context. In: Checkel J T, Katzenstein P T (eds) European Identity. Contemporary European Politics. Cambridge University Press, Cambridge, pp 213–227

Confucius (1998) The Analects (Lau D C (transl)). Penguin Classics, Harmondsworth/New York. Book XIII, Chapter 3, verses 4–7, para 13.3

Devi B (2020) Negotiating Identity in Albert Camus's the Outsider. Journal of Interdisciplinary Cycle Research 12(12):351–356

De Witte B (2006) Sovereignty and European Integration: The Weight of Legal Tradition. In: Campbell T D, Walker N (eds) Relocating Sovereignty. Routledge

Doroga S (2020) Understanding Constitutional Identity Through the Language of Courts. In: Mercescu A (ed) Constitutional Identities in Central and Eastern Europe. Peter Lang, Berlin, pp 91–116

Drace-Francis A (2013) European Identity: A Historical Reader. Red Globe Press, London

Eckes C (2020) The Autonomy of the EU Legal Order. Europe and the World: A Law Review 4(1):1–19

Erasmus D (1917) The Complaint of Peace (Paynell T (transl)). Translated from the Querela Pacis (A.D. 1521) of Erasmus. Open Court, Chicago

Fabbrini F, Sajó A (2019) The Dangers of Constitutional Identity. European Law Journal 25(4):457–473

Faraguna P (2017) Constitutional Identity in the EU—A Shield or a Sword? German Law Journal 18(7):1617–1640

Fukuyama F (2018) Why National Identity Matters. Journal of Democracy 29(4):5–15

Gašperin Wischhoff J (forthcoming) Forgetting Identity Claims – The New Constitutional Paradigm in Multilevel Fundamental Rights Standards. In: Sahadžić M et al (eds) Legal Mechanisms of Divergence and Convergence: Accommodating Diversity in Multilevel Constitutional Orders. Routledge, pp 91–112

Gehring M (2020) Ius Obstacles to European Constitutionalization. In: Europe's Second Constitution: Crisis, Courts and Community. Cambridge Studies in Constitutional Law. Cambridge University Press, Cambridge, pp 155–222

Habermas J (1995) Address: Multiculturalism and the Liberal State. Stanford Law Review 47(5):849–853

Habermas J (1996) The European Nation State. Its Achievements and Its Limitations. On the Past and Future of Sovereignty and Citizenship. Ratio Juris 9:125–137

Habermas J (1997) Between Facts and Norms: Contributions to a Discourse Theory of Law and Democracy. Blackwell Publishers, Cambridge

Häcker B, Freedland M R, Enchelmaier S, Weatherill S (2012) Constitutional Pluralism in the European Union and Beyond. In: Avbelj M, Komárek J (eds) The Enforcement of EU Law and Values, UK edn. Oxford

Hard R (2019) The Routledge Handbook of Greek Mythology, 8th edn. Routledge

Hart H L A (1958) Positivism and the Separation of Law and Morals. Harvard Law Review 71(4):593–629

Hohnerlein J (2020) Recht Und Demokratische Reversibilität. Mohr Siebeck, Tübingen

Holtman R B (1981) The Napoleonic Revolution. Baton Rouge. Louisiana State University Press

Howard J A (2000) Social Psychology of Identities. Annual Review of Sociology 26(1):367–393

Jacobs D, Maier R (1998) European Identity: Construct, Fact and Fiction. In: Gastelaars M, De Ruijter A (eds) A United Europe: The Quest for a Multifaceted Identity. Shaker, Maastricht, pp 13–34

Jacobsohn G J (2010) Constitutional Identity. Harvard University Press, Cambridge

John Paul II (2003) Ecclesia in Europa. Catholic Truth Society

Kaina V, Karolewski I P, Kuhn S (eds) (2016) European Identity Revisited. New Approaches and Recent Empirical Evidence. Routledge

Klabbers J, Peters A, Ulfstein G (2009) The Constitutionalization of International Law. Oxford University Press, Cambridge

Krunke H (2019) Constitutional Identity in Denmark. In: Calliess C, van der Schyff G (eds) Constitutional Identity in a Europe of Multilevel Constitutionalism. Cambridge University Press, Cambridge, pp 114–133

Kumm M (2011) How Does European Union Law Fit into the World of Public Law? Costa, Kadi, and Three Models of Public Law. In: Neyer J, Wiener A (eds) Political Theory of the European Union. Oxford University Press, Oxford/New York, NY, pp 111–138

Kumm M (2012a) Rethinking Constitutional Authority. On the Structure and Limits of Constitutional Pluralism. In: Avbelj M, Komárek J (eds) Constitutional Pluralism in the European Union and Beyond. Studies of the Oxford Institute of European and Comparative Law, Vol. 14. Hart Publishing, Oxford/Portland, OR, pp 39–65

Kumm M (2012b) The Idea of Thick Constitutional Patriotism and Its Implications for the Role and Structure of European Legal History. In: Porsdam H, Elholm T (eds) Dialogues on Justice.

European Perspectives on Law and Humanities. Law & Literature, Vol. 3. Walter de Gruyter, Berlin/Boston, MA, pp 108–137

Kumm M (2012c) The Moral Point of Constitutional Pluralism 1: Defining the Domain of Legitimate Institutional Civil Disobedience and Conscientious Objection. In: Dickson J, Eleftheriadis P (eds) Philosophical Foundations of European Union Law. Oxford University Press, Oxford, pp 216–246

Kumm M (2013) The Cosmopolitan Turn in Constitutionalism: An Integrated Conception of Public. Indiana Journal of Global Legal Studies 20(2):605–628

Millet F X (2013) L'Union européenne et l'identité constitutionnelle des États membres, Bibliothèque constitutionnelle et de science politique. Paris. Available from Cadmus, European University Institute Research Repository, at: http://hdl.handle.net/1814/27788. Accessed 1 December 2021

Millet F X (2019) Constitutional Identity in France: Vices and – Above All – Virtues. In: Calliess C, van der Schyff G (eds) Constitutional Identity in a Europe of Multilevel Constitutionalism. Cambridge University Press, Cambridge, pp 134–152

Millet F X (2021) Successfully Articulating National Constitutional Identity Claims: Strait Is the Gate and Narrow Is the Way. European Public Law 27(3):571–596

Newman E (1976) A Civil Tongue. Bobbs-Merrill Co, Indianapolis

Passchier R, Stremler M (2016) Unconstitutional Constitutional Amendments in European Union Law: Considering the Existence of Substantive Constraints on Treaty Revision. Cambridge Journal of International and Comparative Law 5(2): 337–362

Pech L, Wachowiec P, Mazur D (2021) Poland's Rule of Law Breakdown: A Five-Year Assessment of EU's (In)Action. Hague Journal on the Rule of Law 13(1):1–43

Pinelli C (2016) Theories Concerning the Hierarchy of Norms. Max Planck Encyclopedia of Comparative Constitutional Law, https://doi.org/10.1093/law-mpeccol/e307.013.307. Accessed 1 December 2021

Piris J C (2006) The Constitution for Europe, A Legal Analysis. Cambridge University Press, Cambridge

Plato (360 BCE) Cratylus 402a (Jowett B (transl)). http://classics.mit.edu/Plato/cratylus.html

Polzin M (2017) Constitutional Identity as a Constructed Reality and a Restless Soul. German Law Journal, Volume 18, Issue 7: Special Issue: Constitutional Identity in the Age of Global Migration: 1595–1616

Polzin M (2018) Verfassungsidentität, Ein normatives Konzept des Grundgesetzes? Jus Publicum 272. Mohr Siebeck

Rawls J (1993) Political Liberalism. Columbia University Press, New York

Rosenfeld M (2012) Constitutional Identity. In: Rosenfeld M, Sajó A (eds) The Oxford Handbook of Comparative Constitutional Law. DOI: https://doi.org/10.1093/oxfordhb/9780199578610.013.0037. Accessed 1 December 2021

Roznai Y (2019) Unconstitutional Constitutional Amendments: The Limits of Amendment Powers. Oxford University Press, New York

Sarmiento D (2013) The EU's Constitutional Core. In: Saiz Arnaiz S, Alcoberro Llivina C (eds) National Constitutional Identity and European Integration. Intersentia, Cambridge/Antwerp/Portland, 177–204

Schneider L (2020) Responses by the CJEU to the European Crisis of Democracy and the Rule of Law. re:constitution Working Paper, Forum Transregionale Studien 2/2020

Scholtes J (2021) Abusing Constitutional Identity. German Law Journal 22(4):534–556

Spieker L D (2019) Breathing Life into the Union's Common Values: On the Judicial Application of Article 2 TEU in the EU Value Crisis. German Law Journal 20(8):1182–1213

Spieker L D (2021) Defending Union Values in Judicial Proceedings. On How to Turn Article 2 TEU into a Judicially Applicable Provision. In: von Bogdandy A, Bogdanowicz P, Canor I, Grabenwarter C, Taborowski M, Schmidt M (eds) Defending Checks and Balances in EU Member States: Taking Stock of Europe's Actions. Springer, Berlin/Heidelberg, pp 237–268

Taylor C (1992) Sources of the Self: The Making of the Modern Identity. Harvard University Press, Cambridge

Troitskaya A (2021) Constitutional Identity, and Where (and Why) to Find It, Round Table of the IACL-AIDC Constitutional Identity: Universality of Constitutionalism vs. National Constitutional Traditions? St. Petersburg, Russia, 10–13 June 2021 https://www.youtube.com/watch?v=pG_uNXl5y0U. Accessed 1 December 2021

van der Schyff G (2021) Constitutional Identity of the EU Legal Order: Delineating Its Roles and Contours. Ancilla Iuris 1–12

von Bogdandy A (2021) Towards a Tyranny of Values? In: von Bogdandy A, Bogdanowicz P, Canor I, Grabenwarter C, Taborowski M, Schmidt M (eds) Defending Checks and Balances in EU Member States: Taking Stock of Europe's Actions. Springer, Berlin/Heidelberg, pp 73–103

von Bogdandy A, Antpöhler C, Dickschen J, Hentrei S, Kottmann M, Smrkolj M (2017a) Reverse Solange–Protecting the Essence of Fundamental Rights Against EU Member States. Common Market Law Review 49(2):489–519

von Bogdandy A, Antpöhler C, Ioannidis M (2017b) Protecting EU Values: Reverse Solange and the Rule of Law Framework. In: Jakab A, Kochenov D (eds) The Enforcement of EU Law and Values: Ensuring Member States' Compliance. Oxford University Press, pp 218–233

Walker N (2008) Post-Constituent Constitutionalism? The Case of the European Union. In: Loughlin M, Walker N (eds) The Paradox of Constitutionalism: Constituent Power and Constitutional Form. Oxford University Press

Weiler J H H (2005) On the Power of the Word: Europe's Constitutional Iconography. International Journal of Constitutional Law 3(2–3):173–190

Weiler J H H, Haltern U R (1996) The Autonomy of the Community Legal Order—Through the Looking Glass. Harvard International Law Journal 37:411–448

Whitehead A N (1929) Process and Reality. Free Press, New York

Williams C J F (1979) Is Identity a Relation? In: The Aristotelian Society, Proceedings of the Aristotelian Society, New Series, Vol. 80 (1979–1980). Oxford University Press, Oxford, pp 81–100

Zimmermann R (2015) Roman Law in the Modern World. In: Johnston D (ed) The Cambridge Companion to Roman Law. Cambridge University Press, Cambridge, pp 452–480

Jakob Gašperin Wischhoff is a researcher at the DFG Graduate Program DynamInt at the Humboldt-Universität zu Berlin, where he completed his PhD.

Chapter 4
The Constitutional Identity of the EU as a Counterbalance for Unconstitutional Constitutional Identities of the Member States

Tímea Drinóczi⬤ and Pietro Faraguna⬤

Contents

Abstract This chapter examines the concept of constitutional identity of the EU from the perspective of public law. As the term appears in the TEU and, in the last 15 years, has been used by different apex courts, it draws on the trend of using constitutional identity as a legal argument against EU obligations or creating constitutional law arguments for this purpose. Thus, the chapter claims that the mandate to respect constitutional identities, as stated in Article 4(2) TEU, finds a limit in

T. Drinóczi
Faculty of Law, Federal University of Minas Gerais, Belo Horizonte, Brazil
e-mail: tdrinoczi@direito.ufmg.br

P. Faraguna (✉)
Department of Constitutional Law, University of Trieste, Trieste, Italy
e-mail: pfaraguna@units.it

© T.M.C. ASSER PRESS and the authors 2023
J. de Poorter et al. (eds.), *European Yearbook of Constitutional Law 2022*,
European Yearbook of Constitutional Law 4,
https://doi.org/10.1007/978-94-6265-595-9_4

the respect for EU constitutional identity. The chapter argues that the EU constitutional identity could be identified in the same manner most Member States identify constitutional identity. Therefore, it argues that constitutional identity is a concept both applicable to the EU and the EU Member States, and to make these concepts compatible, Member States' constitutional identities are to be respected as long as they are not incompatible with EU constitutional identity, consisting of fundamental principles of constitutionalism.

Keywords Constitutional identity · European Union · Democratic backsliding · Regression · Abuse · Misuse

4.1 Introduction

The scholarly literature on the concept of "constitutional identity" of the Member States in the European Union (EU) recently formed an autonomous scholarly literary genre,[1] leading to what has been paradoxically labelled an "excess"[2] of literature by some of the authors contributing to it. It is because European treaties explicitly mention "identity", and the EU is a firmly integrated legal space against the background of profound cultural, linguistic, political, and constitutional contrasts within a relatively small territory. Respect for constitutional identities has long been considered a safety valve to make legal integration and constitutional peculiarities compatible.

On the contrary, the notion of an EU constitutional identity[3] is largely under-investigated in the constitutional legal literature. Although this under-investigation affected the related studies also before Euro-scepticism flourished in the EU, the current situation further marginalises such an analysis. However, in recent times, the debate around Member States' constitutional identities seems to be turning the corner again, revealing possible unexpected space for analysis of the constitutional identity of the EU. In fact, Member States' constitutional identity is being increasingly used to justify departures from fundamental values of constitutionalism, including European constitutionalism, particularly in Central and Eastern European (CEE) Member States. "Illiberal constitutionalism" emerged in Poland and Hungary: in these Countries, the construction of a particular constitutional identity, legally obstructing the implementation of some EU obligations [and specifically those stemming from Article 2 of the Treaty on European Union (TEU)], are phenomena that need to be interrogated for the sake of maintaining the unity of EU law and further advancing European integration, as it is stated in the TEU preamble.

---

[1] E.g., European Public Law Vol. 27 (2021) Issue 3; Van der Schyff 2016; Śledzińska-Simon 2015; Millet 2013; Saiz Arnaiz and Alcoberro Llivina 2013; Kostadinov 2012.

[2] Burgorgue-Larsen 2013, p. 275.

[3] In this chapter, we use "EU constitutional identity" and "European constitutional identity" interchangeably.

Identity is a "polysemic concept",[4] one that can be explored within and by many different social sciences.[5] This chapter explores the concept of identity from the perspective of comparative constitutional law, constitutional theory, and European constitutional law, while it also acknowledges and appreciates other, more descriptive, definitions of the term that does not imply immutability.[6] Nevertheless, when the investigation of the concept of identity is limited to the public law realm, it is usually considered an "essentially contested concept".[7] In fact, the "scope and meaning [of identity] seem rather vague and undetermined".[8] Vagueness and ambiguity are the most common adjectives attached to the noun "identity".[9]

This chapter thus takes a legal perspective and is conscious of the contested nature of the term constitutional identity. As the term appears in the TEU and, in the last 15 years, has been used by different apex courts, it draws on the mentioned trend of using constitutional identity as a legal argument against EU obligations or creating constitutional law arguments for this purpose. Thus, the chapter claims that the mandate to respect constitutional identities, as stated in Article 4(2) TEU, finds a limit in the respect for EU constitutional identity. The fact that the concept of EU constitutional identity received recognition in two recent decisions of the Court of Justice of the EU (CJEU), issued in February 2022, makes this claim even more timely and relevant. It is also proposed that the EU constitutional identity could be identified in the same manner most Member States identify constitutional identity. Therefore, it is argued that constitutional identity is a concept both applicable to the EU and the EU Member States, and to make these concepts compatible, Member States' constitutional identities are to be respected as long as they are not incompatible with EU constitutional identity, consisting of fundamental principles of constitutionalism. In other words, EU constitutional identities are to be respected as long as they are not unconstitutional constitutional identities.

To this end, the chapter will first move from the state of the art of the scholarly debate around Member States' constitutional identities. In Sect. 4.2, the chapter locates the concept(s) of constitutional identity within a strict theoretical frame and identifies the European specificities of the discourse around constitutional identity. It investigates how the concept of constitutional identity was constitutionalised and

---

[4] Toniatti 2013, p. 62.

[5] Appiah 2018; Fukuyama 2018; Lawler 2008; Parekh 2008; Gutman 2003; Benhabib 1988; Tajfel 1982; Madell 1981.

[6] For instance, Jacobsohn argues that constitutional identity does not only require to be discovered but it emerges dialogically and intends to transcend the past (Jacobsohn 2010, 7), while Rosenfeld explains that constitutional identity first emerges as a lack that must be overcome through a discursive process that relies on negation, metaphor, and metonymy. (Rosenfeld 2010, 45–64, most recently in Rosenfeld 2022, 2). Nevertheless, in their scholarship, constitutional identity appears to serve as a special "mechanism" or "procedure" that facilitates the understanding of constitutional change. The scope of this chapter is to conceptualise the legal application of the term constitutional identity.

[7] Levinson 1998; Rosenfeld 2010; both referring to WB Gallie's notion.

[8] Saiz Arnaiz and Alcoberro Llivina 2013, p. 2.

[9] Burgorgue-Larsen 2011, p. 156.

applied at the EU level. The following section deals with the abuse of constitutional identity by the two renegade Members States of the EU, Hungary and Poland, and contrasts them with the German and Italian dialogical approaches. Section 4.4 conceptualises European constitutional identity by locating its "untouchable core" into the broader context of a wider conceptual map, by analysing different dimensions of the concept at the European level. It also explains why this identity is important for the European integration project.

4.2 Constitutional Identity: A Global Concept and Its "European Sonderweg" as a Fundamental Legal Concept

4.2.1 Constitutional Identity: An Ambiguous, Malleable, Universal, and Fundamental Legal Notion

The uncertainty concerning the concept of constitutional identity notwithstanding, or maybe exactly because of this conceptual flexibility, studies on identity are recently "blooming"[10] in the public law literature. Nonetheless, the theoretical roots of this concept are far from new. Already in his Politics, Aristotle wrote: "on what principle ought we to say that a State has retained its identity, or, conversely, that it has lost its identity and become a different State?".[11] If we only focus on modern constitutional law scholarship, the concept already emerges in post-WWI literature. Carl Schmitt dedicated an important part of his *Verfassungslehre* to the concept of constitutional identity, as a limit to the amendment power to the Weimar Constitution (Schmitt 1928, § 11[12]). The traditional task of constitutional legal scholars has also been delineated in finding the distinction between the very core of the constitution and the ordinary constitutional laws.[13]

The growing success, application, and migration[14] of the concept led some scholars not only to conceptualise the models the constitutional courts have developed and attitudes they have displayed in their jurisprudence on constitutional identity,[15] but also to criticise its side effects. The critics focus on "dangers"[16] coming from

---

[10] Toniatti 2013, p. 62.

[11] Quoted by Jacobsohn 2006, p. 7.

[12] On the German roots of this concept, see Polzin 2016.

[13] Beaud 1994.

[14] On the successful migration of the concept, see Roznai 2013; Perju 2012; Perju 2020, p. 256.

[15] The three models are confrontational with EU law (Germany), confrontational individualistic detachment (Hungary), and cooperation with embedded identity (Italy); the two attitudes are EU-friendly (Germany and Italy) and antagonistic (Hungary). Drinóczi 2020. Based on its most recent case law, the Polish CT would join Hungary (see *infra*).

[16] Fabbrini and Sajó 2019.

constitutional identity and identify it as an "inherently dangerous concept"[17] prone to abuses and misuses.

However, in our opinion, abuses and misuses are, on the contrary, a further symptom of the success of constitutional identity as a legal notion. In fact, to a certain extent, the same fact that the clause is increasingly more and more subject to abusive domestic manipulations is a clear symptom of its success. The same is true for many other key concepts of public law, such as democracy, freedom, and liberalism: these are all indeterminate, and, as such, they are and have been prone to abusive misinterpretations.

The ambiguity and malleability of the concept facilitate its universal and global vocation: identity is a key concept that may apply in any constitutional system, regardless of its specific features and ideological orientation.

Constitutional identity was successfully, but still somewhat vaguely, described as a legal notion including a "general" and a "particular" aspect. As for the former, it "derives its force from the fact of having an entrenched and written constitution containing the basic moral commitments of the community".[18] As for the latter, it "arises from the concrete constitutional spirit or tradition and refers to the specific constitutional experience of the community in question".[19] Therefore, constitutional identity is, indeed, as one of us proposed it elsewhere, the identity of a constitution.[20]

4.2.2   The European "Sonderweg" of Constitutional Identity

4.2.2.1   The Constitutionalisation of Constitutional Identity at the EU Level

Empirical evidence shows a European special path ("Sonderweg") in the way of approaching the concept of constitutional identity. However, a legally conceptualised epiphany of identity seems to be "a Global North—more specifically EU—phenomenon".[21] Among the many reasons that may illustrate this peculiarity, two of them seem particularly remarkable. First, Europe is a small continent with deep legal integration and wide differentiation of legal regimes. Second, EU law provides for an identity clause in Article 4(2) TEU, a unique example of the constitutionalisation of the legal concept of identity in modern supranational constitutionalism. The two elements are, of course, intertwined: the EU has an identity clause, as the EU needs one. The EU needs one because the EU is a relatively small territory characterised by significant legal heterogeneity.

---

[17] Pech and Kelemen 2019.

[18] Tripkovic 2017, p. 31.

[19] Ibid.

[20] Drinóczi 2020.

[21] Drinóczi 2018, p. 77.

The identity clause in EU law was firstly introduced in the Treaties in 1992. Ahead of the introduction of the clause with the Treaty of Maastricht, some constitutional courts of EU Member States (particularly the Italian Constitutional Court—hereafter ICC—and the German Constitutional Court—hereafter GCC) had already engaged in a judicial dialogue with the CJEU around possible tools of protection of national constitutional peculiarities before 1992. However, it was only with the approval of the Treaty of Maastricht that the Treaties were complemented with an explicit clause providing for the principle of respect for Member States' national identities.[22] At the time of the Maastricht Treaty, the terms of the clause were rather vague and ambiguous. The introduction of the clause was considered a wise point of balance of colliding forces: on the one side, the centripetal force pushing in the direction of stronger and deeper political integration; on the other side, a state-centred centrifugal reluctance to transfer too many state competences to the supranational level. Against this background, and to make a long story short, the political turn marked by the Treaty of Maastricht has been counterbalanced through the introduction of some legal tools. The aim was to reassure the Member States and their concerns about the impact of the new path of the European integration process on the integrity of their statehood. These legal tools include the protocol on subsidiarity, a significant number of opt-outs, the design of differentiated integration tools, and, finally, the principle of respect for Member States' national identities.[23]

For some decades, the value of the identity clause has mostly been considered only as a political statement: among the reassuring tools in the process of balancing mentioned above, the identity clause was the less legally impacting tool within the package. The clause did not make any explicit reference to constitutional elements and textually referred to "national identity", and—above all—it was kept outside the jurisdiction of the CJEU. Therefore, the clause was considered an interpretative complement or a political statement rather than a proper legal and constitutional provision. However, as it appears in the literature, which retrospectively conceptualises the necessity of the identity clauses of the Maastricht and Lisbon Treaties, it could be interpreted as a very clear and historically very appropriate political message. Especially if we consider that, in the 1990s, the EU was in the middle of a significant process of enlargement with the accession of Central and Eastern European countries that, after decades of limitation of sovereignty due to the Soviet influence, were ready to join the EU. Within this context, the identity clause[24] could be viewed as a reassurance for these new Member States that the accession to the EU did not imply a similar violation of the freshly gained sovereign powers but something completely different. This was a good reason not to adopt the language of sovereignty in the Treaties: in fact, the reference to the respect of national identities,

---

[22] According to some authors, the introduction of the clause was a consequence of the case law of the Italian and German Constitutional Courts in the previous years. See, e.g., von Bogdandy and Schill 2011, p. 1426; Martinico 2013, pp. 93, 95.

[23] On this process, see Faraguna 2016.

[24] Bartole 2020, p. 34.

then considered a far less potentially devastating legal notion, brought the debate into a different ground.[25]

The legal impact of the identity clause in its Maastricht formulation has been rather limited. Between 1992 and 2009 (when the Treaty of Lisbon amended its formulation), the clause has never been used in any decision of the Court. However, implicit references to the identity clause are usually recognised in a group of decisions issued before the reformulation of the clause by Treaty of Lisbon in 2009: among these cases, *Anita Groener*,[26] *Omega*,[27] *Grogan*,[28] *Re Azores*,[29] *Gibraltar*[30] are the most famous. In this stream of case law, the CJEU did not make explicit reference to the identity clause, but implicitly referred to it.

The situation has changed, both in the Treaties and in the legal consequences, after the reformulation of the identity clause by the Treaty of Lisbon in 2009. The Treaty of Lisbon rephrased the identity clause and enhanced its legal and constitutional nature. In its current formulation, the clause makes explicit reference to the Member States' "fundamental structures, political and constitutional". Moreover, the Treaty of Lisbon brought Article 4(2) TEU under the jurisdiction of the CJEU.

Nonetheless, if we screen in detail the most important cases where the identity-clause and identity-related arguments made it into the legal reasoning of the Court, we realise that the legalisation of the identity-clause did not have a revolutionary impact on the CJEU case law. The CJEU adopted a cautious and self-restrained approach to the interpretation of the clause even after its constitutionalisation: the clause appeared in the legal reasoning of some decisions of the CJEU, however, the number of cases is limited, and their constitutional tone is rather poor.

4.2.2.2 The Application of Constitutional Identity

On a different yet connected front, there are many more cases in which the identity clause was invoked by the referring courts and/or by national governments intervening in the hearings but were not picked up by the CJEU: *Torresi*[31] and *M.A.S. and M.B.*[32] (also known as *Taricco II*) are quintessential examples of this dynamic. Paradoxically, but understandably, the "constitutionalisation" of the identity clause provided for by the Treaty of Lisbon had a much higher impact on the

---

[25] Weiler 2002, p. 569.

[26] Case C-379/87, *Anita Groener and the Minister for Education and the City of Dublin Vocational Education Committee*, 1989 E.C.R. 3967.

[27] Case C-36/02, *Omega Spielhallen und Automatenaufstellungs-GmbH v. Oberbürgermeisterin der Bundesstadt Bonn*, 2004 E.C.R. I-9641.

[28] Case C-159/90, *Society for the Protection of Unborn Children Ireland Ltd. v. Stephen Grogan and Others*, 1991 E.C.R. 4685.

[29] Case C-88/03, *Portugal v. Commission*, 2006 E.C.R. I-7145.

[30] Case C-145/04, *Spain v. United Kingdom*, 2006 E.C.R. I-7961.

[31] Joined Cases C-58/13 and C-59/13 *Angelo Alberto Torresi and Pierfrancesco Torresi v Consiglio dell'Ordine degli Avvocati di Macerata*, 17 July 2014.

[32] Case C-42/17, *M.A.S. and M.B.*, 5 December 2017.

case-law of Member States' supreme and constitutional courts.[33] The number of cases where Member States' constitutional and supreme courts raised some constitutional objections to the principle of primacy of EU law significantly increased after 2009.

After the famous (for someone: infamous) *Lisbon* decision of the GCC,[34] where identity review was first theoretically designed as a new test of compatibility of EU law with a national constitution, a trend of "constitutional resistance" emerged in the jurisprudence of many Member States' constitutional courts.

In its seminal decision, the GCC identified an essential constitutional core that is not subject to any modification. The Court in Karlsruhe stated that this constitutional core sets a limit to European integration that not even a constitutional amendment may remove. The content of this core is enshrined in the so-called "eternity clause" in accordance with Article 79(3) of the German Basic Law, which was extended to the European matters pursuant to Article 23 of the Basic Law. Hence, within the constitutional core, the eternity clause includes the principle of democracy, the essence of which exists in the constitutional voting rights of German citizens. Against this background, the GCC stated that the German Basic Law impedes the conferral of those competences on the EU that would bear a risk of deprivation of the right to vote and the principle of democracy of their substantive contents. In the view of the GCC:

> Particularly sensitive for the ability of a constitutional state to democratically shape itself are decisions on substantive and formal criminal law (1), on the disposition of the monopoly on the use of force by the police within the state and by the military towards the exterior (2), fundamental fiscal decisions on public revenue and public expenditure, the latter being particularly motivated, inter alia, by social policy considerations (3), decisions on the shaping of living conditions in a social state (4) and decisions of particular cultural importance, for example on family law, the school and education system and on dealing with religious communities (5).[35]

The *Lisbon* decision of the GCC is even now a judicial manifesto of national constitutional identity and had a large and significant impact on the jurisprudence of other Member States' constitutional courts, which increasingly referred to the notion in the last decade. Particularly in the last five years, the trend of objecting to national constitutional reservations regarding the application of EU law in the Member States has escalated. In fact, some early signals emerged when the Czech Constitutional

---

[33] In this analysis, we will consider both groups of cases where constitutional identity emerges openly and cases where it emerges in disguise (under different tags as sovereignty control, *ultra vires* review, fundamental rights review, counterlimits, and similar notions…). In fact, the legal reasoning of many of these decisions does not rely on constitutional identity as a central argument to support its legal effects, but is rather based on the principle of conferral and the connected *ultra vires* review, "a rather clear-cut concept that limits actions emanating from the EU to its competences manifested in the Treaties": in this sense, Spieker 2020. However, the identity and *ultra vires* reviews are independent, but related concepts, in particular when a violation of the democratic principle is at stake. See GCC, BvR 2728/13, *OMT I*, para 27. See further Calliess 2019, p. 175.

[34] GCC, 2 BvE 2/08, 30 June 30 2009, *Lisbon* decision.

[35] Ibidem, at 252.

Court issued its famous *Landtova* judgment,[36] declaring a decision of the CJEU *ultra vires*. Then, the German GCC engaged in a rough judicial dialogue with the CJEU in the famous *OMT* saga,[37] submitting its first reference for a preliminary ruling in 2014, and finally, in its "final decision" of the case in June 2016, decided not to declare any act of European institutions *ultra vires*, after the CJEU issued its reassurances with its decision in 2015.[38] In the same year, the GCC issued an important decision on the European Arrest Warrant,[39] where identity-related arguments were used to perform a peculiar "national constitutional identity-oriented interpretation" of EU law. Some years later, the GCC was involved in a new saga. In the so-called *Weiss* saga, the GCC—for the first time in the history of its European case law—declared an act of the European Central Bank, along with the *Weiss* decision of the CJEU[40] (upholding the validity of the mentioned act of the ECB) to be *ultra vires*.[41]

Some years earlier, in 2016, the Hungarian Constitutional Court (HCC) issued a substantially EU law "unfriendly" decision.[42] which we will specifically explore in detail below along with another recent decision of the HCC adopting identity-related arguments and a decision of the Polish Constitutional Tribunal (PCT) issued in October 2021.

On the other side of the Alps, the ICC engaged in a vibrant judicial dialogue with the CJEU in the so-called *Taricco* saga,[43] which seems to provide the most topical example of the above-illustrated slightly paradoxical developments. While the ICC, in its reference for a preliminary ruling, expressly invoked the protection of "constitutional identity", and explicitly referred to Article 4(2) TEU, the CJEU avoided referring to identity in its legal reasoning, while grounding its accommodating decision on the notion of common constitutional traditions. It is extremely telling that the CJEU decision in *M.A.S. and M.B.*[44] (also known as "Taricco II") did not even mention the word "identity" once.

The saga was initiated by a decision of the CJEU, interpreting Article 325 TFEU as generating an obligation with direct effect, requiring the disapplication of the Italian legislation providing for relatively short limitation periods in the matter of criminal prosecution of financial frauds. In its decision issued in September 2015,[45] the CJEU stated that the contested rules on statutory limitation could result in a violation of Article 325 TFEU. This decision could have led to the disapplication of national

---

[36] Czech Constitutional Court, Judgment of 31 January 2012, case no. Pl. ÚS 5/12, *Slovak Pensions XVII*. See comments by Kühn 2016; Komárek 2012.

[37] On the impact of the OMT saga on the national constitutional identity discourse, see Claes and Reestman 2015,

[38] Case C-62/14, *Gauweiler and others*.

[39] GCC, Order of 15 December 2015, 2 BvR 2735/14.

[40] Case C-493/17, *Weiss and Others*, 11 December 2018, ECLI:EU:C:2018:1000.

[41] GCC, BvR 859/15 - 2 BvR 1651/15 - 2 BvR 2006/15 - 2 BvR 980/16, 5 May 2020.

[42] Constitutional Court of Hungary, Decision 22/2016 (XII. 5.) AB.

[43] ICC, order 24/2017 (in the so-called *Taricco* saga).

[44] Case C-42/17, *M.A.S. and M.B.*, 5 December 2017.

[45] Case C-105/14, *Ivo Taricco and others*, 8 September 2016.

rules on limitation periods, potentially also with retroactive effects. These effects were held incompatible with the essential core of the legality principle as interpreted by a long-standing legal tradition in Italy. Both the fact that the "legal rule" emerged from a discretionary interpretation of the CJEU, pushing the meaning of a provision of the Treaty quite far from its literal meaning, and the supposed retrospective effects of this interpretation generated new controversies on this matter. The ICC was called to decide upon the compatibility of the *Taricco* rule, as interpreted by the CJEU, with Italian constitutional identity.

In a seminal decision, the ICC opted for a dialogical approach, consisting of a new reference for a preliminary ruling. The Court emphasised the substantive understanding of the limitation period and the broad interpretation of the principle of legality in criminal matters as a peculiarity of the Italian legal tradition to be reconnected to constitutional identity. On the one hand, the ICC introduced its arguments through an accommodating incipit, where the European composite constitution was depicted in a rather irenic way. Then the ICC noticed that the primacy of EU law mirrors the idea that the objective of unity in EU law necessarily requires a minimum tolerance of diversity in a legal system that is characterised by pluralism. In the ICC's view, a margin of tolerance is necessary to preserve the national constitutional identities of the Member States, explicitly referring to the TEU constitutional identity clause. In the ICC's view, constitutional identity included its (wide) interpretation of the principle of legality, covering the regulation of the statute of limitation: practically, the ICC offered the CJEU the opportunity to recalibrate its previous decision, or—to put it bluntly—pushed the CJEU to revise its jurisprudence on the interpretation of Article 325 TFEU, advocating an exemption based on constitutional identity. On the other hand, the ICC reference for a preliminary ruling also relied on arguments grounded in EU law, specifically in common constitutional traditions. In fact, the ICC held that the *Taricco* rule, as interpreted—if not created—by the CJEU, was at odds with another aspect inherent to the principle of legality, *i.e.*, the requirement that the provision on the regime of punishment must be sufficiently precise. On this ground, the ICC did not claim any peculiarity of Italian constitutional identity. On the contrary, it argued that the lack of precision of the *Taricco* rule was incompatible with a key principle that is "common to the constitutional traditions of the Member States, which also features within the ECHR system of protection and as such encapsulates a general principle of EU law"[46] and that is inherent to the principle of legality enshrined in Article 49 of the Nice Charter.

Against this background, and to sum it up, on the one hand, the strategy of the CJEU not to play on the constitutional identity table seems wise, as it avoids the risk of strong judicial conflict over the interpretation of a notion that national actors would probably consider to be under their ultimate authority. On the other hand, the same strategy seems to be a missed opportunity for the CJEU to develop its own jurisprudence on an autonomous concept of the constitutional identity of the EU, which, in the case at hand, would not have been necessarily in conflict with the domestic interpretation of national constitutional identity invoked by the ICC.

---

[46] ICC, order 24/2017, para 9.

Lastly, the case law on constitutional identity also shows the key role played by constitutional dialogue between national constitutional courts and the CJEU through the preliminary ruling procedure.

4.3 Unconstitutional Constitutional Identities

4.3.1 What Constitutes (Un)constitutional

In the history of European integration, constitutional identity has been conceived for a long time as a notion that perfectly fits the picture of post-war nation-state constitutionalism. To a certain extent, it represented the ultimate boundary of protection of the essential core of a constitutional design of the nation-state in Western constitutionalism. Both in the German and Italian interpretation of the concept, constitutional identity had been subject to a judicial construction that aimed at developing a tool of protection of fundamental principles of constitutionalism within the picture of the ongoing process of European integration.

In these constitutional experiences, constitutional identity has two sides. There is an internal side, where constitutional identity represents the essential core of a given constitutional order and consists of the (explicitly or implicitly) unamendable provisions. At the same time, constitutional identity also has an external side, where constitutional identity represents a legal tool of protection of the same fundamental principles against possible threats or limitations originating from the *ultra vires* effect and application of European or international norms.

However, in both senses, constitutional identity is conceived as functional to the protection of fundamental principles of constitutionalism or substantive constitutional democracy (the rule of law, democracy, and human rights). Some recent developments have put this normative assumption at risk and invite us to open up the descriptive claim on what constitutional identity is. More precisely, what type of constitutionalism and constitutional principles are the subjects of the identity discourse, how we can distinguish between constitutional and unconstitutional constitutional identity, and how we can identify abusive practices. To this end, we will focus on three seminal episodes of abusive manipulation of constitutional identity.

4.3.2 Abusive Domestic Case Laws

4.3.2.1 First Episode

The first episode occurred in 2016, after an unsuccessful referendum initiated by the Hungarian government against the EU measures on migration ("quota-referendum"). In this political environment, in which Fidesz (the governing political party) also lost its constitutional majority for a short period, the HCC was more than happy to help in the government's attempts to fight against the migration policy of the EU. The HCC, in its first decision on constitutional identity (22/2016 (XII. 5)), stated that it could examine whether the joint exercise of competences under Article E)(2) of the Fundamental Law (FL) infringed human dignity, other fundamental rights (fundamental right review), the sovereignty of Hungary (*ultra vires* review), or Hungary's self-identity based on its historical constitution (identity review). This constitutional identity, according to the HCC, is a fundamental value that had not been created but only recognised by the FL. Therefore, it could not be renounced by an international treaty and needs to be defended. In this decision, the HCC, arguably, created an implicit eternity clause (the internal aspect of constitutional identity), which is called constitutional identity based on the historical constitution of Hungary.[47] Some months later, when Fidesz regained its constitutional majority, it amended the FL (2017),[48] which now, also as a result of further amendments (2019), contains provisions explicitly mentioning "constitutional identity".[49]

Nevertheless, the concept of constitutional identity has not been activated by the HCC against any EU measures, but used to stall some politically sensitive constitutional reviews by "discovering" existing internal procedures. In 2018, it suspended its procedures in the cases of the Central European University[50] and the Act on foreign-funded NGOs,[51] submitted in 2017. The HCC argued that it must wait until the case is decided before the CJEU, as judicial dialogue is vital in the European integration context, as expressed in decision 22/2016 (XII. 5).[52] The HCC also claimed that it wanted to improve its procedure and better its dialogue with the CJEU. Nevertheless,

---

[47] Drinóczi 2020.

[48] E.g., Article E)(2) was enriched with the last sentence: "With a view to participating in the European Union as a Member State and on the basis of an international treaty, Hungary may, to the extent necessary to exercise the rights and fulfil the obligations deriving from the Founding Treaties, exercise some of its competences arising from the Fundamental Law jointly with other Member States, through the institutions of the European Union. Exercise of competences under this paragraph shall comply with the fundamental rights and freedoms provided for in the Fundamental Law and shall not limit the inalienable right of Hungary to determine its territorial unity, population, form of government and state structure."

[49] National Avowal: "We hold that the protection of our identity rooted in our historic constitution is a fundamental obligation of the State." Article R)(4): "The protection of the constitutional identity and Christian culture of Hungary shall be an obligation of every organ of the State." Article XVI (1) "Every child shall have the right to the protection and care necessary for his or her proper physical, mental and moral development. Hungary shall protect the right of children to a self-identity corresponding to their sex at birth, and shall ensure an upbringing for them that is in accordance with the values based on the constitutional identity and Christian culture of our country."

[50] Case C-66/18 *Commission v Hungary*, ECLI:EU:C:2020:792, Decision 3199/2018. (VI. 21.) of the CC, Decision 3200/2018. (VI. 21.) of the CC.

[51] Case C-78/18, *European Commission v Hungary*, ECLI:EU:C:2020:476, Decision 3198/2018. (VI. 21.) of the CC.

[52] After the decision in Case C-66/18 Commission v Hungary (6 October 2020) of the CJEU, in which it declared the conditions introduced to enable foreign higher education institutions to carry out their activities in Hungary incompatible with EU law, it took one year for the HCC to continue its procedure. It terminated the constitutional review process of Lex CEU because, in its view, the

it was not on the HCC's mind earlier, in the case of, *e.g.*, the retirement of judges (2012)[53]—when the need for dialogue also existed. Moreover, the HCC did not suspend its proceedings but upheld the constitutionality of the "Stop Soros" law,[54] claiming that this process was in a different procedural stage before the CJEU as it had not decided whether or not to take the case forward. The HCC has never used the preliminary ruling procedure, and—as we can see—abused the idea of constitutional dialogue.

4.3.2.2   Second Episode

The second episode occurred in October 2021, when the Polish Constitutional Tribunal (CT), following its already developed case law on the relationship between domestic and EU law, explained[55] first how the TEU should not be interpreted. It stated that it could not be interpreted as authorising the EU to act outside the conferred powers, preventing the 1997 Constitution from being the supreme law of the land and Poland from functioning as a sovereign and democratic state. If interpreted this way, the TEU must be considered inconsistent with the Polish Constitution. It also stated that it is inconsistent with the Polish Constitution to interpret Article 19 TEU as entailing that national courts can, in order to protect the EU judicial order, "bypass the provisions of the Constitution in the course of adjudication", "adjudicate on the basis of provisions which are not binding, having been revoked by the Sejm and/or ruled by the Constitutional Tribunal to be inconsistent with the Constitution", review the legality of judicial appointments, review resolutions by the National Council of the Judiciary, or determine the judicial appointments invalid. These could be legitimate claims of domestic constitutional courts in the European context. However, suppose we put this interpretation into context[56] and do not forget about the European clause of the Polish Constitution and its previous European-friendly interpretations. In this case, it is clear that the PCT, similarly to the political communication, rejected the relevant CJEU judgments[57] and, arguably, all the EU rules that they, *i.e.*, the judges of the non-independent PCT, would deem to be contrary to the 1997 Constitution. Therefore, there is also a fear that, in the future, the PCT would not behave differently than before, and it would please the PiS-led government.

This decision is not unique but has been preceded by other PCT decisions already indicating this direction—not with the activation of constitutional identity but of the

---

CJEU decision, the fact that the Hungarian Parliament amended the Act in spring 2021, and the lack of a new initiative by the original petitioner made the case redundant.

[53] 33/2012. (VII. 17.) CC decision, *European Commission v Hungary*, Case C-286/12, ECLI:EU:C:2012:687.

[54] Decision 3/2019. (III. 7.) of the CC.

[55] See the blog symposium at http://www.iconnectblog.com/tag/poland/. Constitutional Tribunal, Judgment of 7 October 2021, K 3/21, https://trybunal.gov.pl/s/k-3-21.

[56] For a broad contextualisation, see Bartole 2020.

[57] Krogel 2021.

national (state) sovereignty argument. Even if it does not use these concepts, the PCT has delivered an *ultra vires* review for the protection of the core of the 1997 Constitution, which is its overall, EU-unfriendly supremacy/not-EU-law-compatible supremacy—as the PCT sees it. In 2020, contrary to its earlier jurisprudence, the PCT delivered two rulings related to the CJEU's November 2019 judgment on the independence of the judiciary in Poland and the implementation of this judgment by the independent chambers of the Supreme Court (SC). The Tribunal held that the SC had emphasised a primary duty of loyalty to EU law and rulings of the CJEU, thus disregarding the Polish Constitution. Further, the PCT held that the SC wrongly assumed the absolute binding nature of CJEU judgments on issues that the Member States have not transferred to the EU. This logic led the PCT to assess the CJEU judgment and consider it to be non-binding.[58]

4.3.2.3 Third Episode

The third episode of abusive manipulation of the concept of constitutional identity emerged in December 2021, as a continuation of the migration issue, when the HCC delivered its newest decision on constitutional identity. The Hungarian Minister of Justice sought an interpretation of the FL because, in her view, the implementation of the judgment of the CJEU in case C-808/18[59] may lead to a foreign national illegally staying in Hungary (in the territory of a Member State) for an indefinite period, and thus becoming part of the population of that state. The CJEU found that the Hungarian legislation on the rules and practice in the transit zones situated at the Serbian-Hungarian border was contrary to EU law, in particular, breaches of provisions of the related directives (on asylum procedures, reception conditions, and return) were identified. The Minister of Justice based this claim on the fact that the relevant EU laws are ineffective because only one-third of the returned persons actually leave the territory of the EU, and because of the CJEU's decision, Hungary did not have effective tools to expel these people.

The HCC assessed whether the implementation of the judgment (which is also called incomplete effectiveness of the joint exercise of competences) could lead to a violation of Hungary's sovereignty, constitutional identity, and fundamental rights and freedoms (including, in particular, human dignity) enshrined in the FL.

The HCC took a *prima facie* politically neutral position by emphasising that it neither reviewed the CJEUs decision nor interpreted the relationship between EU and domestic law. It indicated that it did not take any position on the actual occurrence of the violation of Hungary's sovereignty, etc., either as this latter is for the political branch to decide, but it only interpreted the FL.

---

[58] See more on this: Bień-Kacała 2021.

[59] Asylum Procedures Directive (Directive 2013/32/EU); Reception Conditions Directive (Directive 2013/33/EU); Return Directive (Directive 2008/115/EC).

Consequently, the result of the interpretation of the FL is as follows: considering the limits of a joint exercise of power,[60] where the joint exercise of competences is incomplete, Hungary can, due to the presumption of reserved sovereignty, exercise the relevant non-exclusive field of competence of the EU, until its institutions take the measures necessary to ensure the effectiveness of the joint exercise of competences. Just like in the case of the PCT, it could be a legitimate interpretation of the jointly exercised competencies in the European legal order. However, if we, again, contextualise the decision and look at how the HCC reached its conclusion, the picture is already more subtle and nuanced.

To achieve this interpretative result, the HCC conducted all three reviews developed in 2016. As a result of the "fundamental rights review", it found that the incomplete effectiveness of the joint exercise of competences could result in an infringement of the right of identity of people living in Hungary. Therefore, the state must protect this right. The "self-identity of the people" is actually a newly created constitutional right. In the view of the HCC, it finds its origin in a determinism approach that denies individualism and autonomy, and cultural change, and yet the HCC links it to the right to human dignity. The HCC stated that all men "are born into a given social environment, which can be defined as their traditional social environment, especially through their ethnic, linguistic, cultural and religious determinants. These circumstances create natural ties, determined by birth, which shape the identity of community members,"[61] and "these circumstances cannot or hardly can be changed by the individual, and forms an integral part of the human quality that stems for human dignity".[62]

The HCC, showing a quite activist—nevertheless, also *prima facie* legitimate— approach, extended the *ultra vires* control to situations "in which there is no (effective) EU rule. In this case, the state must act, if without its action, fundamental rights were violated, or the exercise of state power were prevented."[63] The HCC offered limitations of this action, as well: this domestic exercise of power must be time-bounded (until the adoption of the relevant and effective EU measure) and result-oriented (assisting the achievement of the implementation of the treaties of the EU).[64]

Under the identity review, the HCC, while reviewing the FL and Hungarian history, noticed that Hungary has a European identity (National Avowal),[65] and realised that the constitutional identity of Hungary and national (state) sovereignty are terms that do not supplement one another but are intertwined in many respects.[66] Against this

---

[60] The joint exercise of competences has to be in harmony with the fundamental rights as enshrined in the FL (fundamental rights review) and cannot restrict the alienable right of Hungary to its territorial unity, population, form of state, and governance (sovereignty review). Cf 22/2016 CC decision.

[61] http://hunconcourt.hu/kozlemeny/decision-of-the-constitutional-court-on-the-interpretation-of-the-provisions-of-the-fundamental-law-allowing-the-joint-exercise-of-powers.

[62] Decision [34]. Translation by the authors.

[63] Decision [80] Translation by the authors.

[64] Decision [80].

[65] Decision [96].

[66] Decision [99].

background, the HCC stated that the protection of the inalienable right of Hungary to determine its territorial unity, population, form of government, and state structure [Article E)(2)] form part of its constitutional identity.[67]

4.3.3 Analyses

If we accept that illiberal constitutionalism[68] has emerged in Hungary and Poland, we need to realise that, from the perspective of illiberal constitutionalism, the development and (ab)use of the legal concept of constitutional identity is a kind of abusive/ neo-militant tool[69] to protect the illiberal state against constitutionalism and its "principles". In this constitutional design, the rule of law is given only a very limited and formalistic view, thus, it indicates the use of a very thin and re-interpreted concept. Democracy is basically identified with pure and mere majoritarianism. Human rights are not only unnecessarily and disproportionally restricted in some cases, but also are viewed as less individual and more communitarian demanding a traditional view of gender roles and family and overemphasising culture, as in the Hungarian case. Moreover, also the role of national (state) sovereignty is exaggerated, and both the concept of national (state) sovereignty and the related nationalistic sentiments are abusively invoked in the context of the European project at the political and the legal level as well.

4.3.3.1 Commonalities of the Hungarian and Polish Jurisprudence

In the last couple of years, the captured constitutional courts of Hungary and Poland,[70] as a reaction to certain EU legal measures and by a more or less evident political invitation, "discovered" Article 4(2) TEU and the related emerging case law in other Member States. They have started to use the term constitutional identity (Hungary[71]) or the essence of the term without referring to it (Poland[72]), seemingly in harmony with foreign case law but in a different constitutional context, *i.e.*, illiberal constitutionalism.

The three most important decisions (2016 and 2021 HCC, and 2021 PCT) have been abusively initiated or unduly influenced. As these actions characterise illiberal constitutionalism, they are contrary to a substantive constitutional democracy that would expect its constitutional court to be independent and political actors to respect this independence. The 2016 HCC decision was delivered in a heated political debate

---

[67] Decision [110].

[68] Drinóczi and Bień-Kacała 2022.

[69] Rak and Baecker 2022.

[70] See Davies 2018; Analysis 2015.

[71] 22/2016 (XII. 5) CC decision, 32/2021. (XII. 20.) CC decision.

[72] October decision of the PCT, decisions of the PCT from April 2020.

around migration, although the motion was filed before the HCC already one year earlier. Unlike other, Polish, cases illustrated above, the main problematic aspect of the 2016 decision of the HCC was not the actor initiating the process. Conversely, in both 2021 rulings (of the HCC and the PCT), actions were initiated by members of the government, seeking constitutional approval for their anti-EU law measures or agenda.

Both courts pretended to rely on constitutional identity in normative terms, *i.e.*, they interpreted unamendable provisions in their respective constitutions and posited (HCC) and used (PCT) them as a legal tool against allegedly *ultra vires* EU measures. At the same time, they used it not intending to achieve greater harmony in the EU legal sphere or unity in diversity through constitutional dialogue. They have thus abused the term to advance their governments' political agenda[73] in line with their characteristics as illiberal, thus non-independent, constitutional courts.[74]

The result of this kind of constitutional review is an abuse of the notion of constitutional identity. This abuse emphasises the detachment of both the Hungarian and Polish legal systems from common European constitutional traditions and integration and gives much ammunition to the political branch of government to pretend that their anti-EU actions are actually constitutional.

However, this result, first, is different in its immediate effect, as the HCC still seems to serve two masters, while the PCT serves only one. A constitutional court serves two masters when it keeps the appearance of being a constitutional court respecting individual rights and commitments stemming from the EU, but at the same time, it delivers deferential decisions never annulling laws deemed important for the ruling majority. When a constitutional court serves only one "master", it completely disregards maintaining even this "façade" of constitutionalism. This occurs in the Polish understanding of their national sovereignty review vis-à-vis EU law.

Second, the departure from the European common constitutional heritage, as a result, has been achieved through different judicial decisions, constitutional changes, and legal procedures. The Hungarian one is more sophisticated and misleading, as long as it leaves the decision to the government (2021 HCC decision). The government already reinforced its commitment to respect the HCC's decision, which it interpreted as allowing Hungary to disregard laws and judicial decisions of the EU ("as Hungarians have the right to their own country").[75] The Polish ruling is just a slam in the face of the EU. It also seems that the CT took more responsibility for detaching the Polish legal system from the EU than the HCC did - but the end result is no different.

---

[73] Bień-Kacała 2021.

[74] Illiberal constitutional courts attack the ethos of liberal democratic constitutionalism indirectly, as they are already more interested in maintaining the illiberal order, in which they believe—mainly because they have already been packed. The characteristics of illiberal constitutional courts can be found in their composition; procedures, which are abusively initiated or invented or reinvented at discretion; and the content of their decisions whose quality of reasoning has become low, and which clearly show how they serve either one or two masters. Drinóczi 2022.

[75] https://hu.euronews.com/2021/12/20/orban-az-alkotmanybirosag-szerint-a-magyaroknak-joguk-van-sajat-hazajukhoz.

So, as said, none of these differences alter the fact that the constitutional identities apparently emerging in Hungary and Poland, in both its substance and procedural aspects, are contrary to the constitutional identity of the EU.

4.3.3.2 Differences in Light of the German and Italian Dialogical Approaches

After comparing the case law of illiberal constitutional courts and their effect on the European project, we can also highlight some differences in their approaches to constitutional identity when compared with the dialogical approach of the German and Italian constitutional courts. The issue of constitutional identity cannot be separated from its context, which is the multi-layered constitutionalism requiring judicial or constitutional dialogue.

Among the differences emerging from such a comparison, some are especially worthy of attention. While Karlsruhe affirms that the EU Treaties should be respected and supports a strict interpretation of EU law, Warsaw openly challenges the foundational principle of the primacy of EU law through its CT, while Hungary implicitly—through its political branch of government—does the same.

The GCC intervenes in a contested space and invokes a space of decision for political actors against technocratic institutions in the context of multi-layered constitutionalism and constitutional democracy. The HCC pretends to act similarly but in defence of illiberal constitutionalism and illiberal values. The PCT does not even pretend but abusively uses foreign, *e.g.*, German related case-law while putting into question fundamental principles which the German Court intends to protect, and the Italian one relies on, *i.e.*, common constitutional traditions.

The GCC has been accused of a sort of political alliance with political actors, aiming to protect national interests.[76] However, this connection has nothing to do with the action of captured courts, such as the PCT or the HCC lacking any independence from political power. The debate on the decisions of the GCC remains in the territory of the so-called juristocratic turn in a constitutional democracy,[77] while the actions of PCT and HCC need to be viewed and assessed in a different, illiberal, constitutional setting. Moreover, the PCT questioned the primacy of EU law, contrasting it with the whole national Constitution, not only with its unamendable and non-transferrable core.

Another notable difference lies in the institutional background of these decisions. In fact, the institutional position of both the PCT and HCC is remarkably different from both their German and the Italian counterparts. The PCT itself is an unlawfully

---

[76] Already in 2012, pending the decision of the GCC on the European Stability Mechanism, Christine Lagarde, the then managing director of the International Monetary Fund (IMF) was quoted as threatening to leave a meeting, were she to hear again 'Bundesverfassungsgericht': see Medick and Wittrock 2012.

[77] Hirschl 2007.

established court, and the HCC has been packed for years now.[78] The decisions, both issued in 2021, on the relationship between domestic and EU law were triggered by governmental actors, specifically the Polish Prime Minister, and the Hungarian Minister of Justice. The PCT played a far from counter-majoritarian role. On the contrary, the case law of the Italian and German Constitutional Courts was issued by institutions, the independence of which has never been put seriously into doubt. Additionally, the very first steps of the judicial doctrines theorising constitutional limits to the application of EU law have been taken by these courts in times of almost unanimous political consensus in favour of the European integration process.

Finally, both the GCC and the ICC not only stressed the importance of judicial or constitutional dialogue, but also took it seriously. For instance, the *Taricco* saga consisted of two consecutive preliminary ruling procedures—one from an ordinary court, the other from the ICC. Neither the PCT nor the HCC used this procedure, but the latter only formally referred to its importance in 2018.[79] Moreover, ordinary judges in Poland have been punished for initiating preliminary ruling procedures, and the Hungarian ordinary judges have been seriously discouraged from doing the same.[80]

4.4   European Constitutional Identity

4.4.1   The Reason for Discussing the Notion

Moving from these episodes, the scholarly discourse around constitutional identity was subject to new rapid transformations. In fact, in the last decade of the 20th century, constitutional identity seemed to serve as a useful safety clause to reassure Member States' concerns ahead of a qualitative shift in the process of European integration, starting with the introduction of the Treaty of Maastricht, which enhanced the political and constitutional dimension of the EU. At present, the reputation of the identity clause seems to be turning the corner, with many scholars now advocating its lack of utility, or its immanent "dangers".[81] Some scholars demanded that Member States engaging in constitutional identity talks should not take part in the EU legal integration at all and leave the EU entirely.[82]

Abandoning the notion of constitutional identity because of its recent abuses seems far from a wise option.[83] First of all: constitutional identity is nowadays a

---

[78] See e.g. Case of *Xero Flor w Polsce sp. z o.o. v. Poland* (application No. 4907/18), 7 May 2021; Analysis 2015.

[79] Drinóczi and Bień-Kacała 2022, 132.

[80] Matos 2019. On the rule of law situation in Poland and Hungary, see Drinóczi and Bień-Kacała 2021.

[81] Fabbrini and Sajó 2019.

[82] Pech and Kelemen 2019, p. 61.

[83] In the same sense, see Scholtes 2021.

matter of blackletter EU law—Article 4(2) TEU is part of the Treaties, and it is also subject to the jurisdiction of the CJEU. Treaty reform resulting in the abrogation of Article 4(2) TEU is a completely unrealistic scenario, and therefore—as lawyers— we should acknowledge that constitutional identity exists as a legal notion. Second: advancing a sort of theoretical abjuration of identity because of the risks emerging from abuses is counterproductive and more dangerous than the dangers this strategy aims to neutralise.

In our view, there is a much more effective and simpler alternative, which is acknowledging the legal success of the process of legalisation and "positivisation"[84] of constitutional identity in the EU and focusing on abuses and misuses of the notion.

4.4.2 Constitutional Identity of the EU—Conceptualising the Term

4.4.2.1 "Untouchable Core"

The destructive potential of constitutional identity is not its essential character, but is a possible consequence of its abuse. The challenge is then conceptualising the term, recognising abuses (which we have done above), and building legal remedies against them. As legal scholars, we might have some responsibilities on each of these fronts. As for the recognition of abuses of constitutional identity, we should rely on the massive literature on constitutional identity. Therefore, the option advocated by some scholars of abandoning the discourse on constitutional identity just because the notion might be open to abuse sounds rather absurd.

First, we could say that constitutional identities shall be respected as far as they are constitutional and not unconstitutional constitutional identities. Keeping a play on words aside, respecting constitutional identities is a blackletter fundamental principle of the EU that shall be balanced with other fundamental principles of the EU.[85] Among these, the fundamental principles mentioned in Article 2 TEU are certainly to be included, as core principles identifying EU constitutional identity.

Article 2 TEU reads as follows:

> The Union is founded on the values of respect for human dignity, freedom, democracy, equality, the rule of law and respect for human rights, including the rights of persons belonging to minorities. These values are common to the Member States in a society in which pluralism, non-discrimination, tolerance, justice, solidarity and equality between women and men prevail.

Article 2 and Article 4(2) TEU are on the same level: therefore, claiming that Article 4(2) TEU protects a national measure that violates Article 2 TEU shall be recognised as an abusive application of the identity clause.

---

[84] On this process, see Faraguna 2021.

[85] Spieker 2020.

To a certain extent, principles enshrined in Article 2 TEU have been identified by the CJEU as the untouchable core of the European legal order.[86] The idea of an untouchable core is indissolubly linked to the idea of the EU as a constitutional order: since the CJEU started to conceptualise the notion of the autonomy of the EU legal order, commentators suggested that fundamental EU law principles, such as respect for human rights, democracy and the rule of law, may be deemed as untouchable.[87] However, the legal discourse around this untouchability did not find fertile ground in the scholarly debate, and while the literature on the protection of constitutional identities of the Member States soon became very popular, the same might not be said with regard to the emergence of a European constitutional identity. Only some limited exceptions in the literature applied traditional theories of unamendability to theorise a margin of unamendability of the European treaties,[88] thus exploring the existence of an autonomous concept of European constitutional identity.

Such a dimension of constitutional identity as the untouchable core of the EU constitution emerges as a recent trend from the case law of the CJEU. In the seminal twin decisions[89] issued by the Court with regard to the legality of the rule of law mechanism, the Court took a firm position regarding the preliminary ruling asking to ascertain whether the challenged regulation violated the "national identities" of Hungary and Poland according to Article 4(2) TEU.

In the two decisions, the CJEU referred explicitly to Article 2 TEU as a provision containing the values that "define the very identity of the European Union as a common legal order".[90] The Court argues that the Member States "enjoy a certain degree of discretion in implementing the principles of the rule of law". However, it firmly specifies that Article 4(2) TEU does not mean that "the obligation as to the result to be achieved" (*i.e.*, the respect for the rule of law) varies from one Member State to the other. On the contrary, the Court specifies that, even if the Member States maintain their own peculiar national identities, they also "adhere to a concept of 'the rule of law' which they share, as a value common to their own constitutional traditions, and which they have undertaken to respect at all times".[91]

4.4.2.2 Dimensions of the Constitutional Identity of the EU

Latest developments seem to reinforce the idea of shaping European constitutional identity by looking at the external and internal sides of identity.

---

[86] For an account of constitutional identity as attached to unamendable provisions of any constitutional system, regardless of the legal label attached to those principles, see Roznai 2017, pp. 105–178.

[87] Da Cruz Vilaça and Piçarra 1993; Bieber 1993; Curtin 1993; Weiler and Haltern 1996.

[88] Passchier and Stremler 2016; Sichert 2005.

[89] Case C-156/21, *Republic of Poland v European Parliament and Council of the European Union*, 16 February 2022; Case C-157/21, *v European Parliament and Council of the European Union*, 16 February 2022.

[90] Case C-156/21, para 145 (and, in similar terms, para 265).

[91] Case C-157/21, para 233 (and, in similar terms, Case C-156/21, para 265).

As for the external side of identity, the CJEU affirmed in its *Kadi* jurisprudence that limitations implying a "derogation from the principles of liberty, democracy and respect for human rights and fundamental freedoms enshrined in Article 6(1) TEU [now Article 2 of the TEU] as the foundation of the Union"[92] are not permitted. In this way, the CJEU discerned between limitations placed on fundamental freedoms of the internal market, which are to be held permissible under exceptional circumstances, and limitations entailing a violation of the untouchable core of EU fundamental principles, which should be rejected under all circumstances.

Due to the supranational character of the EU, we could identify another, supranational dimension of the identity of the EU, in the Article 7 TEU procedure and the new conditionality mechanism (Reg. 2020/2092). The Article 7 TEU procedure can be launched when there is a clear risk of a serious breach by a Member State of the values referred to in Article 2. If Article 2 is considered as a provision in which core principles identifying EU constitutional identity are found, the Article 7 TEU procedure should also be considered as a constitutional design element (procedural safeguard) to protect this very identity - regardless of its flaws.[93]

The new rule of law conditionality mechanism allows the suspension of payments and budgetary commitments to the Member States in which breaches of the rule of law "affect or seriously risk affecting" the management of EU funds.[94] The mechanism, *prima facie* outside of the context of constitutional identity, provides for specific safeguards covering the principles included in Article 2 TEU, and foresees legal measures (withholding funds) upon the violation of any of these principles. Even if the legal bases of sanctions and their consequences only affect the management of EU funds, the mechanism results in a differentiation between the rule of law-abiding Member States and those which do not respect the European understanding of the rule of law.[95] Thus, it describes a need for self-identification (EU) as opposed to others (*e.g.*, Hungary and Poland).[96] Therefore, from the perspective of constitutional identity, we could propose that, first, this mechanism is a substantive design element for safeguarding the constitutional identity of the EU. We could also suggest that the mechanism, by focusing on the rule of law, has legally supported the claim that the rule of law, and indirectly Article 2 TEU, form part of the constitutional identity of the EU. The fact that the rule of law has been chosen is explained by the severe rule of

---

[92] Joined cases C-402/05 P and C-415/05 P *Yassin Abdullah Kadi and Al Barakaat International Foundation v Council of the European Union and Commission of the European Communities* [2008] ECR I-06351 (*Kadi* I), para 303.

[93] Of course, this would not amount to identifying Article 7 as an unamendable provision of the Treaty. The essential element of the EU constitutional system should be considered the very existence of a procedural safeguard of fundamental values of the EU: then, a specific safeguard should be considered amendable, at least as long as the amendment aims at strengthening the protection of EU fundamental values.

[94] Article 4, Regulation (EU, Euratom) 2020/2092 of the European Parliament and of the Council of 16 December 2020 on a general regime of conditionality for the protection of the Union budget.

[95] Drinóczi and Bień-Kacała 2021, pp. 3–41.

[96] For identification of the "self", see *e.g.*, Jacobsohn 2010; Rosenfeld 2012; Tushnet 2010, pp. 672–75.

law deterioration in Hungary and Poland, which has already affected the cooperation among the domestic courts of Member States in the field of criminal justice. It correlates to the observation that constitutional identity itself has a dialogical nature.[97] The idea that the Commission may also suspend approving both the Polish and Hungarian Recovery Plan until the rule of law breaches have been fixed, which would have significant economic consequences for citizens, civil society and businesses, and the state budget, also supports the idea that the constitutional identity of the EU is already recognisable and that the rule of law is certainly part of this identity.

As for the internal side of constitutional identity, while Article 48 TEU on the ordinary and simplified revision procedure of the Treaties does not provide any textual hints to determine a European "eternity clause", substantive constraints to the Treaty amending power may derive from theories of implicit unamendability. On this point, three premises are necessary: first, these theories acknowledge the power of constitutional or high courts to identify a certain core of the constitution that cannot be abrogated through ordinary constitutional amendment procedures.[98] Second, they have been articulated from the perspective of national constitutional studies, which, until now, have not necessarily considered multi-layered constitutionalism that features in the supranational EU legal order. Third, they are obviously based on case law, and this condition is (still?) missing at the EU level.

The theoretical basis of this global trend[99] lies in foundational structuralism, which has three tenets and requires two preconditions—that are, in our view, despite the limitations we have indicated above, applicable to the EU constitutional system. The tenets, as identified in the legal scholarship for the national constitutional amendments, are as follows: the amendment power, as it is a derivative power, (i) cannot destroy the constitution or (ii) its foundational principles, and (iii) it must act in a bona fide manner. The preconditions are (i) the acknowledgment of the hierarchy of constitutional principles, and (ii) constitutional identity. For foundational structuralism, the idea of a hierarchy of norms examines "whether a constitutional principle or institution is so basic to the constitutional order that changing it—and looking at the whole constitution—would be to change the entire constitutional identity."[100] In the same context of foundational structuralism, "the identity is 'the normative identity of the Constitution, supported by a coherent interpretation of its core constitutional principles or basic features'",[101] without which the constitutional order would lose its "sameness" and need to be viewed as a different constitution(al system).

---

[97] Jacobsohn 2010.

[98] Roznai 2017; Albert 2019.

[99] Roznai 2017, p. 148.

[100] Roznai 2017, p. 148. The acknowledgment of a hierarchy of constitutional principles should not lead to a construction of a permanently fossilised notion of constitutional identity. In fact, constitutional identity itself has a dialogical nature (Jacobsohn 2010), and it is result of a process of balancing of constitutional principles. This process is continuously moving, due to transformations connected to social, economic, and political developments impacting on constitutional interpretation. These transformations continuously shape the point of balance in potentially conflicting constitutional principles, thus modelling a notion of living constitutional identity.

[101] Krishnaswamy 2010, p. 118 cited by Roznai 2017, pp. 148–9.

While it is true that explicit reference to EU constitutional identity emerged rarely and only very recently, these preconditions seem to be already apparent in and supported by the *Kadi* judgment and in some scholarly works, as mentioned above, while the constitutional nature and structure of the EU have not been doubted for decades. Moreover, over the years, both the CJEU and the constitutional legislator (Member States acting jointly when adopting the treaty amendments or new treaties) have developed and strengthened the basic principles of the EU legal system, such as, *e.g.*, supremacy and direct effect of EU law and protection of fundamental rights, which have been also enriched by considerations of national constitutional and high courts. Older Member States have been participating in these changes; new ones have joined the EC/EU knowingly by changing their own national constitutional structure and legal system. The bona fide requirement manifests in the mentioned supranational (procedural) dimension of the EU's constitutional identity, which brings us back to Article 4(2) TEU. In this context, our claim is that if an identity is to be constitutional, it needs to refer to the specific principles of a given constitution of a specific member state, including its European clause or provisions in participation in international/ supranational organisation, and also to the principles attaining at having a constitution in general. According to a normative conception of the concept of constitution, this requires that "Any society in which the guarantee of rights is not assured, nor the separation of powers determined, has no Constitution".[102] According to this normative conception of constitutional identity, the "particular" aspect of constitutional identity could not contradict its "general"[103] aspect, as "[w]ithout the constraints of a prior conception of constitutionalism, constitutional identity collapses into a mere statement of fact".[104]

4.4.3   Constitutional Identity of the EU—Protecting It with Legal Remedies and/or Political Measures

Once we have tried to identify and discern the uses and abuses of constitutional identity, the next challenge is to identify legal and political remedies to tackle abuses and, consequently, ensure the constitutional identity of the EU. Recent developments have not only put legal categories in danger, but have also raised the issue of a more palpable formation of the EU's constitutional identity. Therefore, these challenges also provide for a formidable occasion to test legal remedies in action.

Some of the options already applied are the Article 7 TEU procedure and the Article 258 TEU infringement procedures. However, even though the former could be viewed as a promising theoretical access for the definition of a European constitutional identity, it has proved to be far from an effective option as it is paralysed by the requirement of unanimity for the effective activation of remedies within a

---

[102] Article 16 of the French Declaration of the Rights of Man and of the Citizen of 1789.

[103] In the sense meant by Tripkovic 2017.

[104] Halmai and Scholtes 2021.

political circuit. The infringement procedure is one of the most likely options to be activated, as happened with the *Weiss* decision for Germany and with the recent decision of the PCT.[105] However, as for the *Weiss* case, the matter seems to have been eventually settled within a non-judicial circuit. The European Central Bank (ECB) decided to offer the Bundesbank and Bundestag some unpublished documents, including excerpts from minutes of the Governing Council's meetings concerning the evaluation of the potential side effects of the public sector purchase programme (PSPP), corroborating the adequacy of the proportionality assessment underpinning the challenged ECB policy choices.[106]

After this act of cooperation, the Bundestag passed a resolution, where it found these documents sufficiently convincing, thereby affirming that the requirements set by the PSPP decision of the GCC were met through the additional justification provided by the ECB, which amounted to a satisfying stating of reasons.

As for the Polish saga, and considering the jurisprudence of the illiberal PCT and the illiberal politics in Poland, it is uncertain that there would be any actual results of the procedures initiated by the EU.[107] As said, applying the new rule of law conditionality mechanism could be another option. On 15 February 2022, the CJEU eventually upheld the rule of law conditionality regulation, deciding on the actions brought by Poland and Hungary. In these decisions, as we have briefly summarised above, the Court "embraced the language of constitutional identity".[108] It also affirmed in clear terms that when the sound financial management of the EU budget or the protection of the EU's financial interests are at stake, "the European Union cannot be criticised for implementing, in defence of its identity, which includes the values contained in Article 2 TEU, the means necessary to protect that sound financial management or those financial interests by adopting appropriate measures which, in accordance with Article 5(1) of the contested regulation, relate exclusively to the implementation of the Union budget".[109]

---

[105] This was the immediate reaction after the Weiss decision and seems to be the intention also with regard to the decision of October 7 of the PCT: see the statement of the EU Commission where it states that "We will analyze the ruling of Polish Constitutional Tribunal in detail and we will decide on the next steps. The Commission will not hesitate to make use of its powers under the Treaties to safeguard the uniform application and integrity of Union law": https://ec.europa.eu/commission/presscorner/detail/en/statement_21_5142 then followed by the action launched in December 2021: see https://ec.europa.eu/commission/presscorner/detail/en/ip_21_7070.

[106] For an overview of the official act corroborating this summary, see the following acts of the German Parliament Deutscher Bundestag Drucksache 19/20621 19. Wahlperiode 01.07.2020 Antrag der Fraktionen CDU/CSU, SPD, FDP und BÜNDNIS 90/DIE GRÜNEN Urteil des Bundesverfassungsgerichts zum Anleihekaufprogramm PSPP der Europäischen Zentralbank, available at https://dip21.bundestag.de/dip21/btd/19/206/1920621.pdf. On these developments, see Wendel 2020, p. 981.

[107] See more on the failed legal measures and scholarly suggestions in Drinóczi and Bień-Kacala 2022.

[108] Bonelli 2022.

[109] Case C-157/21, para 268.

Additionally, financial measures have already been adopted, with the order of the Vice-President of the CJEU to condemn Poland to pay a periodic penalty of €1,000,000 euros per day, which Poland refused to pay.[110]

However, EU actors adopting legal remedies and/or political measures should consider that their efficiency can only be expected in connection with constitutional democracies and not illiberal states. The reason is that, due to the historical development and legal requirements of EU integration, constitutional identities of the long-established constitutional democracies in the EU and the emerging constitutional identity of the EU have common core elements. By contrast, illiberal states have already started developing and applying their own legally conceptualised constitutional identity that is not compatible with that of the EU.

Therefore, we could require or demand that these remedies are aimed at "restoring the rule of law" rather than "only punishing, isolating and perhaps expelling Poland" and any other Member States violating EU constitutional identity,[111] but we also should be realistic. Nevertheless, as one of us has already stated,[112] revising procedures, strengthening the protection of the values of the EU,[113] and trying to make them more enforceable are for the future, for truly democratic leaders to be. It is unclear how these new political and legal mechanisms could help if future autocratic leaders follow the Polish (and Hungarian) example: gradually transforming their systems through (formal and) informal constitutional changes based on democratic legitimacy won in an (initially) fair, competitive and free election(s), abusively invoking national sovereignty arguments (or their constitutional identity) at both a political and legal level, maintaining their support with right-wing populistic rhetoric, and always being one step ahead of the reactions to their wrongdoings.

Political measures coming from the EU could be counterproductive. These would be communicated as attacks from Brussels and would trigger a more severe defence using national sovereignty or constitutional identity narratives (as it happened in the EU-Polish "dialogue" on judicial reform). Legal measures could be ineffective, too: the "value-oriented" EU law infringement procedures will not make these governments rectify their infringements but could result in the same political response: non-compliance and pushing the limits even further. A more effective way that could contribute to the fight against the ever-growing illiberalisation and autocratisation of Hungary and Poland, and thus the departure of their constitutional identity (identity of the constitution) from EU common values, is the strengthening of the resilient factors within these countries, so that Hungarians and Poles can help themselves. What is needed for this, is the identification of Hungarians and Poles with the core values of the EU, as they appear in the Treaties. Eventually, it should lead to the development and maintenance of the constitutional identity of these Member States.

---

[110] CJEU: Press Release No. 192/21, Luxembourg, 27 October 2021 Order of the Vice-President of the Court in Case C-204/21 R.

[111] Bonelli 2021.

[112] Drinóczi 2021.

[113] Pech et al. 2021.

4.5 Conclusion

This chapter claimed that the mandate to respect constitutional identities finds a limit in the respect for EU constitutional identity. We defined constitutional identity, in the legal sense, as the ultimate boundary of protection of the essential core of a constitutional design of the nation-state in Western constitutionalism, more specifically, in multi-layered constitutionalism that features the EU. In this conceptualisation, the constitutional identity of states has two sides. The internal side represents the essential core of a given constitutional order and consists of the (explicitly or implicitly) unamendable provisions. Its external side means a legal tool of protection of the same fundamental principles against possible threats or limitations originating from the *ultra vires* application of European or international norms. This concept of constitutional identity has been used (*e.g.*, in Germany and Italy) and abused (in Hungary and Poland). Developing and applying the concept of constitutional review (identity review, *ultra vires* review) with the view of ascertaining whether the EU stays within its powers while respecting the constitutional core of Members States and trying the resolve the disagreements through the mechanisms of constitutional dialogues (*e.g.*, preliminary ruling procedures), unfortunately, invited illiberal constitutional courts to abuse the concept and conduct abusive reviews. If these decisions are read superficially, they could be seen in line with the case law of other constitutional courts. When, however, we contextualise them, we realise that the case-law of the constitutional courts of Hungary and Poland abuse the term. Both Hungary and Poland use constitutional identity to limit the application of EU law because it provides more protections of some values (*e.g.*, gender, discrimination, and human rights), which have been viewed as contrary to their national constitutional traditions and the current state of illiberal constitutionalism. This is completely in contrast to what the EU is and stands for.

Given the nature of the EU and its establishing treaties, we assumed that also the EU has a constitutional identity, which has similar components. We found that its internal aspect consists of the explicit or implicit limits to amendments of the treaties, and its "legal" external aspect is present in certain CJEU jurisprudence (*e.g.*, *Kadi*) and the "political" external, or supranational, dimension of the EU constitutional identity appears in the use of the rule of law conditionality regime. Conceptualising constitutional identity in this manner within the EU and considering the abuse of the concept by illiberalising states, such as Hungary and Poland, we concluded that Member State constitutional identities are to be respected as long as they are not unconstitutional constitutional identities in the light of EU constitutionalism, as determined by the main principles and values of the EU itself.

Within this picture, the rejection of abusive, illiberal, in short, "unconstitutional" constitutional identities, which appear in the misuse of Article 4(2) TEU and related domestic legal actions, would moreover lead to an affirmation of a European constitutional identity. It is a relatively overlooked topic that still needs to be theoretically framed and strongly affirmed in European legal scholarship[114]—with this chapter, we have intended to contribute to this scholarly effort.

Disclaimer This chapter is the result of joint thought and an extended scholarly conversation on these matters between the two authors. Pietro Faraguna wrote Sects. 4.2, 4.4.1 and 4.4.2.1, while Tímea Drinóczi wrote Sects. 4.3, 4.4.2.2 and 4.4.3. Sections 4.1 and 4.5 were drafted jointly.

References

Albert R (2019) Constitutional Amendments: Making, Breaking, and Changing Constitutions. Oxford University Press, Oxford, UK/New York

Analysis (2015) Analysis of the performance of Hungary's "one-party elected" Constitutional Court Judges between 2011 and 2014, https://helsinki.hu/wp-content/uploads/EKINT-HCLU-HHC_Analysing_CC_judges_performances_2015.pdf

Appiah KA (2018) The Lies That Bind: Rethinking Identity. Liverlight, New York

Bartole S (2020) The Internationalisation of Constitutional Law: A View from the Venice Commission. Bloomsbury Publishing, London

Beaud O (1994) La puissance de l'Etat. Presses Universitaires de France, Paris

Benhabib S (1988) Democracy and identity: In search of the civic polity. Philosophy & Social Criticism 24:85–100

Bieber R (1993) Les limites matérielles et formelles à la révision des traités établissant la Communauté Européenne. Revue du Marché Commun et de l'Union Européenne 367:343–350

Bień-Kacała A (2021) Symposium—Part I: How to unfriend the EU in Poland. Int'l J. Const. L. Blog, 16 October 2021, at: http://www.iconnectblog.com/2021/10/symposium-part-i-how-to-unfriend-the-eu-in-poland/

Bonelli M (2021) I·CONnect—Symposium | Part III | Let's Take a Deep Breath: On the EU (and Academic) Reaction to the Polish Constitutional Tribunal's Ruling (I·CONnect Blog of the International Journal of Constitutional Law) http://www.iconnectblog.com/2021/10/sympos ium-part-iii-lets-take-a-deep-breath-on-the-eu-and-academic-reaction-to-the-polish-constitut ional-tribunals-ruling/, accessed 5 November 2021

Bonelli M (2022) 'Has the Court of Justice embraced the language of constitutional identity?'. Diritti comparati, 26 April 2021, at https://www.dirittticomparati.it/has-the-court-of-justice-embraced-the-language-of-constitutional-identity/

Burgorgue-Larsen L (2011) L'identité constitutionnelle en question. In: Burgorgue-Larsen L (ed) L'identité constitutionnelle saisie par les juges en Europe. Pedone, Paris, pp 155–168

Burgorgue-Larsen L (2013) Huron at the Kirchberg Plateau or a Few Naive Thoughts on Constitutional Identity in the Case-law of the Judge of the European Union. In: Saiz Arnaiz A, Alcoberro Llivina C (eds) National Constitutional Identity and European Integration. Intersentia, Cambridge, UK, pp 275–304

Calliess C (2019) Constitutional Identity in Germany. One for Three or Three in One? In: Calliess C, van der Schyff G (eds) Constitutional Identity in a Europe of Multilevel Constitutionalism. Cambridge University Press, Cambridge, UK/New York, pp 153–181

Claes M, Reestman JH (2015) The Protection of National Constitutional Identity and the Limits of European Integration at the Occasion of the Gauweiler Case. German Law Journal 16:917–970

---

[114] For a notable exception to this trend of overlooking the topic, see Passchier and Stremler 2016, p. 342, where they signal that "[c]onsidering the idea of substantive constraints on the Member States' power of Treaty revision may be especially important, moreover, at a time when constitutional democratic norms and values are under considerable pressure in certain European countries".

Curtin D (1993) The Constitutional Structure of the Union: A Europe of Bits and Pieces. Common Market Law Review 30:17–69

da Cruz Vilaça, J.L. , Piçarra N (1993) Y a-t-il des limites matérielles à la révision des traités instituant les Communautés Européennes? Cahiers de Droit Européen 37:3–37

Davies C (2018) Hostile takeover: how Peace and Justice captured Poland's court, https://freedomhouse.org/report/analytical-brief/2018/hostile-takeover-how-law-and-justice-captured-polands-courts

Drinóczi T (2018) The Identity of the Constitution and Constitutional Identity: Opening up a Discourse between the Global South and Global North. Iuris Dictio 21:63–80

Drinóczi T (2020) Constitutional Identity in Europe: The Identity of the Constitution. A Regional Approach. German Law Journal 21:105–130

Drinóczi T (2021) The EU Cannot Save Us: Why Poland and Hungary need resilience, not future-oriented reforms of EU enforcement mechanisms, VerfBlog, 2021/7/07, https://verfassungsblog.de/the-eu-cannot-save-us/

Drinóczi T (2022) Illiberal constitutional courts and the danger they pose. Państwa i Prawa 8:3–25

Drinóczi T, Bień-Kacała A (2021) Illiberal Constitutionalism and the European Rule of Law. In: Drinóczi T, Bień-Kacała A (eds) Rule of Law, Common Values and Illiberal Constitutionalism. Poland and Hungary within the European Union. Routledge, pp 3–41

Drinóczi T, Bień-Kacała A (eds) (2021) Rule of Law, Common Values and Illiberal Constitutionalism. Poland and Hungary within the European Union. Routledge, Abingdon-on-Thames

Drinóczi T, Bień-Kacała A (2022) Illiberal Constitutionalism in Poland and Hungary: The Deterioration of Democracy, Misuse of Human Rights and Abuse of the Rule of Law. Routledge, Abingdon-on-Thames, UK

Fabbrini F, Sajó A (2019) The Dangers of Constitutional Identity. European Law Journal 25:457–573

Faraguna P (2016) Taking Constitutional Identities Away from the Courts. Brooklyn Journal of International Law, 41:491–579

Faraguna P (2021) On the Identity Clause and Its Abuses: 'Back to the Treaty'. European Public Law, 27:427–446

Fukuyama F (2018) Identity: The Demand for Dignity and the Politics of Resentment. MacMillan Publishers, New York

Gutman A (2003) Identity in Democracy. Princeton University Press, Princeton

Halmai G, Scholtes J (2021) Illiberal Constitutionalism and the Abuse of Constitutional Identity. In: Roznai Y, Hirschl R (eds) Deciphering the Genome of Constitutionalism. Essays in honor of Gary Jacobsohn

Hirschl R (2007) Towards juristocracy? The Origins and Consequences of the New Constitutionalism. Harvard University Press, Cambridge MA

Jacobsohn G (2006) Constitutional Identity. The Review of Politics 68:361–397

Jacobsohn G (2010) Constitutional Identity. Harvard University Press, Cambridge MA

Komárek J (2012) Czech Constitutional Court Playing with Matches: The Czech Constitutional Court Declares a Judgment of the Court of Justice of the EU Ultra Vires; Judgment of 31 January 2012, Pl. ÚS 5/12, Slovak Pensions XVII. European Constitutional Law Review 8:323–337

Kostadinov B (2012) Constitutional identity. Iustinianus Primus Law Review 4:1–20

Krishnaswamy S (2010) Democracy and Constitutionalism in India: A Study of the Basic Structure Doctrine, Oxford University Press, Oxford, UK/New York

Krogel M (2021) Symposium—Part IV—After the decision of the captured Polish Constitutional Tribunal: jurists trying to have and eat their cake. Int'l J. Const. L. Blog, 17 October 2021, available at: http://www.iconnectblog.com/2021/10/symposium-part-iv-after-the-decision-of-the-captured-polish-constitutional-tribunal-jurists-trying-to-have-and-eat-their-cake/

Kühn Z (2016) Ultra Vires Review and the Demise of Constitutional Pluralism: The Czecho-Slovak Pension Saga, and the Dangers of State Courts' Defiance of EU Law. Maastricht Journal of European and Comparative Law 23:185–194

Lawler S (2008) Identity: Sociological Perspectives. Polity Press,. Cambridge, UK

Levinson S (1988) Constitutional Faith. Princeton University Press, Princeton

Madell G (1981) The Identity of the Self. Edinburgh University Press, Edinburgh

Martinico G (2013) What Lies Behind Article 4(2) TEU? In: Saiz Arnaiz A, Alcoberro Llivina C (eds) National Constitutional Identity and European Integration. Intersentia, Cambridge, UK, pp 93–108

Matos J I JI (2019) Judicial independence in Poland and Hungary—Going, going, gone? Preliminary requests and disciplinary procedures—A shocking development, https://officialblogofu nio.com/2019/11/18/judicial-independence-in-poland-and-hungary-going-going-gone-prelim inary-requests-and-disciplinary-procedures-a-shocking-development/

Medick V, Wittrock P (2012) Karlsruhe lässt Kanzlerin zappeln. Der Spiegel, 16 July 2012, available at http://www.spiegel.de/politik/deutschland/esm-und-fiskalpakt-bundesverfassungsgericht-lae sst-sich-mit-euro-urteil-zeit-a-844573.html

Millet F (2013) L'Union européenne et l'identité constitutionnelle des états membres. LGDJ, Paris

Parekh B (2008) A New Politics of Identity: Political Principles for an Interdependent World. Palgrave Macmillan, London

Passchier R, Stremler M (2016) Unconstitutional Constitutional Amendments in European Union Law: Considering the Existence of Substantive Constraints on Treaty Revision. Cambridge Journal of International and Comparative Law 5:337–362

Pech L, Kelemen RD (2019) The Uses and Abuses of Constitutional Pluralism: Undermining the Rule of Law in the Name of Constitutional Identity in Hungary and Poland. Cambridge Yearbook of European Legal Studies, 21:59–74

Pech L, Wachowiech P, Mazur D (2021) Poland's Rule of Law Breakdown: A Five-Year Assessment of EU's (In)Action. Hague Journal on the Rule of Law 13:1–43

Perju V (2012) Constitutional Transplants, Borrowing and Migrations. In: Rosenfeld M, Sajo A (eds) Oxford Handbook of Comparative Constitutional Law, pp 1304–27

Perju V (2020) Identity Federalism in Europe and the United States. Vanderbilt Journal of Transnational Law, 53:207–273

Polzin M (2016) Constitutional Identity, Unconstitutional Amendments and the Idea of Constituent Power: The Development of the Doctrine of Constitutional Identity in German Constitutional Law. International Journal of Constitutional Law, 14:411–438

Rak J, Baecker R (eds) (2022) Neo-militant Democracies in the Post-communist Member States of the European Union. Routledge

Rosenfeld M (2010) The Identity of the Constitutional Subject: Selfhood, Citizenship, Culture and Community. Routledge, Milton Park, Abingdon-on-Thames, Oxfordshire, UK

Rosenfeld M (2012) Constitutional Identity. In: Rosenfeld M, Sajó A (eds) The Oxford Handbook of Comparative Constitutional Law. Oxford University Press, pp. 756–775

Rosenfeld M (2022) Deconstructing Constitutional Identity in Light of the Turn to Populism. In: Hirschl R, Roznai Y (eds) Deciphering the Genome of Constitutionalism: Essays on Constitutional Identity in Honor of Gary Jacobsohn. Cardozo Legal Studies Research Paper No. 659. Available at SSRN: https://ssrn.com/abstract=4031008

Roznai Y (2013) Unconstitutional Constitutional Amendments—The Migration and Success of a Constitutional Idea. The American Journal of Comparative Law, 61:657–719

Roznai Y (2017) Unconstitutional Constitutional Amendments. Oxford University Press, Oxford/ New York

Saiz Arnaiz A, Alcoberro Llivina C (eds) (2013) National Constitutional Identity and European Integration. Intersentia, Cambridge, UK

Schmitt C (1928) Verfassungslehre. Duncker & Humblot, Berlin

Scholtes J (2021) Abusing Constitutional Identity. German Law Journal 22:534–556

Sichert M (2005) Grenzen der Revision des Primärrechts in der Europäischen Union, Duncker & Humblot, Berlin

Śledzińska-Simon A, (2015) A Constitutional identity in 3D: A model of individual, relational, and collective self and its application in Poland. International Journal of Constitutional Law, 13:124–155

Spieker L D (2020) Framing and Managing Constitutional Identity Conflicts: How to Stabilize the Modus Vivendi between the Court of Justice and National Constitutional Courts. Common Market Law Review 57:361–398

Tajfel H (1982) Social Identity and Intergroup Relations. Cambridge University Press, Oxford/New York

Toniatti R (2013) Sovereignty Lost, Constitutional Identity Regained. In: Saiz Arnaiz A, Alcoberro Llivina C (eds) National Constitutional Identity and European Integration. Intersentia, Cambridge, UK, pp 49–74

Tripkovic B (2017) The Metaethics of Constitutional Adjudication. Oxford University Press, Oxford, UK/New York

Tushnet M (2010) How do Constitutions Constitute Constitutional Identity? International Journal of Constitutional Law, 8: 671–676

van der Schyff G (2016) EU Member State Constitutional Identity. A Comparison of Germany and the Netherlands as Polar Opposites. Zeitschrift für ausslandisches öffentliches Recht und Völkerrecht 76:167–191

von Bogdandy A, Schill S (2011) Overcoming Absolute Primacy: Respect for National Identity under the Lisbon Treaty. Common Market Law Review, 48:1417–1453

Weiler JHH (2002) A Constitution for Europe? Some Hard Choices. Journal of Common Market Studies 40:563–580

Weiler JHH, Haltern H (1996) The Autonomy of the Community Legal Order: Through the Looking Glass. Harvard International Law Journal 37:411-ff

Wendel M (2020) Paradoxes of Ultra-Vires Review: A Critical Review of the PSPP Decision and Its Initial Reception. German Law Journal, 21:979–994

Tímea Drinóczi is Visiting Professor at the Faculty of Law at the Federal University of Minas Gerais, Brazil, and a Doctor of the Academy of Sciences of Hungary. She is an independent expert of OSCE ODIHR on constitutional and legislative matters. Her newest co-authored book is about Illiberal Constitutionalism in Poland and Hungary: The Deterioration of Democracy, Misuse of Human Rights and Abuse of the Rule of Law (Routledge 2022). Besides illiberal constitutionalism, her research interest covers constitutional identity, constitutional change, and the quality of legislation.

Pietro Faraguna is Associate Professor of Constitutional Law at the University of Trieste, law clerk at the Constitutional Court of Italy and member of the Center for Parliamentary Studies at LUISS University in Rome. His research interests cover a wide area in the field of public law. His main research focus is the exploration of national constitutional identity in Italy and Europe. He authored or co-authored academic publications in major national and international law journals and published a monograph on constitutional identity in Italy and Europe.

Chapter 5
Parameters of EU and Member State Constitutional Identity: A Topic in Development

Gerhard van der Schyff

Contents

Abstract Various identity-based arguments are used in EU law. This contribution argues that terms such as 'national identities' in Article 4(2) TEU and the 'identity of the European Union as a common legal order' in CJEU case law are best considered through the lens of constitutional identity. It is further argued that while the EU is called upon to respect the 'national identities' of the Member States, such respect is to be conditioned by the 'identity of the European Union as a common legal order'. For their part, Member States have to respect the common identity when exercising their respective identities. The background of this interaction is one of a multi-level legal order in which sovereignty is shared between the EU and the Member States in the growing number of fields subject to European integration.

Keywords Constitutional identity · European Union · Multi-level constitutionalism · Primacy of EU law · Rule of law

G. van der Schyff (✉)
Department of Public Law and Governance, Tilburg Law School, Tilburg, The Netherlands
e-mail: g.vdrschyff@tilburguniversity.edu

© T.M.C. ASSER PRESS and the authors 2023
J. de Poorter et al. (eds.), *European Yearbook of Constitutional Law 2022*,
European Yearbook of Constitutional Law 4,
https://doi.org/10.1007/978-94-6265-595-9_5

5.1 Identity Arguments on the Map

On 16 February 2022, the CJEU for the first time referred to the 'identity of the European Union as a common legal order' in two landmark judgements on the rule of law conditionality regulation.[1] Hungary and Poland sought the annulment of the regulation which allows for the protection of the EU budget in the event of rule of law breaches by Member States.[2] The CJEU rejected the actions brought by these states, reasoning that the EU must be able to defend its identity in this way.[3]

Until these judgements, the attention had usually been focused on the EU's duty in Article 4(2) TEU to respect the 'national identities' of the Member States and the numerous judgements by Member States' constitutional courts on protecting their respective 'constitutional identities' in the framework of European integration.[4] In particular, the judgements passed in 2021 by the Romanian, Polish and Hungarian constitutional courts have raised important questions about the constitutional architecture of the EU, especially in relation to identity-based arguments.[5]

The purpose of this contribution is to critically analyse the use of identity-based arguments in the EU in order to understand their proper application and parameters. These arguments, it will become apparent, are best considered through the lens of constitutional identity. By which is meant the fundamental values or elements expressed by a constitutional order itself.[6] It will be argued that although the EU is called upon to respect the 'national identities' of the Member States according to Article 4(2) TEU, such respect is to be conditioned by the 'identity of the European Union as a common legal order', as recently explained by the CJEU. On their part, Member States have to respect this common identity when exercising their respective identities. The background of this interaction is one of a multilevel legal order in which sovereignty is shared between the EU and the Member States in the fields subject to European integration.

In approaching the topic, the initial focus will be on Article 4(2) TEU and the identities of the Member States. This is because for a proper understanding of the identity of the EU, it is important to make sense of the emergence of identity-thinking in EU law on account of the introduction of Article 4(2) TEU. In this regard, the attention will first turn to the scope and content of the term 'national identity' in

---

[1] Court of Justice of the European Union, Case C-156/21, *Hungary v. Parliament and Council*, judgement of 16 February 2022, ECLI:EU:C:2022:97; Court of Justice of the European Union, Case C-157/21, *Poland v. Parliament and Council*, judgement of 16 February 2022, ECLI:EU:C:2022:98.

[2] Regulation (EU, EURATOM) 2020/2092 on a general regime of conditionality for the protection of the Union budget. On the Regulation, see Chamon 2022.

[3] *Hungary v. Parliament and Council*, para 127; *Poland v. Parliament and Council*, para 145.

[4] See the country studies in Calliess and Van der Schyff 2020a.

[5] Romanian Constitutional Court, Case No. 390/2021, judgement of 8 June 2021; Polish Constitutional Tribunal, Case No. K 3/21, judgement of 7 October 2021; Hungarian Constitutional Court, Case No. X/477/2021, judgement of 7 December 2021.

[6] See Van der Schyff 2012, p. 578.

Article 4(2) TEU (Sect. 5.2), after which the nature of the EU's duty to respect such identity will be considered by reference to two different approaches (Sect. 5.3) and national case law in this regard (Sect. 5.4). These approaches and the case law will then be confronted by constitutional law theory and CJEU case law (Sect. 5.5), before concluding the discussion (Sect. 5.6).

5.2 National Identity in Article 4(2) TEU

The first sentence of Article 4(2) TEU provides in part that the EU 'shall respect' Member States' 'national identities, inherent in their fundamental structures, political and constitutional, inclusive of regional and local self-government'. The term national identity was first used in the Maastricht version of the TEU in 1992. Article F(1) TEU provided that the EU 'shall respect the national identities of its Member States, whose systems of government are founded on the principles of democracy'. After the Treaty of Amsterdam in 1997, the clause now in Article 6(3) TEU simply came to read that the EU 'shall respect the national identities of its Member States'. In 2007, the Lisbon Treaty extended the wording in the current version of the TEU. In contrast to its predecessors, Article 4(2) TEU is justiciable, which has led to an increasing number of judgements.

The immediate question concerns the meaning of 'national identities'. Advocate General Collins opined in *RS* that 'the term national identity referred to in Article 4(2) TEU is an umbrella concept which may cover both societal/cultural and political/constitutional identity'.[7] This characterisation is too broad and cannot be supported. Instead, the provision is best understood as requiring the EU to respect what may be described as the national constitutional identities of the Member States.[8] As Monica Claes and Bruno De Witte have noted, since its very first incarnation, the notion of 'national identities' was linked to the 'Member States'.[9] This means that the EU has to respect the national identities of the Member States, as opposed to people, nations or citizens.[10] Apart from the Amsterdam version, the Maastricht and Lisbon versions of the TEU linked the notion of national identity to politico-constitutional topics, thereby turning the attention away from cultural markers. This has been confirmed by other authors too, such as Armin von Bogdandy and Stephan Schill who explain that the wording of Article 4(2) TEU directs the object of protection to the 'content of domestic constitutional orders', instead of 'cultural, historical, or

---

[7] Opinion of Advocate General Collins of 20 January 2022 in *RS (Effet des arrêts d'une cour constitutionnelle)*, Court of Justice of the European Union, Case C-403/21, ECLI:EU:C:2022:44, footnote 30.

[8] Van der Schyff 2012, pp. 567–569. For a different view, see Cloots 2015, who contends that Article 4(2) TEU intends to protect national identity, and not constitutional identity as such.

[9] Claes 2012, p. 216; De Witte 2021, p. 563.

[10] Claes 2012, p. 216.

linguistic criteria'.[11] These authors explain that the 'constitution itself constitutes national identity', as the identity at issue is *inherent* to the applicable structures, at least according to the English and French texts of the TEU.[12] This does not mean that cultural or linguistic identities are left unprotected, as Article 3(3) TEU provides for such protection.

The view that Article 4(2) TEU should be read as protecting the national *constitutional* identity of Member States can also be deduced from CJEU case law and opinions. Already in 2005, Advocate General Maduro wrote in *Marrosu and Sardino* about Article 6(3) TEU (Amsterdam), which only referred to 'national identity', that 'national authorities, in particular the constitutional courts (...) are best placed to define the constitutional identity of the Member States which the European Union has undertaken to respect'.[13] In the CJEU's first judgement in the *Sayn-Wittgenstein* case in 2010, the Court held that in the context of 'Austrian constitutional history' the law on abolition nobility in that country formed a part of its national identity.[14] And in later judgements constitutional links can be observed too, such as protecting Lithuanian as an 'official national language', which was described as a 'constitutional asset' by the country's government.[15] The object of protection is therefore not language as national cultural identity, but as constitutional identity. Insightful is also the recent opinion by Advocate General Kokott in *Stolichna obshtina, rayon 'Pancharevo'*.[16] She explained that Article 4(2) TEU is meant to protect a plurality of views and therefore the differences characteristic of each Member State.[17] But instead of subscribing to a definition as broad as Advocate General Collins did in *RS*, she described the phrase 'fundamental political and constitutional structures' in Article 4(2) TEU as a 'limitation' of the term 'national identities'.[18] She also explained that the objective of national identity was to 'preserve' the 'fundamental political and constitutional structures' of each state and that the current provision reduced 'the scope of national identity' in comparison to Article 6(3) TEU.[19]

When it comes to fleshing out the national constitutional identities of the Member States, it is important to note that such identity is not to be equated with a national constitutional order as such.[20] The notion of identity is not the same as the entire

---

[11] Von Bogdandy and Schill 2011, p. 1427. See also Besselink 2010, p. 44.

[12] Ibid. See also Blanke 2013, p. 195.

[13] Opinion of Advocate General Maduro of 20 September 2005, Court of Justice of the European Union, Case C-53/04, *Marrosu and Sardino*, ECLI:EU:C:2005:569, para 40.

[14] Court of Justice of the European Union, Case C-208/09, *Sayn-Wittgenstein v. Landeshauptmann von Wien*, judgement of 22 December 2010, ECLI:EU:C:2010:806, para 83. See also paras 84, 92.

[15] Court of Justice of the European Union, Case, C-391/09, *Runevič-Vardyn and Wardyn*, judgement of 12 May 2011, ECLI:EU:C:2011:291, paras 84, 86.

[16] Opinion of Advocate General Kokott of 15 April 2021, CJEU, Case C-490/20, *Stolichna obshtina, rayon 'Pancharevo'*, ECLI:EU:C:2021:296.

[17] Ibid., para 71.

[18] Ibid., para 70.

[19] Ibid., paras 87, 88, 90.

[20] Besselink 2010, p. 44.

content of an order, but it refers to its essential elements only.[21] Otherwise, the term would have no additional analytical value apart from being a synonym for a constitution broadly conceived. This is also borne out of Article 4(2) TEU which refers to Member States' identities in relation to their 'fundamental structures'.[22] The point can also be deduced from the *Sayn-Wittgenstein* judgement, where the CJEU noted that Austria had pursued a 'fundamental constitutional objective' in applying the law on the abolition of the nobility.[23] By contrast, in the *O'Brien* case the CJEU found that Article 4(2) TEU had not been engaged in a dispute about a pension scheme for judges, as the independence or governance of the judiciary had not been undermined.[24] In other words, Article 4(2) TEU cannot be triggered if the judiciary is involved in a general sense, but only if an essential element linked to the judiciary is at issue.

In addition to being 'fundamental', Article 4(2) TEU requires a norm to be contained in a Member State's 'structures, political and constitutional, inclusive of regional and local self-government'. The effect is to require an open approach in determining the sources and types of fundamental constitutional norms.[25] When it comes to constitutional orders, the scope of Article 4(2) TEU should not be limited to written, codified or entrenched norms, or to judicially enforceable norms only.[26] As the United Kingdom's membership of the EU illustrated, an order based on an unwritten constitution and a political principle such as parliamentary sovereignty can qualify under the provision. The notion of 'structures' is therefore wide enough to cover a Member State's framework of political and legal norms providing for constitutional governance, such as the separation of powers and the protection of fundamental rights.[27] However, a narrower reading of 'structures' in Article 4(2) TEU has also been proposed. It has been claimed by De Witte that the reference to 'structures' limits the scope of what the EU has to respect to 'constitutional structures', instead of 'national diversity and national constitutional values'.[28] The emphasis on

---

[21] Van der Schyff 2012, p. 576.

[22] See Von Bogdandy and Schill 2011, p. 1430.

[23] *Sayn-Wittgenstein*, para 93. In *Stolichna obshtina, rayon 'Pancharevo'*, Advocate General Kokott (paras 92, 96) applied Article 4(2) TEU not to 'every expression of national identity', but only to its 'fundamental expression'.

[24] Court of Justice of the European Union, Case C-Case 393/10, *O'Brien*, judgement of 1 March 2012, ECLI:EU:C:2012:110, paras 47–49.

[25] On the different sources of constitutional identity, see Van der Schyff 2020, pp. 306–313.

[26] Van der Schyff 2012, p. 576. Compare the view by Von Bogdandy and Schill 2011, p. 1430 that 'only elements somehow enshrined in national constitutions or in domestic constitutional processes can be relevant for Article 4(2) TEU'.

[27] Ibid.

[28] De Witte 2021, pp. 563–564. Similarly, Garben 2020, p. 49, has written that Article 4(2) TEU 'requires respect of independent statehood in terms of internal organizational and institutional autonomy but does not refer to self-determination on substantive issues'. De Witte writes that apart from regional and local self-government, '"fundamental structures" can be understood as referring to such things as the choice between parliamentary or semi-presidential political regimes, the existence or not of a mechanism for the constitutional review of legislation, the proportional or majoritarian nature of the electoral system, etc' (p. 561).

'structures' would encompass institutional diversity and exclude self-determination on substantive issues.[29] This argument derives from the textual differences between Article 4(2) TEU and the proposal made by Working Group V of the Convention on the Future of the EU. The current provision links national identity only to Member States' fundamental structures, and not also to their essential functions, basic public policy choices and social values as suggested by the Group.[30] Article 4(2) TEU makes no reference to public policy choices or social values, while the provision's second sentence creates a separate duty to respect 'essential State functions'.

The view that 'national identity' excludes 'national diversity' in its cultural dimensions can be supported, as it aligns with the argument that the identity to be respected is a *constitutional* one. However, a focus on constitutional structures to the exclusion of other constitutional elements or values, such as human rights questions, cannot be shared. The object of respect in Article 4(2) TEU is not national structures as such. Had this indeed been the intention, the provision could simply have stated as much without reference to identity. The straightforward formulation in the next sentence requiring respect for Member States' 'essential State functions' could have been copied, or the two sentences even combined. Instead, the provision clarifies and emphasises that the fundamental political and constitutional structures of a Member State create its identity, which then requires respect by the EU.[31] It is as a necessary precondition for generating and expressing identity under Article 4(2) TEU that the division and reorganisation of competences within a Member State deserve recognition, as happened in *Remondis*.[32] This includes the vertical separation of powers in a state, as supported by the reference to 'regional and local self-government' in Article 4(2) TEU.

A consequence of the term 'fundamental structures' in Article 4(2) TEU is that there is no single paradigm when it comes to national constitutional identity. As Stelio Mangiameli explains about such structures, a Member State builds its own democracy and rule of law through its constitution without having to follow 'a predetermined type'.[33] The range and content of a Member State's constitutional identity is therefore dependent on that polity's subjective choices, as opposed to the objective guarantee of 'essential State functions' such as territorial integrity.[34] This corresponds with CJEU case law, which has considered a wide range of quite different national expressions under the identity provision, such as the principle of republicanism in

---

[29] De Witte 2021, p. 561.

[30] Final Report of Working Group V on Complementary Competencies of 4 November 2002, CONV 375/1/02 REV, pp. 10–12. The proposal has been dubbed the 'Christophersen clause' after the chairman of the Working Group.

[31] Blanke 2013, p. 228 speaks of 'identity-creating' fundamental structures.

[32] Court of Justice of the European Union, Case C-51/15, *Remondis*, judgement of 21 December 2016, ECLI:EU:C:2016:985, paras 40–41. See also Court of Justice of the European Union, Case C-156/13, *Digibet and Albers*, judgement of 12 June 2014, EU:C:2014:1756, para 34.

[33] Mangiameli 2013, p. 142.

[34] Blanke 2013, p. 228.

Austria or the status of official national languages in Lithuania and Belgium.[35] Advocate General Kokott noted similarly in *Stolichna obshtina, rayon 'Pancharevo'* that national identity in Article 4(2) TEU could not be interpreted abstractly at the EU level, as its content would vary between Member States depending on their own conceptions.[36] This fits the general understanding of a constitution as acquiring its identity through its own experience, as Gary Jacobsohn has argued.[37] Identity on this reading is however not to be equated with constitutional uniqueness, as some contend.[38] Although a Member State's identity may be exclusive to that particular order, that is not a requirement. The object is also not to describe difference between orders. Constitutional identity, also in Article 4(2) TEU, centres instead on finding the core or fundamental elements or values as expressed by a given national order itself, which may or may not be shared with other orders.[39]

5.3 Respecting National Constitutional Identity

Member States enjoy the prerogative to each develop and express their own national constitutional identity, as do all states.[40] The function of Article 4(2) TEU is to require the EU to respect such identity according to the terms of the provision. Given the wide approach adopted to what may be included under such identity, as explained above, the possible interface between EU law and national constitutional law is particularly broad. Consequently, the duty of respect resting on the EU is a broad one too. For national constitutional identity to be accorded respect though, it must be a 'considered manifestation' by the Member State and not simply amount to 'vague, general and abstract assertions'.[41] The EU's duty under Article 4(2) TEU can be said to be broad in its scope, but specific in its application.

Once manifested, it is often accepted that the EU's duty does not amount to according national constitutional self-expression automatic and full respect without further investigation. CJEU judgements on Article 4(2) TEU are illustrative of this point.[42] Invoking national identity in Article 4(2) TEU is not the same as playing a constitutional trump card which matches and disables the application of EU law as a matter of course.[43] Instead of unconditional protection, what has been termed a 'proportional balance' must be struck between the relevant provisions of EU law and

---

[35] *Sayn-Wittgenstein*, para 92; *Runevič-Vardyn and Wardyn*, para 86; Court of Justice of the European Union, Case C-202/11, *Las*, judgement of 16 April 2013, ECLI:EU:C:2013:239, para 26.

[36] Opinion of Advocate General Kokott in *Stolichna obshtina, rayon 'Pancharevo'*, paras 70, 72.

[37] Jacobsohn 2006, pp. 363, 365.

[38] E.g., Drinóczi 2020, p. 127.

[39] Calliess and Van der Schyff 2020b, p. 7.

[40] Van der Schyff 2012, p. 572.

[41] Opinion of Advocate General Collins in *RS*, paras 62–63.

[42] I.e. *Sayn-Wittgenstein*, paras 83–84, 93, 95.

[43] Van der Schyff 2012, p. 579.

the particular national constitutional identity at play.[44] This covers both the interpretation and application of EU primary and secondary law, including the possibility to invalidate the latter for violating such identity.[45]

Opinions on Article 4(2) TEU start to differ markedly on the proper relationship between the CJEU and Member State constitutional courts in deciding whether the EU fulfilled its duty to respect national constitutional identity. As a matter of fact, ever since the adoption of the provision, it has become a focal point in studying the interaction between EU law and national constitutional law.[46] In this regard, the discussion is usually limited to the primacy of EU law, when in fact it is broader. Although this contribution also focuses on the doctrine of primacy, the general conclusions apply equally to other relevant principles, such as the direct effect of EU law. Two main views can be distinguished in this regard.

According to the one view, the CJEU because of its mandate in Article 19(1) TEU will ultimately have to decide on whether the EU fulfilled its duty in Article 4(2) TEU to respect national constitutional identity. This entails that Article 4(2) TEU falls under the doctrine of the primacy of EU law, as formulated by the CJEU and recognised in Declaration No. 17 concerning primacy as attached to the Treaties. The effect is to affirm that EU law has primacy over Member State law, under the conditions set out by case law. This includes the explanation by the CJEU in 1970 in *Internationale Handelsgesellschaft mbH* that the primacy of EU law covered 'fundamental rights as formulated by the constitution' and 'the principles of a national constitutional structure'.[47] It is in this sense that Article 4(2) TEU has an autonomous meaning, as Advocate General Kokott wrote in *Stolichna obshtina, rayon 'Pancharevo'*.[48]

With regards to the primacy of EU law as described above, another view can be distinguished. In this regard, Armin von Bogdandy and Stephan Schill have argued that Article 4(2) TEU integrates the 'thrust' of numerous national constitutional court judgements, which favour a relative conception of primacy, into EU law.[49] In explaining this view, the authors refer to the familiar Italian *controlimiti* and German *Solange* jurisprudence of the 1970s and later decisions including from Ireland, Denmark, Hungary and Poland.[50] From a comparison of such judgements they conclude that national constitutional courts recognise the primacy of EU law, but allow for national constitutional limits under exceptional circumstances, which can be understood as protecting constitutional identity.[51] The innovation brought about

---

[44] Von Bogdandy and Schill 2011, p. 1441.

[45] Ibid., p. 144; Schnettger 2020, p. 30.

[46] See for instance the discussion by Dobbs 2015.

[47] Court of Justice of the European Union, Case C-11/70, *Internationale Handelsgesellschaft mbH v. Einfuhr- und Vorratsstelle für Getreide und Futtermittel*, judgement of 17 December 1970, ECLI:EU:C:1970:114, para 1134.

[48] Opinion of Advocate General Kokott in *Stolichna obshtina, rayon 'Pancharevo'*, para 70.

[49] Von Bogdandy and Schill 2011, pp. 1418–1419.

[50] Ibid., pp. 1433–1434.

[51] Ibid., p. 1434.

by Article 4(2) TEU would be that it ratifies such national constitutional limits.[52] The provision would then permit national courts to invoke constitutional identity limits to the primacy of EU law.[53] The 'absolute' primacy of EU law so becomes what may be termed a 'relative' one. The two authors stress the exceptional nature of this power, which has to be exercised in line with the duty of sincere cooperation between the EU and its Member States in Article 4(3) TEU.[54]

5.4 National Constitutional Courts and Article 4(2) TEU

Writing in 2011, Von Bogdandy and Schill submitted that the use by national constitutional courts of their alleged power to limit the absolute primacy of EU law would be exceptional because of the congruence between Member States' constitutional identities and the EU's foundational values in Article 2 TEU.[55] They also noted that the 'danger of a constitutional cacophony on national identity' had not materialised at that stage.[56] Contrary to the expectations and optimism of such views, a cacophony surrounding the EU's duty in Article 4(2) TEU to respect national constitutional identity is arguably taking place at present. The purpose here is not to discuss all the relevant case law in this regard, but to illustrate how some national courts are linking constitutional identity arguments to Article 4(2) TEU in challenging the primacy of EU law. This essentially amounts to an institutional contest between the CJEU and national courts on whether national constitutional identity is implicated in a particular matter and what consequences should be attached to its use. The issue centres not so much on the meaning and contents of national constitutional identity, as this plausibly falls to national courts and other authorities to decide, but centres on the importance to be attached to such identity in the field of EU law.

The theory and practice of the German Federal Constitutional Court probably comes closest to what Von Bogdandy and Schill envisaged with Article 4(2) TEU. In its *OMT* judgement of 2016, the German Court affirmed that its own constitutional identity review does not violate the duty of sincere cooperation in Article 4(3) TEU.[57] On the contrary, the Court argued, Article 4(2) TEU even provides for identity review by national constitutional courts.[58] Consequently, the Court conducted an identity review and found that German constitutional identity had not been violated by EU law. This was because the Outright Monetary Transactions (OMT) programme did not impair the overall budget responsibility of the federal parliament, which formed

---

[52] Ibid., p. 1449.

[53] Ibid.

[54] Ibid., pp. 1419, 1447.

[55] Ibid., pp. 1432–1433.

[56] Ibid., pp. 1435.

[57] German Constitutional Court, Case No. 2 BvR 2728/13, judgement of 21 June 2016, ECLI:DE:BVerfG:2016:rs20160621.2bvr272813 (*OMT*), para 140.

[58] Ibid., paras 140, 210.

a part of Germany's constitutional identity.[59] The primacy of EU law was therefore left intact. In 2020, in the much-discussed *PSPP* judgement, the German Federal Constitutional Court declared that by passing the *Weiss* judgement in 2018 the CJEU exceeded its judicial mandate in Article 19(1) TEU.[60] According to the German Court, the CJEU failed to subject the European System of Central Banks and the European Central Bank to a 'comprehensible review' when it came to 'observing the limits of their monetary policy mandate' regarding the Public Sector Purchase Programme (*PSPP*).[61] The German Court did not refer to Article 4(2) TEU and ruled that constitutional identity had not been violated as such, as the CJEU judgement had been *ultra vires* instead.[62] There is nonetheless a close relationship between the two forms of review in Germany, as it has been argued that *ultra vires* review is best understood as a sub-category of identity review.[63] Essentially, the *PSPP* judgement shows that in Germany challenging the primacy of EU law, as interpreted by the CJEU, is not simply theoretical and can indeed take place under limited circumstances.[64]

While the *PSPP* judgement did not explicitly threaten identity conflict between the German Constitutional Court and the CJEU, three judgements passed in 2021 by the Constitutional Courts of Hungary, Romania and Poland did move in that direction.[65] Of these judgements, the Hungarian judgement of December 2021 in Case No. X/477/2021 managed to avoid direct identity confrontation with the CJEU. The judgement concerned a request made by the Hungarian government for an abstract interpretation of the Constitution related to implementing the CJEU's judgement in Commission v. Hungary of 2020.[66] According to that judgement, Hungary had violated EU asylum law through practices which limited the number of foreign nationals capable of applying for international protection and removing such nationals contrary to specific safeguards.[67] The government feared that the CJEU judgement could allow foreign nationals to stay illegally in Hungary for an indefinite period of time, thereby violating the country's constitutional identity which includes the right to determine

---

[59] Ibid., para 228.

[60] German Constitutional Court, Case No. 2 BvR 859/15, judgement of 5 May 2020, ECLI:DE:BVerfG:2020:rs20200505.2bvr085915 (*PSPP*), para 163.

[61] Ibid., para 123.

[62] Ibid., paras 116, 228.

[63] Calliess 2020, pp. 174–175. The argument entails that 'any breach of competence constitutes a violation of the principle of democracy', which is itself a part of German constitutional identity (175).

[64] In 2021, the German Federal Constitutional Court, Case No. 2 BvR 1651/15, judgement of 29 April 2021, ECLI:DE:BVerfG:2021:rs20210429.2bvr165115, rejected two applications for the execution of the *PSPP* judgement, thereby bringing the matter to an end. Apart from a procedural reason, the Court accepted that the German government and parliament had acted in ensuring that a proper review of the contested ECB policy was carried out.

[65] See generally Stremler 2021 regarding the state of the rule of law in Hungary (pp. 163–233), Romania (pp. 111–160) and Poland (pp. 235–311).

[66] Court of Justice of the European Union, Case C-808/18, *Commission v. Hungary*, judgement of 17 December 2020, ECLI:EU:C:2020:1029. See also Chronowski and Vincze 2021; Halmai 2017.

[67] Ibid., paras 315–316.

its population. The Hungarian Court explained that the state had an obligation to protect its constitutional identity, which can be compared to the EU's duty in Article 4(2) TEU to respect national identity.[68] However, it did not pass judgement on the merits of the case at hand, as it only concerned an abstract interpretation of the Constitution.[69] At this occasion the primacy of EU law prevailed because of the nature of the particular national constitutional proceedings.

The Romanian and Polish judgements were more concerning though, especially regarding the protection of judicial independence in line with Article 2 TEU. In June 2021, the Romanian Constitutional Court in Case 390/2021 essentially required national courts to disregard the CJEU ruling of May in *Asociaţia 'Forumul Judecătorilor din România'*.[70] In *Asociaţia*, the CJEU stated EU legal requirements for reviewing Romanian legislation which established a special section in the Public Prosecutor's Office (SIIJ) to investigate offences committed by judges and prose-cutors.[71] These requirements entailed objective and verifiable preconditions for the sound administration of justice and included specific guarantees on judicial inde-pendence and fair trial rights in Articles 47 and 48 of the Charter of Fundamental Rights of the EU.[72] The requirements were linked directly to protecting the rule of law in Article 2 TEU as a common value between Member States.[73] The CJEU also expressed reasonable doubt on whether the SIJJ was free from possible political control, but left the final decision in this regard to the referring courts.[74] According to the Constitutional Court though, national courts were precluded from deciding whether the SIJJ was compatible with EU law, as required in *Asociaţia*. This was partly because the SIJJ was in accordance with the Romanian Constitution, which enjoyed primacy over EU law.[75] The Constitutional Court based such constitutional primacy on the need to protect national constitutional identity.[76] Apart from referring to its own and German case law for support, the judgement also noted that national identity in Article 4(2) TEU limits 'constitutional integration' to the fundamental structures of Member States.[77] Article 4(2) TEU was not viewed as contradicting the Court's view on constitutional primacy, but essentially as its reflection in the Treaties. Unsurprisingly, this controversial judgement soon became the topic of a request to the CJEU for a preliminary ruling. In February 2022 in *RS*, the CJEU gave its ruling

---

[68] Hungarian Constitutional Court, Case No. X/477/2021, para 4.

[69] Ibid.

[70] Romanian Constitutional Court, Case No. 390/2021. See also Selejan-Gutan 2021.

[71] Court of Justice of the European Union, Joined Cases C-83/19, C-127/19, C-195/19, C-291/19, C-355/19 and C-397/19, C-83/19, *Asociaţia 'Forumul Judecătorilor din România'*, judgement of 18 May 2021, ECLI:EU:C:2021:393.

[72] Ibid., para 223.

[73] Ibid., para 195.

[74] Ibid., para 207.

[75] Romanian Constitutional Court, No. 390/2021, para 80.

[76] Ibid., paras 72, 74.

[77] Ibid., paras 72, 74–75.

in which it rejected the claim to constitutional primacy over EU law, the merits of which will be considered more closely in the next section.[78]

Following the Romanian judgement, the Polish Constitutional Tribunal also used constitutional identity reasoning to test and cross fundamental boundaries of EU law. In its judgement on the Lisbon Treaty in 2010, the Tribunal affirmed that in principle the Constitution takes primacy over EU law and explained that the need to protect constitutional identity was equivalent to the EU's duty in Article 4(2) to respect national identity.[79] This implies that the Tribunal ultimately decides whether Polish constitutional identity was respected by the EU. In Case No. K 3/21 in October 2021, the Tribunal put this line of thinking into practice in a matter which forms a particularly worrying episode in the well-documented rule of law decline in Poland.[80] Case No. K 3/21 was essentially a reaction to the CJEU's judgement in *A.B.*[81] EU legal requirements were given in *A.B.* to determine whether the appointment of judges to the Polish Supreme Court also safeguarded their independence, something about which serious concerns existed.[82] In response to this ruling, the Polish government petitioned the Tribunal to rule on the constitutionality of selected TEU provisions. The Tribunal found that Articles 1, 2, 4(3) and 19(1) TEU were unconstitutional as far as they infringed a number of national conditions.[83] This was done without requesting the CJEU for a preliminary ruling, even though the Tribunal claimed to attach importance to mutual and sincere dialogue.[84]

This controversial case centred on Article 19(1) TEU and Article 2 TEU to the extent that they require of Member States to ensure effective legal protection of EU law, including the independence of judges. According to the Tribunal, these treaty provisions do not allow domestic courts to bypass the Constitution, including national parliamentary and judicial findings of unconstitutionality, or to review the legality of the appointment of domestic judges. In arriving at its conclusions, the Tribunal explained that these were organisational topics that belonged to Polish constitutional identity and were not subject to conferral on the EU.[85] The Tribunal also recalled

---

[78] Court of Justice of the European Union, Case C-430/21, *RS (Effet des arrêts d'une cour constitutionnelle)*, judgement of 22 February 2002, ECLI:EU:C:2022:99.

[79] Polish Constitutional Tribunal, Case No. K 32/09, judgement of 24 November 2010 (*Lisbon*), para 2.1.

[80] At the time of writing the Tribunal's reasons for the judgement had not yet been published, only the judgement's operative part had been published together with an extensive press release. The description and analysis here draw on the operative part of the judgement and the press release. On the rule of law decline in Poland and the EU's reaction, see the extensive discussion by Stremler 2021, pp. 235–311.

[81] Court of Justice of the European Union, Case C-824/18, *A.B.*, judgement of 2 March 2021, ECLI:EU:C:2021:153.

[82] Ibid., paras 43, 117, 129–136, 139.

[83] Polish Constitutional Tribunal, Case No. K 3/21.

[84] Polish Constitutional Tribunal, Case No. K 3/21, Press Release, para 21.

[85] Ibid., para 17.

that according to Article 4(2) TEU, the EU had to respect such identities when exercising its competences.[86] The Tribunal also turned to the foundational values of the EU in Article 2 TEU. Of these values it noted that they were 'merely of axiological significance' and not 'legal principles' capable of adjudication by the CJEU.[87] As to their content, it continued that judicial organisation did not fall under 'the common constitutional identity of the Member States', adding that different national procedures for appointing judges applied.[88] This led the Tribunal to conclude that the CJEU's guidelines on judicial independence could not replace national constitutional standards. The effect of these arguments is to expect of the CJEU, when interpreting the contested TEU provisions, to observe the national constitutional identity limits formulated by the Tribunal.

5.5 Identity of the EU as a Common Legal Order

5.5.1 The Meaning and Scope of the EU's Constitutional Identity

The picture emerging from the discussion above is that of national constitutional courts setting clear limits to the primacy of EU law on account of their own interpretations of Article 4(2) TEU. On this approach, Article 4(2) TEU is in principle compatible with Member States limiting the primacy of EU law of their own accord because of national constitutional identity. This view cannot be supported.[89] The criticism of this view will focus on the rulings of the mentioned courts, as they form the frontline in defending 'relative' conceptions of the primacy of EU law. It will become clear when engaging with such conceptions that the national courts depart from a concept of sovereignty that incorrectly favours the Member States over the EU when factoring in the relevance of national constitutional identity to EU law. Their reasoning relies on an incomplete account of sovereignty in the legal framework shared by the EU and its Member States.

Although the national judgements might differ in their wording and approach, the common essence is that state sovereignty warrants constitutional identity limits to EU law. The Hungarian Constitutional Court's judgement, for instance, explains that the joint exercise of competence in the EU is subject to a reservation of such sovereignty.[90] The states remain the 'Masters of the Treaties', according to the German Constitutional Court's judgement on the Lisbon Treaty, a position which has since been referred to by the constitutional courts of Romania and Poland among

---

[86] Ibid., para 7.

[87] Ibid., para 19.

[88] Ibid.

[89] See also the criticism by Claes 2012, p. 221.

[90] Hungarian Constitutional Court, Case No. X/477/2021, para 3.2.

others.[91] This position could only change upon the formal founding of a European federal state, failing which the EU remains a *Staatenverbund* or 'association of sovereign states'.[92] On this approach, the starting point and end goal of European integration is sovereign statehood. The fact that the EU is not a state, and might never turn into one, means that it remains a subject of the participating states. Proponents of this confederal model point to the EU lacking a *demos* or constituent people from which sovereignty may sprout, similar to the Member States.[93] The EU by implication possesses a *derivative* or *proxy* constitutional order, which must ultimately yield to the *sovereign* constitutional orders of the Member States.[94] Following this reasoning, the question whether the EU respected national constitutional identity according to Article 4(2) TEU is in the final instance a national one, and not an EU one.

Although the EU does not have sovereign statehood, it can be argued that it does possess a type of sovereign non-statehood.[95] On this reasoning, the EU is not a typical federal state, or a typical confederation either. Instead, as an intermediate governance model it can best be understood as an 'association of constitutions' or a 'federation of states'.[96] The TEU and TFEU function then as constituent treaties which found a distinct supranational constitutional order, that exists alongside the national orders.[97] This new order is the result of pooling sovereignty at the EU level, while reducing Member State sovereignty accordingly.[98] This construction becomes possible when it is realised that the *people* are the ultimate masters of the Treaties, as much as they are of their national constitutions.[99] The Member States are not the masters of the Treaties, but the instruments used by their citizens in constructing the

---

[91] German Constitutional Court, Case No. 2 BvE 2/08, judgement of 30 June 2009, ECLI:DE:BVerfG:2009:es20090630.2bve000208 (*Lisbon*), para 231 (affirmed in German Constitutional Court, Case No. 2 BvR 859/15, (*PSPP*), paras 111, 157). See also Romanian Constitutional Court, No. 390/2021, para 74; Polish Constitutional Tribunal, Case No. K 3/21, Press Release, para 8.

[92] German Constitutional Court, Case No. 2 BvE 2/08 (*Lisbon*), paras 229, 334.

[93] See Grimm 2016, pp. 296, 329; Rosenfeld 2012, p. 765; Habermas 2003, pp. 264–265.

[94] Compare Barents 2021, pp. 4, 6–7, 9. Consider also Grimm 2016, pp. 157, 275, who explains that the EU's legal basis is externally controlled by the Member States, adding that the basis differs from that of a constitution where a 'political unit autonomously determines the purpose, form, and content of its political union'.

[95] This presupposes that sovereignty is a useful concept in understanding the EU, which is itself open to discussion. In Court of Justice of the European Union, Opinion 2/13 of 18 December 2014 of the Court (Full Court) ECLI:EU:C:2014:2454, paras 49, 156, the CJEU indicated for the first time that the EU was not a state.

[96] Grabenwarter 2009, p. 128; Rummens and Sottiaux 2014, pp. 571–576.

[97] See Pernice 1999, pp. 706–707, describing the EU as a 'divided power system', where each level has 'original' legitimacy (p. 709).

[98] See Van der Schyff 2021, p. 4; Pernice 2002, pp. 511, 518.

[99] See Pernice 2002, pp. 518–519; Pernice 2015, p. 544.

EU.[100] Within the multilevel structure of European integration the people express their sovereignty in part by attributing powers to the EU level, and in part to the Member State level.[101] The establishment of an EU citizenship in Article 8(1) of the Maastricht Treaty, to be found today in Articles 9 TEU and 20(1) TFEU, supports this understanding. The concept of EU citizenship takes on a foundational dimension, thereby distinguishing the EU from traditional international law organisations. As Advocate General Maduro explained in *Rottmann v. Freistaat Bayern*, such citizenship forms a new political arena from which rights and duties emerge according to EU law in a manner independent of the Member States.[102] Citizens in Europe are so members of an EU constitutional order, and of their respective national constitutional orders.[103] Although distinct, these orders are closely intertwined given that Article 2 TEU explains that the EU is founded on fundamental values which are common to the Member States. The failure of the Treaty establishing a Constitution for Europe does not contradict this reading of European integration, as it simply shows that EU citizens where not yet prepared to codify their otherwise substantive constitution.[104]

A consequence of the EU possessing an own constitutional order, is that it can *also* lay claim to a constitutional identity. In conceptualising this identity, notice can be taken of Opinion 2/13 which stressed the *autonomy* of the EU legal order in relation to national and international law in pursuing its specific objectives.[105] The mandate of the CJEU in Article 19(1) TEU and the preliminary ruling procedure in Article 267 TFEU coupled with doctrines such as the direct effect and primacy of EU law take centre stage in ensuring the consistency and uniformity of EU law.[106] In addition to maintaining the autonomous application of EU law as such, the identity of the EU can also be understood as encompassing its *fundamental values* as set out in Article 2 TEU.[107] In rejecting the annulment proceedings brought by Hungary and Poland

---

[100] Ibid.; Van der Schyff 2021, p. 4. Compare Cuyvers 2014, pp. 679–680, who speaks of 'sovereign member peoples' instead of 'citizens', who on the basis of reciprocity delegate a part of their powers to the EU as a non-state actor. See also Cuyvers 2013, p. 365.

[101] See Pernice 2002, p. 518. Compare Cuyvers 2014, p. 680; Cuyvers 2013, p. 367.

[102] Opinion of Advocate General Maduro of 30 September 2009 in Court of Justice of the European Union, Case C-135/08, *Rottmann v. Freistaat Bayern*, ECLI:EU:C:2009:588, para 23. See also Pernice 2015, p. 544; Van der Schyff 2021, pp. 10–11. Cuyvers 2013, p. 367 refers to EU citizenship as an example of the 'direct connection between the individual and the EU'.

[103] See also Calliess 2013, pp. 427–430; Van der Schyff 2021, p. 11. Compare the Opinion of Advocate General Colomer of 11 September 2008 in CJEU, Case C-228/07, *Petersen v. Arbeitsmarktservice Niederösterreich*; ECLI:EU:C:2008:281, para 15.

[104] Van der Schyff 2021, pp. 4–5.

[105] Opinion 2/13, para 170. See too Court of Justice of the European Union, opinion 1/91 of 14 December 1991 of the Court, ECLI:EU:C:1991:490, para 30.

[106] Opinion 2/13, paras 165–167, 170, 174–176.

[107] The autonomy element of the EU legal order's identity and its substantive element can be viewed as flip sides of the same coin. Without autonomy, the EU legal order would not be able to vindicate its content, while without content its autonomy would only serve a formal purpose. This interrelationship is illustrated in the Opinion of Advocate General Sánchez-Bordona of 2 December 2021 in CJEU, Case C-156/21, *Hungary v. Parliament and Council*, ECLI:EU:C:2021:974, para 273, where it is explained that 'the rule of law has an autonomous meaning within the EU legal

against Regulation (EU, Euratom) 2020/2092, the CJEU in 2022 for the very first time used the term 'identity' in relation to these values.[108] This is significant, as the attention is usually focused on the Member States' constitutional identities, in part because of Article 4(2) TEU. By contrast, little attention has been paid to the EU's constitutional identity.[109] For instance, in her View regarding Opinion procedure 2/13, Advocate General Kokott rejected arguments that the CJEU could decline to recognise judgements by the European Court of Human Rights (ECtHR) on account of such judgements conflicting with 'the constitutional identity of the EU—a kind of *ordre public* in EU law'.[110] She noted that such reservations existed in the case law of some Member States regarding the EU, but that no reason existed for the CJEU to make similar reservations in respect of the ECtHR.[111] In the *Gauweiler* case, Advocate General Cruz Villalón approached the concept in a more positive light.[112] He explained that an open attitude to EU law among Member States should over time lead to 'basic convergence between the constitutional identity of the Union and that of each of the Member States'.[113] The notion of an EU constitutional identity was also mentioned by Advocate General Szpunar in the *LG* case.[114] Without clearly defining the concept, he observed that a balance must be maintained 'between safeguarding the European Union's constitutional identity and making sure that EU law does not become hostile to the international community'.[115] And, more recently, the General Court considered the claim that the matter went to the 'heart of the constitutional identity of the European Union' irrelevant to the particular case.[116] If anything, such brief examples serve to highlight the importance of the recent CJEU judgements and their use of the term identity in the context of the EU itself.

In turning to the failed annulment proceedings before the CJEU, the Regulation contested by the Hungary and Poland requires that the EU's budget respects the rule of law as guaranteed in Article 2 TEU.[117] According to the two states, the 'rule of

---

system'. Otherwise, each Member State would be able to determine separate parameters for the rule of law. See also Van der Schyff 2022 and 2021, p. 9.

[108] *Hungary v. Parliament and Council*, para 127; *Poland v. Parliament and Council*, para 145. See Chamon 2022, p. 345.

[109] See Van der Schyff 2021, pp. 5–6.

[110] View of Advocate General Kokott of 13 June 2014 regarding Opinion procedure 2/13, ECLI:EU:C:2014:2475, paras 168.

[111] Ibid., paras 169–170.

[112] Opinion of Advocate General Cruz Villalón of 14 January 2015 in Court of Justice of the European Union, Case C-62/14, *Gauweiler*, ECLI:EU:C:2015:7, para 61.

[113] Ibid.

[114] Opinion of Advocate General Szpunar of 14 January 2020 in Court of Justice of the European Union, Case C-641/18, *LG v. Rina SpA, Ente Registro Italiano Navale*, ECLI:EU:C:2020:3.

[115] Ibid., para 141. See also para 144.

[116] Court of Justice of the European Union, Case T-252/20, order of 8 June 2021, ECLI:EU:T:2021:347, paras 48, 65.

[117] According to Article 2 of the Regulation 'the "the rule of law" refers to the Union value enshrined in Article 2 TEU. It includes the principles of legality implying a transparent, accountable, democratic and pluralistic law-making process; legal certainty; prohibition of arbitrariness of the executive powers; effective judicial protection, including access to justice, by independent and impartial

law' has no specific substantive content in EU law on which to base such budget rules, as there is no universal definition of the concept and the EU has 'very limited competences' to define it.[118] This argument echoes Case No. K 3/21 decided by the Polish Constitutional Tribunal, where following a *Staatenverbund*-like approach, the Tribunal argued that Article 2 TEU did not guarantee 'legal principles' which could be adjudicated by the CJEU.[119] Although the CJEU did not refer to that particular judgement, it rejected such reasoning as entirely unfounded. The CJEU emphasised that the values in Article 2 TEU, such as the rule of law, were legally binding obligations for the Member States and not simply policy guidelines or intentions.[120] And importantly, it added that Article 2 TEU formed an 'integral part of the very identity of the European Union as a common legal order', which the EU had to defend in line with the Treaties.[121] This meant that although Member States could differ on how they each implemented the rule of law, Article 4(2) TEU did not allow them to deviate from their common identity as a result.[122]

Although the CJEU only referred to the EU's common legal identity in the two judgements, this can and should indeed be understood as its *constitutional* identity. This flows from the position, canvassed above, that the EU legal order is more than simply a derivative of the Member States' legal orders. The constitutive nature of the Treaties means that the EU possesses a type of sovereign non-statehood, which exists next to and interacts with the sovereign statehood of each Member State. The European project consequently knows not only 27 individual constitutional identities expressed at the national level, but also a collective constitutional identity expressed at the supranational level. The position taken by various constitutional courts that national constitutional identity takes primacy over EU law because of state sovereignty is so fundamentally contested, as the EU also has a credible sovereignty claim which encompasses a constitutional identity. The two identity pillars of the EU as a common legal order, its autonomy and fundamental values can intersect, but this is not necessarily the case. This is because not all challenges to the autonomy of EU law, such as its primacy over national law, will also involve challenges to its fundamental values in Article 2 TEU. The German Federal Constitutional Court's *PSPP* judgement, as discussed above, is a case in point. The German Court challenged the primacy of EU law and so the autonomy pillar of the EU's identity, while not implicating the substantive pillar of the EU's identity in Article 2 TEU. By contrast, a judgement such as that of the Polish Constitutional Tribunal in Case No. K 3/21

---

courts, also as regards fundamental rights; separation of powers; and non-discrimination and equality before the law. The rule of law shall be understood having regard to the other Union values and principles enshrined in Article 2 TEU.'

[118] *Hungary v. Parliament and Council*, para 205; *Poland v. Parliament and Council*, para 313.

[119] Polish Constitutional Tribunal, Case No. K 3/21, Press Release, para 21.

[120] *Hungary v. Parliament and Council*, para 232; *Poland v. Parliament and Council*, para 264. See Chamon 2022, pp. 342–343.

[121] *Hungary v. Parliament and Council*, paras 127, 232; *Poland v. Parliament and Council*, paras 145, 264. See Chamon 2022, pp. 340–341. On how these values can be defended in EU law, see De Zwaan 2022; Stremler 2021.

[122] *Hungary v. Parliament and Council*, paras 233; *Poland v. Parliament and Council*, paras 265.

challenges both the EU's identity pillars. This is because the Tribunal challenged the primacy of EU law in connection with the values in Article 2 TEU by doubting their legal worth.

5.5.2 The EU's Constitutional Identity in Relation to the Member States' Constitutional Identities

The EU, on the basis of the discussion thus far, can be said to possess its own constitutional identity, as does each of its Member States. The pressing question then becomes whether a possible contest between their identities should be settled in favour of the EU, or in favour of the Member States. A plausible answer can be offered. Within the constellation of the EU and its Member States there is sufficient cause to prefer both pillars of the EU's identity to competing national claims that constitutional courts may disregard EU law in the event of differences over identity. It would otherwise arguably make little sense to construct an overarching common constitutional identity, without requiring each of the Member States to respect it on equal terms.[123] As the CJEU made clear in the cases of Hungary and Poland v. Parliament and Council, the common EU identity requires a common defence, as coordinated by the CJEU in terms of Article 19(1) TEU. Without instruments such as the direct effect and primacy of EU law, the EU's legal order would be overly compromised both in terms of its functionality and substance. Not only would the unity of EU law be compromised, but the EU's fundamental values would risk being reduced to mere symbolism. These dangers are real and not simply hypothetical. For example, in their assessment of the Polish Tribunal's earliest case law, Von Bogdandy and Schill opined that although constitutional law was placed above EU law, the national control of EU law was construed 'in a very limited fashion'.[124] In other words, the possibility of real conflict was judged to be very limited. However, the Tribunal's judgement in Case No. K 3/21 severely contradicted any hopes that national judicial prudence and a common vocabulary on identity would prevent or mitigate constitutional conflict with EU law. Also, the 'constitutional cacophony' outlined above shows that the Polish judgement is not an isolated case either. This state of affairs underlines the warning, given already in 2015 by Advocate General Cruz Villalón in Gauweiler, that it would be impossible to preserve the EU in its current form if it were made 'subject to an absolute reservation, ill-defined and virtually at the discretion of each of the Member States, which takes the form of a category described as "constitutional identity".'[125] His concern becomes all the more relevant in the case of disagreements regarding the foundational values protected

---

[123] Compare Pernice 2002, p. 520, who explains that the primacy (or in his words 'supremacy') of EU law is in part grounded in its reciprocal acceptance by the Member States and their citizens.

[124] Von Bogdandy and Schill 2011, p. 1434.

[125] Opinion of Advocate General Cruz Villalón of 14 January 2015 in CJEU, Case C-62/14, *Gauweiler*, ECLI:EU:C:2015:7, para 59. Compare also Pernice 2002, p. 520 who explains that

in Article 2 TEU, such as that on judicial independence.[126] This is because these topics cut to the substantive core of the EU's common constitutional identity. A lack of unity on these issues would undermine their very inclusion in the TEU. The primacy of EU law therefore becomes not less important the more constitutional an issue becomes, but arguably more important to ensure substantive coherence on fundamental questions.

Consequently, the question whether the EU respected national constitutional identity as required Article 4(2) TEU is to be answered by the CJEU and not by the constitutional courts of the Member States. The claims to the contrary by the constitutional courts of Germany, Hungary, Romania and Poland cannot be followed. As the CJEU held in *RS*, in response to the Romanian Constitutional Court's judgement in Case 390/2021, Article 4(2) TEU:

> has neither the object nor the effect of authorising a constitutional court of a Member State (…) to disapply a rule of EU law, on the ground that that rule undermines the national identity of the Member State concerned as defined by the national constitutional court.[127]

Where a national court considers that the EU did not fulfil its obligation under the provision to respect such identity, the court is required to make a request to the CJEU according to Article 267 TFEU for a preliminary ruling in the matter.[128] Article 4(2) TEU does not qualify the exclusive jurisdiction of the CJEU, derived from Article 19(1) TEU, to provide definite interpretations of EU law and decide on the validity of EU acts.[129] Instead, the provision essentially requires EU organs to take national constitutional factors carefully into account when shaping and developing EU law.[130] The effect is not to qualify the primacy of EU law, but to make such law more receptive of national constitutional identities. While Member State institutions including the courts develop and express such identities, the question whether the EU respected them is ultimately one of EU law only.[131] And importantly, as argued here, the invocation of Article 4(2) TEU by Member States is to be judged mindful of the EU's own identity, as embodied by the autonomy of its legal order and its substantive values in Article 2 TEU.

---

the primacy (or in his words 'supremacy') of EU law stems in part from 'the need to preserve the functioning of the European legal system'.

[126] Consider also the view by Lenaerts 2021, pp. 10–11 that 'national identity may not serve to justify a departure from the values of the Union set out in Article 2 TEU' and where 'EU law itself lays down exhaustively the rules to be applied to a particular issue, those rules—as interpreted by the Court of Justice—must prevail over national law'. See in this regard Court of Justice of the European Union, Case C-896/16, *Repubblika*, judgement of 20 April 2021, ECLI:EU:C:2021:311, paras 61–64.

[127] *RS (Effet des arrêts d'une cour constitutionnelle)*, para 70.

[128] Ibid., para 71.

[129] Ibid., paras 71–72.

[130] Van der Schyff 2012, p. 583.

[131] Ibid.

5.6 Constitutional Identity Parameters

The purpose of this contribution has been to investigate the parameters of identity-based arguments in the multilevel framework inhabited by the EU and its Member States. From the analysis it has become clear that the term 'national identity' in Article 4(2) TEU has to be understood in a *constitutional* sense. The term 'identity' potentially captures the whole range of a Member State's fundamental constitutional expression and is not limited to its constitutional structures only. The duty which this provision imposes on the EU to respect such identity is subject to EU law, as governed by the mandate of the CJEU in Article 19(1) TEU. The provision does not modify this cornerstone of the EU's legal system by creating a window for Member States to act unilaterally in protecting their respective identities. The expression of national constitutional identities must respect the common constitutional identity of which the EU is the product, thereby paring the respect to be shown by the EU to national identities on account of Article 4(2) TEU. In grounding both the EU and the Member States' duties towards each other, the need for sincere cooperation becomes vital, as governed by the provisions set out in Article 4(3) TEU.

The concept of an EU constitutional identity is one which is necessary to fully present and understand the relationship between the EU level and the Member State level. The reliance by the CJEU on the EU legal order's common identity in the cases of Hungary and Poland v. Parliament and Council is therefore to be welcomed. Using this term allows scholars and future judgements to draw on national sources, such as the Member States' constitutional traditions, and on EU sources, such as the Treaties and case law, to fashion the EU's identity more explicitly.[132] What has been implicit for so long, can now be stated in so many words. In this way the EU's constitutional identity can better fulfil its benchmark function in deciding which national constitutional identity expressions should be respected according to Article 4(2) TEU. The importance of this reference function has been all too evident in the concrete challenge to the fundamental values protected in Article 2 TEU by the constitutional courts of Romania and Poland. The usage of term will also allow Member States to better understand and engage with their collective self-image at the EU level through mechanisms such as the preliminary ruling procedure in Article 267 TFEU.

This chapter is a translated and slightly modified version of the author's article: (2023) De ontwikkelende constitutionele identiteit van de EU [The developing constitutional identity of the EU]. SEW: Tijdschrift voor Europees en economisch recht 71:57–67.

---

[132] To date the literature on this topic has been limited, for a selection see Faraguna and Drinóczi 2022; Van der Schyff 2022; Van der Schyff 2021; Martinico 2016; Van Damme 2015.

References

Barents R (2021) Het Hof van Justitie en nationale constitutionele rechters 'Lieb Vaterland magst ruhig sein, fest steht und treu die Wacht, die Wacht am Rhein!'. SEW, Tijdschrift voor Europees en economisch recht 69:2–11

Besselink L F M (2010) National and Constitutional Identity before and after Lisbon. Utrecht Law Review 6:36–49

Blanke H F (2013) Article 4: The Relations Between the EU and the Member States. In: Blanke H F, Mangiameli S (eds) The Treaty on European Union (TEU). A Commentary. Springer, Heidelberg, pp 185–253

Calliess C (2013) The Dynamics of European Citizenship: From Bourgeois to Citoyen. In: Rosas A, Levits E, Bot Y (eds) The Court of Justice and the Construction of Europe: Analyses and Perspectives on Sixty Years of Case-law - La Cour de Justice et la Construction de l'Europe: Analyses et Perspectives de Soixante Ans de Jurisprudence. T.M.C. Asser Press, The Hague, pp 425–441

Calliess C (2020) Constitutional Identity in Germany: One for Three or Three in One? In: Calliess C, Van der Schyff G (eds) Constitutional Identity in a Europe of Multilevel Constitutionalism. Cambridge University Press, Cambridge, pp 153–181

Calliess C, Van der Schyff G (eds) (2020a) Constitutional Identity in a Europe of Multilevel Constitutionalism. Cambridge University Press, Cambridge, 377 pp

Calliess C, Van der Schyff G (eds) (2020b) Constitutional Identity Introduced. In: Calliess C, Van der Schyff G (eds) Constitutional Identity in a Europe of Multilevel Constitutionalism. Cambridge University Press, Cambridge, pp 3–8

Chamon M (2022) De conditionaliteitsverordening: een (beperkte) uitbreiding van het rechtsstaatarsenaal van de EU. SEW, Tijdschrift voor Europees en economisch recht 70:337–350

Chronowski N, Vincze A (2021) Full Steam Back: The Hungarian Constitutional Court Avoids Further Conflict with the ECJ. Verfassungsblog 15 December 2021, https://verfassungsblog.de/full-steam-back/

Claes M (2012) Negotiating Constitutional Identity or Whose Identity is it Anyway? In: Claes M, De Visser M, Van de Heyning C (eds) Constitutional Conversations in Europe: Actors, Topics and Procedures. Intersentia, Cambridge, pp 205–233

Cloots E (2015) National Identity in EU Law. Oxford University Press, Oxford

Cuyvers A (2013) The EU as a Confederal Union of Sovereign Member Peoples: Exploring the Potential of American (Con)federalism and Popular Sovereignty for a Constitutional Theory of the EU. Dissertation Leiden, Meijers Series MI-227

Cuyvers A (2014) Wiens soevereiniteit pakt de EU dan af? Europa als een confederale unie soevereine lid-volkeren. Ars Aequi 63:676–681

De Witte B (2021) Article 4(2) TEU as a Protection of the Institutional Diversity of the Member States. European Public Law 27:559–570

De Zwaan J W (2022) De waarden van de Europese Unie, en de handhaving daarvan. SEW, Tijdschrift voor Europees en economisch recht 70:3–19

Dobbs M (2015) The Shifting Battleground of Article 4(2) TEU: Evolving National Identities and the Corresponding Need for EU management? European Journal of Current Legal Studies 21(2)

Drinóczi T (2020) Constitutional Identity in Europe: The Identity of the Constitution. A Regional Approach. German Law Journal 21:105–130

Faraguna P, Drinóczi T (2022) Constitutional Identity in and on EU Terms. VerfassungsBlog, 21 February 2022, https://verfassungsblog.de/constitutional-identity-in-and-on-eu-terms/, https://doi.org/10.17176/20220222-001059-0

Garben S (2020) Collective Identity as a Legal Limit to European Integration in Areas of Core State Powers. Journal of Common Market Studies 58:41–55

Grabenwarter C (2009) National Constitutional Law Relating to the European Union. In: Von Bogdandy A, Bast J (eds) Principles of European Constitutional Law. Hart/CH Beck/Nomos, Oxford, pp 83–129

Grimm D (2016) Constitutionalism: Past, Present, and Future. Oxford University Press, Oxford

Habermas J (2003) Why Europe Needs a Constitution. In: Eriksen E O, Fossum J E, Menéndez A J (eds) The Chartering of Europe: The European Charter of Fundamental Rights and its Constitutional Implications. Nomos Verlagsgesellschaft, Baden-Baden, pp 256–274

Halmai G (2017) The Hungarian Constitutional Court and Constitutional Identity. Verfassungs-Blog 11 January 2017, https://verfassungsblog.de/the-hungarian-constitutional-court-and-con stitutional-identity/

Jacobsohn G J (2006) Constitutional Identity. The Review of Politics 68:361–397

Lenaerts K (2021) Constitutional Relationships between Legal Orders and Courts within the European Union. Speech to the XXIX FIDE Congress, The Hague, 4 November 2021, https:/ /fide2020.eu/wp-content/uploads/2021/11/FIDE-Opening-Ceremony_-4-November-2021_K oen-Lenaerts.pdf

Mangiameli S (2013) Article 2: The Homogeneity Clause. In: Blanke H F, Mangiameli S (eds) The Treaty on European Union (TEU): A Commentary. Springer, Heidelberg, pp 109–155

Martinico G (2016) Building Supranational Identity: Legal Reasoning and Outcome in Kadi I and Opinion 2/13 of the Court of Justice. Italian Journal of Public Law 8:235–267

Pernice I (1999) Multilevel Constitutionalism and The Treaty of Amsterdam: European Constitution-Making Revisited? Common Market Law Review 36:703–750

Pernice I (2002) Multilevel Constitutionalism in the European Union. European Law Review 27:511–529

Pernice I (2015) Multilevel Constitutionalism and the Crisis of Democracy in Europe. European Constitutional Law Review 11:541–562

Rosenfeld M (2012) Constitutional Identity. In: Rosenfeld M, Sajó A (eds) The Oxford Handbook of Comparative Constitutional Law. Oxford University Press, Oxford, pp 756–775

Rummens S, Sottiaux S (2014) Democratic Legitimacy in the Bund or 'Federation of States': The Cases of Belgium and the EU. European Law Journal 20:568–587

Schnettger A (2020) Article 4(2) TEU as a Vehicle for National Constitutional Identity in the Shared European Legal System. In: Calliess C, Van der Schyff G (eds) Constitutional Identity in a Europe of Multilevel Constitutionalism. Cambridge University Press, Cambridge, pp 9–37

Selejan-Gutan B (2021) A Tale of Primacy, Part III. VerfassungsBlog 17 November 2021, https:// verfassungsblog.de/a-tale-of-primacy-part-iii/

Stremler M (2021) Constitutional Oversight of the Member States by the European Union. PhD Dissertation, Tilburg University

Van Damme T A J A (2015) Advies 2/13 en de constitutionele identiteit van de EU: Over de (niet-)toetreding tot het EVRM van een federale 'non-staat'. SEW, Tijdschrift voor Europees en economisch recht 63:616–627

Van der Schyff G (2012) The Constitutional Relationship between the European Union and its Member States: The Role of National Identity in Article 4(2) TEU. European Law Review 37:563–583

Van der Schyff G (2020) Member States of the European Union, Constitutions, and Identity - A Comparative Perspective. In: Calliess C, Van der Schyff G (eds) Constitutional Identity in a Europe of Multilevel Constitutionalism. Cambridge University Press, Cambridge, pp 305–347

Van der Schyff G (2021) Constitutional Identity of the EU Legal Order: Delineating its Roles and Contours. Ancilla Iuris 1–12

Van der Schyff (2022) The Need for an Explicit EU Constitutional Identity: The Flipside of the Polish Constitutional Tribunal Judgment K 3/21. NederlandRechtsstaat, 14 January 2022, https://www.nederlandrechtsstaat.nl/the-need-for-an-explicit-eu-constitutional-identity-the-flipside-of-the-polish-constitutional-tribunal-judgment-k-3-21/

Von Bogdandy A, Schill S (2011) Overcoming Absolute Primacy: Respect for National Identity under the Lisbon Treaty. Common Market Law Review 48:1417–1453

Chapter 6
St. Augustine and the Court of Justice of the European Union on Citizenship

Gohar Karapetian

Contents

Abstract One of the crucial characteristics of the EU's constitutional identity concerns its citizenship. EU citizenship is established in 1992 and is attributed to every person holding the nationality of a Member State of the EU. This chapter examines EU citizenship from the perspective of Christian theological literature, particularly St. Augustine's political thought. It will be argued that some of the main issues EU citizenship is dealing with in the current EU constitutional debate, specifically in its relation with the national citizenship of the Member States, were touched upon in the 5th Century AD by St. Augustine concerning the relationship between Christian citizenship and secular citizenship. The question will be raised whether disputes on loyalty and transcendence back then were analysed in order to facilitate the coexistence of multiple citizenships. From a political theological angle, this chapter sheds light on the current constitutional debate pertaining to the (arguably secular transcendental) nature of EU citizenship.

Keywords Citizen · City of God · Christian citizenship · EU citizenship · Fundamental status · (Secular) transcendence

G. Karapetian (✉)
Faculty of Law, University of Groningen, Groningen, The Netherlands
e-mail: g.karapetian@rug.nl

© T.M.C. ASSER PRESS and the authors 2023
J. de Poorter et al. (eds.), *European Yearbook of Constitutional Law 2022*,
European Yearbook of Constitutional Law 4,
https://doi.org/10.1007/978-94-6265-595-9_6

6.1 Introduction

The idea of citizenship is one of the crucial legacies of classical antiquity which forms a key notion in contemporary constitutional and political thought.[1] In dealing with inclusiveness and exclusiveness, it regulates the relationship between the citizen and its polity. Generally, this relationship is designed reciprocally: citizenship entails rights and privileges on the one hand, but it brings possible far-reaching obligations on the other hand. State citizenship meets the aforementioned structure by reciprocally regulating the relationship between the citizen and the legal and political order of the concerning state.[2] This relationship requires loyalty from both the state and the citizen.[3] Analogous to state citizenship, also European Union citizenship (EU citizenship) forms a *species* of the *genus* citizenship. EU citizenship is established in 1992 and is attributed to every person holding the citizenship of a Member State of the Union. Although the Treaties suggest otherwise, the legal consequences of EU citizenship are up to the present not reciprocally structured.[4] Citizens of the Union enjoy several rights, varying from the right to vote and to stand as candidate in elections for the European Parliament to the right to move and reside freely within the territory of the Member States of the EU. According to the Treaty on the Functioning of the European Union (TFEU), EU citizenship shall be additional to the citizenship of the Member State and not replace it. This construction entails the potentiality of a radical tension between national citizenship and EU citizenship from an almost Hobbesian perspective: from 1992 onwards, the citizens of the Member States enjoy at least two capacities: as a citizen of their state and as a citizen of the Union. To whom is, or should, the citizen be more loyal: the Member State or the EU? This potentially radical tension was substantially increased by the claim of the Court of Justice of the European Union (ECJ) that EU citizenship is destined to be the fundamental status of citizens of the Member States, entailing ultimate loyalty of the multi-layered citizen towards the EU.[5] Nonetheless, the ECJ also made explicit that the relationship between the EU citizen and his national Member State should be of a profoundly intimate nature.[6] The different capacities of the citizen, therefore, entail a thorough conflict concerning loyalty and transcendence. Why does the ECJ attach value to the secular transcendental character of EU citizenship in its relation to national citizenship? Surprisingly, as will be shown in the chapter, St. Augustine,

---

[1] Manville 1990; Riesenberg 1992; Blok 2017.

[2] Karapetian 2019, chapters II and VI.

[3] Fletcher illustrates three dimensions of loyalty: loyalty to loved ones (friends, lovers, family members), loyalty to a group (nation, political party) and loyalty to God. In the sense of this chapter, attention is paid to the second and third dimension of loyalty. Fletcher 1995, chapter 2.

[4] Article 20(2) of the Treaty on the Functioning of the EU (TFEU) reads: "Citizens of the Union shall enjoy the rights and be subject to the duties provided for in the Treaties. (…)".

[5] Court of Justice of the European Union, C-184/99 *Grzelczyk*, 20 September 2001, I-6229, para 31.

[6] Court of Justice of the European Union, C-221/17, *Tjebbes*, 12 March 2019, ECLI:EU:C:2019:189, para 33.

in developing his theory on Christian citizenship, was confronted with similar questions—albeit, there, the tension occurred between Christian citizenship and worldly citizenship. The existence of the notion of Christian citizenship is traced to Biblical references, such as Ephesians 2:19.[7] It entails a relationship between the citizen, i.e. the Christian, and his heavenly polity, being the Kingdom of God. Additionally, such as recognized by St. Augustine and other Christian theologians as John Chrysostom, ultimate loyalty of the Christian citizen is enrolled in Heaven.[8] Analogous to EU citizenship, similar questions on loyalty and transcendence were being raised in the theological debate: to whom should the Christian citizen by virtue of both his heavenly and worldly citizenship be more loyal: his earthly legal and political order, or God's Kingdom? Which reasons are used by St. Augustine in order to argue that Christian citizenship transcends worldly citizenship? Within which framework does worldly citizenship fit, according to Christian theological writings, particularly St. Augustine's?

It is against this background that the notion of Christian citizenship will be scrutinized in this chapter in order to provide new insights in the EU constitutional debate on the secular transcendental character of EU citizenship and the question this provokes, namely that on ultimate loyalty. The notion of transcendence refers in St. Augustine's works, and in the sense of this chapter, to God's absolute independence of the material world, and thus the circumstance that a Christian theological notion exceeds its secular equivalence.[9] Secular transcendence refers to the circumstance that a notion which is undeniably secular in its content, nonetheless shows theological structure and, thus, exceeds another secular notion. Although at first sight the differences between EU citizenship and Christian citizenship cannot be denied, from a constitutional angle there are various similarities between them. Particularly when it comes to their relationship with other existing citizenships, in the case of EU citizenship the national citizenship and in the case of Christian citizenship the worldly citizenship, arguably both have various characteristics in common. Both EU citizenship and Christian citizenship are, namely, supranational and claim to be the fundamental status of the citizen. Both types of citizenship face, therefore, a dispute on loyalty and transcendence. The first goal of this analysis is to describe the construction of both EU and Christian citizenship. Furthermore, a second goal is to identify parallels between these types of citizenship, particularly when it comes to dealing with the dispute on loyalty and transcendence with other existing citizenships. In so doing, and finally, new insights on loyalty and the secular transcendental character of EU citizenship will be analysed from an Augustinian angle. Carl Schmitt's

---

[7] Ephesians 2:19–20 reads: "So then you are no longer strangers and aliens, but you are citizens with the saints and also members of the household of God, 20 built upon the foundation of the apostles and prophets, with Christ Jesus himself as the cornerstone." See also Acts 11:25–26, when the disciples were called Christians for the first time: "Then Barnabas went to Tarsus to look for Saul, 26 and when he had found him, he brought him to Antioch. So it was that for an entire year they met with[e] the church and taught a great many people, and it was in Antioch that the disciples were first called "Christians.""

[8] St. John Chrysostom, Homilies 17:10–12.

[9] Augustine 1997; Dawson 1994.

quote "Alle prägnanten Begriffe der modernen Staatslehre sind säkularisierte theologische Begriffe" arguably holds true for the nature of EU citizenship.[10] According to the German constitutional lawyer and legal theologian Schmitt (1888–1985), a conceptual notion which is irrevocably secular can nonetheless illustrate a certain theological structure.[11] In this chapter, parallels between EU citizenship and Christian citizenship shall be made, in order to illustrate that EU citizenship, particularly in its relationship with the citizenships of the Member States, contains a theological, more specifically Augustinian, structure. Arguably, St. Augustine's thought on the relationship between Christian citizenship and worldly citizenship will be insightful in understanding the ECJ's viewpoint that EU citizenship is destined to be the fundamental status of the citizen.

The analyses in this chapter is concerned with interpretation of legal sources when it comes to EU citizenship, such as primary legislation (i.a. Treaty on the European Union (TEU), TFEU), case law of the ECJ and literature. With regard to Christian citizenship as analysed by St. Augustine, primary sources (in particular his *De civitate Dei*) and secondary sources on citizenship according to St. Augustine will be interpreted and analysed. The structure of the argument is as follows. In Sect. 6.2 an analysis will be provided on the tension EU citizenship causes between itself and the national citizenships of the Member States. Thereafter, in Sect. 6.3, the tension between Christian citizenship such as developed by St. Augustine and worldly citizenship will be analysed. Having dealt with that, Sect. 6.4 will be devoted to the parallels between both citizenships and, thus, on the (secular transcendental) nature of EU citizenship itself. Finally, a conclusion will follow.

6.2 The European Union, the Member States and the Multi-layered Citizen

The introduction of EU citizenship in the constitutional order of the EU has entailed various consequences for the citizen. One of these consequences is that the citizen of a Member State of the Union obtained a new legal and political capacity. Nowadays, he is—besides his capacity as citizen of the Member State—also a citizen of the EU. This section focuses on these two capacities of the citizen: on the one hand of the Member State, and on the other hand of the EU. Attention shall be paid to firstly (Sect. 6.2.1) the introduction of the notion of EU citizenship in the EU constitutional construct and, secondly (Sect. 6.2.2) its derivative character, the rights associated with it, and the tension it causes with the citizenship of the Member State, particularly when it comes to ultimate loyalty.

---

[10] Schmitt 1922, p. 43.

[11] Ibid; Geréby 2008; Schmidt Pasos 2018.

6.2.1   The Introduction of EU Citizenship in the Maastricht Treaty

The Treaty on European Union of 1992, also referred to as Maastricht Treaty, introduced for the first time *de iure* a concept of citizenship in the ambit of the EU. The way towards the codification of the notion of citizenship in the Maastricht Treaty was, however, not without difficulties. In October 1972, during the first joint summit of the government leaders, the president of the European Commission, made explicit in the European Parliament that the European Commission intended to introduce a European citizenship.[12] This proposal, however, did not receive unanimity since various Member States, such as the Kingdom of the Netherlands, were of the opinion that the introduction of a certain notion would strengthen the federal nature of the Union. Nevertheless, there were also proponents of this proposal. Particularly Italy and Belgium were positive towards the introduction of such a concept in Community law.[13]

After the summit of October 1972, the ideas aimed at active participation of citizens of the Member States in the political unit of the Union became more ambitious.[14] For instance, at the summit in 1974, these ideas concerned among others establishing a passport union and abolishing passport controls on the borders of the Member States.[15] Furthermore, various reports were written after these summits on involving citizens in the political sphere of the Union by virtue of the notion of citizenship. During the second summit of 1974, Belgian prime minister Leo Tindemans was invited to write a report on his view on the EU. This report was published in 1975.[16] In this report, Tindemans argues that two courses of action should be adopted in order to get the EU closer to its citizens: firstly, the rights of Europeans should be protected, where they cannot be guaranteed by the Member States solely anymore, and secondly, a manifestation of European solidarity was needed.[17] After

---

[12] Evans 1982, p. 505; Harryvan and Van der Harst 2018, p. 43.

[13] Bierbach 2017, p. 302. The reasons behind the positive attitude towards EU citizenship differ, however. Italy's interest could, for instance, be triggered by its diaspora of mobile nationals. Belgium's focus, by contrast, was on facilitating new educational programs within the Union and harmonizing diplomas. Harryvan and Van der Harst 2018, p. 45.

[14] Bierbach 2017, p. 303.

[15] Ibid.

[16] Text of Mr. Leo Tindemans' letter to his European Council Colleagues, sent on 29 December 1975, *Bulletin of the European Communities 1976, Supplement 1, Bruxelles: European Communities*. Chapter IV of his report reads "A citizen's Europe". Tindemans argues: "The construction of Europe is not just a form of collaboration between States. It is a *rapprochement* of peoples who wish to go forward together, adapting their activity to the changing conditions in the world while preserving those values which are their common heritage. In democratic countries the will of governments alone is not sufficient for such an undertaking. The need for it, its advantages and its gradual achievement must be perceived by everyone so that effort and sacrifices are freely are freely accepted. Europe must be close to its citizens."

[17] Tindemans 1976, p. 26; Harryvan and Van der Harst 2018, p. 45.

the Tindemans report, other reports followed, such as the Scelba report (1977)[18] and the Adonino reports (1985).[19] These reports elaborated on various aspects of a possible notion of EU citizenship, such as political, educational and cultural.[20]

During the negotiations leading to the Maastricht Treaty, the Spanish memorandum "Towards European citizenship" was of crucial importance.[21] The Spanish delegation argued in this memorandum that the citizens of the Member States were to be qualified as more than aliens who had various privileges.[22] The delegation proposed special rights which should be guaranteed to the citizens of the Member States when they abide in another EU Member State.[23] As a consequence of these guarantees, the EU would explicitly start a legal relationship with its citizens. This new capacity of the citizen would draw attention to multiple advantages connected to the European integration. If the citizen makes use of the possibilities granted by the European integration, such as residing in another Member State, then he will be guaranteed various fundamental rights by virtue of his capacity as an EU citizen.[24] The Maastricht Treaty was signed on 7 February 1992 and entered into force on 1 November 1993. Articles 8-8E of the Maastricht Treaty pertained to EU citizenship. According to Article 8 of the Maastricht Treaty every person holding the nationality of a Member State of the Union is to be considered as a citizen of the Union.[25] This provision follows that EU citizens shall enjoy rights conferred by the Maastricht Treaty and be subject to duties imposed by it.[26] Some of the rights connected to the legal status of EU citizen are the right to free movement on the Member States' territory,[27] the right to vote and stand a candidate in local government and European Parliament elections in the Member State of residence under the same conditions as nationals of the concerning Member State,[28] the right to enjoy

---

[18] Scelba 1977.

[19] Adonino 1985.

[20] See on the Scelba Report and Adonino reports: Harryvan and Van der Harst 2018, p. 47; Mindus 2017, p. 9.

[21] Mindus 2017, p. 10.

[22] Harryvan and Van der Harst 2018, p. 50.

[23] Five special rights were mentioned by the Spanish delegation: the right of travel and residence, exclusive rights in the areas of health, social affairs, education, culture, environment and consumer protection, diplomatic and consular protection by other Member States, strengthening the right of petition and, finally, the appointment of a European Ombudsman. Harryvan and Van der Harst 2018, p. 51.

[24] Harryvan and Van der Harst 2018, p. 51: "[…] the Spanish felt that citizens should become more conscious of the benefits they gained from European integration. Not only businessmen profited from Europe, but also consumers, students, tourists, etc.; this should be made more explicit to the public at large."

[25] Article 8, para 1, second sentence of the Maastricht Treaty. Section 6.2.2 of this chapter will elaborate on the derivative character of EU citizenship.

[26] Article 8, para 2 of the Maastricht Treaty. Although the provision makes explicit that EU citizenship can be designed reciprocally, in practice there are no duties connected to EU citizenship. On EU citizenship and duties, see Kochenov 2014.

[27] Article 8A of the Maastricht Treaty; Article 20(2)(a) TFEU.

[28] Article 8B of the Maastricht Treaty; Article 20(2)(b) TFEU.

diplomatic and consular protection in a third country in which the Member State of which the citizen is a national of is not represented[29] and the right of petition to the European Parliament and appeal to the European Ombudsman.[30, 31]

After the entry into force of the provisions in the Maastricht Treaty on EU citizenship, several scholars qualified the new notion of EU citizenship as a "purely decorative and symbolic institution".[32] The main reason behind this was that EU citizenship at first sight did not contribute substantially to existing Community law before the entry into force of the Maastricht Treaty. For example, already in 1968 with Council Directive 68/360/EEC on the abolition of restrictions on movement and residence within the Community for workers of Member States and their families, and with Regulation no. 1612/68 of the Council on freedom of movement for workers within the Community, economically active citizens of the Member States had the right to free movement on the Member States' territory. In other words, the provisions on Union citizenship mainly codified existing Community secondary law. Therefore, the expectation was that this notion would not add any new value to the daily life of the EU citizen.

The position the ECJ took in the first years of its case law on citizenship reflects this point of view taken by various scholars. Several ECJ judgments after the entry into force of the Maastricht Treaty, such as *Boukhalfa*,[33] *Ströber and Pereira*[34] and *Uecker and Jacquet*,[35] illustrate that the ECJ qualifies EU citizenship as a merely secondary source in confirming precedent.[36] EU citizenship's importance, however, has expanded gradually since the first formalized legal provisions in the Maastricht Treaty. As will be illustrated in Sect. 6.2.2, the institutional change concerning EU citizenship has mainly occurred in the case law of the ECJ.

---

[29] Article 8C of the Maastricht Treaty; Article 20(2)(c) TFEU.

[30] Article 8D of the Maastricht Treaty; Article 20(2)(d) TFEU.

[31] According to Article 8E of the Maastricht Treaty the European Commission was obliged to report to the European Parliament, the Council and the Economic and Social Committee before 31 December 1993 and thereafter every three years on the application of the provisions on EU citizenship. In this report, the Commission should take into account the Union's development. The second paragraph of Article 8E of the Maastricht Treaty clarifies that on the basis of this report, the Council may adopt provisions to "strengthen or to add to the rights laid down in this Part [Part Two on "Citizenship of the Union"]".

[32] Kostakopoulou 2008, pp. 285–286. See also Everson 1995; Jessurun d'Oliveira 1995.

[33] Court of Justice of the European Union, C-214/94, *Boukhalfa,* 30 April 1996, I-2273.

[34] Court of Justice of the European Union, Joined Cases C-4/95 and C-5/95, *Ströber and Pereira,* 30 January 1997, I-531.

[35] Court of Justice of the European Union, Joined Cases C-64/96 and C-65/96 *Uecker and Jacquet,* 5 June 1997, I-3182.

[36] Kostakopoulou 2005, pp. 233–267.

6.2.2   EU Citizenship's Derivative Nature and Evolution: On Ultimate Loyalty

A crucial characteristic of EU citizenship is its derivative character. The Maastricht Treaty clearly stated that a person holding the nationality of a Member State is to be considered as a EU citizen. Therefore, the one and only way to obtain EU citizenship is to be granted the nationality of one of EU's Member States. This principle was also confirmed by Declaration No. 2 on the nationality of a Member State, attached to the Maastricht Treaty.[37] According to this Declaration "the question whether an individual possesses the nationality of a Member State shall be settled solely by reference to the national law of the Member State concerned. Member States may declare, for information who are to be considered their nationals for Community purposes by way of a declaration lodged with the Presidency and may amend any such declaration when necessary".[38] This Declaration in combination with the Maastricht Treaty and all following European Treaties[39] give the impression that Member States are fully autonomous in regulating their nationality law.[40] This point of view, however, cannot be maintained when analysing the case law of the ECJ where the status of EU citizenship and the effects connected to this status are being undermined by the nationality of the Member States. In *Micheletti*,[41] *Zhu and Chen*[42] and *Garcia Avello*[43] the ECJ has clarified that EU citizenship cannot be put into question by other Member States. Member States are, in other words, not allowed to impose additional conditions for the recognition of the nationality of other Member States. These cases illustrate that the ECJ is extremely protective when it comes to the exercise of the fundamental rights connected to the status of EU citizenship. The derivative character of EU citizenship, in other words, does not affect the rights provided by the European Treaties.

---

[37] Treaty on European Union, Declaration on Nationality of a Member State, *Official Journal C 191, 29/07/1992*, p. 0098.

[38] Ibid. The United Kingdom of Great Britain and Northern Ireland made use of the possibility of excluding some nationals for EU purposes, see: Declaration by the Government of the United Kingdom of Great Britain and Northern Ireland on the definition of the term "nationals", which is annexed to the Final Act of the Treaty concerning the Association of the Kingdom of Denmark, Ireland and the United Kingdom of Great Britain and Northern Ireland to the European Communities (*Official Journal* 1972, L 73, p. 196).

[39] The derivative character of EU citizenship has not changed in current EU law. See Article 20 of the Treaty on the Functioning of the European Union: "Every person holding the nationality of a Member State shall be a citizen of the Union."

[40] The principle that each State has full competence in regulating its nationality, is also codified in the European Convention on Nationality (Council of Europe, European Treaty Series, No. 166). According to Article 3 of this Convention "Each State shall determine under its own law who are its nationals".

[41] Court of Justice of the European Union, C-369/90 *Micheletti*, 7 July 1992, I-4258.

[42] Court of Justice of the European Union, C-200/02 *Zhu en Chen*, 19 October 2004, I-9951.

[43] Court of Justice of the European Union, C-148/02 *Garcia Avello*, 2 October 2003, I-11635.

The protective attitude of the ECJ on the exercise of EU citizenship rights can also be traced to *Rottmann*[44] and *Ruiz Zambrano*.[45] In the *Rottmann* case, the ECJ ruled that the Member States have the full competence of withdrawing from a EU citizen the nationality of the concerning Member State acquired by naturalisation when the nationality has been obtained by deception. However, the aforementioned can be done only if the national decision to withdraw the nationality of the Member State observes the EU principle of proportionality.[46] In the latter case, that of *Ruiz Zambrano,* the ECJ went further and ruled that Article 20 TFEU is to be interpreted so that it precludes decisions of Member States which deprive EU citizens of the "genuine enjoyment of the substance of the rights attaching to the status of the European Union citizen".[47]

The citizenship of the Member State is, thus, pivotal for the acquisition of EU citizenship. The abovementioned selected case law illustrates that the ECJ has institutionally designed the notion of EU citizenship. Member States are not fully autonomous in regulating national law on the acquisition and loss of their citizenship. Of particular importance in this framework, especially in the relationship between EU citizenship and national citizenship, is the ECJ's ruling in *Grzelczyk*.[48] In this case, the ECJ ruled that "Union citizenship is destined to be the fundamental status of nationals of the Member States, enabling those who find themselves in the same situation to enjoy the same treatment in law irrespective of their nationality [...]".[49] For the first time in the history of EU law, the ECJ explicitly recognizes in *Grzelczyk* that EU citizenship is the primary capacity of the citizen, implicitly providing a hint that the national Member State status of the citizen is *not* the primary capacity of the citizen. The above-cited sentence on EU citizenship being the fundamental status of the citizen is repeatedly confirmed by the ECJ in its following case law.[50] The Treaty of Lisbon, signed in 2008 has, moreover, progressed the ECJ's claim

---

[44] Court of Justice of the European Union, C-135/08 *Rottmann*, 2 March 2010, I-1467.

[45] Court of Justice of the European Union, C-34/09 *Ruiz Zambrano*, 8 March 2011, I-01177.

[46] Court of Justice of the European Union, C-135/08 *Rottmann*, 2 March 2010, I-1467, para 59.

[47] Court of Justice of the European Union, C-34/09 *Ruiz Zambrano*, 8 March 2011, I-01177, para 45.

[48] Court of Justice of the European Union, C-184/99 *Grzelczyk*, 20 September 2001, I-6229.

[49] Court of Justice of the European Union, C-184/99 *Grzelczyk*, 20 September 2001, I-6229, para 31.

[50] See, for instance, Court of Justice of the European Union, C-413/99, *Baumbast*, 17 September 2002, I-7136, para 82; Court of Justice of the European Union, C-138/02, *Collins*, 23 March 2004, I-2733, para 61; Court of Justice of the European Union, C-224/02, *Pusa*, 29 April 2004, I-5774, para 16; Court of Justice of the European Union, C-145/04, *Kingdom of Spain v. United Kingdom of Great Britain and Northern Ireland*, 12 September 2006, I-7961, para 74; Court of Justice of the European Union, C-520/04, *Turpeinen*, 9 November 2006, I-10704, para 18; Court of Justice of the European Union, C-434/09, *McCarthy*, 5 May 2011, ECLI:EU:C:2011:277, para 47; Court of Justice of the European Union, C-165/14, *Rendón Marín*, 13 September 2016, ECLI:EU:C:2016:675, para 69; Court of Justice of the European Union, C-221/17, *Tjebbes*, 12 March 2019, ECLI:EU:C:2019:189, para 31.

on the autonomous character of EU citizenship. Before the Lisbon Treaty, EU citizenship was said to be "complementary" to national citizenship.[51] This changed in the Treaty of Lisbon.[52] According to the current text of the TFEU, EU citizenship "shall be additional to and not replace national citizenship".[53] In the literature, this change has been interpreted as a confirmation that EU citizenship is not subordinate to national citizenship.[54] Although the ECJ considers EU citizenship as the fundamental status of the citizen, it does not deny the intimate relationship that the citizen has with the legal and political order of his Member State. In, for instance, the earlier cited *Rottmann* case, the Court rules on this matter: "[...] it is legitimate for a Member State to wish to protect the special relationship of solidarity and good faith between it and its nationals and also the reciprocity of rights and duties, which form the bedrock of the bond of nationality".[55] This position is confirmed by the Court in its *Tjebbes* case of 2019.[56]

Two conclusions can be drawn on the basis of the aforementioned analysis. Firstly, institutional change concerning EU citizenship has occurred in the case law of the ECJ. The selected rulings which are cited above, illustrate this statement. Secondly, although EU citizenship has a derivative character, according to the ECJ it is intended to be the fundamental status of the nationals of the Member States. The derivative nature of EU citizenship has not changed since the Maastricht Treaty.[57] Access to EU citizenship is, namely, still gained through the nationality law of the Member State. However, the nationality law of the Member States is, as illustrated in this section, no longer autonomously regulated by the Member State. The autonomy of Member States in nationality matters is, therefore, substantially weakened. National measures entailing the loss of the citizenship of the concerning Member State should namely be reviewed by the national institutions in the light of the EU proportionality principle. Furthermore, the ECJ qualifies the status of the EU citizen as the fundamental status compared to his status as citizen of a Member State. In EU citizenship theory, therefore, on the one hand it is confirmed that the national of the Member State has a special and intimate relationship with his Member State, and on the other hand it

---

[51] Article 8(1) of the Treaty of Amsterdam reads: "Citizenship of the Union is hereby established. Every person holding the nationality of a Member State shall be a citizen of the Union. Citizenship of the Union shall be complement and not replace national citizenship."

[52] The earlier cited Declaration No. 2 on the nationality of a Member State was removed from the annex of the Treaty on the EU after the entry into force of the Lisbon Treaty.

[53] Article 20(1) of the TFEU.

[54] Szpunar and López 2017, p. 113; De Waele 2010; Schrauwen 2008.

[55] Court of Justice of the European Union, C-135/08 *Rottmann*, 2 March 2010, I-1467, para 51.

[56] Court of Justice of the European Union, C-221/17, *Tjebbes*, 12 March 2019, ECLI:EU:C:2019:189, para 33. In an earlier case, that of *D'Hoop*, Advocate-General Geelhoed also recognizes the special relationship between a EU citizen and his legal order of the Member State: "As a Belgian national she [Ms D'Hoop] is undeniably linked to the Belgian legal system." Opinion of Advocate General Geelhoed, Case C-224/98, 20 February 2002, I-6194, para 49.

[57] There are various proposals by scholars who introduce a European nationality law: Orgad and Lepoutre 2019; De Groot 2003.

is demonstrated that EU citizenship is, nonetheless, destined to be the fundamental and primary status of the citizen.[58]

These different capacities of the same citizen entail a conflict concerning loyalty. To whom should the multi-layered citizen be eventually loyal to: his Member State or the EU? The ECJ is convinced in its case law that the citizen should eventually be loyal to the EU, and not the Member State. The question then arises why the ECJ attaches value to the secular transcendental character of EU citizenship in its relation to national citizenship. Furthermore, also the European Commission explicitly confirms the transcending nature of EU citizenship.[59] In the making of the preparatory text of EU citizenship before the entry into force of the Maastricht Treaty, the Commission mentions two principles of EU citizenship. Firstly, according to the Commission, EU citizenship is "a component factor in the move to strengthen democratic legitimacy in the Community, both supplementing and transcending national citizenship".[60] Secondly, EU citizenship "reflects the aims of the Union, involving as it does an indivisible body of rights and obligations stemming from the gradual and coherent development of the Union's political, economic and social dimension".[61] It is interesting to scrutinise why institutions of the Union attach value to the transcendental character of EU citizenship. Section 6.4 will deal with this and similar questions. Before getting to Sect. 6.4, in the next section attention shall be paid to Christian citizenship. As stated in Sect. 6.1, the differences between EU citizenship on the one hand, and Christian citizenship on the other hand cannot be denied. However, in particular the relationship of Christian citizenship with secular citizenship provides us with new insights on the nature of EU citizenship and the ECJ's claim that EU citizenship is destined to be the fundamental status of the citizen. As will be argued in Sect. 6.4, St. Augustine's eschatology of the city of God and the EU's final destination according to the ECJ appear to be pivotal in understanding the (secular) transcendental nature of both Christian and EU citizenship.

---

[58] This is also expressed by Advocate General Poiares Maduro in his Opinion in the *Rottmann* case. Opinion of Advocate General Poiares Maduro, Case C-135/08, *Rottmann*, 30 September 2009, para 23: "This is the miracle of Union citizenship: it strengthens the ties between us and our States (in so far as we are European citizens precisely because we are nationals of our States) and, at the same time, it emancipates us from them (in so far as we are now citizens beyond our States)."

[59] Commission of the European Communities, Intergovernmental Conference on Political Union, Draft Text on Union Citizenship, *Bulletin of the European Communities*, Supplement 2/91, p. 87.

[60] Ibid.

[61] Ibid.

6.3 Christian Citizenship and Secular Citizenship: Dispute on Ultimate Loyalty

In this section, attention shall be paid to Christian citizenship such as developed by St. Augustine. Section 6.3.1 will elaborate on Christian citizenship's birth and its first confrontation with secular citizenship. Thereafter, in Sect. 6.3.2, St. Augustine's political thought will be analysed pertaining to the relationship between Christian citizenship and secular citizenship. The parallels between citizenship from an Augustinian angle and the perspective of the ECJ shall be revealed in Sect. 6.4.

6.3.1 Christian Citizenship and Its First Confrontation with Secular Citizenship

Christian citizenship is traced to Biblical references, such as Ephesians 2:19.[62] Scripture established a new capacity of humans: besides the capacity as a citizen of the earthly political unit, one could also be a citizen according to Biblical purposes.[63] Analogues to citizenship, Christian citizenship regulates a relationship between a citizen and a polity—in this case, being the relationship between the Christian and the heavenly polity. This relationship is regulated reciprocally: the Christian citizen has various rights and obligations.[64]

---

[62] See footnote 7 for Ephesians 2:19.

[63] See, for instance, St. Gregory of Narek, in: Terian 2021, p. 442 (Prayer 93.12): "This amazingly miraculous oil brings the blessing of the Light to the Jew and the Gentile, the Indian and the barbarian, the Scythian and the Greek, the cruel savage and the scary cynocephalus giant in fearsome appearance, the freeborn master and the slave by birth, making them Christians, sealing them in your name, dedicating them to your Holy Spirit, and establishing them as true sons of the Heavenly Father". For the Prayer in Armenian, see St. Gregory of Narek 2016, p. 585:
   "Զարմանահրաշ օրհնալոյս յուղն այս
   Հրեային ու խումին, Հնդիկին ու բարբարոսին,
   Սկյութացուն ու Հելլենին,
   Դժնի դումին ու արհավիրատեսիլ
   Սուկավիրխար շնագլխին,
   Ազատ տիրոջն ու ծառայածին ստրուկին
   Քրիստոնյան դարձնելով`
   Քո անվամբ է կնքում, ընծայում Սուրբ Հոգուդ
   Եվ երկնային Հորդ հարազատ Որդի հաստատում:"

[64] Concerning the obligations of the Christian citizen, Matthew 19:16–21 is of particular importance: "16 Then someone came to him and said, "Teacher, what good deed must I do to have eternal life?" 17 And he said to him, "Why do you ask me about what is good? There is only one who is good. If you wish to enter into life, keep the commandments." 18 He said to him, "Which ones?" And Jesus said, "You shall not murder; You shall not commit adultery; You shall not steal; You shall not bear false witness; 19 Honor your father and mother; also, You shall love your neighbor as yourself." 20 The young man said to him, "I have kept all these;[b] what do I still lack?" 21 Jesus said to him, "If you wish to be perfect, go, sell your possessions, and give the money[c] to the poor, and you will have treasure in heaven; then come, follow me." See also Matthew 22:36–40.

A first confrontation between Christian citizenship and secular citizenship occurred in the 4th century in the discussions of two citizens of Antioch: Libanius and St. John Chrysostom. Libanius, born in Antioch in 314 AD, was a pagan Greek lecturer in rhetoric.[65] During the rise of Christian hegemony in the Roman Empire from the 4th century, when pagan beliefs were replaced by Christian education, Libanius remained unconverted and loyal to paganism.[66] One of Libanius' pupils was John Chrysostom, born in c.349 AD. In contrast to his teacher, John Chrysostom dispraised pagan beliefs and converted to Christianity at the age of eighteen.[67] Thereafter, he lived ascetically.[68] One of the main differences in view between Libanius and St. John Chrysostom concerned the dispute on ultimate loyalty. According to Libanius, the one and only capacity of a human being was his capacity as citizen of (preferably) the *polis*. The *polis* was by Libanius considered as the best living environment for the citizen. St. John Chrysostom, however, disagreed entirely:

> If you are a Christian, no earthly city is yours. Of our City "the Builder and Maker is God". Though we may gain possession on the whole world, we are withal but strangers an sojourners in it all! We are enrolled in heaven: our citizenship is there![69]

The confrontation between Libanius and St. John Chrysostom illustrates that the tension between Christian citizenship on the one hand and secular (earthly) citizenship on the other hand mainly focused on the question to whom the Christian citizen should be loyal to: God's Kingdom or the earthly political order. Several Christian theologians, such as St. John Chrysostom, argued that the Christian's ultimate loyalty should be towards God and his Kingdom, since Christian citizenship transcends secular citizenship. A possible solution for this field of tension between the coexistence of Christian citizenship and secular citizenship was offered by the early Christian theologian St. Augustine.

6.3.2 St. Augustine's View on Christian Citizenship

St. Augustine (Aurelius Augustinus) was born in 354 AD in Tagaste Numidia (in what now is Algeria).[70] Initially, St. Augustine was not substantially influenced by Christianity. This changed, however, when St. Augustine met one of the most influential ecclesiastical figures in the 4th Century: bishop Ambrose of Milan.[71] On

---

[65] Downey 1959, p. 652.

[66] Ibid.

[67] Riesenberg 1992, p. 90.

[68] Ibid.

[69] St. John Chrysostom, Homilies 17:10–12. A similar approach is confirmed by Christ in John 18:36: "Jesus answered, "My kingdom is not from this world. If my kingdom were from this world, my followers would be fighting to keep me from being handed over to the Jews. But as it is, my kingdom is not from here.""

[70] Sizoo 1947, p. 6.

[71] Ibid.

the account of the influence of Ambrose of Milan, St. Augustine was converted to Christianity in 386, at the age of thirty-two, and baptized by Ambrose in Milan in 387.[72] One year later, in 388, he returned to his birth place Tagaste in order to become a so-called *servus Dei*—a servant of God. From this year on, St. Augustine's work has been a substantial influence on Christianity.[73] His works include texts on Christian doctrine, exegetical works, such as his commentaries on Psalms, and a plethora of sermons and letters. Moreover, St. Augustine is probably best known for his autobiography, *Confessions*, as well as *City of God* (*De civitate Dei*). This latter work, *De civitate Dei*, forms part of our study and comprises 22 chapters. This work is written between 412 and 426. As a consequence of the sack of Rome in 410 by the Visigoths, and in order to restore the confidence of Christians in Christianity, St. Augustine wrote *De civitate Dei* as an answer to the ones that held Christianity responsible for the Roman catastrophe. It is, among others, in this work that St. Augustine conceptually elaborates on the role and position of the Christian citizen in his earthly political unit. As a result, as will be illustrated in the following, an attempt is made by St. Augustine in order to reconcile Christian citizenship with secular citizenship.

An essential principle of *De civitate Dei* is St. Augustine's categorization of two metaphysical allegiances: the earthly city (*civitas terrena*) on the one hand and the city of God (*civitas dei*) on the other hand.[74] The basis of this notion of the two cities is scriptural, such as Psalm 87:3 illustrates.[75] In Book 11 of *De civitate Dei*, St. Augustine pays attention to the origin of the two cities. There, he notes that before the fall of the angels, they were all created good. Yet, some of them fell due to their own pride, including the devil.[76] On earth, both cities had their germ in Cain and Abel. The earthly city can be traced to Cain due to the fratricide. The city of God, in contrast, can be traced to Abel.[77] St. Augustine continues:

Accordingly, two cities have been formed by two loves: the earthly by the love of self, even to the contempt of God; the heavenly by the love of God, even to the contempt of self... In the one, the princes of the nations it subdues are ruled by the love of ruling... But in the other city there is no human wisdom, but only godliness, which offers due worship to the true God, and looks for its reward in the society of the saints, of holy angels as well as holy men "that God may be all in all."[78]

---

[72] Other influences of Augustine's thought are Tyconius (an African Donatist writer) and Origen (an early Christian theologian of Alexandria). Lee 2017, p. 78.

[73] The literature on Augustine's works is substantial: Van Oort 1986; Van der Grinten 1930; Wetzel 2012; Toom 2017; Kenyon 2018.

[74] Augustinus 2011, Book I, Book XV:1–8. Also in En. Ps. 61, Augustine identifies the two cities as opposites, each with a king. The earthly city has the devil for its king, and the heavenly city has Christ for its king.

[75] Psalm 87:3 reads: "Glorious things are spoken of you, O city of God."

[76] Augustinus 2011, Book 11:11–22.

[77] Although the earthly city was founded by Cain, St. Augustine makes explicit that the city of God was not found by Abel, but by Christ. Abel "being a sojourner, built none"; *De civitate Dei* XV:1.

[78] Augustinus 2011, XIV:28.

St. Augustine uses various synonyms with regard to both cities. He refers to the earthly city, for instance, as the city of unbelievers, the temporal city, the ungodly city, the beast and the city of mortals. For the city of God, St. Augustine also uses a plethora of synonyms, such as the city of heaven, the eternal city, the holy city, Jerusalem and the most glorious city of God. The symbolic name of Jerusalem refers to "New Jerusalem" in Revelation 21.[79]

This antithesis between the two cities perhaps becomes clearer when elaborating on the human beings in both cities. Each city has according to St. Augustine its citizens. The city of God is populated by Christian believers and the city of the world by unbelievers.[80] In eschatological terms, according to St. Augustine's division, every human being has the citizenship of solely one of the cities. Therefore, it is impossible from St. Augustine's point of view to be a citizen of both the heavenly polity and the earthly polity.[81] It is at the final judgment that God will separate the two cities and their citizens in definite fashion. Only God knows who belongs to each city and will reveal this at final judgment day.[82] The question then arises how the citizen of the heavenly city should behave in the worldly city. In the abovementioned analysis on the first confrontation between Christian citizenship and secular citizenship, between Libanius and St. John Chrysostom, the latter clarifies that the Christian citizen should eventually be loyal to God's Kingdom. Although St. Augustine agrees on this statement with St. John Chrysostom, he goes on to state that the relationship between the Christian citizen and the earthly city should be of a profoundly intimate nature. A crucial theme in St. Augustine's political thought is the extent into which Christian citizens have to influence the political structures of the earthly city, in his days the Roman Empire.[83] Although there is a fundamental disparity between both cities in *De civitate Dei*, St. Augustine makes clear that each human being is an integral part

---

[79] Revelation 21:1–4 reads: "Then I saw a new heaven and a new earth; for the first heaven and the first earth had passed away, and the sea was no more. 2 And I saw the holy city, the new Jerusalem, coming down out of heaven from God, prepared as a bride adorned for her husband. 3 And I heard a loud voice from the throne saying, "See, the home[a] of God is among mortals. He will dwell[b] with them; they will be his peoples,[c] and God himself will be with them;[d] 4 he will wipe every tear from their eyes. Death will be no more; mourning and crying and pain will be no more, for the first things have passed away.""

[80] Therefore, the city of the world is by St. Augustine also named, as cited above, "the city of unbelievers".

[81] See also Griffiths 2012, p. 42.

[82] This is a crucial difference between EU citizenship and Christian citizenship as developed by St. Augustine. Where EU citizenship is derivative, as a consequence of which the EU citizen is also a citizen of a Member State, according to St. Augustine the citizen of the City of God cannot be a citizen of the worldly order. Nonetheless, since from St. Augustine's perspective a Christian citizen is an integral part of the worldly city and, furthermore, both the ECJ and St. Augustine aim to reconcile EU citizenship with the citizenship of the Member States and Christian citizenship with the worldly citizenship, it is still useful to scrutinise the parallels between the ECJ's and St. Augustine's conception of citizenship.

[83] On Rome and Augustine, see: Arbesmann 1954.

of his state and Kingdom.[84] Various scholars thus agree that according to St. Augustine Christians should not avoid public office.[85] A reason for this statement is that when "those who are gifted with true godliness and live good lives also know the art of governing peoples, nothing could be more fortunate for human affairs than that, by the mercy of God, they should also have the power to do so."[86] This principle is confirmed by St. Augustine is his other works, such as in En. Ps. 51.6:

> We find a citizen of Jerusalem, a citizen of the kingdom of God, entrusted with secular administration. He may wear the purple, or be an officer of the state, or a magistrate, or a proconsul, or a general. He discharges civic duties, but he keeps his heart raised above them if he is a Christian, a believer, a Godfearing person, who sets little store by the circumstances in which he finds himself and puts his hope in those he has not attained yet... We should not despair of the citizens of the heavenly kingdom, therefore we see them transacting the business of Babylon or dealing with earthly matters in this earthly political area.[87]

Furthermore, in St. Augustine's correspondence with Macedonius—the imperial vicar for Africa—the abovementioned principle is also confirmed. Macedonius was responsible for the administration of justice in the African civil diocese.[88] During Macedonius' two-year tenure in this post, St. Augustine and Macedonius corresponded with letters. Letter 155 to Macedonius is written between 413 and 414 AD.[89] St. Augustine's fundamental argument in Letter 155 is that Macedonius' piety, which results in his faith, hope, and love for God, requires him to alter his political practices in the earthly city.[90] As a result, Christian statesmen's political behaviour, with faith, hope, and love for God and His Kingdom, entails that his political virtues in the earthly city closely resemble the virtues of the Christian citizen in the city of God.[91] To this end, St. Augustine clarifies that the morality of the Christian citizen requires him to balance his desires for benefits in the earthly city and his longing for the benefits of the heavenly city. Therefore, according to St. Augustine, Christian citizens are given a place to support the faith in the worldly city. In case of collision between the benefits of virtues of the earthly city with that of the heavenly city, the Christian citizen should choose the benefits of the heavenly city. Letter 155, therefore, also illustrates clearly that Christian citizens should not avoid public offices in the earthly city. Instead, because of their Christian morality they are capable of deepening their relationship with God as citizens of the city of God, without abandoning and undermining their obligations following their position in the earthly city.[92]

---

[84] Augustinus 2011, IV:3.

[85] Nevertheless, St. Augustine admits that there are difficulties involved for persons balancing their position in the earthly city and their role as a Christian citizen of the City of God. Dodaro 2004, pp. 431–432, 435.

[86] Augustinus 2011, V.19.

[87] En. Ps. 51; see also Crouse 2017, p. 163.

[88] Dodaro 2004, p. 434.

[89] Ibid., p. 432.

[90] Ibid., p. 443.

[91] Ibid., p. 432.

[92] McCurry 2011, pp. 49–52.

The reading of St. Augustine's political thought illustrates his view with regard to the relationship between Christian citizenship and secular citizenship. As analysed in this section, in his description of this relationship, a crucial duality concerns the division between the earthly city and the city of God. The antithesis between the two cities is substantially increased by the statuses of its citizens: the citizens of the earthly city are the unbelievers while the citizens of the heavenly city are to be qualified as the Christian citizens. Although this division between the citizens of both cities is fundamental for St. Augustine's political thought, he maintains that faith, hope and love will transform the manner in which Christian citizens will deal with earthly matters in the earthly city. In doing so, the Christian citizen anticipates in the fulfilment of his virtues in the city of God. Nevertheless, in situations where the Christian virtues entail a conflict with the earthly conflicts, the former transcends. Consequently, it is of no doubt in St. Augustine's works that Christian citizenship transcends earthly citizenship.

6.4   On Two Parallels

In this section a series of parallels linking St. Augustine's political thought between Christian citizenship and secular citizenship and the ECJ's view on EU citizenship and the citizenship of the Member States shall be set out. This analogy can arguably reveal that the ECJ's claims echo similar ideas on transcendence and loyalty as in Augustinian thought. The first parallel concerns the multiplicity of legal orders and cities respectively, and their citizens according to both the ECJ and St. Augustine. The second parallel is with regard to the (secular) transcendental character of both EU and Christian citizenship.

First Parallel: Two Legal Orders, Two Cities and Their Citizens

Both the EU and the city of God as introduced by St. Augustine deal with a similar construction from an institutional perspective. Within the EU, in any case two political and legal orders can be distinguished: that of the Member States and of the EU respectively. From St. Augustine's perspective, the world is organized into two cities: the city of God and the earthly city. Although both levels in the EU and in St. Augustine's political thought entail a duality, it cannot be denied that an interaction between these levels does take place. Within the EU, the EU is in need of the Member State for *inter alia* the implementation of EU law. A similar approach goes for the earthly city's necessity for the city of God. Until the apocalyptic judgment, the Church represents the city of God in the earthly city.[93] In various texts, St. Augustine maintains that the Church is on pilgrimage in the earthly city. For St. Augustine, the necessity of the earthly city for the city of God becomes clear when scrutinising the position of the citizens of both cities. In the earlier section, it was clarified that the

---

[93] Martin 1972, p. 196; Crouse 2017, p. 152.

city of God and the earthly city make use of the same physical goods: Christian citizens in the city of God and pagans in the earthly city. Although St. Augustine's both cities constitute a dichotomy, the citizens of the city of God should have a profoundly intimate relationship with the earthly city's institutional organs. St. Augustine makes explicit in his Letter 155 to Macedonius that the Christian citizen can be an officer of the state or, for instance, a magistrate. As a result, the Christian citizen anticipates in the fulfilment of his virtues in the city of God. Moreover, the notions of faith, hope and love should according to St. Augustine alter the way the Christian citizen fulfils his duties of his earthly office.[94] Therefore, for St. Augustine, Christian rulers are citizens of the city of God who have providentially been given a place to support the faith of the city of the world.[95] To this end, St. Augustine argues that Christian citizens will strengthen the worldly constitutional and political units, because of their Christian beliefs.[96] A similar comparison goes for the position of the EU citizen in the legal and political order of the Member State. The ECJ has confirmed in multiple rulings that the EU citizen should have an intimate relationship with his Member State.[97] Contrary to Christian citizenship and secular citizenship, a person can be qualified as an EU citizen *because* of his capacity as a citizen of a Member State. Nonetheless, in case of a collision between the capacity of the citizen of the Member State and of the EU, according to the ECJ, the citizen should follow the virtues on the basis of EU citizenship.[98] This claim of the ECJ constitutes a second parallel between EU citizenship and Christian citizenship from an Augustinian perspective: namely the (secular) transcendental nature of EU citizenship and Christian citizenship.

Second Parallel: (Secular) Transcendence of EU Citizenship and Christian Citizenship

Transcendence constitutes, as mentioned in the introduction, the absolute capacity of God to be qualified as fully autonomous of the material world. As a result, theological notions exceed their secular equivalence. As illustrated in Sect. 6.3, the aforementioned is argued by St. Augustine in his political works. In this chapter, the notion of Christian citizenship in its relation to earthly citizenship is scrutinised from an Augustinian perspective. St. Augustine is clear on the hierarchy of these notions: Christian citizenship transcends secular citizenship. A similar reasoning occurs when analysing the relationship between EU citizenship and the citizenship of the Member State of the EU. Secular transcendence occurs when a secular notion, such as EU citizenship, exceeds its secular equivalence within another legal order, being the citizenship of the Member States of the EU. This statement is based on the multiple

---

[94] Dodaro 2004, p. 433.

[95] Crouse 2017, p. 169.

[96] Augustinus 2011, V.19.

[97] Court of Justice of the European Union, C-135/08 *Rottmann*, 2 March 2010, I-1467, para 51; Court of Justice of the European Union, C-221/17, *Tjebbes*, 12 March 2019, ECLI:EU:C:2019:189, para 33.

[98] The conflicts between EU citizenship and the citizenship of the Member States will be intensified if the EU legislator connects obligations to EU citizenship.

confirmations of the ECJ that the capacity of the EU citizen is destined to be the fundamental status of the citizen. As a result, the ECJ maintains that EU citizenship exceeds the citizenship of the Member State. The question then arises why the ECJ arguably invokes this secular transcendental character of EU citizenship. In other words, why does the ECJ attach value to the notion that the EU citizen should eventually be loyal towards the Union and not his Member State? A possible answer to the aforementioned question could be that European integration will fail if the EU's citizens eventually would be loyal to their Member States. As a consequence, the Member States' interests—which vary depending on the Member State—will prevail over the interests of the EU. This observation illustrates the *secular* transcendental character of EU citizenship. This final destination of the Union, i.e. 'an ever closer Union among the peoples of Europe'[99] differs fundamentally from that of St. Augustine's city of God—the latter is enrolled in Heaven. The ECJ has integrated this formula of an ever closer union among the peoples of Europe in its case law. The ECJ ruled that "it is unarguably a principle aim of that treaty [EC Treaty] to put an end to the conflicts of the past between the peoples of Europe by creating 'an ever closer union' among them (...)".[100] In the case law of the ECJ, the Treaty on the EU is being marked as a new stage in the process of creating an ever closer union among the peoples of Europe, in which "decisions are taken as openly as possible and as closely as possible to the citizen".[101] It is, furthermore, made explicit by the ECJ that the EU Treaties' purpose is the creation of an "ever closer union among the peoples of Europe (...) from which it follows that the European Union aims to eliminate the barriers which divide Europe".[102] Where the destination of the city of God is a theological one, the EU's destination is irrevocably secular. Nevertheless, the parallel illustrates that the final destination of both orders (i.e. the EU and the city of God) is a possible reason behind the (secular) transcendental character's relevance of both EU citizenship and Christian citizenship. From the perspective of the ECJ, an 'ever closer union among the peoples of Europe' is possible if these peoples of Europe are more loyal to the EU than to their Member States. Only in this way, the EU can eliminate the barriers which divide Europa. A similar approach goes for the city of God; enrolment in Heaven is possible if the Christian citizen is loyal to God's Kingdom.

The aforementioned two parallels strengthen one of the claims made by Schmitt.[103] According to Schmitt, a conceptual framework, although the concerning

---

[99] Treaty on the Functioning of the European Union, *Official Journal of the European Union,* 26.10.2012, C 326/49, Preamble.

[100] Court of Justice of the European Union, T-306/01 *Yusuf and Al Barakaat International Foundation v. Council of the European Union and Commission of the European Communities,* 21 September 2005, II-3554, para 154.

[101] Court of Justice of the European Union, C-621/18 *Wightman et al v. Secretary of State for Exiting the European Union,* 10 December 2018, para 4; Court of Justice of the European Union, C-761/18 P *Sandberg v. European Parliament,* 21 January 2021, para 36.

[102] Court of Justice of the European Union, C-621/18 *Wightman et al v. Secretary of State for Exiting the European Union,* 10 December 2018, para 61.

[103] Schmitt 1922; Schmitt 1970.

conceptual framework is no longer depended upon the divine, still can illustrate a certain theological structure. [104] In the sense of this chapter, although it is of no doubt that EU citizenship is an irrevocably secularised notion since it regulates the relationship between the EU citizen and the legal and political order of the EU, in its abstract structure EU citizenship does display a theological pattern. In its relationship with the citizenship of the Member State, EU citizenship retains a theological architecture, particularly when it comes to the ECJ's claim that EU citizenship transcends the citizenship of the Member State although it is deprived of the latter. This parallelism entails to argue that the conceptual architecture of EU citizenship in its relationship with the citizenship of the Member State is analogous to Christian citizenship in its relationship to secular citizenship as understood by St. Augustine. St. Augustine's perspective on the relationship between Christian and secular relationship, as a result, can help us in understanding the potentially secular transcendental character of EU citizenship in its relation to the citizenships of the EU's Member States. Analogous to Christian citizenship as scrutinised by St. Augustine, where its final destination is the main reason for its transcendence over worldly citizenship, also with regard to EU citizenship, its final destination is pivotal for its transcendence over the citizenship of the member states. St. Augustine's thought, therefore, can help us in exploring from a political theological perspective the ECJ's view on EU citizenship as the fundamental status of the EU citizen in the aforementioned *Grzelczyk* case and as confirmed in later case law. The EU's and its citizenship's final destination (i.e. an ever closer Union) entails its secular transcendence over the citizenship of the member states. Similarly, given the final destination of Christian citizenship according to St. Augustine (i.e. enrolment in Heaven), Christian citizenship transcends earthly citizenship.

6.5 Conclusion

This chapter concerns EU citizenship from the perspective of St. Augustine's thought. It is argued that from a theological perspective, parallels can be linked when comparing the relationship between EU citizenship and the citizenship of the Member States of the EU to that of Christian citizenship and worldly citizenship as understood by St. Augustine. The dispute in current EU constitutional debate on loyalty and transcendence is analysed from an Augustinian perspective in order to shed light on the arguably political theological patterns of EU citizenship. Two parallels are touched upon to argue the analogy between EU citizenship and Christian citizenship: firstly, the conceptual structure of the two legal orders of the EU and the Member State, the two Augustinian cities and their citizens, and secondly, the (secular) transcendental character of EU citizenship and Christian citizenship. These series of parallels constitute an illustration of Schmitt's claim that a notion which is undeniably derived of the divine can display political theological patterns in its systematic structure. St. Augustine's thought on the structure of Christian citizenship helped

---

[104] Schmitt 1970.

us, in conclusion, in answering the question why the ECJ qualifies EU citizenship as the fundamental status of the citizen, and, why EU citizenship, thus, transcends national citizenship from the ECJ's point of view. From an Augustinian perspective, in attaching value to the EU's and its citizenship's final destination, the ECJ ruled that EU citizenship is to be destined the fundamental status of the citizen. Additionally, similar to the relationship of Christian citizenship with worldly citizenship as developed by St. Augustine, in facilitating the coexistence of EU citizenship with the citizenship of the Member States, the ECJ confirms the intimate relationship the citizen has with the legal and political order of his Member State. The city of God's eschatology and the EU's final destination are, in conclusion, from an Augustinian perspective crucial in comprehending the (secular) transcendence of both Christian citizenship and EU citizenship over other existing citizenships.

References

Adonino P (1985) A People's Europa. Report from the ad hoc Committee. Bulletin of the European Communities, Supplement 7/85

Arbesmann R (1954) The Idea of Rome in the Sermons of St. Augustine. Augustiniana, 4:305–324

Augustine (1997) The Confessions. New City Press, New York

Augustinus (2011) De stad van God. Ambo, Amsterdam

Bierbach J B (2017) Frontiers of Equality in the Development of EU and US Citizenship. T.M.C. Asser Press, The Hague

Blok J (2017) Citizenship in Classical Athens. Cambridge University Press, Cambridge

Crouse R C (2017) Two Kingdoms & Two Cities. Mapping Theological Traditions of Church, Culture, and Civil Order. Augsburg Fortress Publishers

Dawson D (1994) Transcendence as Embodiment: Augustine's Domestication of Gnosis. Modern Theology 10:1–26

De Groot G R (2003) Towards a European Nationality Law – Vers un droit européen de nationalité. Universiteit Maastricht. https://doi.org/10.26481/spe.20031113gg

De Waele H (2010) EU Citizenship: Revisiting its Meaning, Place and Potential. European Journal of Migration and Law 12: 319–336

Dodaro R (2004) Political and Theological Virtues in Augustine, Letter 155 to Macedonius. Augustiniana 54:431–474

Downey G (1959) Libanius' Oration in Praise of Antioch (Oration XI). Proceedings of the American Philosophical Society 103: 652–686

Evans A C (1982) European Citizenship. Modern Law Review 45: 497–515

Everson M (1995) The Legacy of the Market Citizen. In: Shaw J, More G (eds) New Legal Dynamics of European Union. Oxford University Press, Oxford

Fletcher G P (1995) Loyalty: An Essay on the Morality of Relationships. Oxford University Press, New York

Geréby G (2008) Political Theology versus Theological Politics: Erik Peterson and Carl Schmitt. New German Critique 35: 7–33

Griffiths P J (2012) Secularity and the *saeculum*. In: Wetzel J (ed) Augustine's City of God. A Critical Guide. Cambridge University Press, Cambridge

Harryvan A G, Van der Harst J (2018) From free cross-border movement to backing legitimacy: European citizenship in a political-historical perspective 1970-2000. In: Van der Harst J et al (eds) European Citizenship in Perspective. History, Politics and Law. Edward Elgar Publishing, Cheltenham/Northampton, pp 42–61

Jessurun d'Oliveira H U (1995) Union Citizenship: Pie in the Sky? In: Rosas A, Antola E (eds) A Citizen's Europe: In Search of a New Order. Sage Publications, London

Karapetian G (2019) Morganatisch burgerschap. Wolters Kluwer, Deventer

Kenyon E (2018) Augustine and the Dialogue. Cambridge University Press, Cambridge

Kochenov D (2014) EU Citizenship without Duties. European Law Journal 20: 482–498

Kostakopoulou D (2005) Ideas, Norms and European Citizenship: Explaining Institutional Change. The Modern Law Review 68: 233–267

Kostakopoulou D (2008) The Evolution of European Union Citizenship. European Political Science 7: 285–286

Lee J K (2017) Augustine and the Mystery of the Church. Fortress Press, Minneapolis

Manville P B (1990) The Origins of Citizenship in Ancient Athens. Princeton University Press, Princeton

Martin R (1972) The Two Cities in Augustine's Political Philosophy. Journal of the History of Ideas 33: 195–216

McCurry J (2011) To Love the World Most Deeply: The Phenomenology of the World as Gift in Augustine's "Confessions". New Blackfriars 92: 46–54

Mindus P (2017) European Citizenship after Brexit. Freedom of Movement and Rights of Residence. Palgrave Macmillan, Cham

Orgad L, Lepoutre J (eds) (2019) Should EU Citizenship Be Disentangled from Member State Nationality? In: EUI Working Papers (RSCAS), no. 24

Riesenberg P (1992) Citizenship in the Western Tradition. Plato to Rousseau. The University of North Carolina Press, Chapel Hill/London, UK

Scelba M (1977) Report of Mr M Scelba drawn up on behalf of the Political Affairs Committee on the granting of 'special rights' to the citizens of the European Community in implementation of the decision of the Paris Summit of December 1974

Schmidt Pasos E (2018) The Blood of the Martyrs: Erik Peterson's Theology of Martyrdom and Carl Schmitt's Political Theology of Sovereignty. The Review of Politics 80: 487–510

Schmitt C (1922) Politische Theologie. Duncker & Humblot, Berlin

Schmitt C (1970) Politische Theologie II. Duncker & Humblot, Berlin

Schrauwen A (2008) European Union Citizenship in the Treaty of Lisbon: Any Change at All? Maastricht Journal of European and Comparative Law 15: 55–64

Sizoo A (1947) Augustinus over den staat. J.H. Kok N.V, Kampen

St. Gregory of Narek (2016) Book of Lamentations, St. Etchmiadzin [Սբ. Գրիգոր Նարեկացի (2016) Մատյան Ողբերգության, Ս. Էջմիածին]

Szpunar M, López M E (2017) Some Reflections on Member State Nationality: A Prerequisite of EU Citizenship and an Obstacle to its Enjoyment. In: Kochenov D (ed) EU Citizenship and Federalism: The Role of Rights. Cambridge University Press, Cambridge

Terian A (2021) From the Depths of the Heart, Annotated Translation of the Prayers of St. Gregory of Narek. Liturgical Press Academic, Minnesota

Tindemans L (1976) Letter from Leo Tindemans to the European Council. Bulletin of the European Communities 1976, Supplement 1, European Communities, Brussels

Toom T (ed) (2017) Augustine in Context. Cambridge University Press, Cambridge

Van der Grinten J (1930) De Staatsleer van Augustinus. Studia Catholica 6: 49–67

Van Oort J (1986) Jeruzalem en Babylon. Een onderzoek naar Augustinus' De Stad van God en de bronnen van zijn leer der steden (rijken). Uitgeverij Boekencentrum B.V., The Hague

Wetzel J (ed) (2012) Augustine's City of God. A Critical Guide. Cambridge University Press, Cambridge

Gohar Karapetian Assistant Professor in Constitutional Law at the University of Groningen, The Netherlands. An earlier version of this chapter was presented at the 9th Yale Law School Annual Scholarship Conference, 8–9 November 2019, New Haven, CT, USA.

Chapter 7
The Principle of Solidarity Forging the Constitutional Identity of the European Union

Erika Arban

Contents

Abstract In the past few years, the European Union has faced numerous challenges, from the economic and migratory crises to the recent COVID-19 pandemic and the Ukraine-Russia war. Against this backdrop lurks solidarity, a principle that is solidly crystallised in Article 2 TEU and elsewhere in the EU Treaties. This chapter suggests that the principle of solidarity helps shape the EU constitutional identity. Consequently, taking solidarity seriously (as a foundational value and as an element forging the EU constitutional identity) could offer a viable legal answer to invigorate the EU integration and curb the tensions that are traversing the continent. To this end, the chapter first unpacks the concept of constitutional identity and offers one possible working definition of it. Next, it surveys the principle of solidarity, as a moral and constitutional principle. Finally, the chapter works out the idea of solidarity as a principle forging a EU constitutional identity: solidarity is put into practice to tackle

E. Arban (✉)
Melbourne Law School, Centre for Comparative Constitutional Studies, Melbourne, Australia
e-mail: erika.arban@unimelb.edu.au

© T.M.C. ASSER PRESS and the authors 2023
J. de Poorter et al. (eds.), *European Yearbook of Constitutional Law 2022*,
European Yearbook of Constitutional Law 4,
https://doi.org/10.1007/978-94-6265-595-9_7

the various crises, reconcile diversity and social cohesion within the EU, and as a potential way out of the emergency. By adopting a mainly theoretical approach, coupled with doctrinal and comparative perspectives, the core objective of the chapter is to showcase how constitutional identity and solidarity are braided together in the EU constitutional context.

Keywords Constitutional identity · European Union · EU constitution · EU integration · EU treaties · National identity · Solidarity

7.1   Introduction

In the past decade or so, both the European Union ("EU") and its member states have faced unprecedented challenges that have threatened the EU project as a whole as well as the integrity of some of its limbs: the economic crisis started in 2008, the migration crisis with its bulk of humanitarian implications and political tensions, Brexit and the Catalan independence referenda, and most recently the dramatic unfolding of the COVID-19 pandemic and the Ukraine-Russia war, are just some of the most flagrant examples of tensions crossing the Union. Against this intricate backdrop lurks solidarity, a principle and a value that is not only ingrained in the constitutions of some of the EU member states, but is also firmly crystallised in Article 2 of the Treaty on European Union ("TEU") as well as elsewhere in other EU Treaties, with the intent to profoundly infuse the EU model.

In this chapter, I contend that the principle of solidarity, so deeply embedded in the EU Treaties, helps shape and define what can be referred to as the EU constitutional identity. The argument further developed in the contribution is that, taking solidarity seriously—as a foundational/historical value and as an element forging the EU constitutional identity—could represent the legal answer to invigorate the EU integration and curb the tensions that are traversing the continent, threatening its very essence.

The chapter proceeds as follows. First, the concept of constitutional identity is unpacked: to this end, I propose one possible working definition of constitutional identity, also probing the conceptual difference between *constitutional* and *national* identity, and then I contend that it is possible to talk about an EU *constitutional* identity even absent a codified EU constitution. Section 7.2 is devoted to a survey of the principle of solidarity, both in general terms and as a legal and constitutional principle, within the EU *acquis* but also within a selection of EU jurisdictions. In Sect. 7.3 I work out the idea of solidarity as a principle contributing to forge the EU constitutional identity: solidarity is put into practice to tackle the various crises, reconcile diversity and social cohesion within the EU, and as a potential way out of the emergency. In terms of methodology, the chapter adopts a mainly theoretical approach, coupled with some analytical, doctrinal and comparative perspectives.

While the core objective of this chapter is to showcase how constitutional identity and solidarity are braided together in the EU constitutional context, at the same time such purpose presents some conceptual and definitional challenges: in fact, both constitutional identity and solidarity are rich and multifaceted concepts, thus meaning different things to different people in different contexts since no universal agreement currently exists among scholars on their definition. To avert such challenges, the chapter espouses a conceptualisation of constitutional identity that draws on the theory elaborated by Gary Jacobsohn, which is thus put to a test within the EU framework. As for solidarity, the chapter embraces a holistic understanding of the principle, one that merges moral and legal facets.

7.2   Defining Constitutional Identity

Constitutional identity is a rather fluid and elusive concept that presents several conceptual and normative challenges. In this section, I will expound the notion of constitutional identity and propose one possible definition of it; in doing so, I will also reveal who contributes to shape constitutional identity, in which ways constitutional identity differs from national identity, and to what extent we can talk of a constitutional identity within the EU legal scheme.

7.2.1   Constitutional Identity in General

As noted, constitutional identity is an abstract notion that is often difficult to capture in its full and true core, also because there is no universally accepted definition of it, and no agreement exists on what it really entails, since constitutional law theorists often refer to constitutional identity in various terms.

In this chapter, I maintain that there is a *thin* and a *thick* definition of constitutional identity that could be employed. Constitutional identity in thin terms may refer to the explicit or implicit limits to constitutional amendment ingrained in the constitution itself. The *Ewigkeitsklausel* ("Eternity Clause") of Article 79(3) of the German *Grundgesetz* is a good illustration of it: by indicating the inadmissibility of any amendment to the federal nature of Germany and to the fundamental principles enshrined in Articles 1 and 20, the provision protects what are considered essential features of the German constitutional system, the core of its constitutional identity. However, a thin definition of constitutional identity can also refer to those parts of the constitution that, although not protected by an unamendability or eternity clause, they remain nonetheless outside of the reach of constitutional change. This often happens by express judicial statement: for example, the Italian Constitutional Court has reiterated that the principle of "unity and indivisibility" of the Republic, ingrained in Article 5 of the constitution, is beyond constitutional amendment even if not protected by a specific eternity clause. In other words, because some sections of a constitution are sacred, they are considered the soul (or constitutional identity) of a nation and thus cannot be touched.

But eternity clauses and unamendability statements by the judiciary are not the only way to distinguish or locate constitutional identity, also because not all constitutions contain such clauses and not all courts have engaged in unamendability declarations. To fully grasp the core meaning of constitutional identity, we thus need a thicker understanding of the concept, one that moves away from the constitution or express judicial declarations (mindful however that constitutions and national apex courts remain key players in determining the true soul of constitutional identity, as will be further explained below).

On a theoretical level, attempts to conceptualise constitutional identity have been made by a number of constitutional law scholars. Among others, the work of American theorists Gary Jacobsohn and Michel Rosenfeld has been particularly influential and illuminating in this regard. I will thus briefly canvass the core of their respective arguments.

In his work *Constitutional Identity*,[1] Jacobsohn embraces a rather sophisticated understanding of constitutional identity, one that transcends the written text of the constitution and that is fluid, changing and open to discussion.[2] For Jacobsohn, "a constitution acquires an identity through experience" as "identity emerges *dialogically* and represents a mix of political aspirations and commitments that are expressive of a nation's past, as well as the determination of those within the society who seek in some ways to transcend that past";[3] furthermore, identity is "changeable but resistant to its own destruction, and it may manifest itself differently in different settings."[4]

Jacobsohn further maintains that a key role of constitutional identity is to deal with the constitutional disharmonies that can emerge in the text of the constitution or in the ambit of historical change or political contestation.[5] Disharmony can be found in the "contradictions and imbalances internal to the constitution itself, and sometimes in the lack of agreement evident in the sharp discontinuities that frame the constitution's relationship to the surrounding society."[6] But disharmony can be defined also as "contradictory visions"[7] in a constitution, or the "incongruities lodged within a constitution."[8] Constitutional identity is thus "not a static or fixed thing", but has a "dynamic quality, which results from the interplay of forces seeking either to introduce greater harmony into the constitutional equation or ... to create further disharmony."[9] Constitutional disharmony also "creates a need for adaptation and coping with conflict and dissonance, and constitutional identity must be

---

[1] Jacobsohn 2010.

[2] *Ibid.*, p. 13.

[3] *Ibid.*, p. 7.

[4] *Ibid.*

[5] Rosenfeld 2012, p. 760.

[6] Jacobsohn 2010, p. 87.

[7] *Ibid.*, p. 122.

[8] *Ibid.*, p. 335.

[9] *Ibid.*, p. 88.

shaped dialogically with a view to overcoming the causes of such disharmony."[10] Consequently, a constitution is never a "perfectly harmonious" piece, and disharmony becomes one of the features of constitutional identity:[11] in fact, disharmony is "the main impulse behind the shaping of constitutional identity".[12] For Jacobsohn, constitutional identity is thus braided together with constitutional disharmony and dissonance: because it emerges from—and is forged by—experience, it can fluctuate over time, or competing constitutional identities can emerge at different times in the same jurisdiction.

To establish the identity of a constitution, Jacobsohn suggests to start from the text itself, as a document that offers the vision of the framers for the governance of the polity and the aspirational values that guided the endeavour.[13] But then the judiciary becomes a key player in the shaping of constitutional identity, along with policy-makers, practitioners and other political actors which are called to construe, implement and extend the constitution.[14]

For Michel Rosenfeld, "the place and function of constitutional identity is determined by the need for dialectical mediation of existing, evolving, and projected conflicts and tensions between identity and difference", something that shapes "the dealings between self and other within the relevant polity committed to constitutional rule and favorably disposed toward the aims of constitutionalism."[15] Constitutional identity depends on the constitutional model involved, but also on "the type of constitution-making that led to its adoption" (*e.g.* violent revolution as opposed to peaceful transition).[16] Furthermore, "constitutional interpretation produces constitutional identity and is at the same time shaped, filled, and molded by the latter."[17] Also, constitutional identity is partly conscious and partly unconscious: in fact, although "the process of the formation and evolution of constitutional identity is varied and complex", the constitution-making moment is important, as it "usually involves a conscious act of negation", accompanied by "unconscious acts of incorporation", and this moment of negation and incorporation is of fundamental importance in determining the core and trajectory of constitutional identity.[18]

In light of the above, both Jacobsohn and Rosenfeld share the view of constitutional identity as a dynamic concept, one that is constantly in dialogue—and often in tension—with other factors. For Jacobsohn, such other factors are the constitutional disharmonies and dissonance intrinsic in any constitution, while for Rosenfeld it is the differences internal to the polity that contribute to shaping constitutional identity. Both agree, however, on the fact that courts and judges—along with other policy

---

[10] Rosenfeld 2012, p. 760.

[11] Jacobsohn 2010, p. 349.

[12] *Ibid.*, p. 335.

[13] *Ibid.*, p. 348.

[14] *Ibid.*, p. 351.

[15] Rosenfeld 2012, p. 761.

[16] *Ibid.*, p. 766.

[17] *Ibid.*, p. 771.

[18] Rosenfeld 2005, pp. 317–318.

makers—are *key* (although by no means the *only*) players in forging the identity of a constitutional order.

This chapter proposes to adopt a thick concept of constitutional identity that builds on Jacobsohn's theory: constitutional identity will thus be construed as a combination of political aspirations and commitments expressing a nation's past,[19] a fluid and changeable concept forged by experience, emerging dialogically and manifesting itself differently in different settings,[20] whose main function is to deal with contradictions and imbalances internal to the constitutional text (what Jacobsohn refers to as constitutional disharmonies and dissonances, as defined above).[21] As such, constitutional identity is not fixed but has a dynamic quality and can fluctuate over time, or competing constitutional identities can emerge at different times in the same jurisdiction. Finally, it has multiple creators with potentially competing agendas.

Of course, this conceptualisation of constitutional identity may appear broad and indeterminate and somehow difficult to operationalise; furthermore, as a conceptualisation it remains open to further probing. For example, divergent opinions might arise among theorists and/or the judiciary on which core elements, principles and values are actually reflected by constitutional identity at a given time in a specific jurisdiction: but this should not be perceived as an insurmountable obstacle, as constitutional identity is, by definition, changing, evolving and multifaceted and has multiple creators with potential competing agendas.

7.2.2 Constitutional Identity Versus National Identity

Both in legal scholarship and judicial case law, one conceptual problem that often arises is represented by the interchangeable use, by theorists and commentators, of *constitutional* and *national* identity, as if the two concepts were perfectly coterminous. In this section, I draw on Rosenfeld and suggest that the two notions shall be kept separate and distinct, although some inevitable overlapping exists and they may comprise the same membership.[22]

Quite importantly, constitutional identity presupposes—and is premised on—a constitution, something that does not necessarily apply to national identity, which can instead be construed and understood as an uncodified set of beliefs, practices and traditions that are not obviously constitutional in character.[23] As posited by Rosenfeld, while drawing on national, ethnic, cultural, historical or political identities,

---

[19] Jacobsohn 2010, p. 7.

[20] *Ibid.*, p. 7.

[21] *Ibid.*, p. 4.

[22] Rosenfeld 2012, p. 758.

[23] For a more detailed illustration of the concept of national identity see, *ex multis*, Rieder 2021, p. 12.

constitutional identity differs from each of them.[24] This because the latter is "constructed over time through a dynamic process that involves negation of these other identities accompanied by a rearrangement and reincorporation of salient features of the latter";[25] at the same time, "constitutional identity must constantly remain in dynamic tension with other relevant identities" as it emerges in the context of a dynamic process.[26]

In the EU-specific case, von Bogdandy has noted how an essential element of collective identity is a "mutual perception of belonging"[27] and is normally "based on social constructs".[28] In this regard, a common history is an important element forging this collective (or national) identity,[29] as are other social constructions.[30] To this end, the Treaty on the Functioning of the European Union ("TFEU") contains a declaration by 16 member states recognising a number of symbols expressing "the sense of community of the people in the European Union and their allegiance to it."[31] Such symbols include: the EU flag (a circle of twelve golden stars on a blue background), the anthem based on the "Ode to Joy" from Beethoven's Ninth Symphony, the motto "united in diversity", the Euro as the common currency and a "Europe Day" (9 May, to remember the Schuman Declaration of 1950).[32] Language or symbols like mottos, flags and anthems often contribute to shaping the collective or national identity of a group, as are common or shared values:[33] consequently, the aforementioned EU symbols may be encompassed in a broader European collective (rather than strictly "national") identity, but technically speaking they would be distinct from a EU constitutional identity.

A constitution can contribute to this process of collective identity formation, and sometimes some of the shared values may be entrenched as constitutional values. But constitutional identity is different, as it encompasses doctrines, values and principles, written and unwritten, that are normally used by judges to interpret constitutional norms, or by policy makers to draft domestic policies and that may, or may not, coincide with some of the values that also shape the national or collective identity.[34]

---

[24] Rosenfeld 2005, p. 317.

[25] *Ibid.*, pp. 317–318.

[26] Rosenfeld 2012, p. 758.

[27] Von Bogdandy 2005, p. 298.

[28] *Ibid.*

[29] *Ibid.*, p. 299.

[30] *Ibid.*, p. 306.

[31] Declaration 52 by 16 member states on the symbols of the European Union.

[32] *Ibid.*

[33] Von Bogdandy 2005, p. 307.

[34] To illustrate the concept of national identity, Rieder brings the example of the UK's National Health Service (NHS), often viewed as the secular counterpart of the Anglican Church and as such as a "talismanic institutional pillar of English identity"; Rieder 2021, p. 12. This is obviously different from constitutional identity, construed as a set of written or unwritten constitutional principles, values or doctrines used by judges in their case law or otherwise informing policies and laws (in the UK, it may be parliamentary sovereignty).

7.2.3 Paving the Way Towards an EU Constitutional Identity

Ambitious as it is to conceptualise and define constitutional identity in broad terms, and determine in what it differs from similar (yet not identical) doctrines like national identity, the task is further complicated in the specific EU context by a number of additional reasons. First, as noted, by its own definition constitutional identity presupposes the existence of a constitution, something that is not so obvious within the EU, where a traditionally codified constitution is still lacking. Second, because the EU is a multilevel supranational entity composed of sovereign states with their own constitutional and national identities, these can (and often do) compete with the broad EU collective and/or constitutional identity. Finally, while lots of discussion has occurred at doctrinal, judicial and theoretical levels on national and constitutional identity within the various EU member states, very little thinking has been devoted to the topic of an overarching EU constitutional identity.

Dissecting these elements further, the first tension (to what extent we can talk of a EU constitutional identity absent a properly codified EU constitution) can be easily demystified. As Van der Schyff, among others, has noted, although the attempt to draft a EU constitution has failed, this does not mean that the EU lacks its own constitutional order.[35] In fact, a codified constitution "is not a precondition for the existence of constitutional law" as testified for example by the United Kingdom,[36] which lacks a codified constitution but has a very rich constitutional history and law. Within the EU, the various EU Treaties—while technically drafted under international law—are normally regarded as the equivalent of "constitutional charters" perhaps not in form but in substance, as also repeatedly affirmed by the European Court of Justice (as it then was) since the *Les Verts* decision in 1986.[37] Specifically, the two main EU Treaties, the TEU and the TFEU, represent the constitutional-like edifice which includes "a framework for governance comprising institutions and a system of checks and balances, including the protection of fundamental rights."[38] In light of this, this chapter takes the view that the EU Treaties have constitutional nature, and create a supranational, multi-level system of governance.[39]

Once an agreement is reached that the EU has its own—albeit *sui generis*—constitutional order, and therefore it is possible to talk of a EU constitutional identity even absent a codified constitution, the other points of tension identified above can also be easily resolved. As for potential conflicts between constitutional and/or collective/national identities at the EU and member states level, this should be of no concern, once we accept the definition of constitutional identity proposed above, as it admits dissonances, disharmony and conflicts. This point is further elaborated in Sect. 7.3

---

[35] Van der Schyff 2016, p. 235.

[36] *Ibid.*, p. 235.

[37] *Ibid.*, p. 235, citing ECJ, Case 294/83 *Les Verts* [1986] ECR 1365, para 23.

[38] Van der Schyff 2016, p. 235.

[39] This is also confirmed by the fact that universities across Europe offer courses and seminars on EU constitutionalism.

below, along with the third point of tension (the little attention devoted until now to an overarching EU constitutional identity).

7.3   The Principle of Solidarity

This chapter advances the view that solidarity is a fundamental value that contributes to forge the EU constitutional identity. After unpacking in the previous section the concept of constitutional identity, I will now illuminate the principle of solidarity, first in general terms, and then as an aspirational constitutional principle. It shall be pointed out, however, that an extensive scholarship already exists that explores the many facets of solidarity in the EU context.[40] My aspiration is thus not to revisit this vast literature in great detail. Rather, I would like to briefly point to the pervasiveness of solidarity in the EU legal framework (as well as in the constitutional architecture of a selection of member states) through a textual analysis of Treaty provisions and a brief engagement with the case law of the Court of Justice of the European Union ("CJEU"), with the intention to prove how it contributes to forging the EU constitutional identity.

7.3.1   Solidarity in General

Solidarity is a universal value, a virtue, a meta-principle that has had various meanings, synonyms and conceptualisations throughout history. It is multi- and cross-disciplinary, and displays moral, ethical, political as well as legal and constitutional implications. The semantic richness and polymorphism of solidarity, as well as its epistemological link with other concepts (such as friendship, charity, fraternity) and with legal principles (loyalty, cooperation, cohesion) makes it difficult to define the concept, and invites a distinction between solidarity and close but not synonymic notions.[41] Like constitutional identity, solidarity is thus also a fluid and elusive concept presenting several conceptual and normative challenges.

First, as I have extensively explained elsewhere,[42] it is possible to distinguish between moral and legal solidarity. In fact, as Ottmann posits, moral solidarity can be construed as a voluntary charitable act premised on mutual assistance or philanthropy.[43] Rieder refers to this as an expression of "altruistic solidarity" as used

---

[40] In addition to the literature specifically cited in this chapter, what follows is a rather preliminary, non-exhaustive list of scholarly work—in several languages—on solidarity in the EU: Biondi et al. 2018; Borger 2020; Boutayeb 2011; Kadelbach 2014; Karagiannis 2007; Lahusen and Grasso 2018; Ross and Borgmann-Prebil 2010; Stiernø 2004.

[41] For a short history of the concept of solidarity in general, see Liedman 2020, p. 11. For a Durkheimer, Weberian and Habermasian conceptualisation of solidarity, see Schiek 2020, p. 260.

[42] Arban 2017, p. 243, 2021, pp. 109–110.

[43] Ottmann 2008, p. 40; Eijsbouts and Nederlof 2011, p. 172; Arban 2017, p. 243, 2021, p. 109.

especially in a religious context.[44] Legal solidarity, on the other hand, could be understood as an "obligatory act based on legal rights and duties"[45] although always interspersed with sentiments of mutual assistance.[46] This type of solidarity is based on reciprocity,[47] or *do ut des*. It is precisely its reciprocal character that distinguishes legal solidarity from other notions such as charity, philanthropy or altruism. In other words, solidarity is not the same as altruism or similar concepts,[48] although some common sentiments are shared: in fact, solidarity "refers to the common exercise of interests, for example in risk prevention or in a political struggle, while altruism finds its roots in an individual attitude which is totally unselfish."[49] Egoism is thus key in distinguishing between solidarity and altruism, since the former "has many egoistic traits" whereas altruism "is characterized by a total lack of egoism."[50] As Rieder further posits, reciprocal solidarity is a form of cooperation and therefore requires mutual trust.[51]

However, even in this legal acceptation, solidarity takes different nuances depending on whether it is ingrained in international law, private law, constitutional law, or federalism theory.[52] For example, in international law, solidarity is intertwined with the French concept of *fraternité* which, together with *liberté* and *égalité*, represented epitome values of the French revolutionary political engineering.[53] Such values were then embedded in the French constitution and later in the Universal Declaration of Human Rights.[54] As some scholar has suggested, solidarity in international law could be construed as the legalisation of fraternity.[55] In private law, on the other hand, solidarity comes from the Latin word *in solidum* connoting a shared responsibility for the whole common objective (*solidum*) and not just the care for an individual. Roman civil law institutionalised the "obligation in *solidum*" implying that each debtor owed an identical thing to that to which his co-obligor is held.[56]

In its public law understanding, which interests us more closely, solidarity can be considered as "an aspirational principle and all-encompassing concept", one that promotes "equality, social rights, well-being, and friendship" among and between constitutional actors.[57] More specifically, solidarity can be (implicitly or explicitly)

---

[44] Rieder 2021, pp. 5–6.

[45] Ottmann 2008, pp. 39–40.

[46] Arban 2017, p. 243, 2021, p. 109.

[47] Rieder 2021, p. 5.

[48] Hilpold 2015, p. 261.

[49] *Ibid.*, p. 262.

[50] *Ibid.*, p. 262.

[51] Rieder 2021, p. 11.

[52] Arban 2017, p. 243, 2021, p. 109.

[53] Gonthier 2000, p. 572.

[54] *Ibid.*; Arban 2021, p. 109.

[55] Carlassare 2016, p. 47, fn. 8, also reported in Arban 2021, p. 109.

[56] Arban 2021, p. 109.

[57] Arban 2021, p. 101.

spelled out in welfare provisions or in provisions on socio-economic rights.[58] Likewise, the spirit of solidarity can penetrate provisions on natural or man-made disasters and emergencies, or terrorist attacks.[59] Also, solidarity may shape the responsibility of an individual in her interactions with the community: for example, political solidarity entails a duty to vote, while socio-economic solidarity implies a duty to obtain proper education, work or contribute to public expenses.[60] Finally, solidarity assumes a very unique hue in federal theory, where it inspires equalisation provisions whose purpose is to curb socio-economic imbalances among territories.[61] More broadly, solidarity in federal theory draws upon the German doctrine of *Bundestreue*, whose literal meaning is fidelity or loyalty to the federal compact:[62] in this specific meaning, federal solidarity implies a duty of the various layers of government to respect the federal character of the state, with its division of powers and responsibilities and the duty to work harmoniously and constructively together.

7.3.2 Solidarity in the EU Treaties

The Union is founded on the values of respect for human dignity, freedom, democracy, equality, the rule of law and respect for human rights, including the rights of persons belonging to minorities. These values are common to the Member States in a society in which pluralism, non-discrimination, tolerance, justice, solidarity and equality between women and men prevail [Article 2 TEU] (emphasis added)

After dissecting the notion of solidarity in broad terms, it is now time to sharpen focus on solidarity within the communitarian *acquis*.

As is well known, what is now the European Union emerged in the early 1950s as a community of six original states, who agreed to come together for economic purposes to try and rebuild a common social and economic fabric that the Second World War had devastated. The need to strengthen solidarity among states and people was an absolute necessity. Solidarity has thus informed the European project since its early stages, as confirmed also by the Schuman Declaration of 1950 which already talked about the creation of "de facto solidarity" in Europe, and also of "solidarity in production" for coal and steel.[63] For this reason, the principle was recognised by the original European Court of Justice as paramount in what was then the legal architecture of the

---

[58] Ottmann 2008, p. 39; Arban 2017, p. 244, 2021, p. 109.

[59] Arban 2017, pp. 244–245, 2021, p. 109.

[60] Arban 2021, pp. 109–110.

[61] *Ibid.*, p. 110.

[62] Arban 2017, p. 245, 2021, p. 110.

[63] Hilpold 2015, p. 258, citing Schuman's exact words "L'Europe ne se fera pas d'un coup ni dans une construction d'ensemble: elle se fera pour des réalisations concrètes, créant d'abord une solidarité de fait."

European Economic Communities.[64] The Treaty of Lisbon, chronologically the last significant addition to the EU treaty system, has strengthened the notion of solidarity as also embedded in the TEU.

Within the various EU Treaties and legal documents, solidarity is referred to both as a "principle" and as an "objective".[65] Besides its entrenchment in Article 2 TEU (as reproduced above), solidarity has come to occupy a prominent role in the communitarian acquis. First, the preamble of the TEU explicitly aspires to deepen the "solidarity between their peoples" while Article 3(3) TEU mandates that the EU shall—among other things—"promote ... solidarity between generations and ... among Member States." Article 3(5) TEU invites the EU to "contribute to ... solidarity and mutual respect among peoples". In Title V TEU on the Union's external action and on the common foreign and security policy, solidarity plays a prominent role: for example, Article 21(1) mandates that solidarity as a fundamental principle shall guide the "Union's action on the international scene"; pursuant to Article 24(2), the EU shall develop "mutual political solidarity among Member States"; likewise, Article 24(3) mandates that each member state shall "support the Union's external and security policy actively and unreservedly in a spirit of loyalty and mutual solidarity"; also, member states shall "work together to enhance and develop their mutual political solidarity"; finally, Articles 31(1) and 32 make reference to solidarity among member states when acting in the EU scene.

The preamble of the TFEU also emphasises how solidarity "binds Europe and the overseas countries", but a very interesting provision is enshrined in Title V on Freedom, Security and Justice: here, Article 67(2) posits that the whole EU common policy on asylum, immigration and external border control shall be based on solidarity among member states. Article 80 mandates that solidarity and the principle of fair sharing of responsibility between member states shall govern the policies of the EU in the same area.

As mandated by Article 122(1) on economic and monetary policy, a solidarity spirit among member states shall be the guiding principle for the Council in decisions on economic measures, particularly in the energy sector. In the section devoted to the Union's external action, Title VII contains a so-called solidarity clause among the EU and member states in the event of a terrorist attack or of a natural or man-made disaster. Finally, Protocol (No 28) on Economic, Social and Territorial Cohesion recalls Article 3 TEU and its objectives to promote economic, social and territorial cohesion and solidarity between Member States.

Also the Charter of Fundamental Rights of the European Union contains references to solidarity. First, the preamble reinforces the idea that solidarity is one of the fundamental values on which the Union rests. Chapter IV is devoted to solidarity, and under this heading several rights are protected (*e.g.* workers' right to information and

---

[64] See European Court of Justice, *Commission v France*, judgment of 10 December 1969, para 16, ECLI:EU:C:1969:68: "The solidarity which is at the basis of these obligations as of the whole of the Community system in accordance with the undertaking provided for in Article 5 of the Treaty ..." as cited in Hilpold 2015, p. 258 (fn. 1).

[65] *Ibid.*

consultation; right of collective bargaining and action; right of access to placement services, etc.).

The scope of solidarity in the EU Treaties is further supported by the provision ingrained in Article 7 TEU, which provides for a special procedure to be followed in case of risk of a breach—or actual breach—by a member state of one or more of the values referred to in Article 2 TEU. Once such determination has been made following all the procedures detailed in Article 7, some of the rights deriving from the application of the treaties to the member state in question can be suspended. Normatively, Article 7 provides for a preventive and a sanctioning mechanism. The two scenarios are not formally linked with each other: preventive sanctions do not necessarily have to come first, and the same member state could be sanctioned for a clear risk of a serious breach and/or a serious and persistent breach.[66] Since 2009, the Commission has been repeatedly confronted with critical events in some EU countries and it has addressed them by exerting political pressure, as well as launching infringement proceedings in case of violations of EU law. Incidentally, a question could be asked whether this mechanism would be appropriate to enforce the principle of solidarity. As previously mentioned, solidarity occupies a preeminent position in the communitarian legal structure and acquis. This relevant status is legally materialised with the inclusion of solidarity among the fundamental values listed in Article 2 TEU: therefore, the basic normative requirement to engage the proceedings of Article 7 TEU is probably fulfilled.

Solidarity within EU law is mostly characterised by a "strongly reciprocal nature, a do ut des character".[67] However, when member states "are required to act prevailingly in an altruistic way and no reciprocity is in sight, the 'island of solidarity' is in danger of being washed away as is the case with refugee and asylum policy",[68] as further discussed in Sect. 7.3 below.

In any event, as maintained by Hilpold, while EU Treaties contain a constellation of references to solidarity, at the end of the day the exact meaning of this principle depends on "the specific circumstances of the sector in which it shall apply and from the period of time to which the examination refers."[69]

7.3.3 Solidarity in the CJEU Case Law

As often happens with similar broad-reaching principles, one of the problems of solidarity is its justiciability. In fact, the CJEU has generally been "unwilling to develop a general understanding of solidarity as a discrete ground for European

---

[66] Communication from the Commission to the Council and the European Parliament on Article 7 of the Treaty on European Union. Respect for and promotion of the values on which the Union is based: COM (2003) 606.

[67] Hilpold 2015, p. 284.

[68] *Ibid.*, p. 284.

[69] *Ibid.*, p. 284.

obligations."[70] For example, in a recent string of decisions on responses to the Euro crisis, the CJEU has refused to offer any interpretation of the "meaning or scope of solidarity as a legal principle."[71] Also in the field of asylum law (particularly, Article 80 TFEU), the CJEU has refrained from using solidarity to decide cases concerning the Dublin Regulation.[72] The decrease in the importance of transnational solidarity in the CJEU case law has been pointed out by Rieder in reference to a string of decisions such as *Grzelczyk, Förster* and *Dano.*[73] In a thorough survey of the CJEU's case law engagement with solidarity, Schiek has compellingly proved how the CJEU has until now missed the opportunity to clarify the many hues of solidarity as a EU constitutional principle,[74] thus failing to develop a "consistent approach" towards the principle which, in his opinion, could be used in several fields, from EU citizenship to social policy, to antidiscrimination law.[75]

7.3.4 A Brief Comparative Survey of (Constitutional) Solidarity in Some EU Member States

To a certain extent, the pervasiveness of solidarity as a fundamental principle of the EU architecture can be buttressed by the prominence that the principle has in some of the EU member states. For example, in jurisdictions like Italy, Spain and Germany, the principle of solidarity could also be considered part of their constitutional identity, a constitutional principle that is not only embedded, but one that has been elaborated upon by courts and developed by constitutional scholarship, and informing all relationships among state and local actors: as such, solidarity does not

---

[70] Linden-Retek 2021, p. 511.

[71] *Ibid.* The author cites the following: European Court of Justice, *Thomas Pringle v. Government of Ireland and Others*, judgment of 27 November 2012, ECLI:EU:C:2012:756, paras 142–144; European Court of Justice, *Peter Gauweiler et al v. Deutscher Bundestag*, judgment of 16 June 2015, ECLI:EU:C:2015:400; Linden-Retek 2021, p. 512.

[72] Linden-Retek 2021, p. 512. See for example European Court of Justice, *Zuheyr Frayeh Halaf v Darzhavna agentsia za bezhantsite pri Ministerskia savet*, judgment of 30 May 2013, ECLI:EU:C:2013:342, para 25; European Court of Justice, joined Cases C-643/15 and C-647/15 *Slovak Republic and Hungary v. Council of the European Union*, judgment of 6 September 2017, ECLI:EU:C:2017:631, para 253; European Court of Justice, Joined Cases C-411/10 and C-493/10 *N.S. v. Sec. of State for the Home Department*, judgment of 21 December 2011, ECLI:EU:C:2011:865, para 87 (all cited in Linden-Retek 2021, p. 512).

[73] Rieder 2021, p. 3. The specific cases mentioned are: European Court of Justice, *Rudy Grzelczyk v Centre public d'aide sociale d'Ottignie-Louvain-la-Neuve* of 20 September 2001, ECLI:EU:C:2001:458; European Court of Justice, *Jacqueline Förster v Hoofddirectie van de Informatie Beheer Groep*, judgment of 18 November 2008, ECLI:EU:C:2008:630; Court of Justice of the European Union, *Elisabeta Dano and Florin Dano v Jobcenter Leipzig*, judgment of 11 November 2014, ECLI:EU:C:2014:2358.

[74] Schiek 2020, p. 297.

[75] *Ibid.*, p. 299.

assume only a moral, aspirational gloss, but it can be considered a fully enforceable legal value.

As an example, in the framework represented by the 1948 Italian constitution, solidarity immediately acquired a prominent place among the fundamental principles of the constitutional edifice. Solidarity is expressly spelled out as such in Article 2[76] and Article 119 on fiscal federalism;[77] however, both the Italian Constitutional Court and most constitutional scholars acknowledge that solidarity infuses several other constitutional provisions.[78] It thus occupies a prominent place in the constitutional system, and it also informs the relationship between the central state and regional governments when it comes to fiscal issues,[79] since Article 119 requires the central government to play a pivotal role in assisting disadvantaged regions and contain the imbalances between richer and poorer areas through equalization payments.

Also the Spanish constitution of 1978 offers interesting insights into solidarity. Article 2 mandates for a general solidarity duty among the nationalities and regions that compose the Spanish nation, while Article 138(1) postulates how to implement the solidarity principle of Article 2.[80] Solidarity as entrenched in Article 2 has been defined as a principle of territorial organization of the state in association with the principles of autonomy and unity, and the point of balance between centripetal and centrifugal forces.[81] According to Alonso de Antonio, the constitutional principles of unity, autonomy and solidarity represent the main pillars on which the autonomic state is premised.[82] Article 156(1) of the constitution also mentions solidarity in relation to fiscal federalism and the financial autonomy of the self-governing communities.

---

[76] Article 2 provides that "The Republic recognises and protects the inviolable rights of the person, both as an individual and in the social groups where human personality is expressed, and expects that the fundamental duties of political, economic and social solidarity be fulfilled."

[77] The first two paragraphs of Article 119 Const. mandate that local governments shall enjoy financial autonomy of revenues and expenses, and shall set and levy taxes and collect revenues of their own; furthermore, regions and other local entities share in the tax revenues related to their respective territories. Article 119(3) introduces equalization payments, mandating that national legislation shall provide for equalization funds (with no allocation constraints) for territories having a lower per-capita taxable capacity. Article 119(5) provides that the central government shall allocate supplementary resources and adopt special measures in favour of specific regions or other local governments to promote economic development, social cohesion and solidarity, to reduce economic and social imbalances, to foster the exercise of individual rights or to achieve goals other than those pursued in the ordinary implementation of their functions.

[78] Besides Article 2, the spirit of solidarity infuses provisions on the right to work (Articles 4 and 36(1) Const.); the right to an equal salary treatment for working men and women for the same job (Article 37 Const.); the right to welfare and/or support services to citizens unable to work (Article 38 Const.); the right of the family (Articles 29 and 31 Const.); the right to health (Article 32(1) Const.); and the right to education (Article 34 Const.).

[79] Arban 2021, p. 101.

[80] Article 138(1) mandates that "[t]he State guarantees the effective implementation of the principle of solidarity proclaimed in Section 2 of the Constitution, by endeavouring to establish a fair and adequate economic balance between the different areas of the Spanish territory and taking into special consideration the circumstances pertaining to those which are islands."

[81] Fernández Segado 2012, pp. 154–155; Alonso de Antonio 1984, p. 32.

[82] Alonso de Antonio 1984, p. 46.

Article 158(2) provides for the solidarity-based tool of compensation funds to redress "interterritorial economic imbalances" and implement solidarity. Like Italy, besides the provisions where solidarity is expressly entrenched, the Spanish constitution also contains sections where solidarity is implicit.[83]

Finally, the German Basic Law ("GG") also contains interesting solidarity-related features. Similarly to other federal states, Articles 107(1)(2) contain provisions on distribution of tax revenue, financial equalisation among *Länder* and supplementary grants that can be directly linked to solidarity values.[84] Furthermore, Article 35 details the legal and administrative type of support that *Länder* shall offer to each other in the event of a disaster. Article 91(1) also deals with solidarity-based provisions in case of internal emergency. Similarly to the previous countries examined, the GG also carves out a well-articulated notion of solidarity, one that binds not only the central institution with the periphery, but also the *Länder* among themselves, although it does so primarily in the event of an adversity.

To conclude, with its roots in Roman civil law, and further developments in French constitutional law as an expansion of principles like equality, fraternity, and liberty, solidarity is now solidly ingrained in the EU acquis and as a constitutional and aspirational principle in several EU constitutions, where it also contributes to shape the constitutional identity of such jurisdictions. The next section sharpens focus on the core argument made in this chapter, braiding together the notions of solidarity and constitutional identity in the specific EU context.

7.4 The Principle of Solidarity and EU Constitutional Identity

In this last section, I elaborate on two key claims made in this chapter: first, the principle of solidarity as ingrained in the EU Treaties is a fundamental value that contributes to forge the EU constitutional identity; and, second, by construing solidarity as part the EU constitutional identity, it is possible to invigorate the EU integration and curb the many tensions that cross the Union.

---

[83] See *ex multis* the provisions protecting basic socio-economic rights (*e.g.* the right to employment (Article 35); socio-economic and legal protection of the family (Article 39); social security system (Article 41); health protection (Article 43)). Article 30 enshrines the right and duties of Spanish citizens to defend Spain as a solidarity-based principle which also includes a duty in cases of serious risks, catastrophes or public calamity.

[84] Vega García 2014, p. 249.

7.4.1 A Case for Solidarity Shaping EU Constitutional Identity

As anticipated in Sect. 7.1 above, very little intellectual and scholarly discussion has occurred within the EU about an EU constitutional identity. This immediately brings to light an interesting contradiction, since within EU member states, apex courts have often resorted to the doctrine of constitutional identity,[85] where constitutional identity claims have been used both as a "shield to protect national constitutional identities against further European integration" and as a "sword to fend off the authority of EU law over a Member State jurisdiction".[86] This approach has been facilitated by the protection of national identity as recognised by Article 4(2) TEU mandating, in relevant part, that [t]he Union shall respect the equality of Member States before the Treaties as well as their national identities, inherent in their fundamental structures, political and constitutional, inclusive of regional and local self-government.

To be sure, in the years when the (failed) EU constitution was being drafted, theorists and scholars had engaged in discussions on matters of EU identity, since the supranational constitution that was under preparation represented the ideal occasion for such intellectual exchange. Most importantly for our discussion, the EU experience afforded the basis for a reflection on the possibility of sketching a *supranational* constitutional identity:[87] this was unprecedented, because until that moment constitutional identity had been discussed as a matter of domestic constitutional law only. As remarked by Jacobsohn, the issue in Europe was not so much "how extra-national precepts and principles [could] be integrated into the jurisprudence of nations possessing unique histories and ways of doing things, but how—or whether— the distinctive political and legal cultures of a diverse group of nations [could] be incorporated within an over-arching framework of international governance such as to create a constitutional identity for the new entity as a whole."[88]

The focus of such debates, however, was mainly the extent to which an EU constitution would contribute to create and shape an EU *collective* identity, and not so much the formation and existence of a EU *constitutional* identity. For example, von Bogdandy explored issues of EU collective identity, asking whether the EU needed a common EU identity to shape EU citizens, and whether a constitution would help in that endeavour.[89] Grimm asked similar questions, that is, whether the EU constitution could "foster the integration of EU citizens."[90]

As part of this intellectual engagement, it was actually Rosenfeld who explored the issue of how an EU constitutional identity would look like.[91] On the one hand, he

---

[85] Fabbrini and Sajó 2019, p. 457.

[86] Faraguna 2017, p. 1631.

[87] Rosenfeld 2012, p. 774.

[88] Jacobsohn 2010, p. 114.

[89] Von Bogdandy 2005, p. 295.

[90] Grimm 1995, p. 282.

[91] Rosenfeld 2012, p. 774.

remarked how several values and factors already existed that could shape a common EU identity: "common origins, common values, common destiny, and a common differentiation from American identity."[92] On the other hand, he wondered whether such values could actually serve to "sustain a viable constitutional identity".[93] In the end, Rosenfeld suggested that an EU constitutional identity "could easily ground its narrative of origins on a repudiation of Nazism and Soviet communism and on the need to create a political order that would minimize the chances of any return to tyrannical totalitarian rule."[94]

From the perspective of constitutional identity, Rosenfeld continues, origins partially depend on negation, although negation alone is not enough to create "a distinct image of origins".[95] Consequently, while important, the rejection of both Nazism and Communism alone was not enough, in and of itself, to explain the need to build a supranational or transnational constitutional order coexisting with several other national constitutional regimes.[96] For Rosenfeld, then, the EU constitutional identity could be grounded in the repudiation of Nazism and Soviet communism, followed by an act of reincorporation into a "transnational multiethnic order".[97] He further contended that elements such as a community of values, which were featuring in the Treaty Constitution, could "well figure in a European constitutional identity at some point in the future", but at that point, they sounded "hollow", because they remained "abstract and largely generic"[98] (Rosenfeld was writing at a time when the EU appeared to be at a "constitution-making stage" so it was difficult to clearly identify which values would forge the specific EU constitutional identity).[99]

More recently, Van der Schyff reverted to the question of an EU constitutional identity, suggesting that Article 2 TEU—which as noted includes solidarity—"must be central to efforts at understanding and articulating this identity, as the provision clearly aims at grounding the entire constitutional order."[100]

Drawing on these intuitions, I thus purport that, in light of its pervasiveness in the EU Treaties and as a value that has inspired the building of EU integration, the principle of solidarity could be considered as part and parcel of the constitutional identity of the European Union. As such, solidarity may represent the element that bridges together the rejection or negation of the past (represented by the horrors of Nazism and Communism) with the creation of a Union solidly grounded on a multi-ethnic and diverse order, as suggested by Rosenfeld.

This also fits—at least partially—into the thick conceptualisation of constitutional identity offered in Sect. 7.1 above: solidarity could be seen as contributing

---

[92] *Ibid.*, p. 774.

[93] *Ibid.*, p. 774.

[94] *Ibid.*, pp. 774–775.

[95] *Ibid.*, p. 775.

[96] *Ibid.*, p. 775.

[97] Rosenfeld 2005, p. 329.

[98] Rosenfeld 2012, p. 775.

[99] Rosenfeld 2005, p. 318.

[100] Van der Schyff 2016, p. 235.

to forging the EU constitutional identity as it is a political aspiration and commitment expressive of the EU's past; it is also a fluid and changeable concept, emerging dialogically and manifesting itself differently in different settings, as we saw from the holistic approach to solidarity as ingrained in the EU *acquis*. In fact, in the EU Treaties solidarity is the animating force that inspires all types of dynamics: among citizens, among member states, among member states and central institutions, and between the Union and the international community at large. Such constitutional identity forged by solidarity has the function to deal with constitutional disharmonies and dissonances represented by competing national identities and by a transnational multiethnic order composed of several nation states with competing socio-economic and political agendas, but all united in repudiating a totalitarian past. As such, solidarity could help reconcile diversity and social cohesion within the variegated EU context, thus cementing the idea of unity in diversity, which is the EU motto.[101] This seems to be the position maintained also by Hilpold, when asserting that "European integration itself can be seen as an expression of insights into the merits of solidarity. After the Second World War peoples in Europe realized that a solidarity integration project might greatly reduce the risk of falling back into conflict and war and creating a new sense of cohesion."[102] I further elaborate on this idea in the section below. However, for solidarity to really become the beacon of an EU constitutional identity, a more substantive engagement of the CJEU on this matter would greatly help. To this end, it was only very recently that the CJEU made a direct reference to Article 2 TEU and EU identity (but not to an EU *constitutional* identity) in cases C-156/21 and C-157/21. In the first case, the CJEU alleged that "Article 2 TEU is not merely a statement of policy guidelines or intentions, but contains values which … are an integral part of the very identity of the European Union as a common legal order, values which are given concrete expression in principles containing legally binding obligations for the Member States."[103] The same idea of Article 2 TEU containing values that express the very identity of the EU as a legal order is replicated in the second case.[104] The court, however, does not elaborate any further on this concept of EU identity.

7.4.2 Bridging the Gap: Solidarity as an EU Constitutional Identity to Invigorate Integration and Curb Tensions

One final question remains to be addressed: which purpose would serve the identification of solidarity as contributing to forge an EU constitutional identity, separate from

---

[101] Von Bogdandy 2005, p. 310.

[102] Hilpold 2015, p. 263.

[103] Court of Justice of the European Union, *Hungary v European Parliament and Council of the European Union*, judgment of 16 February 2022, ECLI:EU:C:2022:97, paras 232 and 127.

[104] Court of Justice of the European Union, *Republic of Poland v European Parliament and Council of the European Union*, judgment of 16 February 2022, ECLI:EU:C:2022:98, paras 145, 264, 268.

the various constitutional identities at the level of member states? Debating issues of constitutional identity might appear to most as an abstract or futile endeavour of little practical use, interesting perhaps only to constitutional theorists. Yet, I maintain that reflecting on an EU constitutional identity is far from being a pointless exercise: rather, it would greatly help assessing the very nature and purpose of the integration process, for member states and peoples alike, especially at this challenging time, with the EU project under threat on many different fronts.

Section 7.2 above illuminated the various meanings that solidarity assumes as a legal/constitutional principle. Such semantic richness and polymorphism have been well transplanted in the EU Treaties, thus justifying the relevance and maturity that the principle has acquired at EU level. In fact, as previously suggested, the entire EU legal framework is interspersed with solidarity-based provisions, especially after the modifications brought by the Treaty of Lisbon.[105]

Taking solidarity seriously as part and parcel of constitutional identity—of this set of values that infuse the EU constitutional edifice—might help invigorate integration and curb the tensions that are threatening the EU project, and that reflect the endemic tensions emerging from contextual differences and dissonances. The economic crisis started in 2008, the migration crisis, Brexit and other withdrawal threats coming from various directions, and of course the COVID-19 pandemic and the Ukraine-Russia war are all indicators of conflicts within the continent causing disharmonies and tensions. Solidarity as a principle has been included in the Treaties (and in many member states constitutions) exactly as a tool to combat such problems. Solidarity as part and parcel of an EU constitutional identity can and should therefore represent the dialogical mediation essential to face such crises, as was the original intention that led to the entrenchment of the principle in the communitarian acquis.

As an example, the current migration and asylum crises could be the point of departure to start building a more solidarity-based system. Here, two types of solidarity are in tension. On the one hand, a more charitable form of solidarity, one that invites EU institutions to welcome and help people experiencing dramatic circumstances and in search of a better life. On the other hand, a more "legal" form of solidarity, one that binds member states in offering this help. As many scholars have observed, in spite of treaty provisions, the current asylum policies infringe upon solidarity, in that they overburden certain member states only, as an effect of the Dublin Regulations.[106] In fact, as is known, Mediterranean countries are more exposed to requests for asylum by refugees than northern countries, a situation that is further aggravated by the fact that "asylum applications have to be treated in the state where the asylum seeker

---

[105] Corre 2014, p. 2.

[106] Küçük 2016, p. 448; Hilpold 2015, p. 272. It shall be recalled that, as explained by Linden-Retek, according to the Dublin Regulation, requests of asylum are allocated among member states based on several criteria, from family unity to place of application. However, in case of mass migration as experienced in the EU in recent years, the main allocation criterion has been the first country of irregular entry; Linden-Retek 2021, p. 519. Consequently, especially for migratory flows coming from Africa, the most exposed countries have been Mediterranean member states, and particularly Italy.

first enters the EU".[107] Although there is awareness of the problem, a real solidarity among EU Member States in this area has not been attained yet.[108]

Perhaps imbuing solidarity with a more concrete and practical meaning in this context, and insisting on the importance of such value for a general EU constitutional identity, could assist in the effort to create better policies reflecting the solidarity-based principle of fairly sharing responsibilities among member states.

Second, reflecting on what is the true constitutional identity of the EU could be used to counter the use of national constitutional identity discourses at the level of member states which, as explained *supra*, is often used as shield against EU legislation by domestic courts. The dangers of such an abuse might potentially lead to the disaggregation of the EU.[109] In this sense, an EU constitutional identity premised on solidarity might help mending or fixing such centrifugal threats and avert further withdrawals from the Union after Brexit.

Finally, the EU is often described as a multi-level supranational system that displays several federal-like features. As noted in Sect. 7.2, in order to function successfully, federal systems are premised on *federal solidarity*, a doctrine mandating that all levels of government respect each other, the assigned areas of jurisdiction, and collaborate together for the common good. In other words, even if they have their own constitutionally entrenched autonomy, constituent units of the member states are not isolated entities, but are part of a common project and are bound by this duty to respect and be faithful to the federal bond. In a federalising order like the EU, solidarity could thus acquire a new gloss as federal solidarity, part and parcel of the EU constitutional identity.

7.5 Conclusion

The EU originated as a common market and as an economic community. The forging of an ever-closer Union occurred over time and incrementally; but such a project also required the building of a European community, identity and constitutional order. Echoing Van der Schyff, "the EU is not simply a constellation of states amounting to no more than the sum of its components, but a constellation with its own distinct constitutional order."[110] However, in spite of such efforts, many citizens still perceive the EU as a distant, complex and overtly bureaucratic apparatus of very little use to them. The encroachment of EU law in the jurisdiction of many member states does not help improve such negative perception, as the calls for withdrawal from the Union testify.

In this chapter, I suggested that the principle of solidarity could be considered as informing the EU constitutional identity. In advancing this claim, I proposed a

---

[107] Hilpold 2015, p. 272.
[108] Hilpold 2015, p. 272.
[109] Fabbrini and Sajó 2019, p. 457.
[110] Van der Schyff 2016, p. 236.

definition of constitutional identity that draws on the conceptualisations offered by Jacobsohn and Rosenfeld, and then charted the various meanings of solidarity as a moral and legal principle. While solidarity might not be the only element infusing the constitutional identity of the EU, the pervasiveness of this principle in the EU Treaties, coupled with its entrenchment in a number of member states constitutions, suggests that it represents a foundational element of EU identity. Not only is solidarity enshrined in Article 2 TEU, but it also enjoys the special protection prescribed by Article 7 TEU and it appears in many other sections of the EU Treaties (in addition to being embedded in many constitutions of EU member states).

In suggesting solidarity as an element of the EU constitutional identity, I also focused on the current humanitarian, political and democratic crises threatening the Union. The conclusion puts into practice the principle of solidarity proposed in the paper and its potentialities to tackle the various crises, thus contributing to balance diversity and social cohesion within the EU. This proposal offers an alternative way out of the existential crises that is affecting the EU, at the same time offering an opportunity to shed light on intricate principles such as solidarity and constitutional identity in the EU.

References

Alonso de Antonio J A (1984) El principio de solidaridad en el estado autonomico. Sus manifestaciones juridicas. Revista de Derecho Político 21: 31–81

Arban E (2017) Exploring the Principle of (Federal) Solidarity. Review of Constitutional Studies 22: 241–260

Arban E (2021) Italy: The Principle of Solidarity as a Principle of Equality. In: Belser E M et al (eds) The Principle of Equality in Diverse States. Reconciling Autonomy with Equal Rights and Opportunities. Brill Nijhoff, Leiden/Boston, pp 101–129

Biondi A, Dagilyte E, Küçük E (eds) (2018) Solidarity in EU Law: Legal Principle in the Making. Edward Elgar, Cheltenham

Borger V (2020) The Currency of Solidarity. Cambridge University Press, Cambridge, UK

Boutayeb C (ed) (2011) La Solidarité dans l'Union Européenne. Éléments Constitutionnels et Matériels. Dalloz, Paris

Carlassare L (2016) Solidarietà: un progetto politico. Costituzionalismo.it 1: 45–67

Corre P (2014) La conception de la solidarité entre États membres par la Cour de Justice de l'Union européenne, obstacle à la fédéralisation? Paper presented at the World Congress of the International Association of Constitutional Law held in Oslo, Norway, 16–20 June 2014

Eijsbouts W T, Nederlof D (2011) Editorial: Rethinking Solidarity in the EU, from Fact to Social Contract. European Constitutional Law Review 7: 169–172

Fabbrini F, Sajó A (2019) The Dangers of Constitutional Identity. European Law Journal 25: 457–473

Faraguna P (2017) Constitutional Identity in the EU – A Shield or a Sword? German Law Journal 18: 1617–1640

Fernández Segado F (2012) La Solidaridad Como Principio Constitucional. Teoria e Realidad Constitucional 30: 139–181

Gonthier C D (2000) Liberty, Equality, Fraternity: The Forgotten Leg of the Trilogy, or Fraternity: The Unspoken Third Pillar of Democracy. McGill Law Journal 45: 567–589

Grimm D (1995) Does Europe Need a Constitution? European Law Journal 1: 282–302

Hilpold P (2015) Understanding Solidarity Within EU Law: An Analysis of the 'Islands of Solidarity' with Particular Regard to Monetary Union. Yearbook of European Law 34:257–285
Jacobsohn G (2010) Constitutional Identity. Harvard University Press, Cambridge/London
Kadelbach S (ed) (2014) Solidarität als Europaische Rechtsprinzip? Nomos, Baden-Baden
Karagiannis N (ed) (2007) European Solidarity. Liverpool University Press, Liverpool
Küçük E (2016) The Principle of Solidarity and Fairness in Sharing Responsibility: More than Window Dressing. European Law Journal 22: 448–469
Lahusen C, Grasso M (eds) (2018) Solidarity in Europe. Citizens' Responses in Times of Crisis. Palgrave Macmillan, London
Liedman S (2020) Solidarity. A Short History from the Concept's Beginnings to the Present Situation. In: Krunke H et al (eds) Transnational Solidarity. Concept, Challenges and Opportunities. Cambridge University Press, pp 11–21
Linden-Retek P (2021) The Refugees We Are: Solidarity, Asylum, and Critique in the European Constitutional Imagination. German Law Journal 22: 506–533
Ottmann J (2008) The Concept of Solidarity in National and European Law: The Welfare State and the European Social Model. Vienna Journal on International Constitutional Law 2: 36–48
Rieder C (2021) The Relationship Between Solidarity and National Identity. https://papers.ssrn.com/sol3/papers.cfm?abstract_id=3918269
Rosenfeld M (2005) The European Treaty-Constitution and Constitutional Identity: A View from America. The International Journal of Constitutional Law 3: 316–331
Rosenfeld M (2012) Constitutional Identity. In: Rosenfeld M, Sajó A (eds) The Oxford Handbook of Comparative Constitutional Law. Oxford University Press, Oxford, pp 756–776
Ross M, Borgmann-Prebil Y (eds) (2010) Promoting Solidarity in the European Union. Oxford University Press, Oxford
Schiek D (2020) Solidarity in the Case Law of the European Court of Justice. Opportunities Missed? In: Krunke H et al (eds) Transnational Solidarity. Concept, Challenges and Opportunities. Cambridge University Press, pp 252–300
Stiernø S (2004) Solidarity in Europe. The History of an Idea. Cambridge University Press, Cambridge
Van der Schyff G (2016) Exploring Member State and European Union Constitutional Identity. European Public Law 22: 227–242
Vega García A (2014) El principio constitucional de solidaridad interterritorial in España y en Alemania: aplicación y límites. REAF 20: 214–277
Von Bogdandy A (2005) The European Constitution and European Identity: Text and Subtext of the Treaty Establishing a Constitution for Europe. The International Journal of Constitutional Law 3: 295–315

Erika Arban Senior Research Associate, Centre for Comparative Constitutional Studies, Melbourne Law School. E-mail address: erika.arban@unimelb.edu.au. The author gratefully acknowledges the support of the Australian Government through the Australian Research Council (ARC) Laureate Program "Balancing diversity and social cohesion in democratic constitutions" that fully funded this research. The author is also indebted to Antoni Abat Ninet for previous discussions on the topic and for sharing thoughts and ideas, many of which were included in this chapter.

Chapter 8
"United in Diversity"—Homogeneity and Differentiation as Parts of the Union's Constitutional Identity

Robert Böttner

Contents

Abstract The European Union is primarily regarded as a project of common integration aimed at forming an "ever closer union". Indeed, some of the most important architectural elements are those of uniform application of the law and primacy. Policy-making aims at building a common European space and a level playing field for enterprises and citizens. In addition, the Union is based on a set of values shared by its members that require a certain degree of homogeneity. On the other hand, there have always been elements in the law that allowed for legal differentiation. Over time, other elements were added and at least with the introduction of enhanced cooperation as an instrument for differentiation at the level of secondary law, differentiation has outgrown its status as "exception". Today, "united in diversity" is not only the Union's motto; it is also at the core of the Union's very identity.

Keywords Differentiation · Enhanced cooperation · Harmonisation · National identity · Primacy · Safeguard clauses · Unity · Values

R. Böttner (✉)
University of Erfurt, Erfurt, Germany
e-mail: robert.boettner@uni-erfurt.de

© T.M.C. ASSER PRESS and the authors 2023
J. de Poorter et al. (eds.), *European Yearbook of Constitutional Law 2022*,
European Yearbook of Constitutional Law 4,
https://doi.org/10.1007/978-94-6265-595-9_8

8.1 Introduction

The discussion about "identity" in the context of EU law and politics has focused on the identities of the Member States. As set out in this yearbook's issue, the Union itself, however, has over time developed an identity of its own,[1] not least with the development of a European citizenship.[2] The Union's motto—one of its symbols— is "united in diversity".[3] As harmless as these three words may seem, upon closer inspection they are emblematic of the EU's constitutional DNA: On the one hand, the Member States are connected through common legal provisions and a set of shared values on which the Union is founded. They are an indispensable entry requirement for membership in the Union and their upholding is a common undertaking, both internally and internationally. What is more, the Union was founded for the attainment of common objectives, such as the internal market, the Economic and Monetary Union or the Area of Freedom, Security and Justice. Through enhanced integration, the Member States aim to form an ever closer union among the European peoples. The European Union shall be an integrated economic, social, and political space where Union citizens and undertakings enjoy the same rights independent of their origin or place of action.

On the other hand, hardly anyone would argue today that the Union will—much less so should—evolve into a federation in the constitutional sense of the word. Instead, it will remain a (highly integrated) association of sovereign States. This must take account of different attitudes towards integration and the willingness to cooperate. As a prominent obligation, Article 4(2) TEU requires the Union to respect the national identities of the Member States. Pushing uniformist approaches too far can even lead to a member's leaving the Union, as the discussions surrounding Brexit have shown.

The development of the common European project has always tried to strike a balance between sovereignty and integration, reflected first and foremost in unanimity and qualified majority voting in the Council. The widening of the group of Member States and the enhanced depth of integration increasingly leads to situations where a step forward in integration may not be taken—at least not by all Member States. Differentiation and flexible integration may serve as means to overcome deadlocks, but at the expense of uniform integration. Enhanced cooperation under Article 20 TEU, as one emanation of differentiation, may serve as a tool in this respect.

Looking at some aspects of the legal history of European integration, it seems that "those who want more, do more", formulated by the European Commission as one scenario in its White Paper on the future of Europe, is not only a theoretical approach. Against this background, the chapter sets out to explore some elements of "unity" and "diversity" and their interplay as two equally valid strands of the Union's

---

[1] See e.g. Claes 2013, pp. 115 f.

[2] Fromage and De Witte 2021, p. 413.

[3] Proclaimed by the European Parliament on 4 May 2000 and later inserted in Article I-8 of the Constitutional Treaty, now part of a political declaration (no. 52) by 16 Member States annexed to the Treaties.

constitutional identity, taking into account their potentials and risks for the evolution of European integration.

8.2 United …

Unity and uniformity is but one paradigm of European integration in a community of law. It can be found in various areas of the Treaties and in the relationship between the Union and its members. This chapter can highlight but a few, among which are— most prominently—the unity of the legal order (Sect. 8.2.1) and the common values of the Member States founding the Union (Sect. 8.2.2). Apart from the constitutional implications for unity, it extends also to the level of secondary law. The establishment of the internal market (Sect. 8.2.3) is probably the most important aspect of economic integration.

8.2.1 "Legal Unity" and Uniform Interpretation of EU Law

A basic idea of integration within the European Communities and the Union has always been the unity of Union law, *i.e.*, the uniform application of European law standards in all Member States.[4] The objective of establishing an "ever closer Union" has been part of European integration from the outset. The preamble of the ECSC Treaty proclaimed that the Community was founded as an economic community to lay the foundation of a European order intended to secure and maintain peace in Europe and the world.[5] The 1958 EEC Treaty proclaimed the determination of the Contracting Parties "to establish the foundations of an ever closer union among the European peoples" in order to "guarantee steady expansion" and "strengthen the unity of their economies".[6] This wording has remained the same over time and is now found in the Preamble (13th recital) and Article 1(2) TEU. The idea of ever closer union points to the further development of the integration process. It assigns to the Union a mandate for integration in which the supranational *acquis* is safeguarded

---

[4] Cf. Solar 2004, p. 513; Blanke 2013c, para 24; Haratsch 2017, para 2. See in more detail also Sielmann 2020, pp. 284 ff.

[5] Cf. the preamble to the ECSC Treaty: "[…] CONVINCED that the contribution which an organized and vital Europe can bring to civilization is indispensable to the maintenance of peaceful relations; CONSCIOUS of the fact that Europe can be built only by concrete actions which create a real solidarity and by the establishment of common bases for economic development; […] RESOLVED to substitute for historic rivalries a fusion of their essential interests; to establish, by creating an economic community, the foundation of a broad and independent community among peoples long divided by bloody conflicts; and to lay the bases of institutions capable of giving direction to their future common destiny […]."

[6] See the first, fourth and fifth recitals of the preamble to the EEC Treaty.

and extended by removing remaining derogations[7] and by leading to consolidation. After all, the European Community/Union is a legal community which requires uniform application of legal rules.[8] An ever closer union is characterised by the axiom of uniform integration of differing *national* legal orders towards a *European* legal order in which rules and obligations are equally binding for all Member States,[9] but which does not necessarily mean centralisation of power or full harmonisation of legislation.

Though founded as a classical international organisation, the Community evolved into what we now call a supranational organisation. Rather early, the rule making at European level was emancipated by the case law of the European Court of Justice, developing the idea of primacy of European law over national law. In the well-known decision regarding *Costa v. E.N.E.L.*, the Court of Justice ruled that the Member States through the EEC Treaty have created their own legal system which has become part of their internal legal order. Moreover, by transferring sovereign power to the European level, the Member States have agreed to give precedence to legal acts stemming from that level. In the words of the Court: "The executive force of Community law cannot vary from one State to another in deference to subsequent domestic laws, without jeopardizing the attainment of the objectives of the Treaty … and giving rise to … discrimination …"[10] At another occasion, the Court held the "attainment of the objectives of the Community requires that the rules of Community law established by the Treaty itself or arising from procedures which it has instituted are fully applicable at the same time and with identical effects over the whole territory of the Community without the Member States being able to place any obstacles in the way."[11] In this context, uniform integration means uniform *legal* integration, *i.e.*, the adoption and application of legal rules for all Member States.[12] The foundations for this uniform integration are the principles of direct effect and primacy and the single institutional framework.[13] Rules of Union law therefore should apply to all Member States at the same time and with the same content.[14] In other words: either every single member or no-one at all.[15] In this respect, the ECJ pointed out that the preamble to the EEC Treaty required "common action in eliminating the barriers which divide Europe".[16] It declared incompatible with this concept of common action the complete exclusion, even voluntary, of a specific Member State from any participation in a relevant project

---

[7] Cf. Blanke 2013a, para 26; Calliess 2020a, b, paras 12 f.

[8] Martenczuk 2000, pp. 359 f.

[9] Becker 1998, p. 33; Bender 2001, pp. 731 f.; Hatje 2001, p. 160.

[10] ECJ, Case 6/64, *Flamino Costa v. E.N.E.L.*, judgment of the Court of 15 July 1964, ECLI:EU:C:1964:66, pp. 593 f.

[11] ECJ, Case 48/71, *Commission v. Italy*, judgment of the Court of 13 July 1972, ECLI:EU:C:1972:65, para 8.

[12] Cf. Beck 1995, p. 51; Linke 2006, pp. 25 f.

[13] Bender 2001, p. 731; Linke 2006, p. 26.

[14] Scharrer 1984, p. 12.

[15] Cf. Linke 2006, p. 27.

[16] Second recital of the preamble to the EEC Treaty.

or the power reserved to certain Member States to take no part in a matter which comes within a common policy.[17] What is more, it has been argued that the principle of primacy of European law (and its full recognition by the national legal orders, including national constitutional courts) contributes to ensure equality of the Member States because it makes sure that all members of the Union remain equally bound to the terms they have unanimously agreed to.[18]

Within the European Union, both the European and the national courts are called upon to apply European law. In other words, also national courts are functional European courts. However, in order to ensure that European law is applied uniformly throughout the Community, only a court at European level can authoritatively interpret and—if necessary—declare invalid an act of European authority.[19] To this end, the unity of the legal order is supplemented by the preliminary ruling procedure between the ECJ and the national courts.[20] Article 267 TFEU confers jurisdiction on the ECJ to rule on the validity of (secondary) Union law at the request of a national court and to give an interpretation of European secondary and primary (constitutional) law.[21]

At the same time, the preliminary reference procedure serves as a means to review the compatibility of national law against obligations stemming from EU law. Taking account of the different legal orders in the multilevel governance system that is the EU, the ECJ may not, however, rule on the *validity* of national law. Therefore, within the preliminary ruling procedure, the ECJ gives its interpretation on European law, concluding that "a provision like the one presented by the national court" may or may not be compatible with European law.[22] The European Court thus offers a "helpful interpretation of [Union] law"[23] for the national court to determine the validity of the national law provisions.

In order to ensure the uniform application of Union law, the ruling given in a preliminary ruling procedure does not only bind the referring court in its proceeding at hand (*inter partes* effect). Instead, it is a binding interpretation of Union law and thus binding on all national courts and institutions beyond the national dispute (*erga omnes* effect). This has been well explained already back in 1977 by AG *Warner* when he wrote that the preliminary ruling procedure as a "dialogue between the courts"

---

[17] Opinion 1/76, *Draft Agreement establishing a European laying-up fund for inland waterway vessels*, Opinion of 26 April 1977, ECLI:EU:C:1977:63, para 11.

[18] Fabbrini 2015, p. 1015.

[19] Cf. Lenaerts et al. 2014, paras 3.59–3.60, 10.13. See also ECJ, Case 314/85 *Foto-Frost v. Hauptzollamt Lübeck-Ost*, judgment of the Court of 22 October 1987, ECLI:EU:C:1987:452, para 17; Case C-366/10, *Air Transport Association of America and Others*, judgment of the Court (Grand Chamber) of 21 December 2011, ECLI:EU:C:2011:864, paras 47–48 with further references.

[20] See, inter alia, Arnull 2003.

[21] See on the interpretative function of the preliminary ruling procedure Lenaerts et al. 2014, paras 6.01 ff.

[22] See on this issue Lenaerts et al. 2014, paras 6.21 and 6.23 with extensive references from the ECJ's case law.

[23] ECJ, Case 244/78, *Union Laitière Normande*, judgment of the Court of 12 July 1979, ECLI:EU:C:1979:198, para 5.

(nowadays commonly referred to as "judicial dialogue"[24]) aims to secure uniformity in the interpretation and application of Community law throughout the Member States by binding all national courts to the *ratio decidendi* of an ECJ judgment. Primacy and uniform interpretation thus ensure that the European Union as a union of law confers the same rights and obligations on all its members and guarantees the unity of the legal order.[25]

8.2.2 A Union Based on Common Values

While the principle of primacy of EU law serves to ensure uniform applica-tion of the legal rules and thus provide for legal homogeneity throughout the Union, the supranational order has evolved into what is termed a "Union of values". Article 2 of the TEU lists the values on which the Union is founded: respect for human dignity, freedom, democracy, equality, the rule of law and respect for human rights, including the rights of persons belonging to minorities. The provision further claims that "these values are common to the Member States in a society in which pluralism, non-discrimination, tolerance, justice, solidarity and equality between women and men prevail". It was not without cause that the Commission, when this provision was negotiated for the Amsterdam Treaty, called for this European model—values shared by all its societies and combining the characteristics of democracy with those of an open economy, internal solidarity and cohesion—to be strengthened and made more explicit.[26] While we cannot elaborate on the individual principles and values here, suffice it to say that they reflect the achievements of modern constitutionalism[27] in liberal-democratic States. In fact, some national constitutions impose requirements on the Union's set up.[28]

Article 2 TEU is operationalised and sanctioned at two stages of the integration process. First of all, it is an essential requirement for accession to the European Union. Article 49 of the TEU states that any European State may apply to become a member of the Union, provided that it respects the values referred to in Article 2 and is committed to promoting them. The Union's values thus become a convergence point for candidate States. Adherence to these constitutional principles safeguards the Union's identity as a community of law and backs the legitimacy of the power

---

[24] See, among many, Groussot 2008.

[25] ECJ, Case 112/76, *Manzoni*, Opinion of AG Warner of 20 September 1977, ECLI:EU:C:1977:133, p. 1662.

[26] European Commission, *Reinforcing Political Union and Preparing for Enlargement*, COM(96) 90, para 8.

[27] Nettesheim 2003, p. 38.

[28] For example, Article 23 of the German Basic Law requires the Union to be "committed to democratic, social and federal principles, to the rule of law, and to the principle of subsidiarity, and that guarantees a level of protection of basic rights essentially comparable to that afforded by this Basic Law." See also Schorkopf 2000, pp. 46 ff., on the homogeneity clauses of the (then fifteen) Member States.

exercised by the Union and its members.[29] However, the values are not only an entry requirement. Instead, they are a membership requirement *per se*, as non-compliance can be sanctioned. Under Article 7 TEU, a Member State can be deprived of its rights deriving from the application of the Treaties, including the voting rights of its representative in the Council, in case there is a serious and persistent breach by that Member State of the values referred to in Article 2 TEU. In most recent years, the Court of Justice has referred to Article 2 TEU more frequently, most prominently in cases against Poland and Hungary regarding rule-of-law concerns,[30] and it has thus contributed to the operationalization of the values contained in that provision.

In sum, Member States must adhere to certain values in order to become a member of the Union in the first place, but they must also adhere to these values in order to not get sanctioned under Article 7.[31] For this reason, the provision of Article 2 TEU has been characterised by some authors as a "homogeneity clause"[32] similar to those found in federal systems, for example in the German Basic Law.[33]

8.2.3 The "Common" Market as an Example for a Level Playing Field

The establishment of an economic level playing field was at the start and core of European integration *sensu stricto*.[34] In fact, Article 2 of the 1957 EEC Treaty stipulated that it "shall be the aim of the Community, by establishing a Common Market and progressively approximating the economic policies of Member States, to promote throughout the Community a harmonious development of economic activities […] and closer relations between its Member States". Still today Article 3(3)(1) of the TEU declares the establishment of the internal market as one of the Union's (persistent) objectives.

One way to achieve this—and still the cornerstones of today's internal market—are the free movement of goods, persons, services and capital. As a form of "negative" integration,[35] the four freedoms aim to ensure that economic factors can move freely

---

[29] Cf. Nettesheim 2003, p. 36; Calliess 2004, pp. 1039 f.; Ohler 2017, para 15.

[30] See, *inter alia*, Case C-619/18, *Commission v Poland (Independence of the Supreme Court)*, judgment of the Court (Grand Chamber) of 24 June 2019, ECLI:EU:C:2019:531, and most recently Case C-156/21, *Hungary v Parliament and Council*, judgment of the Court (Full Court) of 16 February 2022, ECLI:EU:C:2022:97.

[31] Cf. Nettesheim 2003, p. 38 f.

[32] Schorkopf 2000, pp. 101 ff.; Mangiameli 2013, paras 1, 42 ff.

[33] Article 28(1) of the German Basis Law provides: "The constitutional order in the *Länder* must conform to the principles of a republican, democratic and social state governed by the rule of law, within the meaning of this Basic Law."

[34] Cf., among others, de Búrca 2000, p. 134; Blanke and Böttner 2020, para 8; Blanke 2021, para 6.

[35] Cf. Schütze 2015, pp. 473 ff.

within the territories of the Union's Member States. They remove obstacles to inter-State trade that result from different national rules and guarantee access to the market as well as equal treatment between nationals and EU foreigners.[36] Based on the direct effect of the fundamental freedoms, it was mostly thanks to the European Court of Justice that over the decades most national obstacles to free trade within the Union have been abolished.

Negative integration, however, does not suffice to establish a true economic "area without internal frontiers in which the free movement [...] is ensured" (Article 26(2) TFEU), but instead needs to be complemented by means of positive integration, which is the adoption of common rules and "integration through legislation".[37] Article 26(1) TFU endows the Union with the competence to adopt measures for the establishment and functioning of the internal market. Moreover, the EEC has always had the competence to "adopt the measures for the approximation of the provisions laid down by law, regulation or administrative action in Member States which have as their object the establishment and functioning of the internal market" (now Article 114(1) TFEU). Frankly, "approximation" is not synonymous to legal unification (or harmonisation *sensu stricto*),[38] but Article 114 TFEU grants the Union extensive legislative capacity to create a (legal) level playing field in the internal market.

As a general rule, States acceding to the Union are obliged to accept and implement the *acquis communautaire*, *i.e.* the totality of the rules already established by the Union (arg. *e contrario* Article 20(4) TEU). This means that they must accept the level of integration already achieved by the incumbent members of the club. Article 49(2) TEU (as did all predecessors since Article 237(2) TEEC) provides that the conditions of admission and the adjustments to the Treaties, which the accession entails, shall be the subject of an agreement. In the words of the ECJ, "the provisions of the Act of Accession affirm the results of the accession negotiations which constitute a totality intended to resolve difficulties which accession entails either for the Community or for the Applicant State".[39] Frankly, the accession of new Member States could and can lead to arrangements which include derogations from primary law and thus from uniform integration.[40] This does *prima facie* not exclude the possibility of *permanent* derogations, but temporary derogations correspond more to the spirit of the Treaties.[41]

---

[36] Blanke 2021, para 9.

[37] See Schütze 2015, pp. 527 ff.

[38] Blanke and Böttner 2020, paras 126 f.

[39] Joined Cases 31 and 35/86, *LAISA v. Council*, judgment of 28 April 1988, ECLI:EU:C:1988:211, para 15.

[40] Cf. Hanf 2001, pp. 7 f.

[41] Cf. Schauer 2000, pp. 43 f. See in more detail also Ott 2017.

8.3   … in Diversity

The unity of the legal system, however, is not an end in itself, but "rather has a serving function, which is exhausted in the achievement of the integration goal".[42] With the accession of more Member States to the Community, uniform integration was also harder to achieve. More members to the club simply means more voices and—potentially—more veto players. At the same time, a widening geographical scope and set of competences makes it harder to sustain a degree of homogeneity, commonality and unity of purpose and method that characterised the earlier Community, but instead brings political, economic and cultural heterogeneity to the institutions and the exercise of competences.[43] To overcome this general obstacle, the Union has pursued two basic routes.

On the one hand, over the years and through the treaty reforms, unanimity voting was successively replaced by qualified majority voting. Starting with the Single European Act in 1986, the Member States have agreed to more and more areas in which decision making would not require the positive vote by each member of the club. Interestingly, in practice qualified majority voting does not lead to situations in which Member States are simply outvoted. Instead, the mere *possibility* of being outvoted leads Member States to being more open to compromise.[44] Secondly, various forms of differentiation have been introduced to accommodate special situations of Member States or to allow for progress in the integration process that not all members of the Union are willing to pursue, at least not for the moment.

This section aims to highlight a few areas in which national diversity and differentiation have made their way into the Union legal order. It will first deal with differentiation as contained in or determined by primary law (Sect. 8.3.1). Furthermore, it will try and elaborate on the national identity discourse that has been troubling the Union and its members for decades and has increased as integration deepened (Sect. 8.3.2). Finally, the chapter will discuss differentiation at the level of secondary Union law, most prominently by means of the instrument of enhanced cooperation (Sect. 8.3.3).

8.3.1   Primary-Law Based Differentiation

The primary law of the Communities and the Union contained from the beginning[45] specific safeguard clauses that could lead to legal differentiation between the Member

---

[42] Bender 2001, p. 766 (my translation); cf. also Becker 1998, p. 42.

[43] Cf. De Búrca and Scott 2000, p. 2.

[44] Cf. Commission Communication, *A stronger global actor: a more efficient decision-making for EU Common Foreign and Security Policy*, Brussels, 12 September 2018, COM(2018) 647 final, p. 3; see also Böttner 2020, p. 496.

[45] On differentiation in the EC and EU over the years, see in detail Tuytschaever 1999.

States.[46] Specific possibilities for derogations were introduced by the Single European Act and subsequent Treaty revisions. These include, amongst others, Articles 36, 45(3) and 52 as well as Articles 45(4) and 52 TFEU (and their predecessors), which allow for derogations from the fundamental freedoms either for exercise of public authority or for reasons of public policy.[47] Through the (exhaustive) justifications found in primary law, Member States may derogate from the free movement rights for reasons of domestic policy. Apart from these reasons, the European Court of Justice has acknowledged implied justifications ("mandatory requirements" or "overriding reasons relating to the public interest") for non-discriminatory restrictions on trade, such as consumer protection, environmental protection or fundamental rights. These exceptions allow for legal differentiation among the Member States. However, the Court of Justice has always interpreted these justifications narrowly[48] so as to not let "domestic partisanship" or "political obstructionism" gradually undermine the idea of commonality which underpins not just the common market.[49]

Another set of rules are Articles 114(4), (5) and (10), 153(4), 168(4)(1), 169(4), and 193 TFEU, which allow for the maintenance or introduction of more stringent protective measures for specific national, non-economic reasons and thus to derogate from (harmonised) rules of secondary Union law.[50] Ironically, these provisions, especially Article 114 TFEU and its predecessors, have led to extensive legislative differentiation in a branch of decision-making which has normally been thought to exemplify the classic, traditionally conceived Community aims of integration, harmonisation and unity.[51] Indeed, a derogation clause within a harmonising competence is a special expression of accepting diversity in the Union.[52] Again, however, Member States are not free to adopt whatever measure they seem fit under national policy. Instead, it is subject to strict oversight by the Commission ad eventually the Court of Justice and thus by the common interest of the Union. As in the case of derogations from the fundamental freedoms, these exceptions are interpreted strictly.[53]

While the Court of Justice has tried, through its case law, to limit derogations based on primary law, the Member States decided to give European integration a new spin when they introduced primary-law based opt-outs and accompanying extra-EU agreements. The first great turning point in the process of uniform and simultaneous integration came about with the Schengen Agreements (1985/1990). Five of the ten EEC Member States decided to deepen integration in the field of free movement of

---

[46] Guilloud-Colliat 2016, p. 156: "Differentiation within the Union is as old as the construction of Europe itself". On other "legal avenues of differentiated integration", see Sielmann 2020, pp. 295 ff.

[47] See in detail Barnard 2016, pp. 152 ff. and 449 ff.

[48] See already Case 46/76, *Bauhuis*, judgment of the Court of 25 January 1977, ECLI:EU:C:1977:6, para 12; Case 113/80, *Commission v. Ireland*, judgment of the Court of 17 June 1981, ECLI:EU:C:1981:139, para 7.

[49] De Búrca 2000, p. 138.

[50] Cf. Schauer 2000, pp. 75 ff. and 79 ff.

[51] De Búrca 2000, p. 140.

[52] Cf. Vos and Weimer 2017, p. 308.

[53] Cf. Vos and Weimer 2017, pp. 312 ff.

persons and to abolish internal border controls. Since not all States wanted to participate, the willing Member States had to revert to cooperation outside the Community's legal and institutional framework by means of an international treaty regime. It was only with the Treaty of Amsterdam that the Schengen *acquis* was transferred into the Union's legal framework by means of a Protocol (Schengen Protocol, now Protocol No. 19). For those Member States not willing to participate, namely Denmark, the United Kingdom and Ireland, the Treaty revision of Amsterdam provided for a complex system of permanent legal opt-outs.[54] According to the system of the Amsterdam Treaty and the Schengen Protocol, Ireland (and the United Kingdom) opted-out of the Schengen *acquis*.[55] However, according to Article 4 of the Schengen Protocol, Ireland (and the United Kingdom) can (and could) at any time request to take part in some or all of the provisions of the Schengen *acquis*. The Council then decides on the request with the unanimity of the members of the Schengen Group[56] and the representative of the government of the State concerned. Both States have previously made use of this option.[57] The position or non-participation in the Schengen *acquis* is supplemented by Protocol No. 21, which serves as a general opt-out for Ireland from the Area of Freedom, Security and Justice. It can nevertheless decide on a case-by-case basis to participate or later accede to a proposal, initiative or measure under that Title V.

According to Article 3 of the Schengen Protocol, however, the participation of Denmark in the adoption of measures constituting a *development* of the Schengen *acquis*, as well as the *implementation* of these measures and their *application* to Denmark, shall be governed by the relevant provisions of Protocol No. 22 on the position of Denmark. As for Ireland, the Denmark Protocol provides in a comprehensive manner that Denmark shall not take part in the adoption of, nor be bound by, rules under Title V of Part Three of the TFEU. Unlike the position of Ireland, Denmark cannot participate on a case-by-case basis. It has an opt-out from all measures adopted under the Area of Freedom, Security and Justice but can nonetheless decide within six months after the decision of the Council to implement a measure in its national law. However, in accordance with Articles 7 and 8 of the Danish Protocol, Denmark may, at any time and in accordance with its constitutional requirements, inform the other Member States that it no longer wishes to avail itself of all or part of this Protocol. It

---

[54] See in detail Böttner 2021, pp. 282 ff. with further references.

[55] Cf. in this respect Case C-77/05, *United Kingdom v. Council*, judgment (Grand Chamber) of 18 December 2007, ECLI:EU:C:2007:803, paras 57 ff.; Case C-482/08, *United Kingdom v. Council*, judgment (Grand Chamber) of 20 October 2010, ECLI:EU:C:2010:631, paras 42 ff.; Case C-44/14, *Spain v. Parliament and Council*, judgment (Grand Chamber) of 8 September 2015, ECLI:EU:C:2015:554, paras 26 ff.

[56] The Schengen Group, according to Article 1 of the Schengen Protocol, comprises Belgium, Bulgaria, the Czech Republic, Denmark, Germany, Estonia, Greece, Spain, France, Italy, Cyprus, Latvia, Lithuania, Luxembourg, Hungary, Malta, the Netherlands, Austria, Poland, Portugal, Romania, Slovenia, Slovakia, Finland and Sweden as well as Croatia in accordance with Article 4 of its Act of Accession (OJ 2012 L 112, pp. 21, 36).

[57] Council Decision 2000/365/EC, OJ 2000 L 131, p. 43 and Council Decision 2002/192/EC, OJ 2002 L 64, p. 20.

may also decide to replace its position with regard to the Area of Freedom, Security and Justice with a set of rules that is similar to that of the Irish Protocol No. 21.

Without asynchronicity and flexible integration, it may not have been possible for the European Union to include in its framework and later supranationalise large parts of the area of justice and home affairs. Without the concessions given to the Member States not ready or not willing to deepen integration in this area, the Union's competence would most likely still be of an intergovernmental nature. The history of the Schengen Agreement and the Area of Freedom, Security and Justice shows that, given the political will for intensified cooperation, the Member States will find a way for its establishment and implementation, if necessary outside the Union's framework but with the aim to eventually integrate it into the Treaty structure. In this respect, Ireland (and formerly the United Kingdom) was granted the right to opt-in to the areas from which they were granted an opt-out, and they have readily made use of this option.[58]

Another important area of asynchronicity of European law is the Economic and Monetary Union as it was agreed in the Treaty of Maastricht.[59] The idea of a non-simultaneous establishment of the monetary union dates back to the early 1970s, when the six EEC Member States and the three accession candidates (Denmark, United Kingdom, Ireland) agreed to narrow fluctuations between the national currencies with the aim of creating parity between the currencies (the "snake").[60] International turbulences, *inter alia* the collapse of the Bretton Woods system, led six of the States to maintain the stable exchange rates and concerted floating of the currencies towards third States while the remaining three maintained isolated floating but with the aim of eventually joining the agreement of the other six.[61]

The 1975 Tindemans report[62] suggested that, with regard to economic and monetary policy and with a view to the divergence of the national economic and financial situations of the Member States, "it is impossible at the present time to submit a credible programme of action if it is deemed absolutely necessary that in every case all stages should be reached by all the States at the same time." Instead, he held that "those States which are able to progress have a duty to forge ahead" while the others will temporarily remain behind. The Member States staying behind then receive from the progressing States "any aid and assistance that can be given [to] them to enable them to catch the others up".[63]

The 1992 Treaty of Maastricht introduced the Economic and Monetary Union into EU law. However, not all Member States were willing to participate in this new step of integration in all stages (*i.e.*, in the third stage, eventually) but were ready to let the remaining Member States proceed. The consensus was that the EMU

---

[58] See in more detail Monar 2010; Tekin 2012.

[59] On flexibility in EMU, see further Deubner 2017; Lacchi 2017.

[60] See Council Decision 71/143/EEC, OJ 1971 L 73, p. 15.

[61] Linke 2006, p. 51.

[62] Report by Mr *Leo Tindemans*, Prime Minister of Belgium, to the European Council, Bulletin of the European Communities, Supplement 1/76, available at http://aei.pitt.edu/942/.

[63] Tindemans Report, see n. 62, p. 20.

would not be based on a "pick and choose" model. Thus, it should not be up to every Member State to decide separately whether to participate or not.[64] While the majority of Member States agreed on binding rules on economic cooperation and, more importantly, the establishment of a single European currency area (Eurozone), Denmark and the United Kingdom were granted opt-outs that were guaranteed by means of Protocols attached to the Treaties.

Taking into account the original idea of uniform integration and participation in the EMU, every acceding Member State since Maastricht is under the obligation to eventually join the third stage and introduce the euro currency. In the meantime, they are treated as Member States with derogations[65]; the special rules are found in the chapter entitled "transitional provisions" (Articles 139 ff. TFEU). All of this highlights the exceptional character of being outside the euro area. In that respect, Denmark can renounce their opt-outs by notifying the Council and by complying with the conditions and procedure of Article 140 TFEU.[66] Participation in the third stage of the EMU is dependent on the meeting of a certain set of criteria (convergence criteria) now set out in Article 140 TFEU and Protocol No. 13 on the Convergence Criteria (*i.a.* price stability and absence of an excessive deficit). Similar to Schengen, participation in the final stage of EMU is an obligation that a Member State assumes upon accession to the Union and the full application of which is suspended only temporarily, subject to a certain set of objective criteria. However, unlike Schengen, while the rules on EMU may in theory be judicially enforceable and subject to review by European Courts, the establishment of synchronicity in the monetary Union by joining the third stage of EMU depends to a large degree on political factors. The most prominent example may be Sweden, whose national legislation still does not allow for participation in the third stage of emu.

Differentiation between Member States is reflected also in the institutional setting of EMU.[67] The European Central Bank (ECB) and the national central banks form the European System of Central Banks (ESCB), but only the national central banks of States whose currency is the euro, together with the ECB, form the Eurosystem (Article 282(1) TFEU). Another element of institutional differentiation with regard to EMU is the Council: Composed of the ministers of those Member States whose currency is the euro (the "Euro Group"), the Council shall adopt measures specific to the euro area Member States (Article 136 TFEU). The Member States forming the Eurozone shall elect a president for the Euro Group (Article 2 of Protocol No. 14) and only members of the Council representing Member States whose currency is the euro shall take part in the vote for adopting the measures.

The 2008 financial crisis, which developed into a "euro crisis", led to further dynamic development and the need to enhance cooperation among the euro area

---

[64] Louis 1995, p. 148.

[65] See, most recently, Article 5 of the Act of Accession of Croatia, OJ 2012 L 112, pp. 21, 36.

[66] Point 2 of Protocol No. 16. The same applied to the United Kingdom in accordance with point 9 of Protocol No. 15.

[67] See in more detail Zilioli and Selmayr 2001, chapter 4 (The European Central Bank and Differentiated Integration).

members in order to overcome the situation and strengthen the EMU framework.[68] Because the Union did not possess the required competences, and as consensus among all Member States on a necessary Treaty amendment could not be reached, the willing Member States again had to resort to cooperation outside the Union's framework.[69] This led to the negotiation of two international agreements, namely the Treaty establishing a European Stability Mechanism (ESM Treaty) and the Treaty on Stability, Coordination and Governance in the Economic and Monetary Union (the so-called "Fiscal Compact").[70] The proposed fiscal union and economic governance may be the starting point for a whole new range of enhanced cooperation,[71] for example, the financial transaction tax.[72]

Another major achievement of the Treaty of Maastricht was the introduction of a Common Foreign and Security Policy (CFSP)[73] under the roof of the newly founded European Union. Due to the impact of foreign and security policy on domestic sovereignty, the provisions set the default rule for decision-making to unanimity (Article J.8(2) TEU Maastricht). However, even at the time, Contracting Parties were aware that unanimity or better yet, granting a veto position to every Member State, would be a high obstacle for this policy area.[74] This resulted in Declaration No. 27 which provided that "with regard to Council decisions requiring unanimity, Member States will, to the extent possible, avoid preventing a unanimous decision where a qualified majority exists in favour of that decision". It is safe to assume that the inclusion of Common Foreign and Security Policy in the Treaty of Maastricht was possible only because of the absence of majority voting, or more generally speaking, the inapplicability of the "Community method".[75]

The Treaty of Amsterdam introduced in Article 23(1)(2) TEU (now Article 31(1)(2) TEU) another novelty in the form of *qualified* abstention.[76] According to this provision, a member of the Council may qualify its abstention by making a formal declaration with the effect that it shall not be obliged to apply the decision, but shall accept that the decision commits the Union.[77] Hence, the use of qualified abstention is not subject to any further conditions as regards the form of the declaration or the substantiating of reasons. The instrument of qualified abstention is supplemented by

---

[68] Blanke 2011, p. 402.

[69] Uerpmann-Wittzack 2013.

[70] On the Fiscal Compact and the ESM, see in more detail Lo Schiavo 2017; Pilz 2016; on most recent developments, see Manger-Nestler and Böttner 2019. On the new EMU architecture see most recently Pilz 2021.

[71] Cf. Blanke 2013c, para 57; Messina 2014.

[72] See also Böttner 2021, pp. 300 ff.

[73] On flexibility in CFSP, see also Graf von Kielmansegg 2017.

[74] Böttner and Wessel 2013, para 3.

[75] See Böttner and Wessel 2013, para 8.

[76] As Rinke 2015, p. 170 points out, the provision has been included with a view to the newly acceded States of Austria, Finland, and Sweden, which have a rather neutrality-oriented foreign policy. Cf. also Blockmans 2018, pp. 1805 f.

[77] See in detail Böttner and Wessel 2013, paras 16 ff.; Böttner 2021, pp. 313 ff.

a quorum for a sort of blocking minority,[78] which, if reached, means the decision shall not be adopted. Moreover, Member States relying on qualified abstention are exempt from the financing of operations with military or defence implications (now Article 41(2)(2) TEU).[79]

At the time, qualified abstention was meant as an alternative to closer cooperation, which was not (yet) possible in foreign policy.[80] Since the introduction of this possibility, CFSP actions were no longer dependent on the approval and implementation of all Member States and this more flexible approach allowed for smaller groups of States to engage in a certain action or to adopt a position. Qualified abstention thus may be seen as a realisation of the idea of Europe *à la carte*.[81]

With the Treaty of Nice, the instrument of enhanced cooperation was extended to the area of CFSP (Articles 27a through 27e TEU Nice), enabling a group of Member States to increase cooperation for the implementation of a joint action or a common position. However, an important exception was made: such enhanced cooperation shall not relate to matters having military or defence implications (Article 27b TEU Nice). This restriction was lifted with the Treaty of Lisbon and enhanced cooperation is now possible in CFSP, including all areas with military or defence implications.[82] It is questionable, however, if enhanced cooperation will ever be used in the area of military and defence since the Treaty of Lisbon has introduced new forms of flexible cooperation in the (intergovernmental) area of security and defence as a sort of "inbuilt closer co-operation".[83] The most important innovation may be the introduction of "permanent structured cooperation" (PESCO, Articles 42(6), 46 TEU and Protocol No. 10), which has been activated in late 2017.[84]

Over the decades, primary law has incorporated more and more elements that lead to a legal differentiation between the Union's members. Clearly, the number of members has grown considerably, from originally six States to almost thirty and counting. Progress in integration became more difficult and differentiation, used both boldly and cautiously, enabled to take further steps along the road to an ever closer union.

---

[78] The quorum is reached if the members of the Council qualifying their abstention in this way represent at least one third of the Member States comprising at least one third of the population of the Union.

[79] See Schmidt-Radefeldt 2013, para 18.

[80] Cf. Novi 2019, p. 373 (fn. 27).

[81] In this sense Thym 2004, p. 154.

[82] Blanke 2013c, para 31.

[83] For this terminology, see Piris 2010, pp. 90 f.; see further Böttner 2021, pp. 313 ff.

[84] Council Decision (CFSP) 2017/2315, OJ 2017 L 331, p. 57. See further Böttner 2021, pp. 63 ff. and 320 ff.

8.3.2   National Constitutional Identity as Constitutional Limit for Federal Homogeneity

Article 4(2) TEU states that the Union shall respect the Member States' national identities, "inherent in their fundamental structures, political and constitutional, inclusive of regional and local self-government [and] their essential State functions". Moreover, the Charter of Fundamental Rights states in its preamble that the Union contributes to the preservation and to the development of its common values (Article 2 TEU) "while respecting the diversity of the cultures and traditions of the peoples of Europe as well as the national identities of the Member States and the organisation of their public authorities at national, regional and local levels". The (national) identity clause contains the key notion of legal and institutional pluralism within the EU and in fact the nexus between identity and integration, statehood and supranationality.[85] As an idea or concept, national identity is descriptive and refers to structures from the past, but as a legal term it has to be filled with meaning in order to shape the future.[86] It is further complicated by the fact that quite naturally it draws on ideas and understandings of the individual Member States, but as a legal *topos* from the Treaties it has to be given individual (*i.e.*, European) meaning.[87]

The key element of the provision is the concept of 'identity', which for good reason was not defined in the Treaties, because the concept implies above all a self-definition of national identity by each Member State that cannot be interpreted uniformly alongside EU criteria. It can comprise common elements, but how the individual Member State legally, institutionally and culturally designs and implements the pillars and mechanisms of national identity is an attribute of the State and this cannot be overridden by the scope of a supranational market, governed by market-efficiency considerations. Member States' legal-institutional frameworks build unique systems, embedded in values that are strongly culturally rooted. Due to its strong cultural embeddedness, national identity must be defined by reference to the national constitutional law of each Member State. Meanwhile, national constitutional identity (and counterparts in national constitutional law) has been used by several national constitutional courts to delimit Union from State competences and define the nature of the multilevel governance system of EU and Member States.

While this is not the place to go into detail on the justiciability of the identity clause,[88] the Court of Justice provided so far a very narrow room for the Member States to define national identity in terms of public policy, demanding that "genuine

---

[85] Cf. Grawert 2012, pp. 196 f. But see also De Witte 2021, who argues for a very narrow reading of Article 4(2) TEU, limited to institutional diversity.

[86] Blanke 2013b, para 18.

[87] On the national discourses on the identity clause, see most recently the contributions in Calliess and van der Schyff 2020.

[88] See, among many, von Bogdandy and Schill 2011, p. 1445; Konstadinides 2011, p. 206; more recently Martinico 2021, pp. 457 f.

and sufficiently serious threat to a fundamental interest of the society"[89] must occur, and also stressed that the scope of public policy shall not be unilaterally determined by the Member States, but will be subject to the review of any of the EU institutions.[90] In *Taricco II*, the ECJ prominently acknowledged that reasons of national identity may be invoked in order to abstain from implementing EU rules.[91] This, however may only occur in exceptional circumstances and is bound to the situation in a specific Member State. In this context, national identity, in combination with the reiteration of the equality of Member States (Article 4(2), sentence 1 TEU) serves as a limitation to complete convergence and equalisation of the Member States' constitutional traditions as it demands from the Union to regard every Member State as equal and therefore to respect (only to a certain degree, of course) that Member States have different forms of government, different democratic traditions or specifications of the rules of law. This applies also to candidates applying for membership in the Union.[92] However, national identity should not be construed as a unilateral derogation from primacy of EU law[93] or as excluding certain areas from EU law *per se*.[94] All actors involved have to be thorough and find the right balance in order to avoid that this sort of differentiation leads to a drifting apart of the members of the common project. The identity claim thus allows for diversity[95] (and indeed, from the very outset of European integration[96]), but this diversity is limited by the requirements of unity under the homogeneity clause of Article 2 TEU as a common standard.[97]

8.3.3 Secondary-Law Based Differentiation

With the Treaty of Amsterdam, the logic of differentiation has been transposed to the level of secondary EU law; this time, however, not in the sense of individual derogations from uniform law, but as the possibility for a group of Member States to forge ahead. Initially unused, it was only after the reform of the Lisbon Treaty, which included some changes to enhanced cooperation, that this instrument was awakened from its slumber. More specifically, under the instrument of enhanced cooperation, the Council in its entirety (with the consent of the European Parliament) can authorise

---

[89] Case C-208/09, *Sayn-Wittgenstein v. Landeshauptmann von Wien*, judgment of the Court (Second Chamber) of 22 December 2010, ECLI:EU:C:2010:806, para 23.

[90] Case C-208/09, *Sayn-Wittgenstein*, para 96.

[91] ECJ, Case C-42/17, *M.A.S and M.B. (Taricco II)*, judgment of 5 December 2017, ECLI:EU:C:2017:936; on this case, see among others Faraguna 2021, pp. 438 ff.

[92] Ohler 2017, para 15.

[93] Wendel 2011, p. 135; Bonelli 2021, p. 538.

[94] Cf. Di Federico 2019, p. 355; Bonelli 2021, p. 538.

[95] Cf. Bonelli 2021, p. 555.

[96] Case C-160/03, *Spain v. Eurojust*, Opinion of AG Poiares Maduro of 16 December 2004, ECLI:EU:C:2004:817, para 31.

[97] Cf. Schorkopf 2000, p. 212.

a group of at least nine Member States to adopt among themselves rules of secondary EU law that is binding only on the participating States and does not affect those States wishing to abstain from the cooperation.

Since its introduction by the Treaty of Amsterdam, enhanced cooperation has been used in no fewer than five cases: the law applicable to divorce and legal separation,[98] unitary patent protection,[99] financial transaction tax,[100] property regimes of international couples,[101] and the European Public Prosecutor's Office (EPPO).[102] Moreover, permanent structured cooperation (PESCO) has been established on the basis of Article 46 TEU.[103] The files are all characterised by different timeframes and intensity of discussions and different levels of political controversy, all of which are factors that eventually led to enhanced cooperation.[104] While the EPPO had been established only after thorough and profound discussions between all Member States that lasted for several years, enhanced cooperation in other cases was established relatively quickly due to the fundamental opposition by some members.

The picture would be incomplete, however, if we did not take into account those files in which—although not put into place—enhanced cooperation had been considered at some point and then had been abandoned: either because agreement was reached by all Member States or because the dossier was abandoned altogether.[105] For example, already back in 2005, enhanced cooperation was considered as a potential tool to overcome the deadlock regarding the proposal for passenger car-related taxes.[106] It was one part of a larger strategy to reduce CO_2 emissions in order to meet the standards set by the Kyoto Protocol. The legal basis, Article 93 TEC (now Article 113 TFEU) required a unanimous decision in the Council. Due to the fiscal nature and budgetary implications of the measure, the Member States did not reach an agreement. In this situation, the rapporteur in the European Parliament

---

[98] Council Decision 2010/405/EU, OJ 2010 L 189, p. 12 and the implementing Council Regulation (EU) No. 1259/2010, OJ 2010 L 343, p. 10.

[99] Council Decision 2011/167/EU, OJ 2011 L 76, p. 53 and the implementing Parliament /Council Regulation (EU) No. 1257/2012, OJ 2012 L 361, p. 1, as well as Council Regulation (EU) No. 1260/2012, OJ 2012 L 361, p. 89.

[100] Council Decision 2013/52/EU, OJ 2013 L 22, p. 11. No implementing act has yet been adopted, but discussions are still ongoing on the basis of the Commission's proposal COM(2013) 71 and a Franco-German proposal of 2019.

[101] Council Decision (EU) 2016/954, OJ 2016 L 159, p. 16 and the implementing Council Regulation (EU) 2016/1103 and Council Regulation (EU) 2016/1104, OJ 2016 L 183, pp. 1 and 30.

[102] See the implementing Council Regulation (EU) 2017/1939, OJ 2017 L 283, p. 1. There is no authorising decision as enhanced cooperation for the EPPO has been established by a fast-track procedure.

[103] Council Decision (CFSP) 2017/2315, OJ 2017 L 331, p. 57. See also European Council of 14 December 2017, Conclusions, EUCO 19/1/17 REV 1, p. 1.

[104] On the legislative history of the dossiers, see in detail Böttner 2021, pp. 47 ff.; see also Heber 2021, pp. 44 ff.

[105] See in more detail Böttner 2022.

[106] Proposal for a Council Directive on passenger car related taxes, COM(2005) 261 final.

proposed to use enhanced cooperation by the EU members favouring the Commission's proposal.[107] Nevertheless, the dossier was abandoned altogether without any further explanation[108] but it is likely that the more integration-friendly Member States were not willing to carry a burden while others were not ready to do the same.

Finally, there are cases in which enhanced cooperation was considered but eventually Member States could agree on uniform integration. In 1997, the Commission proposed a directive on energy taxation based on what is now Article 113 TFEU, which requires unanimity in the Council.[109] In the following four years and after considerable work was done, the Council was unable to reach an agreement, which led the Commission to publicly consider the use of the enhanced cooperation mechanism.[110] By the end of the year, the Council noted that there was still no agreement on the issue.[111] The matter had been discussed by the European Council in March 2002[112] and the Council was finally able to reach an agreement in October 2003 to adopt the directive.[113] An interesting example where enhanced cooperation has *not* been used is the case of the European arrest warrant.[114] The Commission proposed a framework decision in 2001[115] whose adoption was subject to unanimity in the Council. Italy opposed the initial proposal and demanded a reduced list of offences for which double criminality would not be checked. Italy's opposition met strong resistance by the other Member States, the Commission, and national media. Both the European Parliament and the European Commission advocated for enhanced cooperation without Italy's participation should unanimity not be possible. Outside pressure and high domestic reputation costs eventually led Italy to give in so that the European arrest warrant could be adopted as an instrument by the Union as a whole.[116]

At first it seemed that the first cases of enhanced cooperation were only a test run, which then quickly dried up again. In the recent past, however, enhanced cooperation has again moved more into the focus of political discussion as a means of

---

[107] European Parliament, 10 July 2006, Rapporteur's position. European Parliament Report on the proposal of a Council directive on passenger car related taxes, A6-0240/2006.

[108] Cf. Heber 2021, p. 58.

[109] Proposal for a Council Directive restructuring the Community framework for the taxation of energy products, COM(97) 30 final.

[110] Agence Europe, Bulletin Quotidien Europe No. 7897 of 7 February 2001.

[111] Council Doc. 15288/01 of 5 February 2002, p. 6, as corrected by Council Doc. 15288/01 COR 1 REV 1 of 23 April 2002.

[112] Barcelona European Council of 15–16 March 2002, Presidency Conclusions, point 12.

[113] Council Doc. 14140/03 ADD 1 of 24 November 2003, pp. 4 ff.; Council Directive 2003/96/EC, OJ 2003 L 283, p. 51.

[114] See on this case Kroll and Leuffen 2015, pp. 366 f.; Böttner 2021, p. 346.

[115] Proposal for a Council Framework Decision on the European arrest warrant and the surrender procedures between the Member States, COM(2001) 522 final.

[116] Council Framework Decision 2002/584/JHA of 13 June 2002 on the European arrest warrant and the surrender procedures between Member States—Statements made by certain Member States on the adoption of the Framework Decision, OJ 2002 L 190, p. 1.

overcoming the so-called poly-crisis.[117] The Commission added to this debate with its White Paper on the Future of Europe.[118] In this reflection paper, the Commission presented five scenarios on the state of the Union by the year 2025. Scenario 3 ("Those Who Want More, Do More") is of particular interest: In this scenario, coalitions of willing Member States cooperate in various policy areas by agreeing on legal and budgetary arrangements within the Union, similar to the Schengen or the euro area arrangements. Interestingly, in most recent times enhanced cooperation has been considered for subjects with major political implications. While eventually not put to use, enhanced cooperation has been discussed as an option for the reform of the Dublin system or the implementation of the NextGenerationEU instrument.[119] Furthermore, with regard to the "rule of law crisis" in Poland, some authors discuss whether enhanced cooperation could be used as a means of *de facto* expulsion of an EU Member State,[120] because the Union is lacking the tools for actually expelling a member from the organisation.

While enhanced cooperation cannot be used to make major political areas subject to differentiated integration (like Schengen or EMU), the inclusion of this instrument in primary law (Amsterdam) the anchoring of the basic norm in the TEU (Article 20)—the Union's constitution,[121] as well as its use (and consideration) at least since the Treaty of Lisbon differentiation must be recognised as a constitutional principle of the Union.[122] It may be used to reconcile, at the level of secondary legislation, the need for uniform integration with the desire to deepen integration and to recognise different approaches to specific policy issues by the Member States.

8.4 Concluding Remarks

The focus on the individuality of the Member States within a supranational community is expressed in the Union's motto "united in diversity"; the origin of which also dates back to the early years of European integration.[123] Flexible integration and

---

[117] Cf. Speech by President *Jean-Claude Juncker* at the Annual General Meeting of the Hellenic Federation of Enterprises (SEV) of 21 June 2016, https://ec.europa.eu/commission/presscorner/det ail/de/SPEECH_16_2293.

[118] European Commission, *White Paper on the Future of Europe—Reflections and scenarios for the EU27 by 2025*, COM(2017) 2025 of 1 March 2017.

[119] Giegold and Repasi 2020; Graf von Luckner 2020.

[120] Chamon and Theuns 2021.

[121] Cf. Blanke 2013a, para 61.

[122] Cf. already Chaltiel 1998, p. 289; Wessels 1998, p. 197; Dougan 2009; Becker 2015, para 24 ("constitutionalisation of flexibility"); Zeitzmann 2015, p. 105; Böttner 2021, p. 2; with an opposing view Bender 2001, p. 766.

[123] The first President of the Commission, *Walter Hallstein*, had already acknowledged that "Europe presents an example of unity in diversity". See the speech addressed to the Second Congress of the European Foundation for Cultural Purposes on 13 December 1958, Milan, The Unity of European Culture and the Policy uniting Europe, available at: http://aei.pitt.edu/14887/1/s51.pdf.

thus a departure from the apparent need to uniform integration tries to find a balance between the widening and the deepening of integration. At first glance, it seems that unity and diversity are contradictory in nature, and one is reminded of the famous quote made by *Dr. Faust* in *Goethe*'s classic: "Two souls, alas, dwell in my breast/ each seeks to rule without the other". However, the opposite is true. In the context of European integration, they are two sides of the same coin: unity is the ideal of European integration, but diversity is a strength of the EU.[124]

Only recently, the leaders of the Union and of its Member States in their Rome Declaration underlined that "our Union is undivided and indivisible" and that "unity is both a necessity and our free choice". At the same time, however, they stated their commitment to "act together, at different paces and intensity where necessary, while moving in the same direction, as we have done in the past, in line with the Treaties and keeping the door open to those who want to join later".[125] A minimum degree of conformity is necessary for the States to accept in order for the EU to maintain an identity as a polity.[126] "United in diversity" is thus not only the Union's motto; it is also at the core of the Union's very identity.

References

Antoniolli L (2019) "United in Diversity"? Differentiated Integration in an Ever Diverse European Union. In: Antoniolli L, Bonatti L, Ruzza C (eds) Highs and Lows of European Integration. Sixty Years After the Treaty of Rome. Springer, Heidelberg, pp 83–102

Arnull A (2003) The Past and Future of the Preliminary Rulings Procedure. In: Andenas M, Usher J (eds) The Treaty of Nice and Beyond - Enlargement and Constitutional Reform. Bloomsbury Publishing, pp 345–354

Barnard C (2016) The Substantive Law of the EU: The Four Freedoms, 5th edn. Oxford University Press, Oxford

Beck H (1995) Abgestufte Integration im Europäischen Gemeinschaftsrecht unter besonderer Berücksichtigung des Umweltrechts. Peter Lang, Frankfurt

Becker U (1998) Differenzierungen der Rechtseinheit durch abgestufte Integration. In: Schwarze J, Müller-Graff P-C (eds) Europäische Rechtseinheit durch einheitliche Rechtsdurchsetzung. Nomos, Baden-Baden, pp 29–57

Becker U (2015) Artikel 20 EUV. In: von der Groeben H, Schwarze J, Hatje A (eds) Europäisches Unionsrecht, 7th edn. Nomos, Baden-Baden

Bender T (2001) Die Verstärkte Zusammenarbeit nach Nizza: Anwendungsfelder und Bewertung im Spiegel historischer Präzedenzfälle der differenzierten Integration. Zeitschrift für ausländisches öffentliches Recht und Völkerrecht, 61(4):729–770

Blanke H-J (2011) The European Economic and Monetary Union: Between Vulnerability and Reform. International Journal of Public Law and Policy, 1(4):402–433

---

[124] Calliess 2020a, p. 29.

[125] The Rome Declaration, Declaration of the leaders of 27 member states and of the European Council, the European Parliament and the European Commission of 25 March 2017, https://www.consilium.europa.eu/en/press/press-releases/2017/03/25/rome-declaration/; Cf. also Antoniolli 2019, pp. 97 f.

[126] De Búrca 2000, p. 137.

Blanke H-J (2013a) Article 1 TEU. In: Blanke H-J, Mangiameli S (eds) The Treaty on European Union – A Commentary. Springer, Heidelberg

Blanke H-J (2013b) Article 4 TEU. In: Blanke H-J, Mangiameli S (eds) The Treaty on European Union – A Commentary. Springer, Heidelberg

Blanke H-J (2013c) Article 20 TEU. In: Blanke H-J, Mangiameli S (eds) The Treaty on European Union – A Commentary. Springer, Heidelberg

Blanke H-J (2021) Article 26 TFEU. In: Blanke H-J, Mangiameli S (eds) Treaty on the Functioning of the European Union – A Commentary, Volume I. Springer, Heidelberg

Blanke H-J, Böttner R (2020) § 13 Binnenmarkt, Rechtsangleichung, Grundfreiheiten. In: Niedobitek M (ed) Europarecht – Grundlagen und Politiken der Union, 2nd edn. De Gruyter, Berlin

Blockmans S (2018) The EU's Modular Approach to Defence Integration: An Inclusive, Ambitious and Legally Binding PESCO? Common Market Law Review, 55(6):1785–1826

Bonelli M (2021) National Identity and European Integration Beyond 'Limited Fields'. European Public Law, 27(3):537–558

Böttner R (2020) The Commission's Initiative on the Passerelle Clauses – Exploring the Unused Potential of the Lisbon Treaty. Zeitschrift für europarechtliche Studien, 483–503

Böttner R (2021) The Constitutional Framework for Enhanced Cooperation in EU Law. Brill Nijhoff, Leiden

Böttner R (2022) The Instrument of Enhanced Cooperation – Pitfalls and Possibilities for Differentiated Integration. European Papers 7(3): 1147–1164

Böttner R, Wessel R (2013) Article 31 TEU. In: Blanke H-J, Mangiameli S (eds) The Treaty on European Union – A Commentary. Springer, Heidelberg

Calliess C (2004) Europa als Wertegemeinschaft: Integration und Identität durch europäisches Verfassungsrecht? Juristenzeitung, 59(21):1033–1045

Calliess C (2020a) The Future of Europe After Brexit - The Principles of Efficiency, Subsidiarity, Solidarity and Flexibility as Drivers for the Reform of the European Union and Its Euro Area. Berliner Online-Beiträge zum Europarecht, No 120

Calliess C (2020b) Artikel 1 EUV. In: Calliess C, Ruffert M (eds) EUV/AEUV mit Grundrechtecharta, 6th edn. C.H. Beck, Munich

Calliess C, van der Schyff G (eds) (2020) Constitutional Identity in a Europe of Multilevel Constitutionalism. Cambridge University Press, Cambridge

Chaltiel F (1998) Le traité d'Amsterdam et la coopération renforcée. Revue du marché commun et de l'Union européenne, 418:289–293

Chamon M, Theuns T (2021) Resisting Membership Fatalism: Dissociation Through Enhanced Cooperation or Collective Withdrawal. Verfassungblog, 11 October 2021, available at https://verfassungsblog.de/resisting-membership-fatalism/

Claes M (2013) National Identity: Trump Card or Up for Negotiation? In: Saiz Arnaiz A, Alcoberro Llivina C (eds) National Constitutional Identity and European Integration. Intersentia, Cambridge, pp 109–139

de Búrca G (2000) Differentiation Within the Core: The Case of the Common Market. In: de Búrca G, Scott J (eds) Constitutional Change in the EU: From Uniformity to Flexibility? Hart, Oxford, pp 133–171

de Búrca G, Scott J (2000) Introduction. In: de Búrca G, Scott J (eds) Constitutional Change in the EU: From Uniformity to Flexibility? Hart, Oxford, pp 1–8

De Witte B (2021) Article 4(2) TEU as a Protection of the Institutional Diversity of the Member States. European Public Law, 27(3):559–570

Deubner C (2017) Deepened Integration in the Eurozone? In: Giegerich T, Schmitt D, Zeitzmann S (eds) Flexibility in the EU and Beyond. Nomos, Baden-Baden, pp 183–194

Di Federico G (2019) The Potential of Article 4(2) TEU in the Solution of Constitutional Clashes Based on Alleged Violations of National Identity and the Quest for Adequate (Judicial) Standards. European Public Law, 25(3):347–380

Dougan M (2009) The Unfinished Business of Enhanced Cooperation: Some Institutional Questions and Their Constitutional Implications. In: Ott A, Vos E (eds) Fifty Years of European Integration – Foundations and Perspectives. T.M.C. Asser Press, The Hague, pp 157–179

Fabbrini F (2015) After the OMT Case: The Supremacy of EU Law as the Guarantee of the Equality of the Member States. German Law Journal, 16(4):1003–1023

Faraguna P (2021) On the Identity Clause and Its Abuses: 'Back to the Treaty'. European Public Law, 27(3):427–446

Fromage D, De Witte B (2021) Guest Editors' Introduction: National Constitutional Identity Ten Years On: State of Play and Future Perspective. European Public Law, 27(3):411–424

Giegold S, Repasi R (2020) Budget Blockade by Hungary/Poland: EU Council Presidency Should Start "Enhanced Cooperation" to Ensure Corona Aid Flows, 26 November 2020, available at https://sven-giegold.de/en/budget-blockade-hungary-poland/

Graf von Kielmansegg S (2017) The Common Foreign and Security Policy - A Pool of Flexibility Models. In: Giegerich T, Schmitt D, Zeitzmann S (eds) Flexibility in the EU and Beyond. Nomos, Baden-Baden, pp 139–160

Graf von Luckner J (2020) A Novel "Reinforced Cooperation" in the EU: The Viable Option of a NextGenEU Without Poland and Hungary. Verfassungsblog, 9 December 2020, available at https://verfassungsblog.de/a-novel-reinforced-cooperation-in-the-eu/

Grawert R (2012) Homogenität, Identität, Souveränität. Positionen jurisdiktioneller Begriffsdogmatik. Der Staat, 51:189–213

Groussot X (2008) Spirit, Are You There?: Reinforced Judicial Dialogue and the Preliminary Ruling Procedure. Europarättslig tidskrift, 11(4):934–966

Guilloud-Colliat L (2016) Le principe majoritaire et les coopérations renforcées. In: Picod F (ed) Le principe majoritaire en droit de l'Union européenne. Bruylant, Brussels, pp 155–177

Hanf D (2001) Flexibility Clauses in the Founding Treaties, from Rome to Nice. In: De Witte B, Hanf D, Vos E (eds) The Many Faces of Differentiation in EU Law. Intersentia, Antwerp, pp 3–26

Haratsch A (2017) Artikel 20 EUV. In: Pechstein M, Nowak C, Häde U (eds) Frankfurter Kommentar zu EUV, GRC und AEUV. C.H. Beck, Munich

Hatje A (2001) Die institutionelle Reform der Europäischen Union: der Vertrag von Nizza auf dem Prüfstand. Europarecht, 36(2):143–184

Heber C (2021) Enhanced Cooperation and European Tax Law. Oxford University Press, Oxford

Konstadinides T (2011) Constitutional Identity as a Shield and as a Sword: The European Legal Order Within the Framework of National Constitutional Settlement. The Cambridge Yearbook of European Legal Studies, 13:195–218

Kroll DA, Leuffen D (2015) Enhanced Cooperation in Practice. An Analysis of Differentiated Integration in EU Secondary Law. Journal of European Public Policy, 22(3):353–373

Lacchi C (2017) How Much Flexibility Can European Integration Bear in Order to Face the Eurozone Crisis?: Reflections on the EMU inter se International Agreements Between EU Member States. In: Giegerich T, Schmitt D, Zeitzmann S (eds) Flexibility in the EU and Beyond. How Much Differentiation Can European Integration Bear? Nomos, Baden-Baden, pp 225–250

Lenaerts K, Gutman K, Maselis I (2014) EU Procedural Law. Oxford University Press, Oxford

Linke G (2006) Das Instrument der verstärkten Zusammenarbeit im Vertrag von Nizza. Peter Lang, Frankfurt

Lo Schiavo G (2017) The Treaty on Stability, Coordination and Governance and the ESM Treaty: Intergovernmental Arrangements Outside EU Law, but for the Benefit of the EMU? In: Giegerich T, Schmitt D, Zeitzmann S (eds) Flexibility in the EU and Beyond. How Much Differentiation Can European Integration Bear? Nomos, Baden-Baden, pp 195–224

Louis J-V (1995) L'Union européenne et sa monnaie. Commentaire J. Mégret, 2nd edn. Éd. de l'Université de Bruxelles, Brussels

Manger-Nestler C, Böttner R (2019) Der Europäische Währungsfonds nach den Plänen der Kommission. Zeitschrift für ausländisches öffentliches Recht und Völkerrecht, 79(1):43–84

Mangiameli S (2013) Article 2 TEU. In: Blanke H-J, Mangiameli S (eds) The Treaty on European Union – A Commentary. Springer, Heidelberg

Martenczuk B (2000) Die differenzierte Integration und die föderale Struktur der Europäischen Union. Europarecht, 35(3):351–364

Martinico G (2021) Taming National Identity: A Systematic Understanding of Article 4.2 TEU. European Public Law, 27(3):447–464

Messina M (2014) Strengthening Economic Governance of the European Union Through Enhanced Co-operation: A Still Possible, but Already Missed, Opportunity. European Law Review, 39(3):404–417

Monar J (2010) The 'Area of Freedom, Security and Justice': 'Schengen' Europe, Opt-outs, Opt-ins and Associates. In: Dyson K, Sepos A (eds) Which Europe? Palgrave Macmillan, London, pp 279–292

Nettesheim M (2003) EU-Beitritt und Unrechtsaufarbeitung. Europarecht, 38(1):36–64

Novi C (2019) L'attuazione della cooperazione strutturata permanente (PESCO) nella prospettiva di una difesa europea più autonoma ed effettiva. Studi sull'integrazione europea, 14(2):365–386

Ohler C (2017) Artikel 49 EUV. In: Grabitz E, Hilf M, Nettesheim M (eds) Das Recht der Europäischen Union, 62th supplement. C.H. Beck, Munich

Ott A (2017) Differentiation Through Accession Law: Free Movement Rights in an Enlarged European Union. In: De Witte B, Ott A, Vos E (eds) Between Flexibility and Disintegration. Edward Elgar, Cheltenham, pp 146–178

Pilz S (2016) Der Europäische Stabilitätsmechanismus. Mohr Siebeck, Tübingen

Pilz S (2021) Supplement to Title VIII: Introduction. In: Blanke H-J, Böttner R (eds) The Treaty on the Functioning of the European Union, Volume II. Springer, Heidelberg

Piris J-C (2010) The Lisbon Treaty: A Legal and Political Analysis. Cambridge University Press, Cambridge

Rinke B (2015) Formen differenzierter Integration und ihre Konsequenzen in der GASP/GSVP. In: Stratenschulte E (ed) Der Anfang vom Ende? Nomos, Baden-Baden, pp 165–185

Scharrer HE (1984) Abgestufte Integration - Eine Einführung. In: Grabitz E (ed) Abgestufte Integration. Eine Alternative zum herkömmlichen Integrationskonzept? Engel, Kehl, pp 1–30

Schauer M (2000) Schengen - Maastricht - Amsterdam: Auf dem Weg zu einer flexiblen Union. Verlag Österreich, Vienna

Schmidt-Radefeldt R (2013) Article 41 TEU. In: Blanke H-J, Mangiameli S (eds) The Treaty on European Union – A Commentary. Springer, Heidelberg

Schorkopf F (2000) Homogenität in der Europäischen Union. Duncker & Humblot, Berlin

Schütze R (2015) European Constitutional Law, 2nd edn. Cambridge University Press, Cambridge

Sielmann CM (2020) Governing Difference: Internal and External Differentiation in European Union Law. Nomos, Baden-Baden

Solar N (2004) Neues totes Recht?: die "verstärkte Zusammenarbeit" im Entwurf einer Verfassung für Europa. In: Köck H, Lengauer A, Ress G (eds) Europarecht im Zeitalter der Globalisierung. Linde, Vienna, pp 511–528

Tekin F (2012) Opt-outs, opt-ins, opt-arounds?: Eine Analyse der Differenzierungsrealität im Raum der Freiheit, der Sicherheit und des Rechts. integration, 35(4):237–257

Thym D (2004) Ungleichzeitigkeit und europäisches Verfassungsrecht. Nomos, Baden-Baden

Tuytschaever F (1999) Differentiation in European Union Law. Hart, Oxford

Uerpmann-Wittzack R (2013) Völkerrecht als Ausweichordnung - am Beispiel der Euro-Rettung. In: Hatje A (ed) Die Einheit des Unionsrechts im Zeichen der Krise. Nomos, Baden-Baden, pp 49–60

von Bogdandy A, Schill S (2011) Overcoming Absolute Primacy: Respect for National Identity Under the Lisbon Treaty. Common Market Law Review, 48(5):1417–1454

Vos E, Weimer M (2017) Differentiated Integration or Uniform Regime? National Derogations from EU Internal Market Measures. In: De Witte B, Ott A, Vos E (eds) Between Flexibility and Disintegration - The Trajectory of Differentiation in EU Law. Edward Elgar, Cheltenham, pp 304–335

Wendel M (2011) Lisbon Before the Courts: Comparative Perspectives. European Constitutional Law Review, 7(1):96–137

Wessels W (1998) Verstärkte Zusammenarbeit. Eine neue Variante flexibler Integration. In: Jopp M, Maurer A, Schmuck O (eds) Die Europäische Union nach Amsterdam. Europa-Union-Verlag, Bonn, pp 187–218

Zeitzmann S (2015) Zuviel gewollt, zu wenig geregelt? Das komplizierte Verhältnis der Verstärkten Zusammenarbeit zum acquis communautaire. In: Stratenschulte E (ed) Der Anfang vom Ende? Nomos, Baden-Baden, pp 103–134

Zilioli C, Selmayr M (2001) The Law of the European Central Bank. Hart, London

Chapter 9
European Constitutional Identity as a Normative Concept: Pointing to the Core of European Democracies

Giuliano Vosa

Contents

Abstract Whereas national identity has enjoyed considerable success in the debates on the Union and *identitarian arguments* are often deployed to limit the Union law's applicative priority on national laws, a 'European identity' struggles to acquire relevance, let alone normative value, in either discourse. Nevertheless, arguments have been recently raised to back a non-limited Union law's priority in the assumption of, or building on, a normative conception of European identity derived from sociology or political science. Pursuant to an examination thereof, this chapter argues that a European identity concept of that kind would pave the way for an overwhelming Union law's primacy based on moral-rationalist arguments only, political conflicts then being silenced rather than resolved. Conversely, both a historical and a literal-systematic reading of the Treaties reveal that a European identity should rather defend a constitutional equilibrium between the Union and the States based on respect for national democratic self-government and on the protection of rights by equivalent standards. Such a concept would foster a European public sphere as the place for accountable decisions of supranational relevance and link the Union law's applicative priority with a reinforced, actual consent of the (peoples of the) Member States.

G. Vosa (✉)
Department of Law, University of Catania, Catania, Italy
e-mail: Giuliano.vosa@unict.it

© T.M.C. ASSER PRESS and the authors 2023
J. de Poorter et al. (eds.), *European Yearbook of Constitutional Law 2022*,
European Yearbook of Constitutional Law 4,
https://doi.org/10.1007/978-94-6265-595-9_9

Keywords European constitutionalism · European values · Constitutional identity · Judicial dialogue · Legal principles · Rule of law · Representation · Sovereignty

9.1 Introduction: Why a Normative European Identity?

The concept of European identity regularly eludes a scholarly definition and rarely features in legal texts; it is safe to say that it could hardly be given normative value. In Maastricht, 'European identity' became the trademark of the European Union *vis-à-vis* international actors, with special regard to the prospective construction of a common defence policy that would make Europe independent from geopolitical partners.[1] Yet, as claimed in the Recitals, affirming a European identity on the international scene is instrumental to promoting 'peace, security and progress in Europe and in the world'; thereby, a link emerges with the values that have set in motion the constitutionalisation of the European polity.

In fact, good reasons exist to argue that a normative concept of European identity would not be at odds with the Union law *acquis*, but somehow consistent with the integration path, although the term *identity* became *à la mode* only recently.[2] As Europe's narrative goes, a constitutional motion revolving around a nucleus of common values has triggered the turn from an *economic* Community to a *constitutionalised* Union, in which the protection of fundamental rights is guaranteed by reference to 'common constitutional traditions'.[3] Hence, applicative priority of Union law *vis-à-vis* an ever-expanding array of (even) constitutional cases has been attained by means of general 'inviolable'[4] legal principles that build on such traditions[5] and, as fundamental rights,[6] bind the Union's institutions as well as Member States.[7] This manifold constitutional flow leading to the formulation and adoption of the Charter of Fundamental Rights[8] has been repeatedly associated with a European identity of some kind.[9]

---

[1] See Article B of the Treaty of Maastricht, OJ C 191, 29 July 1992, pp. 1–112.

[2] Weiler 2005, p. 184.

[3] Sadurski 2006, p. 2.

[4] Cartabia 1995, p. 173.

[5] Tridimas 1999, p. 23; see also Liisberg 2001, p. 1.

[6] Lenaerts 1999, p. 423.

[7] Rossi 2002, p. 565.

[8] Alston and Weiler 1998, p. 658; von Bogdandy 2000b, p. 1307; Eeckhout 2002, p. 945; de Búrca and Aschenbrenner 2004, p. 3.

[9] Von Bogdandy 2000a, p. 28.

Be that as it may, today a European identity's normative concept seems somehow neglected as a suitable option to help ease an utterly polarized dispute.[10] While identity talks continue to ignite the debate,[11] the current legal and political state of affairs is affected by diverging tensions. On one side, claims to primacy are as enhanced for they are fragmented. Enhanced, for the Union is seeking applicative priority in areas hardly covered by its own competence,[12] or even quite clearly excluded.[13] Fragmented, as a seesawing approach has been endorsed by the Union institutions before the contrary claims raised by national courts: blunt towards Spain,[14] tolerant with Italy,[15] silent in respect to Denmark,[16] exacerbated towards Germany,[17] harsh *vis-à-vis* Poland[18]—the scale of the reactions mirroring the political characteristics of the issues concerned rather than the intrinsic persuasiveness of the legal arguments brought to the table.

On the other side, national claims are raised, yet in different tones and with diverse content, towards a selective application of Union law. Some envisage a rupture of the Union as such, being ready to pay that price for the sake of their national interests.[19] Radical *Exit* is no longer a pure theoretical option, but a concrete one[20]—successfully practiced, as well-known, by one Member State; but also deployed as a threat before other States who were reluctant to obey certain Union measures.[21]

This chapter aims to interrogate the topic of a European identity to unleash its normative potential, *i.e.* to elucidate the ties between this concept and the Union law's primacy. After a survey of recent scholarly attempts in that field, and a special focus on the 'systemic deficiencies' doctrine, the analysis involves Article 2 TEU as the legal basis of this identity and looks at Articles 4(2) and 9 TEU for a systematic reading thereof. Pursuant to a comparison with the Maastricht's formula—laid down in then-Article F—concerning the relation between the Union and the States, it is argued that a normative concept of European identity ties respect for self-government to compliance with equivalent standards for protection of fundamental rights. Eventually, three claims in favour of such a normative European identity are put forward to highlight the advantages of deploying this tool in the relationships between the (courts of the) Union and (of) the Member States.

---

[10] Cruz Villalón 2013, p. 501.

[11] Martinico and Pollicino 2020, p. 228; Drinóczi 2020, p. 105.

[12] Poulou 2017, p. 991; Steinbach 2019, p. 1363; Bast 2020.

[13] Krajevski 2018, p. 395; Bonelli and Claes 2018, p. 622; Ovádek 2018.

[14] Torres Pérez 2014, p. 308.

[15] Rauchegger 2018, p. 1521; Piccirilli 2018, p. 814.

[16] Krunke and Klinge 2018, p. 157.

[17] Fabbrini 2020.

[18] Lasek-Markey 2021; Uitz 2021.

[19] See Weiler and Lustig 2018, p. 315.

[20] Wilkinson 2017, p. 213.

[21] Habermas 2015.

9.2 From Sociology to Political Science and Law: The European Identity in Search of a Normative Dimension

While 'national identity' is deployed to prevent, or to deflect, the application of Union law,[22] a 'European identity' has hardly been credited with normative force. It may seem paradoxical, but what can be located as lying at the core of the *Euro-unitary* polity remains unclear. Perhaps, one may say, such an indeterminacy is instrumental to the Union's very success, as a typical *tolerance* has allowed Member States to preserve their own constitutional settlements while aiming at an *ever closer union*.[23] Nonetheless, in times of acute social-political fractures and rampant disagreement on prime constitutional concepts,[24] it may seem convenient to supply European identity with a structured legal background in view of better articulating the claims for the Union law's applicative priority—particularly, when rights and interests at stake are of the most sensitive nature.

To be sure, the simple fact that in the passage from Maastricht to Lisbon the Treaties have ventured on the slippery path of multiple national identities entails a certain restraint when endowing a single European one with legal force.[25] Debates incline towards a socio-political understanding of 'identity'.[26] Yet, if this approach is taken, the analysis hardly delves into the conditions under which Union law enjoys applicative priority. Rather, these debates replicate the pattern of the dispute on the possibility, and opportunity, of a Constitution for Europe; therefore, they do not provide a legal answer to the question of whether, and to which extent, Union law must prevail over national laws.

However, in the recent literature, several argumentative paths aim to construe a bridge between a socio-philosophical concept of a 'European identity' and the applicative priority of Union law regarding an ever-expanding range of cases. These arguments hardly refer to identity as such; yet, they revolve around the same pattern— a nucleus of European values to be endowed with normative force—and, although to a different extent, they follow a similar methodological paradigm: relying on sociology and political science as a twofold background to derive legal concepts.

In short, yet conceding to rough schematism, attempts to create, or to assume, a normative concept of European identity can be presented along four lines. The most recent of such attempts can be found in Armin von Bogdandy's work on 'Our European Society' published in English as a post on *Verfassungsblog* in May 2021[27]

---

[22] See Faraguna 2017, p. 1617; most recently, see the Polish Constitutional Court's judgments on the relations between the Polish legal order and the EU (*Trybunał Konstytucyjny Polski*, K 3/21, judgment of 7 October 2021) and the ECHR (K 6/21, judgment of 24 November 2021); comments in Garner and Lawson 2021.

[23] Weiler 2003, p. 7.

[24] Weiler 2009, p. 77.

[25] Kochenov 2013, p. 97.

[26] Rosenfeld 2009, p. 11.

[27] Von Bogdandy 2021a.

and in German as an *Editorial* in *Der Staat* (with an even more revealing title).[28] Building on Niklas Luhmann and Hartmut Kaelble, von Bogdandy points to the progression of the 'European society' from the late '80s onwards. In his account, Kaelble, in 2020, stated that '[s]ince 1987, ... the societies of the Member States have continued to grow together "substantially", despite and because of many crises and major conflicts'. Hence, what is today Article 2 TEU cannot be thought of as a product of 'a few people who, while working in the Brussels bubble in the *Rue de la Loi* area, concocted it for the failed Constitutional Treaty'. Rather, it must be seen as 'an instance of self-description' meeting the self-reflexivity required for a collective European 'we' to arise[29]—hence, for a sort of 'constitutional moment' in the European history.

The work makes ample reference to Ferdinand von Schirach's *manifesto* on Six New Fundamental Rights.[30] While explaining that '[p]olitics no longer seems to be able to cope with six of the greatest challenges of our time: (1) destruction of the environment, (2) digitalisation, (3) the power of algorithms, (4) systematic lies in politics, (5) unchecked globalisation and (6) threats to the rule of law', von Schirach calls for 'an enhanced European citizenship' that comprises these six rights. Then, if one bears in mind the functionalist approach of the European integration, the link between a 'European society' concept and a European identity endowed with normative force looks clearer. To put it roughly: while rights from 1 to 5 present prospective, yet promising paths for legal action, the sixth has already made its way into the current practice of Union law—to the extent that, following the 'rule of law's defence', Poland would first experiment with the applicability thereof, Romania and Hungary being next.[31] The European Courts—first and foremost, the Court of Justice—could therefore impose a supranational law of principles regardless of a State's sovereignty, *i.e.* even against the contrary view of those who are to be bound by that law. Perhaps, the functionalist idea of progression through little steps would make the erosion of national competences more tolerable for sceptics.[32] But however politically desirable it may be, this result would not be without consequences as regards the Union's constitutional settlement. In fact, pursuant to such ground-breaking reasoning, little room would remain for national courts to oppose what would look like 'absolute'[33] primacy of a law of principles elaborated by *experts*[34]— in Courts, in Academia, in the 'competent' *technical* bodies. Such a consequence could satisfy those who, among scholars as well as in the sphere of politics, support

---

[28] Von Bogdandy 2021b, p. 171.

[29] See Poiares Maduro 2004, p. 40.

[30] Available at: https://you.wemove.eu/campaigns/for-new-fundamental-rights-in-europe.

[31] See, as for the Romanian case, ECJ, C-357/19 *et alt.*, *Euro Box Promotion* (et. alt.), 21 December 2021, ECLI:EU:C:2021:170, and comments on that saga at https://verfassungsblog.de/tag/rom anian-constitutional-court/. On the Hungarian case, see the Hungarian Constitutional Court's judgment X/00477/2021 of 10 December 2021; comments by Chronowski and Vincze 2021; Szekeres 2021; Kazai 2022.

[32] Loughlin 2017, p. 57.

[33] Arena 2018, p. 300.

[34] Scharpf 2016, p. 29.

G. Vosa

the continued progress of the European project; yet, doubts as to whether it would be legally acceptable and politically desirable on a general plane are certainly in order.

This insight proves useful when it comes to confronting further arguments that assume a normative concept of European identity. One lies in Spieker's proposal to read the conflicts between national constitutional courts and the Court of Justice as 'conflicts of values'.[35] Launched in an article published in 2020 in the *Common Market Law Review*,[36] this proposal, far from satisfying a frivolous aspiration, carries significant normative ambition. To present such conflicts in terms of values may lead to a situation in which, whatever the solution sought, sacrificed positions would be declared illegal and cancelled from the European legal universe, as contrary to the values the latter is built on. In fact, as far as scholars are concerned, incompatible values hardly coexist in a single order, while principles stemming from such values— by way of balancing—can.[37] 'Reasoning by values', as Norberto Bobbio puts it, is radically different from 'reasoning by principles';[38] then, deriving the former from the latter is hardly a neutral operation. As a result, the *BVerfG*'s position in *PSPP* would be held not only contrary to the position of the Court of Justice, but contrary to the Union values as such; the same goes for the Danish Supreme Court's position in *Ajos*, and for any other position that dissents from the stances the Union takes for each specific case—and the other way around, too, should national positions prevail. A twofold consequence would arise: the interests and rights at stake would be straightforwardly denied, and the arguments concerned likewise disqualified as forbidden, unfounded or irrelevant. Hence, if the national position prevails, the way is paved for further *Exits*; else, absolute primacy would be imposed at the discretion of the Luxembourg Court. Put this way, this looks like a more sophisticated version of the *take-it-or-leave-it* argument that clusters 'Europeanists' and 'sovereigntists' on the opposite banks of a single river:[39] it does not contribute to easing the current tensions, but, on the contrary, it appears to increase polarization.

Another similar proposal, yet perhaps even more sophisticated, is formulated by Giuseppe Martinico in a 2015 article on the 'polemical spirit of EU law'[40] published in the *German Law Journal* and relaunched in 2018 in a chapter in Davies and Avbelj 2017.[41]

Martinico highlights that constitutional pluralism has had troubles in dealing with conflicts. Indeed, both moderate and radical pluralists do not envisage specific legal tools to deal with (and try to solve) conflicts. Rather, they tend either to set aside that question—trusting the *auto-correct function* of pluralist systems[42]—or to phrase it as

---

[35] Spieker 2019, p. 386.

[36] Ibid., p. 361.

[37] Aleinikoff 1987, p. 945; Zagrebelsky 2002, p. 865; Zagrebelsky 2008, p. 205; Petersen 2013, p. 1387.

[38] Bobbio 1999, p. 139.

[39] Loughlin 2013, p. 34; Kelemen 2016, p. 136.

[40] Martinico 2015, p. 1374.

[41] Martinico 2018, p. 78.

[42] Bobić 2020, p. 60.

an evaluation of the 'best fit', *i.e.*, of the best possible way of pursuing goals that are assumed as common, which leads to treating—and eventually eliding—conflicts in a *télos*-oriented perspective.[43] Then, he adds, a better-fitting theoretical framework would be Chantal Mouffe's agonistic pluralism,[44] the key premise of which is an 'agonistic democratic public sphere' that is to be defended against all those 'who put its basic institutions into question'.[45] Hence, the 'friend-foe' divide, though placed at the boundaries of a 'democratic' public sphere, is restored; the acknowledgement of conflicts and the critique to 'irenic' constitutional approaches[46] seem to ultimately draw a line between, so to say, what is 'acceptable' as a conflictive matter and what is not. Such a line is placed with some degree of arbitrariness, as it relies on subjective conceptions of democracy and constitutionalism: a matter of philosophy, political theory, ethics and other such social sciences, more than of law.

As a consequence, value judgments pave the ground for any pluralistic interlocution, and certain positions may be simply ruled out as non-acceptable. To say it openly: positions that, in light of these value judgments, would be held in breach of 'basic democratic institutions', would be held illegal even if they conveyed political issues that could deserve to find shelter in the Union's pluralistic order.

Were such to be the normative yardstick of a European identity, the latter would rest on merely material grounds assumed as an *a priori* to democratic bargaining, which, though highly politically desirable it may be in times of aggravating polarization, might lead to the exclusion of certain positions regardless of the possibly legitimate political points that lay at their roots. Whether the Union can afford it, in moral, political, legal and finally social terms, is certainly a matter for discussion.

9.3 The 'Systemic Deficiencies' Concepts and Its Discontents

Along this line, the journey from sociology and political science to law reached a *crescendo* when the 'systemic deficiencies' concept enters the scene. In Union law, elaborations of such a concept date back to 2014. The term has been used by the Commission in non-binding acts;[47] among scholars, the concept has been studied extensively in the Max-Planck-Institute for Comparative Law and Public International Law from 2016 onwards.[48] Particularly, a proposal to sanction such deficiencies via the infringement procedure was advanced in a 2019 MPI Working

---

[43] Kumm 2005, p. 286.

[44] Mouffe 2000, p. 80.

[45] See Martinico 2018, p. 88.

[46] Luciani 2006, p. 1644.

[47] Communication from the Commission to the European Parliament and the Council. A new EU Framework to strengthen the Rule of Law, COM(2014) 158 final.

[48] Von Bogdandy and Ioannidis 2014, p. 59. See also Spieker 2019, p. 1182, and Schmidt and Bogdanowicz 2018, p. 1061.

Paper delivered by Armin von Bogdandy[49] and then re-launched in 2020 in the *Common Market Law Review* by the same author.[50] The thick theoretical substance and the multiple practical implications of this work ask for an in-depth reading.

The conceptual frame set at the beginning seems that of a communication between legal orders—pluralist, inter-systemic—but it entails 'the exercise of public authority';[51] hence, it can only be produced on the basis of an evaluation that, albeit external to one of the systems—*i.e.* the 'inflamed' one—has the power to unilaterally modify it. This leads to abandoning the pluralist, inter-systemic scenario to embrace a monist, *Verfassungsverbund*-like approach to the Union[52]—as the author reveals by using the term 'European *Verbund*' in the same passage.[53] Yet, crucial conceptual knots of the *Verfassungsverbund*—namely, the link between voluntarism (the 'will of the people') and the law flowing from the multilevel structure[54]—are shadowed by the following magniloquent statement:

> European constitutionalism is perhaps facing a 'constitutional moment': the decision whether it comprises illiberal democracies or whether it fights them. The first case would herald the end of the European Union's current self-understanding, as 'illiberal democracies' would co-inform the common values of Article 2 TEU in the future. The alternative path requires the Union to resist illiberal threats.[55]

The latter leans on the assumption that either 'democratic' values fight, and expulse, 'illiberal' elements, or such illiberal elements enter, and virtually oust, democracy. Only one of the two can survive, and the labels 'democracy' and 'illiberal' are used from a standpoint that does not conceal its partiality. Noticeably, the will of the people(s) and of the States that would have to fight each other or co-exist simply never makes it to the level of relevance. A fully-fledged *friend-foe* paradigm is consciously adopted, and its symbolic force deployed to bluntly elide pluralism in the name of a supreme good for the so-individuated community: 'surviving' the *enemy*.

> To achieve this, European constitutionalism must draw and defend 'red lines', which would also imply a considerable constitutional development: European constitutionalism would gain in profile and develop elements of a militant democracy.[56]

The divide between law and politics is purposely blurred, and the 'purity' of the former renounced with no hesitation; democratic institutions are oriented to combat what is presented as 'illiberal', in a massive, yet partisan, deployment of constitutional resources. Blurred is, furthermore, the distinction between values and principles:

---

[49] Von Bogdandy 2019b, p. 1.

[50] Von Bogdandy 2020, p. 705.

[51] Von Bogdandy 2019b, p. 5; p. 12.

[52] Pernice 1999, p. 703.

[53] Von Bogdandy 2019b, p. 12.

[54] Pernice 1999, p. 709.

[55] Von Bogdandy 2019b, p. 3.

[56] Ibid., p. 12.

It is common to contrast values with law, with the consequence that Article 2 stipulates normative, but non-legal guidelines. Therefore, a deficiency of values would not require a breach of law, according to the dualism of values and the law. The Commission strives to distinguish between law and value: 'The Commission, beyond (!) its task to ensure the respect of EU law, is also responsible (…) for guaranteeing the common values of the Union.'[57]

In the very same words of the Commission, law and values are two different objects, a deficiency in values not necessarily amounting to a breach of law. Nevertheless, the author argues,

> [t]his differentiation is hardly convincing. The values of Article 2 TEU are laid down in the Treaty on European Union, a legal text, and not only in the declaratory part, *i.e.* the preamble, but also in the operative part. They are conceived to be binding and are applied by public institutions in procedures established by law, as stated in Articles 3, 7, or 13 TEU. Violating these values can result in sanctions, which are equally stipulated in the TEU. Whichever concept of the law is used: the values of Article 2 TEU are a part of Union law.[58]

As a result of this terse assumption, the distance between values and principles is annulled: the values of Article 2 TEU 'qualify as fundamental legal principles' and can be used as such by the Court of Justice. The ample literature on the difference between the two is knowingly downplayed for a concrete practical purpose. Against this background, no specific breach of law is required for a systemic deficiency to be detected: the 'illegality' threshold is met even in cases of 'serious risks', or 'threats', to the survivance of the pre-individuated community. As a matter of fact, the author contends,

> Article 7 allows for acting in case of a 'clear risk', and, according to the Rule of Law Framework, the Commission can issue a rule of law recommendation 'if it finds that there is objective evidence of a systemic threat and that the authorities of that Member State are not taking appropriate action to redress it'.[59]

This argument is definitively telling: a framework that is conducive to political action is taken as reference for legal actions that generate binding effects—as the infringement procedure does. Building on an idea that echoes the '*Reverse Solange*' doctrine,[60] this reasoning points to the Union's *constitutional core* with a view to preventing a 'strategic restriction of constitutional rights'—thereby, following a line of reasoning that was also adopted in 2013 by Daniel Sarmiento, albeit in a different fashion.[61]

Eventually, one may say that recent attempts to create, or to assume, a European identity concept as a legal yardstick to support the Union law's applicative priority display three pertinent characteristics.

First, these attempts rely on value-based judgments even at the cost of excluding certain positions that legitimately enjoy a right to voice, and they do so with a view

---

[57] Ibidem, pp. 13–14.

[58] Ibidem, p. 14.

[59] Ibidem, p. 15.

[60] See Antpöhler et al. 2012, p. 489.

[61] Sarmiento Ramírez-Escudero 2013, p. 191.

to treating the concerned conflict as illegal and to impose a given solution thereto. Advocates of such views are aware of the 'tyranny of values' risk[62] and accept it for the sake of defending their own community—although the community they claim to speak for does include *others*, too, who legitimately *dissent*. Then, having regard to that whole community, the gist of this reasoning may be seen as the *pro domo sua* argument of some groups, classes, or otherwise formed circles, who have gained prevalence in a certain society and seek to reinforce it.

Second, they virtually overlook the fact that the holders of the rights recognized by public authorities must have a substantial voice in determining the content of such rights. This pillar of *post*-WWII constitutions undergirds the general proclamation of universal suffrage, and, as a consequence, the imposition of the legality principle on administrative action and the creation of powerful constitutional courts meant to protect rights against the will of the legislature.[63] To deny it would entail a step back towards XIX century constitutions, in which the politically relevant society was defined *ratione census* and, rather than recognized, rights were conceded—*octroyés*—to an inert populace.

Third, they disrupt the balance between *ratio* and *voluntas* in the understanding of law.[64] Throughout time, law has been obeyed because of its intrinsic correspondence to generally felt exigences of justice and rationality, and/or for it corresponded to the will of the sovereign. In *post*-WWII constitutions, a renewed balance is sought between the people's sovereignty and the limitations thereto—hence, between a voluntarist and a moral-rationalist element, the former tied to the *volonté générale*, the latter to scholarly-judicial elaboration. Therefore, should a European identity pave the way to a fully-fledged applicative priority of a Union law of principles of doctrinal-judicial ancestry solely, the link with the initial intent of the Member States would be severed (let alone the link with an actual will of the people(s) involved). This would signpost an over-powering prevalence of moral-rational arguments over arguments based on the will of the law's recipient: in other words, it would lead to law being imposed because of its intrinsic *rightfulness*, no voice rights being necessary, nor consent required for specific binding effects to arise.

That the three characteristics just mentioned indicate a departure, maybe a definitive one, from the political-constitutional arrangements laid down in the constitutions of the Member States, seems hard to deny: the principle of the 'people's sovereignty' features in the prime articles of all of them and yet is being marginalised to a substantive extent.[65]

Thereby, two conclusions are possible. Either Union law is allowed to cut the ties with those political-constitutional arrangements—hence, to depart from States' identities and to replace them with a new one, no act of political responsibility at all being necessary to that purpose—or, conversely, it is not allowed to do so.

---

[62] Von Bogdandy 2019a.

[63] Duong 2020, p. 29.

[64] Campanini 1966, p. 45.

[65] Carlassare 2006, p. 1.

If the first is true, a normative concept of European identity would legitimately serve as a *passepartout* to impose absolute primacy at the expense of national constitutional law, which would only be accepted in the European legal order so long as compatible with what the Court of Justice holds to be part of the European identity.

Contrarily, in the latter case, a European constitutional identity must comprise and protect, rather than overwhelm, national laws, and cherish the links with the effective, actual will of the people(s) and the States involved as much as the integrity of the principles it refers to—both being regarded as elements of a constitutional legacy that ought to be defended and transposed to the supranational level.

9.4 The Positive Grounds for a Normative European Identity

Though it is widely accepted that the interpretive canon of international law departs from strict legal positivism, written texts remain at the core of hermeneutic activity. Hence, it does not seem inopportune to rely on fundamental legal documents, such as the Treaties, to investigate the possible foundational grounds of a normative European identity.

Article 2 TEU is commonly understood as the basic norm in that regard.[66]

> The Union is founded on the values of respect for human dignity, freedom, democracy, equality, the rule of law and respect for human rights, including the rights of persons belonging to minorities. These values are common to the Member States in a society in which pluralism, non-discrimination, tolerance justice, solidarity and equality between women and men prevail.

One may legitimately wonder whether the selected order of the words reflects a specific relation among the concepts that those words express. Indeed, it would have been inappropriate to draft such a crucial provision, utterly rich in axiological implications, randomly. Therefore, one is let to presume that such an order is not random and, absent evidence to the contrary, to expose the logical-systematical connections that the selected order unleashes.

Human dignity occupies, in German fashion, the top of the conceptual pyramid in which these values are structured—a construct, to be sure, of a pure logical-systematic nature, which ought not to imply a *Wertordnung* nor somewhat of a pre-established hierarchy among these values.[67]

From human dignity descend, in this order, freedom, democracy, equality, rule of law and respect for human rights, including the rights of minorities.

As the cornerstone of the values' architecture, human dignity is assumedly the richest in axiological potential. Indeed, having regard to the history of the concept concerned, two lines can be detected which unleash that potential.[68] One considers

---

[66] In OJ C 326, 26 October 2012, pp. 13–390.

[67] See Habermas 2010, p. 464.

[68] Ridola 2010, p. 77.

human dignity as a *gift*, the divine glimmer that makes humans special *vis-à-vis* other creatures; it inclines towards natural rights and entertains a *dialectic* relation with freedom—as human persons may not fully dispose of their own dignity, to the existence of which they did not contribute. The other one argues that human dignity is tied to a conscious self-determination of the human person, both as an individual and as a member of social groups, who is recognized as the master of his or her own destiny: it enjoys a directly proportionate relation with freedom and conceives of rights as products of self-determination, with, in principle, faculty of disposal by their holders.

Yet at the cost of exploring such a massive conceptual edifice with rough superficiality for the sake of brevity, this bipartition gives a hint on the intertwining argumentative lines that lay at the core of European democracies and permeate Europe's most fundamental constitutional grounds.

Human dignity is, first and foremost, coupled with freedom, which marks the choice of the Treaty's drafters towards the second of the abovementioned lines—the 'freedom'; yet, without ignoring the 'gift' by any means. Therefore, freedom of individual self-determination, in the private sphere, adds to freedom of collective self-determination in the public sphere: as democracy and equality come next, there is no room for individualism as an exasperation of the private independence,[69] in Constant's guise.[70] In fact, the link from dignity and freedom to democracy and equality endorses a certain conception of democracy, which is tied to the expression of individual and collective self-determination of free, equal persons—equal in participation (including the duty/right to vote)[71] as well as equal before the democratically-made law, the rule of which is to be protected.[72] The paradigm of '*égaliberté*', *i.e.* freedom of equals in an equal society, points at dignity as conducive to the right to decide for one's own destiny, as a person and as a group.[73]

In this vein, the 'gift' axiological line supplements the 'freedom' one—the 'freedom' line—by pointing at certain rights that must be protected not only as a consequence of individual-collective self-determination, but also as manifestations of a moral-rational *acquis* elaborated by non-democratic, but otherwise legitimized, institutions. Following this line, rights are recognized as belonging not only to those who participate in the law-making, but to humans in general, as holders of an equal dignity. This conclusion, while supporting the recognition of human rights and of the rights of minorities—who, in principle, lack a voice of enough relevance to influence law-making—meets the universal-cosmopolitan aspirations of supranational law.[74]

---

[69] Somek 2008, p. 272.

[70] Constant 1819/1997, p. 589.

[71] Lanchester 1983, p. 31.

[72] See, for instance, *Bundesverfassungsgericht*, Judgment of the First Senate of 15 February 2006 - 1 BvR 357/05, para 121.

[73] Balibar 2010, p. 11.

[74] Stone Sweet 2012, p. 53.

On such grounds, European society proclaims itself plural, aimed at non-discrimination, based on tolerance and pursuing justice, solidarity, and gender equality.

As far as this chapter is concerned, there would be three implications of such a reading of Article 2 TEU.

The first elucidates the *inclusive* attitude of the Union's values, which accept the recognition of rights not only to themselves, but to humans in general, and to minorities:[75] in fact, they endorse the contrary of an *introverted*, exclusive *militant* approach. While the latter would imply that only those who are part of the Union (or anyway make it to the level of being able to influence law-making) could be recognised as genuine holders of rights, the Union's approach ensures that certain rights are understood as belonging to persons as such.

The second strikes a balance between the sovereign will of the people and the protection of rights in continuity with the constitutions of the Member States—*i.e.* prioritizing freedom as a display of human dignity and providing guidance for it to be expressed in both individual and collective forms, while the 'gift' line works as a (necessary) *countermajoritarian* supplement.

The third conveys the idea that the rule of law is not a principle to be imposed regardless of the voluntarist element, rather it acquires the substance of a legal parameter inasmuch as the 'law' meant to 'rule' includes both the elements cited above.[76] As a consequence, one may contend, to impose the 'rule of law' as a principle of pure doctrinal-judicial descent, severed from any voluntarist element, would lead to a logic fallacy, as that 'law' would hardly possess the requirements to qualify as legally binding and the principle concerned would be deprived of legal force.

9.5 Fine-tuning the Normative European Identity: Backing or Denying 'Absolute' Primacy?

Arguments in support of such a reading of Article 2 TEU feature in pertinent links with other provisions of the same Treaty. As well known, Article 4(2) TEU, first line, points to the relations between the Union and the Member States:

> The Union shall respect the equality of Member States before the Treaties as well as their national identities, inherent in their fundamental structures, political and constitutional, inclusive of regional and local self-government.

On this basis, two argumentative lines have been raised to hold that, despite the wording of the Treaty, national law must give way to the applicative priority of Union law. One outlines that, being Article 4(2) a Union law provision, it is solely for the Court of Justice to interpret it—hence, to decide on what exactly the Union is bound

---

[75] Habermas 1995, p. 65.
[76] Zagrebelsky 2008, p. 107.

to 'respect'.[77] The other points to the fact that, should restraints of a substantive sort be articulated by national courts, equality among States would be irreversibly impaired.[78]

Against the first line, a counterargument would rely on the history of the Union integration. In fact, Article 4(2) TEU has a famous antecedent in the Treaty of Maastricht, Article F thereof stating as follows:

> The Union shall respect the national identities of its Member States, whose systems of government are founded on the principles of democracy.
>
> The Union shall respect fundamental rights, as guaranteed by the [ECHR] and as they result from the constitutional traditions common to the Member States, as general principles of Community law.

Following the evolutionary trajectory from Maastricht to Lisbon, it is possible to connect the dots between the two provisions and to discern the elements they have in common.

National identity—the object of the Union's respect—is tied to national democratic self-government; thereby, it lays in the abovementioned balance between people's sovereignty and protection of rights enshrined in the national constitutions, democratic self-government being the expression of individual and collective manifestations of the dignity of the people(s) concerned. At the same time, the Union binds itself to standards of rights protection that are equivalent to those provided for in national constitutions, as the very same Union's general legal principles build on the common constitutional traditions and develop their *acquis* on the supranational plane.[79]

Hence, the voluntarist element is balanced with the moral-rationalist one, continuity with national constitutions being preserved. Respect for the self-determination of the people(s) of the Member States leads to a circular relation between the two levels—the national and the Union one—through which the European people(s) cooperate to determine the content of the rights to be recognized for the benefit of all Union citizens by equivalent standards.

In fact, behind this formulation, the two lines of 'dual supranationalism'[80] are detectable. One is genuinely political, and leads to the renowned '*Exit, Voice & Loyalty*'[81] *trias* Weiler borrows from Hirschman: in this light, more consistent rights of *Voice* must compensate for enhanced demands of *Loyalty* coming from the 'federal', Union level. The other one is legal, and points to the likewise famous *Solange* formula, according to which national legal orders give the green light to a single supranational one as long as the European standard for protection of rights is consistently deemed equivalent, at least in general terms, to the national ones.[82]

---

[77] Many different nuances of such a straightforward assumption exist: see e.g. Tizzano 2012, p. 811; Claes 2013, p. 109; Amalfitano 2017, p. 9.

[78] Fabbrini 2015, p. 1003.

[79] See Di Federico 2019, p. 344.

[80] Weiler 1981, p. 267.

[81] Weiler 1991, p. 2403.

[82] See e.g. Weatherill and Beaumont 1995, p. 367.

Conclusively: as this twofold yardstick is a *prius* for the limitations of national sovereignty to apply and for the duty of prior application of Union law to bind national courts, thinking of the 'respect' paid by the Union to the Member States merely in terms of the Union's self-limitation would be inconsistent with the overall integration path, and—absent any explicit statement to the contrary—most probably extraneous to Union law.[83]

The second argumentative line enumerated above is countered by reference to Article 9 TEU:

> In all its activities, the Union shall observe the principle of the equality of its citizens, who shall receive equal attention from its institutions, bodies, offices, and agencies. Every national of a Member State shall be a citizen of the Union. Citizenship of the Union shall be additional to national citizenship and shall not replace it.

Formal equality among States, in this light, is supplemented by a perspective of substantive equality—the pursuit of which the Union undertakes as a duty of its own.[84] Furthermore, it appears that in pursuing substantive equality the Union does not resort to the imposition of a supranational, uniform law regardless of the 'respect' provided for in Article 4(2). In fact, the duty to pursue substantive equality qualifies as one of 'equal attention' towards the citizens, which does not entail uniformity as an immediate consequence but leaves room for further ponderation of the rights and interests at stake. From this angle, Articles 4(2) and 9 TEU can be looked at as two sides of the same coin and read in conjunction with Article 2 TEU.

In sum: to impose a certain measure of Union law on all Member States without regard of the specificities of each may well satisfy formal equality while violating substantive equality. In fact, it is possible that such measure entails a prejudice for sensitive rights/interests of the citizens of one Member State while giving advantages, even conspicuous in size and extent, to the citizens of another Member State.[85] In this case, the measure of Union law concerned could hardly be considered as legally binding on the latter State.

In this regard, mentioning the Union's citizenship in the second line of the same paragraph underscores the continuity with the political-constitutional settlement enshrined in the constitutions of Member States.[86] As a matter of fact, 'equal attention' refers to the twofold 'citizen' *status* possessed by Member States' nationals. Therefore, European citizens are called on to play a role of the following sort: as 'sovereigns', they participate in law-making at both levels. In fact, they contribute to determining the content of the rights whose protection is sought at each national level and, at the same time, at the supranational one—*i.e.*, by the Union institutions as a result of the above-cited 'equal attention'.

Conclusively, in light of Articles 2, 4(2) and 9 TEU, an equilibrium of constitutional rank welds together the *Euro-unitary* arrangements from the Member States

---

[83] See Komárek 2013, p. 420.

[84] Zaccaroni 2021, p. 20.

[85] Goldoni 2012, p. 385.

[86] See Menéndez and Olsen 2020, p. 20.

to the Union. This equilibrium possesses three salient features. First, it is as much as possible inclusive towards the rights of humans, and of minorities, in the name of human dignity. Second, it actively offers ways to proceed to such inclusion by respecting national democratic self-government before rights and interests of the utmost sensitivity: it aims to create a supranational, multi-layered public sphere where conflicts between Member States and the Union can find, should they exceed the capacities of the multi-level judicial dialogue, space for a sufficiently pondered political solution. Third, it preserves the balance of voluntarism and rationalism-moralism in law-making, so that a doctrinal-judicial elaboration of general principles of Union law finds its counterpart in the genuine consent of those who are to abide by such law.

It seems sensible to say that, should a normative concept of European identity be coined, it ought to consider this overall picture as a benchmark, and to prevent, rather than impose, a straightforward applicative priority of Union law should any of these features be lacking.

9.6 Conclusions: Three Claims in Support of a Normative European Identity

The *golden age* of European constitutionalism[87] became a vibrant autumn by the demise of the Constitutional Treaty and turned into winter following the 2008 crisis.[88] In the aftermaths, numerous claims to oppose the applicative priority of Union law have been raised; some of them aimed at a selective application, some others more radical—one of which ended, as well-known, with the withdrawal of a Member State. By contrast, the Union has continued to impose its law as prior-in-application while seeking to enhance its applicative scope.[89] Contrary to such an enhancement stands the principle of conferral; nevertheless, its theoretical background and operational modalities are in fact a matter for conflict,[90] the language of the European integration entering a stage of utter confusion.[91]

Against this background, deploying a normative European identity as a nuclear weapon to turn the Union law's applicative priority into a fully-fledged federal supremacy could be, and actually is, a tempting option. Signs of the Union institutions consistently brooding on such an idea surface in the Romanian saga: even opinions contained in a recommendation issued by the Commission in the framework of Romania's 'conditioned' adhesion (settled in an *ad hoc* Decision)[92] trigger the

---

[87] Balaguer Callejón 2012, p. 99.

[88] Joerges 2014, p. 985.

[89] Bartoloni 2018, p. 10.

[90] Jakab 2016, p. 65.

[91] Balaguer Callejón 2004, p. 317.

[92] See Commission Decision 2006/928/EC of 13 December 2006 establishing a mechanism for cooperation and verification of progress in Romania to address specific benchmarks in the areas of

non-application of conflicting national law if the Court of Justice drops 'rule of law' as an *ace-wins-all*, making it a yardstick that Member States must comply with even in matters of their own competence.[93]

Yet, at the current state of Union law, such a powerful tool would present a crucial, threefold problem: it would be at odds with the trajectory of the integration, hostile towards the robust constitutional background that arises from a systematic reading of the TEU provisions, and, finally, disrespectful *vis-à-vis* the national identity of the Member States 'inherent in their fundamental structures, political and constitutional, inclusive of regional and local self-government', as far as the wording of Article 4(2) TEU is concerned. In other words: such a normative European identity would have little chance to survive a historical argument to the contrary, and even fewer chances if a systematic and a literal argument were offered as a supplement.

Yet, there is another function that a normative European identity can be asked to play, which goes in the opposite direction: to unveil the delicate mechanisms that bind together people's sovereignty and protection of rights in the passage from a State-based to an 'after-State', *supranational* scenario. In other words: a European normative identity could work as a yardstick for judicial review of those pieces of Union law that lack ties with a sufficiently solid consent of (the people of) the Member States.

There would, in fact, be three benefits of a similar legal tool in disentangling the intricate knot of the relations between the Union and the Member States. First, it would call politics back to the table and re-allocate political responsibility to deal with the conflicts. A comeback of political representation as a support for politically sensitive decisions would revitalize a European public sphere that has often, and rightly, been blamed for inconsistency.

Second, it would neutralize the Schmittian, *introvert* potential of the identity concept, which, far from disappearing, looks even reinforced since the word 'sovereignty' was cancelled from the Treaties—to the extent that Gábor Halmai has reported an 'abuse' of the identity concept.[94] By pointing to the general representation that underpins national sovereignty, a European identity of this sort would prompt a multifaceted integration of the citizens into the structures of public power through multiple institutional layers; consequently, the Union construction, rather than polarized by mutually radical positions, would be seeking 'inter-systemic bridges' for reciprocal communication.[95]

---

judicial reform and the fight against corruption – C(2006) 6569), OJ L 354, 14 December 2006, pp. 56–57.

[93] See ECJ, Joint Cases C-83/19, C-127/19 and C-195/19, *Asociaţia «Forumul Judecătorilor din România» v Inspecţia Judiciară*, 18 May 2021, ECLI:EU:C:2021:393, at para 162.

[94] Halmai 2018, p. 23.

[95] Walker 2012, p. 1185.

Third, it would overcome the post-*PSPP* judgment *impasse* as regards the ways to enforce the conferral principle.[96] *PSPP* demonstrated that proportionality is ultimately unfit for this purpose;[97] on the other hand, when it comes to juridically policing the frontiers of attributed powers, subsidiarity, too, has already exposed irremediable flaws.[98] Hence, such a European identity can be a starting point for rephrasing the respective competences of the Union and of the Member States in terms of political sensitivity on the one hand—with special regard to fundamental rights—and of interpretation of the respective legal bases on the other hand.

In other words, such a European identity would require positive law, backed by adequate political responsibility at the national and supranational level, to support pieces of Union law that would otherwise exceed the boundaries of Union competences 'too evidently' in relation to the political sensitivity of the matter concerned. This reasoning, moulded on the '*reserve de loi*' concept, is not alien to comparative judicial reasoning and features in the case-law of the very same Court of Justice, too, as regards secondary legal bases.[99] Legal certainty, understood as the predictability of legal consequences by the rule-followers, would be enhanced, rather than sacrificed on the altar of Union law's uniform application; and the 'rule of law' as the cornerstone of Union values would enshrine a sound balance between voluntarist and moral-rationalist elements as components of 'law', both equally well-rooted in the constitutional traditions of Europe.[100]

Downplaying political conflicts to legal issues shows the intrinsic weakness of the regimes that do so. Yet, as recent narratives from both the Union and some Member States prove, it is a dangerous strategy: a silenced political conflict is doomed to explode if the conditions that have caused it do not come spontaneously to a solution, which is *per se* uncertain. What can be taken for granted is that such a strategy rapidly consumes the legitimacy resources that law possesses and leaves the ground to unregulated social conflicts—which, as history teaches, are conducive to further limitations of rights and liberties.[101] Then, paradoxically, the *militant* defence of shared values would trigger their restriction; something that could hardly be linked with the national political-constitutional *post*-WWII *acquis*, but—as argued rather convincingly—would possibly unveil the *dark legacy* of a turbulent past.[102]

For the opposite, channelling such conflicts into structured, mutually understandable legal tools could help opening spaces for the positions concerned while monitoring the change that unleashing these conflicts would trigger. To this aim, perhaps,

---

[96] *BVerfG*, Judgment of the Second Senate of 5 May 2020 - 2 BvR 859/15, 'PSPP'.

[97] Petersen and Chatziathanasiou 2021, p. 314; see also Steinbach 2021, p. 7.

[98] Davies 2006, p. 63.

[99] More in Vosa 2020, p. 204.

[100] Palombella 2009, p. 442; Kratochwil 2009, p. 171.

[101] Wilkinson 2021, p. 44.

[102] Joerges and Singh Ghaleigh 2003.

a normative 'European identity' could be of good use: it would offer a chance to overcome the *fear* of 'the sovereign people' that has been exposed as one of the underlying keys of post-war constitutionalism,[103] and it would do so in a most timely manner.

References

Aleinikoff T A (1987) Constitutional Law in the Age of Balancing. Yale Law Journal 96: 943–1005
Alston P, Weiler J H H (1998) An 'Ever Closer Union' in Need of a Human Rights Policy. European Journal of International Law 9: 658–723
Amalfitano C (2017) La vicenda Taricco e il (possibile) riconoscimento dell'identità nazionale quale conferma del primato del diritto dell'Unione europea. EuroJus (22 May 2017) 1–17
Antpöhler C, Dickschen J, Hentrei S, Kottmann M, Smrkolj M, von Bogdandy A (2012) Reverse Solange–Protecting the essence of fundamental rights against EU Member States. Common Market Law Review, 49: 489–519
Arena A (2018) The Twin Doctrines of Primacy and Preemption. In: Schütze R, Tridimas T (eds) The Oxford Principles of European Union Law. Oxford University Press, Oxford, pp 300–349
Balaguer Callejón F (2004) La construcción del lenguaje jurídico en la Unión Europea. Revista de Derecho Constitucional Europeo, 1: 307–320
Balaguer Callejón F (2012) El final de una época dorada: Una reflexión sobre la crisis económica y el declive del Derecho constitucional nacional. In: Alves Correia F (ed) Estudos em Homenagem ao Professor Doutor José Joaquim Gomes Canotilho – Vol. II, Constituição e Estado: entre Teoria e Dogmática. Coimbra Editora, Coimbra, pp 99–122
Balibar É (2010) La proposition de l'égaliberté: essais politiques 1989-2009. Presses Universitaires de France, Paris
Bartoloni M E (2018) Ambito d'applicazione del diritto dell'Unione europea e ordinamenti nazionali – Una questione aperta. ESI, Naples
Bast J (2020) Autonomy in Decline? A Commentary on Rimšēvičs and ECB v Latvia. Verfassun gsblog.de Accessed 13 May 2020
Bobbio N (1999) Teoria generale della politica. In: Bovero M (ed). Einaudi, Turin
Bobić A (2020) Constructive *Versus* Destructive Conflict: Taking Stock of the Recent Constitutional Jurisprudence in the EU. Cambridge Yearbook of European Legal Studies, 22: 60–84
Bonelli M, Claes M (2018) Judicial serendipity: how Portuguese judges came to the rescue of the Polish judiciary – ECJ, 27 February 2018, Case C-64/16, Associação Sindical dos Juízes Portugueses. European Constitutional Law Review, 14: 622–643
Campanini G (1966) Ragione e volontà nella legge. Giuffrè, Milan
Carlassare L (2006) Sovranità popolare e Stato di diritto. Costituzionalismo.it, 1: 1–40
Cartabia M (1995) Principi inviolabili e integrazione europea. Giuffrè, Milan
Chronowski N, Vincze A (2021) Full Steam Back. The Hungarian Constitutional Court Avoids Further Conflict with the ECJ. Verfassungsblog.de Accessed 15 December 2020
Claes M (2013) National Constitutional Identity and European Integration. In: Sáiz Arnaiz A, Alcoberro Llivina C (eds) National Constitutional Identity and European Integration. Cambridge University Press, Cambridge, pp 109–139
Constant B (1819/1997) De la liberté des anciennes comparé à celle des modernes. In: Gauchet M (ed) Écrits politiques. Gallimard, Paris, pp 589–619
Cruz Villalón P (2013) La identidad constitucional de los estados miembros: dos relatos europeos. AFDUAM – Anuario de la Facultad de Derecho de la Universidad Autónoma de Madrid, 17: 501–514

---

[103] Möllers 2007, p. 87.

Davies G (2006) Subsidiarity: The wrong idea, in the wrong place, at the wrong time. Common Market Law Review, 43: 63–84

Davies G, Avbelj M (eds) (2017) Research Handbook on Legal Pluralism and EU Law. Elgar, Cheltenham

de Búrca G, Aschenbrenner J B (2004) European Constitutionalism and the Charter. In: Peers S, Ward A (eds) The EU Charter of Fundamental Rights: Politics, Law and Policy. Hart Publishing, Oxford, pp 3–34

Di Federico G (2019) Il ruolo dell'art. 4, par. 2, TUE nella soluzione dei conflitti interordinamentali. Quaderni Costituzionali, 2: 333–357.

Drinóczi T (2020) Constitutional Identity in Europe: The Identity of the Constitution. A Regional Approach. German Law Journal 21: 105–130

Duong K (2020) What Was Universal Suffrage? Theory & Event, 23: 29–65

Eeckhout P (2002) The EU Charter of Fundamental Rights and the Federal Question. Common Market Law Review 39: 945–994

Fabbrini F (2015) After the OMT Case: The Supremacy of EU Law as the Guarantee of the Equality of the Member States. German Law Journal, 16: 1003–1023

Fabbrini F (2020) Suing the *BVerfG*. Verfassungsblog.de Accessed 13 May 2020

Faraguna P (2017) Constitutional Identity: A Shield or a Sword? German Law Journal 18: 1617–1640

Garner O, Lawson R (2021) On a Road to Nowhere. Verfassungsblog.de Accessed 23 November 2021

Goldoni M (2012) Constitutional Pluralism and the Question of the European Common Good. European Law Journal, 18: 385–406

Habermas J (1995) Die Einbeziehung des Anderen. Studien zur politischen Theorie. Suhrkamp Verlag, Frankfurt

Habermas J (2010) The Concept of Human Dignity and the Realistic Utopia of Human Rights. Metaphilosophy, 41: 464–480

Habermas J (2015) Interview with Philip Oltermann. The Guardian, 16 July 2015

Halmai G (2018) Abuse of Constitutional Identity. The Hungarian Constitutional Court on Interpretation of Article E) (2) of the Fundamental Law. Review of Central and East European Law, 43: 23–42

Jakab A (2016) European Constitutional Language. Cambridge University Press, Cambridge

Joerges C (2014) Europe's Economic Constitution in Crisis and the Emergence of a New Constitutional Constellation. German Law Journal – Special Issue: EU Citizenship: Twenty Years On, 15: 985–1028

Joerges C, Singh Ghaleigh N (eds) (2003) Darker Legacies of Law in Europe: The Shadow of National Socialism and Fascism Over Europe. Hart Publishing, Oxford

Kazai V Z (2022) Constitutional Complaint as Orbán's Tool. Judicial assistance for the reinforcement of the government's interests. Verfassungsblog.de Accessed 1 March 2021

Kelemen R D (2016) On the Unsustainability of Constitutional Pluralism: European Supremacy and the Survival of the Eurozone. In: Fabbrini F (ed) The ECJ, the ECB and the Supremacy of EU Law. Maastricht Journal of European and Comparative Law (Special Issue) 23: 136–151

Kochenov D (2013) The Essence of EU Citizenship Emerging from the Last Ten Years of Academic Debate: Beyond the Cherry Blossoms and the Moon? International and Comparative Law Quarterly, 62: 97–136

Komárek J (2013) The Place of Constitutional Courts in the EU. European Constitutional Law Review, 9: 420–450

Krajevski M (2018) *Associação Sindical dos Juízes Portugueses*: The Court of Justice and Athena's Dilemma. European Papers, 3: 395–407

Kratochwil F V (2009) Has the 'Rule of Law' become a 'Rule of Lawyers'? An Inquiry into the Use and Abuse of an Ancient Topos in Contemporary Debates. In: Palombella G, Walker N (eds) Relocating the Rule of Law, Hart Publishing, Oxford/Oregon, pp 171–196

Krunke H, Klinge S (2018) The Danish *Ajos* Case: The Missing Case from *Maastricht* and *Lisbon*. European Papers, 3: 157–182

Kumm M (2005) The Jurisprudence of Constitutional Conflict: Constitutional Supremacy in Europe before and after the Constitutional Treaty. European Law Journal 11: 262–307

Lanchester F (1983) Il voto obbligatorio da principio a strumento: un'analisi comparata. Il Politico, 48: 31–53.

Lasek-Markey M (2021) Poland's Constitutional Tribunal on the status of EU law: The Polish government got all the answers it needed from a court it controls. www.europeanlawblog.eu Accessed 21 October 2021

Lenaerts K (1999) Le respect des droits fondamentaux en tant que principe constitutionnel de l'Union européenne. In: Dony M (ed) Mélanges en l'honneur à Michel Waelbroeck. Bruylant, Brussels, pp 423–457

Liisberg J B (2001) Does the EU Charter of Fundamental Rights Threaten the Supremacy of Community Law? Jean Monnet Working Paper No. 04/01

Loughlin M (2013) Why Sovereignty? In: Rawlings R, Leyland P, Young A (eds) Sovereignty and the Law: Domestic, European and International Perspectives. Oxford University Press, Oxford, pp 34–50

Loughlin M (2017) The Erosion of Sovereignty. Netherlands Journal of Legal Philosophy, 2: 57–81

Luciani M (2006) Costituzionalismo irenico e costituzionalismo polemico. Giurisprudenza costituzionale, 51: 1644–1669

Martinico G (2015) The 'Polemical' Spirit of European Constitutional Law: On the Importance of Conflicts in EU Law. German Law Journal 16: 1343–1374

Martinico G (2018) Constitutional conflicts and agonistic pluralism: what can we learn from political theory? In: Davies G, Avbelj M (eds) Research Handbook on Legal Pluralism and EU Law. Elgar, Cheltenham, pp 78–94

Martinico G, Pollicino O (2020) Use and Abuse of a Promising Concept: What Has Happened to National Constitutional Identity? Yearbook of European Law, 39: 228–249

Menéndez A J, Olsen E D H (2020) Challenging European Citizenship: Ideas and Realities in Context. Palgrave-McMillan, London

Möllers C (2007) 'We are (Afraid of) the People': Constituent Power in German Constitutionalism. In: Loughlin M, Walker N (eds) The Paradox of Constitutionalism: Constituent Power and Constitutional Form. Oxford University Press, Oxford, pp 87–107

Mouffe C (2000) The Democratic Paradox. Verso, London

Ovádek M (2018) Has the CJEU just Reconfigured the EU Constitutional Order? Verfassungsb log.de Accessed 28 February 2018

Palombella G (2009) The rule of law beyond the state: Failures, promises, and theory. International Journal of Constitutional Law, 7: 442–467

Pernice I (1999) Multilevel Constitutionalism and the Treaty of Amsterdam: European Constitution-Making revisited? Common Market Law Review, 36: 703–750

Petersen N (2013) How to Compare the Length of Lines to the Weight of Stones: Balancing and the Resolution of Value Conflicts in Constitutional Law. German Law Journal, 14: 1387–1408

Petersen N, Chatziathanasiou K (2021) Balancing Competences? Proportionality as an Instrument to Regulate the Exercise of Competences after the *PSPP* Judgment of the *Bundesverfassungsgericht*. European Constitutional Law Review, 17: 314–334

Piccirilli G (2018) The '*Taricco* Saga': the Italian Constitutional Court continues its European journey. European Constitutional Law Review, 14: 814–833

Poiares Maduro M (2004) How Constitutional Can the European Union Be? The Tension Between Intergovernmentalism and Constitutionalism in the European Union. NYU – Jean Monnet WP 5/04, Altneuland: The EU Constitution in a Contextual Perspective, pp 1–52

Poulou A (2017) Financial Assistance Conditionality and Human Rights Protection: What is the Role of the EU Charter of Fundamental Rights? Common Market Law Review, 54: 991–1026

Rauchegger C (2018) National constitutional rights and the primacy of EU law: *M.A.S.* Common Market Law Review, 55: 1521–1547

Ridola P (2010) La dignità dell'uomo e il 'principio libertà' nella cultura costituzionale europea. In: Ridola P (ed) Diritto comparato e diritto costituzionale europeo. Giappichelli, Turin, pp 77–137

Rosenfeld M (2009) The Identity of the Constitutional Subject: Selfhood, Citizenship, Culture, and Community. Routledge, London

Rossi L S (2002) La Carta dei diritti come strumento di costituzionalizzazione dell'ordinamento dell'UE. Quaderni Costituzionali 12: 565–575

Sadurski W (2006) European Constitutional Identity? EUI Working Paper LAW No. 2006/33

Sarmiento Ramírez-Escudero D (2013) The EU's Constitutional Core. In: Sáiz Arnaiz A, Alcoberro Llivina C (eds) National Constitutional Identity and European Integration. Cambridge University Press, Cambridge, pp 177–204

Scharpf F W (2016) The costs of non-disintegration: the case of the European Monetary Union. In: Chalmers D, Jachtenfuchs M, Joerges C (eds) The End of the Eurocrats' Dream: Adjusting to European Diversity. Cambridge University Press, Cambridge, pp 29–49

Schmidt M, Bogdanowicz P (2018) The infringement procedure in the rule of law crisis: How to make effective use of Article 258 TFEU. Common Market Law Review, 55: 1061–1100

Somek A (2008) Individualism. An Essay on the Authority of the European Union. Oxford University Press, Oxford

Spieker L D (2019) Breathing life into the Union's common values: On the judicial application of Article 2 TEU in the EU value crisis. German Law Journal, 20: 1182–1213

Steinbach A (2019) EU Economic Governance after the Crisis: Revisiting the Accountability Shift in the EU Economic Governance. Journal of European Public Policy, 26: 1354–1372

Steinbach A (2021) The Federalism Dimension of Proportionality. European Law Journal, 1: 1–14

Stone Sweet A (2012) A cosmopolitan legal order: Constitutional pluralism and rights adjudication in Europe. Global Constitutionalism, 1: 53–90

Szekeres Z (2021) Don't be fooled: Hungarian court ruling didn't allow pushbacks. Euronews.com Accessed 16 December 2021

Tizzano A (2012) Il nuovo ruolo delle Corti supreme nell'ordine politico e istituzionale: la Corte di giustizia dell'UE. Il diritto dell'Unione Europea, 17: 811–849

Torres Pérez A (2014) *Melloni* in Three Acts: From Dialogue to Monologue. European Constitutional Law Review, 10: 308–331

Tridimas T (1999) The General Principles of EC Law. Oxford University Press, Oxford

Uitz R (2021) The Polish Constitutional Tribunal Asserts the Primacy of National Constitution over EU Law—In Words with No Legal Force. Bridgenetwork.eu Accessed 8 October 2021

von Bogdandy A (2000a) The European Union as a Supranational Federation: A Conceptual Attempt in the Light of the Amsterdam Treaty. Columbia Journal of European Law 1: 27–54

von Bogdandy (2000b) The European Union as a Human Rights Organization? Human Rights and the Core of the European Union. Common Market Law Review, 37:1307–1338

von Bogdandy (2019a) Fundamentals on Defending European Values. Verfassungsblog.de Accessed 12 November 2019

von Bogdandy A (2019b) Principles and Challenges of a European Doctrine of Systemic Deficiencies. MPIL Research Paper Series No. 2019-14, pp 1–33

von Bogdandy A (2020) Principles of a Systemic Deficiencies Doctrine: How to Protect Checks and Balances in the Member States. Common Market Law Review 3: 705–740

von Bogdandy A (2021a) Our European Society and Its Conference on the Future of Europe. Verfassungsblog.de Accessed 14 May 2021

von Bogdandy A (2021b) Editorial: Unsere europäische Gesellschaft und ihr öffentliches Recht. Der Staat, 60: 171–175

von Bogdandy A, Ioannidis M (2014) Systemic deficiency in the rule of law: What it is, what has been done, what can be done. Common Market Law Review 51: 59–96

Vosa G (2020) Il principio di essenzialità. Profili costituzionali del conferimento di poteri tra Stati e Unione europea. FrancoAngeli, Milan

Walker N (2012) The European Union's Unresolved Constitution. In: Rosenfeld M, Sajó A (eds) The Oxford Handbook of Comparative Constitutional Law. Oxford University Press, Oxford, pp 1185–1208

Weatherill S, Beaumont P L (1995) EU Law, 2nd edn. Penguin Books, London

Weiler J H H (1981) The Community System: The Dual Character of Supranationalism. Yearbook of European Law, 1: 267–306

Weiler J H H (1991) The Transformation of Europe. Yale Law Journal, 100: 2403–2483

Weiler J H H (2003) In defence of the *status quo*: Europe's constitutional *Sonderweg*. In: Weiler J H H, Wind M (eds) European Constitutionalism beyond the State. Cambridge University Press, Cambridge, pp 7–24

Weiler J H H (2005) On the Power of the Word: Europe's Constitutional Iconography. International Journal of Constitutional Law, 3: 173–190

Weiler J H H (2009) Fundamental Rights and Fundamental Boundaries: Common Standards and Conflicting Values in the Protection of Human Rights in the European Legal Space. In: Kastoryano R, Emmanuel S (eds) An Identity for Europe: The Relevance of Multiculturalism in EU Constitution. Palgrave Macmillan, London, pp 73–101

Weiler J H H, Lustig D (2018) Judicial Review in the Contemporary World: Retrospective and Prospective. International Journal of Constitutional Law, 16: 315–372

Wilkinson M A (2017) Constitutional Pluralism: Chronicle of a Death Foretold? European Law Journal, 23: 217–233

Wilkinson M A (2021) Authoritarian Liberalism and the Transformation of Modern Europe. Oxford University Press, Oxford

Zaccaroni G (2021) Equality and Non-Discrimination in the EU – The Foundations of the EU Legal Order. Elgar, Cheltenham

Zagrebelsky G (2002) Diritto per: valori, principi o regole? Quaderni fiorentini, 31: 865–897

Zagrebelsky G (2008) La legge e la sua giustizia. Einaudi, Turin

Giuliano Vosa Post-Doc Researcher (tenure-track) in Constitutional Law, University of Catania, Department of Law.

Chapter 10
From Monologues to Dialogue: The US "Certification" Procedure as a Source of Inspiration for EU Cooperative Judicial Federalism

Alberto Nicòtina and Emil Martini

Contents

Abstract Born as a post-modern construction, the European Union does not find its identity defined by positive law nor unilaterally affirmed by means of interpretation of the CJEU. Instead, the notion of identity of the European Union finds a definition and consolidates itself in the institutional capacity of national and supranational courts to engage in a fruitful dialogic relationship. So far, the preliminary reference mechanism has represented the only way for national courts to cooperate with the supranational judiciary in defining a shared understanding of the core values

A. Nicòtina (✉)
Government and Law Research Group, Faculty of Law, University of Antwerp, Antwerp, Belgium
e-mail: alberto.nicotina@uantwerpen.be

E. Martini
College of Europe, Bruges, Belgium
e-mail: emil.martini@coeurope.eu

© T.M.C. ASSER PRESS and the authors 2023
J. de Poorter et al. (eds.), *European Yearbook of Constitutional Law 2022*,
European Yearbook of Constitutional Law 4,
https://doi.org/10.1007/978-94-6265-595-9_10

on which the European identity is based. More recently, however, several national courts and scholars have found this bottom-up mechanism insufficient, and are now advocating for the establishment of new institutional tools to enter into a peer-to-peer judicial dialogue. Through a comparative law perspective, this chapter contributes to the discussion about the possible institutional instruments to enhance the judicial dialogue among courts. We conclude that the US practice of federal courts asking for a "certification" of questions of State law to States' supreme courts could represent a source of inspiration for the CJEU to involve national courts in its decision-making processes with a view to establish a more cooperative judicial federalism in Europe. In particular, we point out that EU law already offers valid tools for such a "reverse preliminary reference" procedure to be implemented in the form of non-binding requests for information or clarification on the interpretation of national law.

Keywords Certification · Certified questions of state law · Constitutional interdependence · Cooperative judicial federalism · Reverse preliminary reference · EU constitutional identity · Judicial dialogue · National identity

10.1   Introduction: The EU as a Post-modern Construction

Since the foundation of the EU legal order, the preliminary reference mechanism has been one of the defining characteristics of EU law.[1] It was meant to create a privileged interaction between national and supranational courts, far away from political interferences. As such, it has constantly attracted the attention of legal scholars. While it has never been uncommon for legal systems to establish mechanisms that could allow national courts to refer to higher courts requests clarification on the interpretation of the legal provisions implied in the cases they heard, it is definitely uncommon to apply this mechanism across national boundaries. In fact, the singularity of the preliminary reference mechanism is only one of the features of the EU legal order which is highly peculiar itself. The innovative, heterarchical constitutional structure of the EU has no counterpart in the world. It is a model on its own, which currently represents a source of inspiration for other supranational organizations in the making.[2]

The peculiar constitutional structure of the EU is the outcome of the historical moment in which it has been conceived and constructed. Indeed, since the second half of the 19th century, postmodern thinking has dominated the public sphere in Western societies. As opposed to modernism, in which the idea of hierarchy and high principles found its application *inter alia* in the Westphalian system of Nation-States, Post-modernism "replaces the antiquated metaphor of the machine with that

---

[1] See Article 267 TFEU.

[2] An example of this is the East African Community (EAC). For a comparison between EU and EAC law and institutions, see Ugirashebuja et al. 2017.

of the network".[3] As Graham pointed out, "Modernity was confident; Postmodernity is anxious. Modernity had all the answers; Postmodernity is full of questions. Modernity revealed in reason, science and human ability; Postmodernity wallows in the incapacity to know anything with certainty".[4]

In this context, postmodern philosophers have tackled the notion of Europe by pointing out the postmodern character of its heterarchical institutional architecture and the impossibility to deal with it through the traditional (modern) categories of sovereignty and identity. Habermas, for instance, argues that the main innovation of the European construction resides in its "dual sovereignty", which creates a "complementary dependence and interconnection"[5] between the national and supranational levels. The two levels are consequently co-original and co-determinate, to the extent that tearing them apart is "neither necessary, nor possible".[6]

The consequence of this heterarchical and horizontal constitutional structure calls, according to another postmodern philosopher, Jacques Derrida, to a "responsibility for the impossible": using the instrument of dialogue with "the other heading" (i.e. national or supranational, depending on the viewpoint) to reach the twofold objective of preserving the unity and strengthening its relationship with both "the other in itself" (i.e. the different national identities within the EU) and "the other with itself" (i.e. the non-European other).[7]

Far from providing a comprehensive account of the philosophical underpinnings of the EU (constitutional) identity, the aim of this chapter is rather to use the methods and the categories of comparative law to offer a reading of the EU constitutional identity as the institutional capacity of national and supranational courts to engage in an authentic two-sided judicial dialogue, understood as an exchange of strategic positions among peers. Accordingly, the fundamental research question this chapter intends to answer can be formulated as follows: *how could judicial dialogue be enhanced in order to let a shared understanding of the EU constitutional identity emerge?*

To this purpose, we will first provide a brief overview of the "national identity" discourse (Sect. 10.2), and subsequently consider as a possible model the US experience of certification of questions of state law to state supreme courts (Sect. 10.3) by putting it in comparison with the current multi-level judicial structure of the EU (Sect. 10.4).

---

[3] Castells 1996, p. 3.

[4] Graham 2001, p. 26.

[5] Habermas 2012, p. 27.

[6] Habermas 2012, p. 91.

[7] Derrida 1992, pp. 76–77. According to the author, "European identity, like identity or identification in general, if it must be equal *to itself and to the other*, up to the measure of its own immeasurable difference with itself, belongs, therefore must belong, to this *experience and experiment of the impossible*". Moreover, always for Derrida, Europe has a "duty to open itself onto an other that cannot relate to itself as *its* other, *the other with itself*. (…) This duty also dictates opening Europe onto that which is not, never was, and never will be Europe (…) in order to recognize and accept their alterity" (italics of the author).

Our contribution is thus limited to one specific aspect of federal theory, namely comparative judicial federalism, with the aim of resorting to comparative legal methodology in order to investigate the opportunity for a legal transplant in the light of the specific features of the EU legal order.

10.2 The "National Identity" Clause: A Case of Failed Dialogue

The notion of identity can now boast a vast literature on it. When it comes to the legal sphere, however, it seems to struggle finding its own real dimension. Yet, also in legal scholarship, it is more *à la mode* than ever.[8] Legal scholars have almost exclusively focused their analyses on what Derrida calls "the other in itself", i.e. the national identity within the EU.

In this section, we will briefly discuss how it has developed from a political concern to an increasingly legalised concept linked to a strict (at least theoretically) division of competences. The Lisbon Treaty has introduced a new formulation of the so-called "national identity clause", but it has not changed the competence-driven approach adopted by the Member States in the interpretation of it, nor the tendency of the CJEU to affirm its monopoly over it.

These considerations will serve as a premise to our contribution, which in turn focuses on the institutional tools that could be put in place to facilitate the dialogue among courts.

10.2.1 Making the Treaties: The Spectre of Competence Creep

The national identity issue made its first appearance in the European legislation with the Maastricht Treaty.[9] The formulation adopted on that occasion reflected the (actually political) concern to defend "national democracy".[10] Until Lisbon, however, its importance was very modest. The current version of the national identity clause dates back to Article I-5 of the Constitutional Treaty.[11]

---

[8] Sarmiento 2013, p. 177.

[9] Article F, para 1: "The Union shall respect; the national identities of its Member States, whose systems of government are founded on the principles of democracy".

[10] Claes 2013, p. 111.

[11] Article I-5 para 1 stated that "the Union shall respect the equality of Member States before the constitution *as well as their national identities, inherent in their fundamental structures, political and constitutional, inclusive of regional and local self-government. It shall respect their essential State functions, including ensuring the territorial integrity of the State, maintaining law and order and safeguarding national security*" (emphasis added).

The new formulation made it clear that the actual meaning of "national identity" was a strictly legal one and was aimed at "carving out core areas of national sovereignty"[12] in which the Union could not interfere. Within the drafting process, this objective was pursued in particular by the fifth working group on "complementary competencies", whose task was to formulate a clearer delimitation of competence between the Union and the Member States.[13] In this context, four solutions were envisaged to protect national prerogatives.[14] The first, called *Community model*, consisted in a negative delimitation of EU competence made policy area by policy area in the text of the Treaty; the second, the *Union model*, required an (over)expansion of the old identity clause including the constitutional and political structure of the Member States, the relationships with religious confessions, taxation, and welfare; the third, referred to as the *constitutional model*, implied the formulation of a provision spelling out the Member States' reserved areas of competence; and, finally, the fourth, *political model*, suggested drafting a separate document, a *Charter of Member States' Rights*, tackling the issue in a more extensive manner, this way providing a catalogue of national competences.[15] Thus, a lot of different solutions were on the table to try to solve the problem of competence creep and to defend Member States' core prerogatives. In the end, the final draft of Article I-5 was, not surprisingly, the result of a compromise between the different actors and visions, and consisted in clarifying what could be included under the notion of national identity.

However, in order to better understand the meaning of the clause, it is necessary to see it in context, considering its positioning within the Treaty. The title of Article I-5, "Relations between the Union and the Member States", confirmed that the identity issue was inserted in a logic of power balance. The second paragraph of the article established the principle of sincere cooperation, according to which "the Union and the Member States shall, in full mutual respect, assist each other in carrying out tasks which flow from the Constitution". However, the Christophersen clause was not considered among the principles on the delimitation of competences;[16] instead, it has been included in Title I on the "definition and objective of the Union", as suggested by the EU Commission.[17] Actually, some Member States would have preferred to move it into the new competence-title, to make it clear that it had not

---

[12] Guastaferro 2012, p. 276.

[13] All along the *travaux préparatoires* Article I-5 was referred to as the *Christophersen clause*, since the first proposal to reform the identity clause came from Henning Christophersen, chairman of the fifth working group.

[14] Christophersen 2002.

[15] Guastaferro 2012.

[16] Title III of the Constitutional Treaty was titled "Union competence". Among the principles driving the competence issue, Article I-11 only mentioned the principles of conferral, subsidiarity and proportionality.

[17] It must be also mentioned that in this Title, at Article I-6, for the first time the "principle of primacy" was meant to be inserted in the Treaties. Nevertheless, this article was not confirmed in the Lisbon Treaty, given the controversies raised around an explicit mention of such clause in primary law. In any case, the Lisbon Treaty still endorses the *acquis jurisprudential* on the principle of primacy through the Declaration No. 17 attached to it. According to the majority of the doctrine, the position of the primacy clause in relation to the identity clause has no influence on the relationship

only a political importance but also a legal one.[18] As a counterbalance, then, the representatives of the Member States were able to expand the identity clause to include some core national prerogatives to be respected by the EU. The model of Article I-5, notwithstanding the unfortunate fate of the Constitutional Treaty, was transposed into the Lisbon Treaty, in Article 4, para 2 TEU. The wording of the two provisions is almost identical, and the new positioning seems to suggest an even closer link to the competence issue.

10.2.2 The Identity of the Nation Versus the Identity of the Constitution

The most evident difference between the current version of the identity clause and its predecessors in the Treaties of Maastricht and Amsterdam is the explicit connection between national identity and the "fundamental political and constitutional structures". This characteristic has led scholars to debate on whether or not to consider the notion of "national identity" as equivalent to that of "constitutional identity". Among the defenders of the idea that national identity should not be limited to constitutional identity, understood as the objectifiable "identity of the constitution", it is affirmed that the new specifications cannot limit a wider interpretation of the values related to national identity, which "should be regarded as the instantiation of basic moral principles that require a multinational political community to show respect for the identity of its constituent national groups".[19] On the contrary, the supporters of constitutional identity state that the new provision clearly distance the notion at stake from cultural, historical and linguistic criteria by turning it into an objective legal notion.[20] A third interpretation is finally proposed by those who, even assuming the shift in emphasis from national identity as such to constitutional identity, stress the importance of not abandoning "the idea that national identities can be multiple and encapsulate cultural identities as well", as it is the case for federal and multi-national Member States.[21]

All these views actually suggest that even though it is not advisable to depart from a legal understanding of the notion of identity, a concept such as constitutional identity should be considered broad enough to include the specificities of each legal

---

between the two principles (see for example Claes 2013, p. 109, also for further bibliographical references; *contra*, see for example Pizzorusso 2002, p. 22; Groppi 2005, p. 5).

[18] European Convention, Working Group V, Working Document 20, 4 September 2002, p. 12. Available at: www.european-convention.europa.eu/docs/wd5/2341.pdf.

[19] Cloots 2017, p. 12.

[20] This is the most widely endorsed viewpoint. See Van der Schyff 2012; Drinóczi 2020; Fabbrini and Pollicino 2017; Fabbrini and Sajó 2019.

[21] See Besselink 2010, p. 44.

order in its socio-political complexity.[22] From our perspective, this last argument seems to be the most convincing one, since the opposite view (the national identity *stricto sensu*) would entail dealing with an unobjectifiable concept deprived of any meaningful legal content.

10.2.3   Breaking the Treaties: Use and Misuse of the National Identity Clause in Court

Even though national identity appeared for the first time in the Maastricht Treaty, it was considered to be justiciable only after the entry into force of the Lisbon Treaty. However, the case law of the CJEU referred to this notion well before 2009, even though the overall number of references to the national identity clause is not remarkable. Even in the absence of a specific identity clause, the judges of Luxembourg tended anyway to recognise the need for respect of diversity among the national constitutional systems.[23] Quite surprisingly, the first reference to national identity emerged in the EU case-law already before the Maastricht Treaty, in a case in which the CJEU held that EU law does not preclude the adoption of national policies aimed at protecting national languages.[24]

From that moment on, the applicability of the national identity clause was acknowledged by the CJEU both as a stand-alone legitimate exemption[25] and as an interpretative support of existing exemptions to the four fundamental freedoms.[26]

Most importantly, in the last few years the national identity clause has also been invoked by some national courts in an "antagonistic" way. So far, the CJEU has denied its applicability in all those cases that Von Bogdandy and Schill, already in 2011, indicated as "a justification by a Member State for non-compliance with, or derogation from, an obligation under secondary EU law without affecting the legality of the EU measure".[27] Indeed, the CJEU has always strongly denied the possibility

---

[22] We thus adhere to the majoritarian trend in constitutional scholarship that considers the notion of national and constitutional identity as interchangeable.

[23] Faraguna 2016, pp. 508–509.

[24] Case C-379/87, *Groener* 1989 E.C.R. 3967.

[25] The protection of national language represented a fertile ground for the applicability of the clause. See for instance case C-391/09, *Runevič* 2011, E.C.R. I-3818. At closer inspection, however, the protection of national language would anyway find a protection in EU law, even beyond the identity clause, to the extent that in such a case Article 4, para 2 TEU does not seem to work as an autonomous ground of derogation.

[26] In several other cases, the CJEU has considered the national identity clause as an argument to strengthen one of the legitimate exceptions to the application of a fundamental freedom already in place. In the *Sayn-Wittgenstein* case (Case C-208/09, *Sayn-Wittgenstein*, 2010, E.C.R. I-131718) for instance, the CJEU affirmed that prohibition under Austrian law to carry on surnames indicating titles of nobility represents a legitimate exemption to the circulation of EU citizens insofar it is the outcome of the peculiar identity and (constitutional) history of that country, protected as such also (but, again, not only) by Article 4, para 2 TEU.

[27] Von Bogdandy and Schill 2011, p. 27.

to invoke the clause for the purpose of limiting the scope of application of EU law measures. In other words, the CJEU's take on the matter is clear: the identity clause must be exercised with due respect for the primacy of EU law. Of a different opinion have lately been some national constitutional courts, namely in Poland and Hungary. In these countries, it is now widely acknowledged that a "rule of law crisis" is taking place. What is interesting, for the purpose of this chapter, is witnessing how the multi-level judicial framework in which this crisis is inscribed seems to lack the appropriate tools for such competing views to be expressed. As a result, both national and EU courts are currently resorting to their official adjudicatory powers to "send signals" to their (supra)national homologues, with the practical result of undermining the implementation of EU law in those countries and to significantly lower the standard of protection of fundamental rights and freedoms. A crucial question, at this point, arises: what is (or could be) the role of judicial dialogue in this context?

10.2.4   A "Reverse" Preliminary Reference?

In the previous subsections of this section, we have tried to provide a brief overview of the debate surrounding the national identity clause. The issue is actually broader, and the national identity clause is only one aspect of it. It concerns the delicate balance between shared and "individual" identity. In particular, addressing EU constitutional identity necessarily involves answering a fundamental question: *what court should have the last word on the interpretation of national constitutions?* This might seem an academic question that could be answered easily: after all, the CJEU's mandate is not to interpret national constitutional provisions. In practice, however, as we have seen in the previous paragraphs, by establishing the scope of application of Article 4(2) TEU (i.e. when assessing whether such provision has been violated) the CJEU is obliged, at least to a certain degree, to interpret national constitutions in order to define what is national identity and what is not.

This seems actually to go in the opposite direction compared to a reading of an identity clause as a *Verbundnorm, i.e.* "a way to achieve unity, effective problem solving, and coherence and integrity within the whole of the European legal system not only through procedural conflict resolving techniques, but mainly also through material ones".[28]

As a consequence, specific procedures are needed to establish not only the content of the identity clause, but also (and more generally) a definition of the EU constitutional identity that is actually shared.

This matter is clearly a complex one and, as far as we are aware, to date two main solutions have so far been proposed to address this issue: the recent proposal for the establishment of a mixed chamber of the CJEU (composed of both national and supranational judges)[29] on one hand, and on the other the establishment of

---

[28] Schnettger 2020, p. 12.

[29] See Weiler and Sarmiento 2020a; 2020b; Zinonos 2020.

a "reverse" preliminary ruling procedure enabling the CJEU to address national constitutional and apex courts with a request for the correct interpretation of the national constitutional law implied in a given case.

In the remainder of this chapter, we focus on the last one, which seems to have gained a lot of attention from scholars over the past years. Several scholars have, indeed, more or less timidly, suggested the introduction of such a "reverse preliminary ruling" mechanism[30] in order to institutionalise, and thus give due recognition, to well-established phenomena, such as the Taricco back-and-forth.

To this purpose, we have actually embraced Marta Cartabia's invitation to look at "the practice of some US federal courts that ask the state courts for 'certification' of the correct interpretation of state legislation implied in federal cases", considered as "an interesting example of dialogue moving from the center to the peripheries which is worth exploring in more detail".[31]

10.3   The "Certified Questions of State Law" in the US Legal System

10.3.1   The US Judicial System: A Brief Overview

Compared to all the other judicial systems in federal countries, American judicial federalism is quite a case on its own. The US dual judicial system implying the co-existence of States' and federal courts has virtually no peer worldwide. A good deal of responsibility for this *sui generis* structure belongs (as for many other characteristics of US federalism) to James Madison. As Calabresi recalls, lower federal courts are indeed Madison's creation: it was his proposal to insert in the US constitution the possibility to create lower federal courts in the event that the workload of the federal judiciary (originally consisting of the Supreme Court only) became unbearable.[32] As a consequence, already since 1795, the US judicial system comprises two separate (and parallel) orders of courts: the federal one, built on three layers (district courts, circuit courts, and the US Supreme Court) and the State one. Each State is free to organize its judicial system, with the consequence that "no two states have identical court structures".[33] State courts handle the vast majority of cases and, compared to lower federal courts, are far better equipped in terms of working capacity, as their caseload is significantly higher.[34]

---

[30] See Von Bogdandy and Schill 2011, p. 1449; Cartabia 2015, p. 1796; Röttger-Wirtz and Eliantonio 2019, p. 19.

[31] Cartabia 2015, p. 1796.

[32] Calabresi 2003, p. 1294.

[33] Oakley and Amar 2009, p. 41.

[34] Manweller 2006, p. 55. According to the author, in 2001 the federal judiciary employed a total of 841 judges, whereas all the State judges combined were more than 29,000 (ibid.).

The consequences of this separate setting are not negligible. As Wells notices, in practical terms, "federal judges are more attuned to the vindication of federal rights and state judges more concerned with implementing the State's interests".[35] These differences can be explained both in the light of the specific role conferred to each set of courts, and by considering the fact that federal judges are normally appointed for their lifetime, whereas state ones are mostly elected, and consequently more inclined to take into account the interests of their electorate.[36]

As Cohen correctly points out, three main differences can be observed between the US and the EU judicial systems: the absence of an "EU court system" like the US federal one; the absence of a right to appeal judgements from the Member States' courts to the CJEU, which by contrast exists in the US; and finally the absence in the US of a bottom-up procedure, like the EU preliminary reference mechanism, that could enable State courts to bring before the US Supreme Court requests for interpretation of the federal law implied in a specific case.[37] What is in place in the US is in fact the exactly opposite (top-down) mechanism, which goes by the name of "certification" procedure.

Before the establishment of certification, the US Supreme Court adopted different approaches in all those cases in which federal courts had to interpret state law provisions. This happened for instance in the 1938 case *Erie Railroad v Tompkins*,[38] in which the Supreme Court held that when a federal court exercises diversity jurisdiction,[39] it must apply the relevant "state decisional as well as statutory law".[40] The practical effect of this decision was that lower federal courts were thus obliged to choose what state's law to apply in the specific case, and subsequently provide their own interpretation of state law provisions.[41] These objective difficulties led the US Supreme Court some years later to change its approach to the issue, and develop what was called the "abstention doctrine". In the 1941 case *Railroad Comm'n v Pullman Co.*,[42] the Supreme Court established that lower federal courts could decline their jurisdiction, and thus refuse to decide a case, when it involved unclear issues of state law not yet solved by the competent state courts, which might raise a federal constitutional question. To some extent, this second approach, also known as *Pullman doctrine*, was even more problematic that the *Erie* one, since it ultimately implied for

---

[35] Wells 2017, p. 716.

[36] Ibid. Most State judges serve in their role for periods of 6 or 8 years.

[37] Cohen 1996, pp. 446–447.

[38] *Erie Railroad v Tompkins*, 304 US 64 (1938).

[39] In US law "diversity jurisdiction" indicates the jurisdiction accorded to the federal judiciary under Article 3, para 2 of the US constitution, establishing that "the [federal] judicial power shall be extended to controversies between citizens of different states (...) and between a state, or the citizens thereof, and foreign states, citizens or subjects".

[40] Chase 1992, p. 411. The expression "decisional and statutory law" refers to both state positive law and the case-law of state courts, which is binding under the *stare decisis* principle.

[41] According to Chase, "determining the law of the forum state proved troublesome" (ibid.).

[42] *Railroad Comm'n v Pullman Co.*, 312 US 496, 499–500 (1941).

federal courts retaining their jurisdiction only *de jure*,[43] and for litigants embarking in lengthy and expansive proceedings to settle their controversy.[44]

To solve the many issues brought up by abstention, some years later the US Supreme Court introduced certification. In the following subsections of this section, we provide an overview of the certification procedure, by focusing on the use of it by the US Supreme Court.

10.3.2   What, When and How: The Certification Procedure and Its Implementation

In *Arizonans for Official English v. Arizona* (1997), the US Supreme Court established a generalised obligation on lower federal courts to ask the state's highest court for the correct interpretation of the relevant state legislation before making a final decision on its constitutionality.[45]

This decision came at a point in which the practice of certification was already widely used. The first State to explicitly authorise the certification procedure was Florida in 1945.[46] However, the explicit endorsement by the US Supreme Court dates back to 1960 only. In *Clay v Sun Insurance Office Ltd.*, indeed, the US Supreme Court applauded "the Florida Legislature [that], with rare foresight, has dealt with the problem of authoritatively determining unresolved state law involved in federal litigation by a statute which permits a federal court to certify such a doubtful question of state law to the Supreme Court of Florida for its decision".[47] Soon afterwards, in 1963, the Federal Supreme Court itself made use of the procedure for the first time in two subsequent cases,[48] but it failed to provide lower federal courts with a guideline on how to make correct use of it. Such guidance was provided only ten years later, with the 1974 seminal *Lehman Bros* decision in which the Supreme Court held that certification "does, of course, in the long run save time, energy and resources and *helps build a cooperative judicial federalism*".[49] As Ripple and Gallagher notice, the main guidance this decision provided to lower federal courts consisted in stimulating judges to pose themselves the questions just recalled: will it save time and money? Are federal judges familiar enough with that specific state law provision to avoid

---

[43] See *Harrison v N.A.A.C.P.*, 360 US 167, 177 (1959), establishing that *"abstention does not, of course, involve the abdication of jurisdiction, but only the postponement of its exercise"*.

[44] In practice, litigants had to start a new proceeding in state courts, exhausting all state's judicial avenues, and only then return to the federal court for the final decision on the case.

[45] *Arizonans for Official English v. Arizona* 520 US 43, 76–79 (1997).

[46] Nash 2003, p. 1674.

[47] *Clay v Sun Insurance Office Ltd.*, 363 US 207, 212 (1960).

[48] *Aldrich v Aldrich*, 375 US 249, 251 (1963); *Dresner v City of Tallahassee*, 375 US 136, 138–39 (1963).

[49] *Lehman Bros*, 416 US 386 (1974).

it? Will that specific certified question help build cooperative judicial federalism by helping the state supreme court to advance state law?[50]

Since then, the US Supreme Court "has consistently championed the cause of state law question certification".[51] This track has been followed by lower federal judges, who nowadays seem to show an "overwhelming judicial support" for the procedure.[52] To date, all States, with the only exception of North Carolina, have rules regulating certification.[53]

As for the content of the certified question, it is for the federal judge to decide. On one hand, "formulating a pure question of law presents a difficult task".[54] on the other, state supreme courts have also been found declining questions that were "too factually specific".[55] It seems that, as it happens with the EU preliminary ruling procedure, a reasonable balance between law and facts of the case should be found by the judges of the referral in order to receive a meaningful answer.

As the US Supreme Court put it, when a federal court deals with State law, it does not provide an interpretation but rather a "speculation".[56] It is however for State courts to decide if and when to reply to certified questions. Indeed, the mere existence of rules foreseeing certification does not impose a duty on courts to answer certification requests.[57] Some States, like New Jersey, for a long time systematically refused to answer certified questions[58] and, according to the federal judiciary, in doing so they "face(d) the threat that federal courts will misanalyse the state's law, already open to various interpretations, by inadvertently viewing it through the lens of their own federal jurisprudential assumptions".[59]

10.3.3 Criticisms

The criticisms to which the certification has been subject over time can be summarized in two main areas: its costs (in terms of both time and money), and the abstract nature of the certified question which is answered behind closed doors.[60]

As Long notices, "certification is more costly (to litigants and the courts) than a direct federal resolution of the state law matter, but—as he also acknowledges—less

---

[50] Ripple and Gallagher 2020, p. 1930.

[51] Cochran 2013, p. 166.

[52] Chase 1992, p. 408. This trend has been recently confirmed by Ripple and Gallagher 2020, p. 1930.

[53] Ripple and Gallagher 2020, p. 1930.

[54] Cochran 2013, p. 184.

[55] Ibid.

[56] *Brockett v Spokane Arcades Inc.*, 472 US 491, 510 (1985).

[57] Cochran 2013, p. 214; Long 2009, p. 116.

[58] Ibid., p. 168.

[59] *Hakimoglu v Trump Taj Mahal Assoc.*, 70 F.3d 291, 302-3 (3rd Cir. 1995).

[60] See Cohen 1996, pp. 457–58; Long 2009.

costly than abstention".[61] It thus depends on the viewpoint, and on the objective pursued.

But the main problem that certification seems to pose is the impossibility for litigants to take part in the state courts' proceedings leading to the certified answer.[62] Unlike the EU preliminary ruling procedure, where the judge of the referral can only interact with the CJEU through the order of referral but the litigants are allowed to be heard before the CJEU, the US certification procedure creates a "judicial-only" dialogue that risks missing significant elements of the case and undermining the litigants' right to defence. This said, it has also to be noted that the purpose of the two procedures is different: the EU preliminary reference mechanism actually bears more resemblance to the *abstention doctrine*, which implied deferring the whole case to another court. By contrast, certification consists of an "internal" procedure aimed at providing the "only" court actually handling the case with the necessary expertise in order for it to take a more informed decision. The ultimate proof of this line of reasoning is the non-binding nature of the certified answer.

According to Calabresi, who advocates for a more intense use of certification, the main virtue of certification consists in letting "each set of courts do what it knows and does best (...) and learn that it is not a matter of 'whom is better than whom', but rather than each should be humble about acknowledging the existence of areas as to which it knows less than other courts".[63] Likewise, Nash stresses how certification is useful in "enlisting the aid of a second court system to resolve a case, while affording the second court system the opportunity to announce a rule of law".[64] Ultimately, what we consider as certification's main asset is its capacity to strengthen federalism since not only "it serves to allocate [but also to] *share* judicial power"[65] between federal and state courts.

10.4 Potential Paths for a European "Certified Question of National Law"

According to Witte, implementing a reverse preliminary reference procedure in the context of the EU would require "legislative changes (most likely at the level of primary law) to put such a novel procedure in place" to such extent that "it cannot be expected for the foreseeable future".[66] We do not necessarily agree with this claim. In fact, the US experience shows that such a mechanism does not need to be established by law: it is mostly for the courts and their internal rules to decide whether such a

---

[61] Long 2009, p. 152.

[62] Ibid.

[63] Calabresi 2003, p. 1308.

[64] Nash 2003, p. 1690.

[65] Cochran 2013, p. 168 (emphasis added).

[66] Witte 2021, p. 240.

procedure can be carried out.[67] Likewise in the EU context, both at the national and supranational level, it is not for constitutional or ordinary law to regulate the cases in which a court can or cannot deliver an opinion, but rather to regulate the legal effects of the decisions taken by courts, i.e. whether such decisions are legally binding or not.

Conscious of this crucial point, Grabenwarter et al advocate for a structural change in EU primary law by inserting in Article 267a TFEU the principle according to which every time the identity clause is brought before the CJEU, national constitutional courts shall be invited to intervene alongside national governments and the EU Commission in order to "render a *binding* decision on the interpretation of the national constitution".[68] According to the authors, "this would allow the CJEU and the national constitutional courts to reach a conclusion jointly, but still independently in the sense that they both adopt a binding decision".[69] Conceived in these terms, such a procedure would definitely require a profound change in the relevant legal framework. But, as the same authors also acknowledge, "no doubt there are other methods to involve the national constitutional courts in relevant proceedings in the CJEU if one begins to look for them".[70]

In the following pages, we engage precisely in the search for these other methods and point out in what ways a similar result can be achieved under both the CJEU Statute and the Rules of Procedure in the form of a "request for information", and a "request for clarification" in the context of a preliminary reference.

10.4.1 Request for Information Under the CJEU Statute

One of the methods Grabenwarter et al refer to had already been indicated by Von Bogdandy and Schill ten years before.[71] According to these authors, on the basis of Article 24 of the CJEU Statute, "the ECJ has the necessary powers to ensure that the government of a Member State submits the relevant view of that State's constitutional court to the ECJ on the interpretation of national, respectively constitutional identity".[72] This would consequently be a procedure confined to the interpretation of Article 4(2) TEU and—more importantly—a procedure that would rely on the mediation of the national governments for its actual modalities and timing.

---

[67] For a recent overview of the individual legal sources (mainly State courts' internal rules and State statutes) authorizing the certification procedure in the US system, see Cantone and Giffin 2020.

[68] Grabenwarter et al. 2021, pp. 59–60 (emphasis added). We cannot help but notice that the authors themselves preferred the "hard way" and consequently decided not to engage in the search for such "other methods".

[69] Ibid.

[70] Ibid.

[71] Von Bogdandy and Schill 2011, p. 1449.

[72] Ibid.

However, the most recent developments in the evolution of EU law show that the expectation that in the context of such a procedure the CJEU would "have the necessary powers *to ensure*" that national governments representing the Member State within the court proceedings actually provide the required national constitutional court's opinions can at least be questioned. If we consider those cases in which the very basic features of constitutional democracy are in jeopardy—including, first and foremost, the separation of powers within certain Member States' internal structure—this might translate into a severe limitation to a smooth judicial dialogue among courts. Indeed, the only way at the disposal of the CJEU under Article 24, para 1 CJEU Statute to sanction a party in the proceedings that refuses to provide the required information is to "take note" of the refusal.[73]

Nonetheless, the second (and last) paragraph of the same Article 24 CJEU Statute enables the Court to "also require the Member States and institutions, bodies, offices and agencies not being parties to the case to supply all information which the Court considers necessary for the proceedings". This general provision indeed already allows the Court to do without the collaboration of the parties in the proceedings, as well as to address directly national courts, thus avoiding any other forms of mediation whatsoever.

With a bit of creativity, further ways can be found to serve the same purpose. Article 25 CJEU Statute, for instance, allows the CJEU to "entrust at any time any individual, authority, committee or other organisation it chooses with the task of giving an expert opinion". As it is evident, the primary aim of this provision is actually to provide the Court with the necessary technical knowledge in the event (and to the extent) that this is required in order for it to perform its adjudicatory duties. But, at the same time, nothing prevents the CJEU to ask national courts, including—why not—subnational constitutional courts,[74] i.e. bodies whose specific mandate is to interpret the constitutions, to share their expertise on constitutional interpretation. Such provision already has a quite wide scope of application, covering also issues that go beyond the technical expertise traditionally supplied to courts, to the extent that it also includes "comparative analyses on the legislation of the Member States on a given legislative concept".[75]

It will be for the specific national court then to decide whether accepting or refusing to issue an opinion. In this sense, the parallelism with the American certification procedure is particularly fitting: as Cohen puts it, "there is no logical connection between certification and mandatory responses".[76] We believe that this should be the case for the European version too.

---

[73] Article 24, para 1 CJEU Statute: "the Court of Justice may require the parties to produce all documents and to supply all information which the Court considers desirable. Formal note shall be taken of any refusal".

[74] We think here of those Member States with multi-tiered constitutional systems where subnational constitutional courts are established, such as the Lander constitutional courts in Germany.

[75] Wägenbaur 2013, p. 92.

[76] Cohen 1996, p. 460.

10.4.2 Request for Clarification Under the CJEU Rules of Procedure

The most evident way in which a direct dialogue between the CJEU and national (constitutional or apex) courts can be established is through Article 101 Rules of Procedure. This provision refers to the opportunity for the CJEU to address national courts with a "request for clarification" in the context of a request for a preliminary ruling.[77]

In this case too, the provision was designed with the aim to provide additional information on the factual background of the case brought before the CJEU.[78] In fact, the CJEU has already demonstrated that a broader interpretation of this procedural rule is possible. It has indeed used it to stimulate a further assessment by the judge of the referral on the relevance of the preliminary ruling in consideration of further elements that emerged in the period between when the request for a preliminary ruling was issued and the moment in which the CJEU had examined the case.[79]

The use of this procedure is strongly advocated by Langer, who considers it as the "obvious course of action" since it "has the potential to bring the dialogue to full maturity".[80] Of course, as he also acknowledges, this procedure might entail some procedural complications, especially regarding the time-length of the proceeding. It seems appropriate, in other words, that its use be dependent upon the importance of the decision at stake. For instance, one might legitimately expect that if the referring court is a constitutional court and the decision requires the interpretation of fundamental constitutional rights, the duration of the proceeding or any other procedural matter would not be among the most important concerns of the CJEU.

Over the past few years, invitations to the CJEU to make a broader use of its prerogatives under Article 101 Rules of Procedure have come from national courts in at least two forms. First, on at least one occasion, judges of national apex courts expressed the need to have a more direct dialogue with CJEU, and even to be heard personally within the proceeding in Luxembourg.[81] Second, during the bilateral meetings organized annually in the context of the Association of the Council of States and

---

[77] Article 101, para 1 of the CJEU Rules of Procedure: "without prejudice to the measures of organisation of procedure and measures of inquiry provided for in these Rules, the Court may, after hearing the Advocate General, request clarification from the referring court or tribunal within a time limit prescribed by the Court".

[78] Wägenbaur 2013, p. 341.

[79] According to Wägenbaur 2013, p. 341 this happened in at least two cases: case C-134/94, *Esso Espanola* [1995] ECR I-4223, para 7, and case C-254/06, *Zürich Versicherungsgesellschaft* [2007], para 1 (not published in the ECR).

[80] Langer 2015, p. 13. It is interesting to note that, in developing such considerations, the author speaks in the twofold capacity of academic and legal agent for the Dutch government before the CJEU.

[81] Ibid. As Langer reports, in 2015 Peter Wattel, Advocate General at the Dutch Supreme Court, proposed to enable referring judges to be heard personally before the CJEU in order to be able to give more information about both the facts of the case and the national law implied in the decision, as well as to respond *viva voce* to the questions posed by the supranational judges.

Supreme Administrative Jurisdictions of the EU, between national (administrative) judges and the CJEU, national judges have specifically "expressed the desire for the Court of Justice to make more use of its powers under Article 101 of the Rules of Procedure to ask the national court for clarification. Most reports mention that the Court of Justice has not, to date, made any such request to the members concerned".[82]

In any case, it has to be noted that beyond the specific cases and provisions already mentioned, the CJEU enjoys a general power to request a clarification on the cases brought to its attention by national courts, proof being its use of it even in the context of the "urgent preliminary ruling procedure" under Article 107 Rules of Procedure.[83] This is why it seems appropriate to conclude that the primary source of the institutional capacity of the CJEU to involve national courts in its decision-making process has to be found not so much in specific procedural provisions, but rather in common sense.

10.4.3 Contextual Adaptations and Possible Scenarios

The procedures referred to above do not require the amendment of the EU primary legislation insofar they do not consist in creating new ways to initiate a court proceeding nor to modify the legal effect of the decisions rendered by the courts involved. Instead, they give the CJEU the opportunity to make full use of the prerogatives it already enjoys in order to involve national (constitutional or apex) courts within its ongoing proceedings in all those cases in which a doubt on the interpretation of national constitutional provisions is at stake.

Also, our proposal for a greater involvement of national courts comes at a moment in which the general trend seems to be for a closer cooperation between supra-national and (apex/constitutional) national judges. As numerous empirical studies show, "the importance attached to different preliminary references by the CJEU reflects a growing preference for cooperation with peak courts".[84] The phenomenon has become evident so as to lead commentators to conclude that "peak courts may just have bolstered their *de facto* position *vis-à-vis* the CJEU in the development of EU law".[85] Also, when it comes to the use of the preliminary ruling procedure, the CJEU seems to be ready to take a less hierarchical stance towards national courts by showing increasingly more respect towards national judges and their margin of appreciation in referring cases to Luxembourg.[86]

---

[82] ACA Seminar "The Preliminary Ruling Procedure", Discussion Paper on *Cooperation between courts prior to a reference being made for a preliminary ruling at national and European level*, The Hague, November 7th 2016, p. 2. Available at: www.aca-europe.eu/seminars/2016_TheHague/Wor kDocEN.pdf.

[83] See for instance case C-92/12 PPU, *Health Service Executive v S.C.* [2012].

[84] Dyevre et al. 2017.

[85] Ovádek et al. 2020, pp. 33–34. See also Pavone and Kelemen 2019; Dyevre et al. 2017.

[86] See for instance the recent judgement rendered by the CJEU in the case C-561/19 *Consorzio Italian Management and Catania Multiservizi SpA*.

Of course, a request for information under the CJEU Statute or a request for clarification under the CJEU Rules of Procedure is not binding, precisely as the answers provided by the US State courts in the context of the US certification procedure are not binding. Nor would the opposite be desirable. This brings to the floor further important elements that need to be considered. These include issues such as: what would happen should a national court refuse to provide an answer to the CJEU's request for information/clarification? What about those constitutional systems in which a constitutional court is not established? Whom should the CJEU address with its request for information/clarification in this case? As it is evident, here we can only provide provisional answers to these questions. To do so, the comparison with the US certification procedure comes again to hand. From an academic point of view, it might be tempting to imagine the CJEU addressing directly the Polish or Hungarian parliaments and governments to ask them what their definition of "rule of law" is, thus unveiling the unconstitutionality (under the respective national constitutions) of potential authoritarian arguments. However, in concrete terms, this would raise several problems. Besides, within the proceeding before the Luxembourg Court the same questions can already be posed to the agents of the Member States' governments. Thus, resorting once again to the American experience, it seems appropriate to say that, in the absence of a constitutional court, supreme courts are the ones charged with the task to interpret the constitution. In case of a refusal to cooperate, then, not many alternatives can be envisaged: the CJEU will keep acting as it did so far and will interpret national constitutional alone to the extent that this is required when establishing, for instance, what is the content and scope of Article 4(2) TEU.

It also seems inevitable to think about what could have already happened if this closer cooperation between the two set of courts was already in place. What would have happened if the recent judgment of the Polish Constitutional Tribunal[87] had been rendered within a mere "request for information" under Article 24, para 2 of the CJEU Statute, rather than in a formal judicial decision? It would probably have had the same echo, but would it have had the practical effect of undermining the enforceability of EU law within national boundaries? In short, the certification procedure is aimed at establishing a dialogue, at creating an arena in which the different judicial systems, national and supranational, can freely exchange positions. And this while maintaining the necessary role of the Court of Justice as the main actor of the European construction through its high duty of ensuring a harmonized implementation of EU law across all Member States.

The same way in which national constitutional courts have broken the glass ceiling and overcame "the fear that a preliminary ruling request might raise the expectation of passive obedience to another court",[88] the CJEU could now take the lead and play a more active and conciliatory role. To be at stake is indeed the possibility of existence itself, more even that the constitutional identity, of the European Union, which depends on the mutual acceptance of the role of each actor within the composite EU multi-level judicial system. Precisely as the preliminary ruling mechanism has

---

[87] Polish Constitutional Tribunal, judgement K 3/21, issued on 7 October 2021.

[88] Cartabia 2015, p. 1795.

demonstrated that constitutional courts can find an active and specific role within the wider national and supranational judicial system, the CJEU has now the opportunity to dismiss every appearance of hierarchical (op)position and to cooperate peer-to-peer with its national homologues to pursue the project of "an ever-closer Union".

We believe that opening the way to the possibility of an authentic two-sided judicial dialogue could serve a twofold purpose: strengthening the already existing trend of cooperation between CJEU and national (constitutional or apex) courts on one side; and reaffirming the heterarchical constitutional architecture of the EU, thus laying down the premises for a deliberative way of understanding and furthering its constitutional identity.

10.5 Conclusion

The European constitutional model, in line with the historical moment in which it was created and developed, seems to reflect a postmodern approach to the issues of sovereignty and identity. In this context, the notion of identity is consequently to be understood as a shared responsibility, a continuous relationship with the "other heading", national or supranational. Such a model seems to rely on an increasingly precarious legal framework. But this precariousness, this continuous succession of crises, is not exceptional, but rather the very existential condition of the postmodern era; an era in which the certainties of modernity (hierarchies, great principles) are supplanted by *aporia*, a condition of puzzlement in which everything struggles to find an unambiguous qualification, and is defined by the need to constantly place itself in relation to the other. The aporetic nature of the European constitutional identity thus finds its meaning defined by the institutional capacity of the various constitutional actors to enter into a dialogical relationship among peers. While this is already possible and obvious in the case of national and supranational parliaments and executives, it is not so in the case of courts.

In this chapter we set out to analyse the possibility for courts to enter into a dialogue and exchange views beyond the rigid bottom-up mechanism of the preliminary reference. In our search for the institutional tools that could ensure this dialogue, our attention was kept by the American model of federal courts "certifying" questions of State law to State courts. Our analysis has led us to point out several practical implications of such a procedure. Questions related to its legal sources, modalities of implementation, courts' behaviour and the effect of the decision taken within this framework have been answered. Ultimately, starting from the general consideration (which applies also to European courts) that it is for courts to decide whether and how to exchange with other courts, we concluded that the EU legal order has already in itself all the necessary means to enable the CJEU to address a request for information or clarification on the interpretation of national law both in general and in the specific context of the preliminary ruling procedure.

Introducing such a "certified question of national law" would also be in line with an ongoing trend in the evolution of the CJEU. For some time now, the tendency seems to be one of greater involvement of national courts in the CJEU's decision-making process. This has so far consisted in a greater attention paid by the CJEU to the preliminary references coming from national peak and constitutional courts.

As a consequence, at least theoretically, there are reasons to suspect that the time might be ripe for such a procedure to be put in place. Whether it will be implemented in practice remains to be seen. In any case, our analysis leads us to believe that strengthening the dialogue between courts by making it two-sided will be crucial to let a shared understanding of the EU constitutional identity emerge, and to preserve it from illiberal drifts.

Acknowledgements An earlier version of this chapter was presented at the International Association of Constitutional Law (IACL) Roundtable on *Constitutional Identity: Universality of Constitutionalism vs. National Constitutional Traditions?* held at St. Petersburg State University (Russia) from 10–13 June 2021. It was also partly written during a research stay at the Complutense University of Madrid thanks to the financial support of the Spanish Ministry of Science and Innovation (project PID2019-108719GB-I00, P.I. Ricardo Alonso García). A special thanks goes to Prof. Ricardo Alonso Garcìa and Prof. Pablo Gonzalez Saquero.

References

Besselink L F M (2010) National and constitutional identity before and after Lisbon. Utrecht Law Review, 6(3), 36

Calabresi G (2003) Federal and State Courts: restoring a workable balance. New York University Law Review, 78(4), 1293–1308

Cantone J A, Giffin C (2020) Certified Questions of State Law. An Examination of State and Territorial Authorizing Statutes. Federal Judicial Center, Washington

Cartabia M (2015) Europe as a Space of Constitutional Interdependence: New Questions about the Preliminary Ruling. German Law Journal, 16(6), 1791–1796

Castells M (1996) The Rise of the Network Society. Vol. 1. Wiley Blackwell

Chase R A (1992) A State Court's Refusal to Answer Certified Questions: Are Inferences Permitted? St. John's Law Review, 66(2)

Christophersen H (2002) Highlighting the limits of EU competence (Working Document 5). Available at: www.ec.europa.eu

Claes M (2013) National Identity: Trump Card or Up For Negotiations? In: Saiz Arnaiz A, Alcoberro Llivina C (eds) National Constitutional Identity and European Integration. Intersentia

Cloots E (2017) National Identity, Constitutional Identity, and Sovereignty in the EU. Netherlands Journal of Legal Philosophy, 45(2), 82–98

Cochran R A (2013) Federal Court Certification of Questions of State Law to State Courts: A Theoretical and Empirical Study. Journal of Legislation, 29(2)

Cohen J C (1996) The European Preliminary Reference and US Supreme Court Review of State Court Judgments: A Study in Comparative Judicial Federalism. The American Journal of Comparative Law, 44(3), 421–461

Derrida J (1992) The Other Heading: Reflections on Today's Europe. Indiana University Press

Drinóczi T (2020) Constitutional Identity in Europe: The Identity of the Constitution: A Regional Approach. German Law Journal, 21, 105–130

Dyevre A, Atanasova A, Glavina M (2017) Who Asks Most? Institutional Incentives and Referral Activity in the European Union Legal Order. SSRN Electronic Journal, 1–24

Fabbrini F, Pollicino O (2017) Constitutional Identity in Italy: European Integration As the Fulfillment of the Constitution. SSRN Electronic Journal

Fabbrini F, Sajó A (2019) The dangers of constitutional identity. European Law Journal, April, 457–473

Faraguna P (2016) Taking Constitutional Identities away from the Courts. Brooklyn Journal of International Law, 492–601

Grabenwarter C, Huber P M, Knez R, Ziemele I (2021) The Role of the Constitutional Courts in the European Judicial Network. European Public Law, 27(1), 43–62

Graham J (2001) Preaching to a Postmodern World: A Guide to Reaching Twenty-first Century Listeners. Baker

Groppi T (2005) La Primauté del Diritto Europeo Sul Diritto Costituzionale Nazionale: Un Punto di Vista Comparato. ASTRID - Rassegna, 13. www.astrid-online.it

Guastaferro B (2012) Beyond the Exceptionalism of Constitutional Conflicts: The Ordinary Functions of the Identity Clause. Yearbook of European Law, 31(1), 263–318

Habermas J (2012) The Crisis of the European Union: A Response. Polity

Langer J (2015) The Preliminary Ruling Procedure: Old Problems or New Challenges? SSRN Electronic Journal

Long J R (2009) Against Certification. George Washington Law Review, 78, 111–154

Manweller M (2006) The Roles, Functions, and Powers of State Courts. In: Hogan S (ed) The Judicial Branch of State Government: People, Process, and Politics. ABC CLIO. 37–96

Nash J R (2003) Examining the Power of Federal Courts to Certify Questions of State Law. Cornell Law Review, 88(6)

Oakley J B, Amar V D (2009) American Civil Procedure: A Guide to Civil Adjudication in US Courts. Kluwer Law

Ovàdek M, Wijtvliet W, Glavina M (2020) Which Court Matters Most? Measuring Importance in the EU Preliminary Reference System. European Journal of Legal Studies, 12(1), 121–155

Pavone T, Kelemen R D (2019) The Evolving Judicial Politics of European Integration: The European Court of Justice and National Courts Revisited. European Law Journal, 25(4), 352–373

Pizzorusso A (2002) Il Patrimonio Costituzionale Europeo. Il Mulino

Ripple K F, Gallagher K A (2020) Certification Comes of Age: Reflections on the Past, Present, and Future of Cooperative Judicial Federalism. Notre Dame Law Review, 95(5)

Röttger-Wirtz S, Eliantonio M (2019) From Integration to Exclusion: EU Composite Administration and Gaps in Judicial Accountability in the Authorisation of Pharmaceuticals. European Journal of Risk Regulation, 10(2), 393–411

Sarmiento D (2013) The EU's Constitutional Core. In: Saiz Arnaiz A, Alcoberro Llivina C (eds) National Constitutional Identity and European Integration. Intersentia, 177–204

Schnettger A (2020) Article 4(2) as a Vehicle for National Constitutional Identity in the Shared European Legal System. In: Calliess C, Van der Schyff G (eds) Constitutional Identity in a Multilevel Constitutionalism. Cambridge University Press

Ugirashebuja E et al. (2017) East African Community Law. Institutional, Substantive and Comparative EU Aspects. Brill

Van der Schyff G (2012) The Constitutional Relationship between the European Union and its Member States: The Role of National Identity in Article 4(2) TEU. European Law Review, 37(563–586)

Von Bogdandy A, Schill S (2011) Overcoming absolute Primacy: Respect for National Identity Under the Lisbon Treaty. Common Market Law Review, 48, 1417–1454

Wägenbaur B (2013) Court of Justice of the EU. Commentary on Statute and Rules of Procedure. Hart

Weiler J H H, Sarmiento D (2020a) The EU Judiciary After Weiss – Proposing A New Mixed Chamber of the Court of Justice. A Reply to Our Critics. EU Law Live, 6 July 2020. www.eulawlive.com

Weiler J H H, Sarmiento D (2020b) The EU Judiciary After Weiss – Proposing A New Mixed Chamber of the Court of Justice. EU Law Live, 15 June 2020. www.eulawlive.com

Wells M L (2017) Judicial Federalism in the European Union. Houston Law Review, 54(3), 697–774
Witte A (2021) The Application of National Law by the ECB, Including Options and Discretions, and its Impact on the Judicial Review. In: Zilioli C, Wojcik K P (eds) Judicial Review in the European Banking Union. Edward Elgar, 236–250
Zinonos P (2020) A Mixed Chamber or an Ad Hoc Advisory Body for the Court of Justice of the EU? EU Law Live, 20 July 2020. www.eulawlive.com

Alberto Nicòtina Ph.D. Candidate in Constitutional Law, Government and Law Research Group, Faculty of Law, University of Antwerp.
     Alberto Nicòtina wrote Sects. 10.3 and 10.4.

Emil Martini LL.M., College of Europe, Bruges.
     Emil Martini wrote Sect. 10.2.

Correction to: Introduction: Exploring the Concept of a Constitutional Identity for the European Union

Gerhard van der Schyff, Ingrid Leijten, Charlotte van Oirsouw, Jurgen de Poorter, Maarten Stremler and Maartje De Visser

Correction to:
Chapter 1 in : J. de Poorter et al. (eds.), *European Yearbook of Constitutional Law 2022*, **European Yearbook of Constitutional Law 4,**
https://doi.org/10.1007/978-94-6265-595-9_1

The original version of chapter 1 was revised: The wrong abstract and keywords have been removed from the online version and replaced by the correct abstract. The correction chapter and the book have been updated with the changes.

The updated version of this chapter can be found at
https://doi.org/10.1007/978-94-6265-595-9_1

© T.M.C. ASSER PRESS and the authors 2023
J. de Poorter et al. (eds.), *European Yearbook of Constitutional Law 2022*,
European Yearbook of Constitutional Law 4,
https://doi.org/10.1007/978-94-6265-595-9_11

Printed and bound by CPI Group (UK) Ltd, Croydon, CR0 4YY

10/10/2024

01043257-0002